HISTORY, POLICY,
——— AND ———
ECONOMIC THEORY

HISTORY, POLICY, AND ECONOMIC THEORY

ESSAYS IN INTERACTION

W. W. ROSTOW

Routledge
Taylor & Francis Group
LONDON AND NEW YORK

First published 1990 by Westview Press

Published 2018 by Routledge
52 Vanderbilt Avenue, New York, NY 10017
2 Park Square, Milton Park, Abingdon, Oxon OX14 4RN

Routledge is an imprint of the Taylor & Francis Group, an informa business

Copyright © 1990 by W. W. Rostow

All rights reserved. No part of this book may be reprinted or reproduced or utilised in any form or by any electronic, mechanical, or other means, now known or hereafter invented, including photocopying and recording, or in any information storage or retrieval system, without permission in writing from the publishers.

Notice:
Product or corporate names may be trademarks or registered trademarks, and are used only for identification and explanation without intent to infringe.

Rostow, W. W. (Walt Whitman), 1916–
  History, policy, and economic theory : essays in interaction / W. W. Rostow.
    p. cm.
  Includes bibliographies.
  ISBN 0-8133-0918-2
  1. Economics. 2. Economic policy. 3. Economic history.
I. Title.
HB171.R673 1990
330—dc20   89-5697
                                                                         CIP

ISBN 13: 978-0-367-00363-0 (hbk)
ISBN 13: 978-0-367-15350-2 (pbk)

In memory of Munia Postan

Contents

Preface ... xi

Part One
Problems of Method

1 James Harvey Rogers, 1886–1939: In Memoriam (1940) ... 3

2 The Interrelation of Theory and Economic History (1957) ... 13

3 Cycles and the Irreducible Complexity of History (1982) ... 27

4 Professor Arrow on Economic Analysis and Economic History (1986) ... 35

Part Two
Issues of Historical Analysis

5 Adjustments and Maladjustments After the Napoleonic Wars (1942) ... 43

6 Some Notes on Mr. Hicks and History (1951) ... 55

7 From Dependence to Interdependence: A Historian's Perspective (1973) ... 64

8 No Random Walk: A Comment on "Why Was England First?" [by N.F.R. Crafts] (1978) ... 77

9 Review of Immanuel Wallerstein, *The Modern World System II: Mercantilism and the Consolidation of the European World Economy, 1600–1750* (1981) ... 81

10	The Terms of Trade and Development (1982)	86
11	Review of Robert L. Heilbroner, *The Nature and Logic of Capitalism* (1986)	106

Part Three
Elaboration of a Dynamic Theory Including the Take-off Debate

12	Trends in the Allocation of Resources in Secular Growth (1955)	113
13	Some General Reflections on Capital Formation and Economic Growth (1956)	126
14	Industrialization and Economic Growth (1960)	142
15	The Konstanz Conference: Leading Sectors and the Take-off (1960) and Epilogue (1963)	161

Part Four
Issues of Current Policy

16	The Problem of Achieving and Maintaining a High Rate of Economic Growth: A Historian's View (1960)	197
17	The Bankruptcy of Neo-Keynesian Economics (1976); A Reluctant Keynesian, a Reply by Abba P. Lerner (1976); A Rejoinder (1976)	211
18	Review of Ernest Mandel, *Late Capitalism* (1979)	235
19	Comment from a Not Quite Empty Box (1982)	238
20	Review of P. T. Bauer, *Equality, the Third World, and Economic Delusion* (1982)	244
21	Technology and Unemployment in the Western World (1982)	249
22	Reflections on the Drive to Technological Maturity (1987)	271

23 Beware of Historians Bearing False Analogies:
    A Review of Paul Kennedy, *The Rise and Fall
    of Great Powers* (1988); Pointers from the Past:
    Kennedy's Comment (1988); Reviewer's Reply (1988) 299

Part Five
The Evolution of Economic Doctrine

24 Technology and the Economic Theorist: Past,
    Present, and Future (1989) 317

25 Development, Efficiency, and Equity in
    Historical Perspective (1989) 354

Preface

Just before I began to write this prefatory note I ran across the following observation by Josef Škvorecký, the expatriate Czech novelist: "Some writers may *think* their only subject is themselves: if they are any good they are telling the history of their time and of their people in the form of a self-portrait. For the self-portrait has an open landscape in the background, with little human figures toiling and frolicking in it, as in a genre painting by a Dutch Master."*

A collection of professional essays spanning a half-century is, inevitably, autobiographical after a fashion; but fellow economists and historians do, indeed, populate these essays. Moreover, one can trace fairly well the sequence of the great issues of public policy that marked these decades. There is also the reflection of a good deal of toil but, unfortunately, not much frolicking.

So far as intellectual autobiography is concerned, I was struck, in reviewing these pieces, by the continuity over the years of my approach to economic analysis. From the beginning, for example, I have been concerned more than most of my contemporaries with the generation and diffusion of technology; the generation of adequate supplies of food, raw materials, and energy; and, above all, by the inescapable role of noneconomic forces in economic analysis. There is no mystery about the source of my emphasis on the effects of noneconomic forces. After an initial focus on history, I turned in my sophomore year at Yale to a systematic effort to link the insights and methods of economics and history. For wholly understandable reasons—at a time of unexampled unemployment in the Western world—the most exciting work in economic theory concerned effective demand and its manipulation by public policy. But I soon found that economic history simply could not be explained in terms of fluctuations in effective demand, under Marshallian short-

---

*"Josef Škvorecký Failed Saxophonist," *Autobiography*, GRANTA no. 14 (Harmondsworth, Middlesex: Granta Publications, Winter 1984), p. 168.

period assumptions, with the supply side frozen or subject to once-over change. Nor could the unfolding of economic events be explained if one abstracted from the noneconomic forces at work. The same propositions have turned out to be valid in the analysis of current problems in the world economy.

From the beginning to end, then, my work as an economist has been an effort to fill these gaps in mainstream economic theory in a systematic way. The challenge incorporated in that effort may explain the ease and excitement with which I had turned back to academic life after three intervals in public service: 1941–1946; 1947–1949; 1961–1969. The task I had chosen was evidently much larger than any one person's capacities. I explored facets of it piece by piece; therefore, on each return to academic life I knew on which unsolved piece of the problem I had to resume. For example, the fragmentary reflections on the noneconomic dimensions of industrialization in my August 1960 Stockholm essay (Chapter 14) clearly foreshadow the subject of my first post-Washington book, *Politics and the Stages of Growth* (1971).

How does one structure a collection of essays like this? After some experiment, my admirable editor at Westview Press, Spencer Carr, and I decided to group the essays under five areas that have concerned me for longer than a half-century:

- Problems of Method
- Issues of Historical Analysis
- Elaboration of a Dynamic Theory Including the Take-off Debate
- Issues of Current Policy
- The Evolution of Economic Doctrine

This organizational method, we hope, will make it easy for the reader to perceive the strands of continuity as well as those of evolution that are reflected in these essays. I should also note that all the essays do not neatly fit our five categories. But that is not wholly inappropriate in a book whose overarching theme is interaction.

The debate with Paul Kennedy (Chapter 23) speaks for itself. At first sight, its ultimate theme—an appropriate military and foreign policy for the United States in the generation now ahead—does not appear to fit the subject matter of this book. But as the prefatory note for that chapter underlines, the ultimate analytic issues center on technology and the stages of economic growth in relation to the contours of global power and politics.

A word about the dedication: Professor M. M. Postan of Cambridge was a close friend from 1938 until his death in 1981. I first met him when he was editor of *The Economic History Review*. I had submitted an article for publication at the suggestion of Humphrey Sumner, then at Balliol College, Oxford. Postan not only accepted the piece but also invited me to join him in Wiltshire for a weekend. The animated dialogue

Preface

that began that weekend continued without significant interruption even during years of war and when I was in the public service in Geneva and Washington. Postan appears at several points in this book.

There have been few academics who did more to nurture their field than did Postan over the long span of his professional life: by his scholarly example and teaching, through *The Economic History Review* and International Economic History Association, and by his editorship of *The Cambridge Economic History of Europe*. His reign had two special characteristics: an extraordinarily infectious enthusiasm and his capacity to inspire young scholars while quite consciously making sure they pursued their own bent. He sought colleagues not disciples. For several generations there was hardly a major economic historian, in any country, whose career had not been touched by Postan and who did not treasure that tie.

In assembling these essays and writing prefatory notes I was greatly helped by my assistant, Lois Nivens, and by Mickey Russell who imperturbably got the typing done while moving an office.

The reader is unknowingly in the debt of my wife, Elspeth Davies Rostow, who read most of these essays in draft form, contributed considerable substance, and measurably improved their style and clarity.

W. W. Rostow

PART ONE

Problems of Method

_____ ONE

James Harvey Rogers, 1886–1939: In Memoriam (1940)

In the autumn of 1933, as a sophomore at Yale, I went to live in Pierson College. This was the first year of the College Plan, and traditions were established every day. In those early years no one did more to enrich the life of the college than a shy South Carolina bachelor, James Harvey Rogers.

Rogers was an economist of distinction, an adviser to President Franklin D. Roosevelt in the early days of the New Deal, and a friend to undergraduates, notably those with an interest in economics. But he even turned up occasionally at intercollege football games, ate with us regularly in the college dining hall, and mounted a good many black tie dinners in his rooms, where we met cabinet ministers, bankers from New York, and assorted other grand figures. We learned to listen, to question, and, even, to debate our elders with civility.

Substantively, Rogers left two enduring memories. The first underlined the reticence appropriate to a presidential adviser. When he returned from Washington on one occasion after a session with FDR that had been reported in the press, an overeager student asked: "What did you talk about?" Rogers answered with a not unkindly smile, "Various economic facts in general," a phrase that promptly passed into local folklore. When Rogers disagreed with FDR's devaluation of the dollar but was associated in the press with its monetarist supporters, his personal cheering squad urged him to speak out. He explained that one did not reveal one's advice to a president and accepted without rancor misinterpretations in the press.

The second lesson was professional. Rogers, as a young economist, had experienced a traumatic shock. As an enthusiastic advocate of the use of

---

This essay was published as a chapter in Arnold Wolfers (ed.), *James Harvey Rogers, 1886–1939. In Memoriam* (Stamford, Ct.: Overbrook Press, 1940). Reprinted with permission.

mathematics in economics, he went off to Geneva to study with Vilfredo Pareto, but he found Pareto thoroughly disabused with mathematical economics and engrossed in sociology. Rogers did not abandon mathematics, but he limited himself strictly to areas where the empty boxes could be filled—where abstract statements could be tested empirically. Rogers's influence helped me focus sharply, at an early stage, on the limitations as well as the virtues of mathematics as a tool in economic analysis—a theme to which I have returned in my Theorists of Economic Growth from David Hume to the Present *(1989).*

Rogers was killed in a flying boat accident on August 14, 1939, in the harbor of Rio de Janeiro. He was on a presidential mission to explore the possibility of enlarging production and trade in essential raw materials in Latin America, should the United States become embroiled in war. Twenty-three, and just out of graduate school, I was asked to write the following essay on Rogers as an economist for a thin memorial volume (James Harvey Rogers, 1886–1939. In Memoriam, *edited by Arnold Wolfers) published in 1940 by the Overbrook Press in Stamford.*

James Harvey Rogers belongs to the distinguished line of economists who were attracted into the field after a considerable formal training in mathematics—the line of Cournot, Marshall, Pareto, and Professor Irving Fisher, among many others. During the past century, economics has offered the mathematician enlarging scope for the rigorous statements of formal propositions. In the years before 1914, the structure of the theory of value and of monetary theory was being subjected to mathematical formulation, notably by Walras and Pareto on the continent, by Professor Fisher in the United States. Professor Rogers entered economics optimistic of the possibilities of creating and applying a body of economic theory stated with scientific precision.

His first advanced course in economics was, somewhat paradoxically, under Professor Alvin Johnson at the University of Chicago (1913–14), where Mr. Rogers had come as a graduate student in mathematics. Professor Johnson emphasized, then as now, the shifting social framework within which economic forces operate. While sympathetic to the purist's spirit, which motivated the mathematical economists of that day, he was keenly aware of the limitations of their method in dealing with those immediate economic problems that were his central concern. He preferred to state issues in their historical and institutional setting, rather than *in abstracto*. He would caution, with Bagehot, against trying "to express various meanings on complex things with a scanty vocabulary of fastened uses."[1]

On one occasion Mr. Rogers was permitted dramatically to judge the merits of the two approaches. Walras had written to Professor Johnson agreeing with a recent article he had written, but urging, in fifteen pages of formulæ, that Johnson's verbal analysis could be more profitably stated in mathematical terms. When shown the correspondence, Mr.

Rogers sided with Walras. It was, nevertheless, Alvin Johnson who recommended him to Geneva and Pareto.

Pareto was then a mathematical economist of first rank. In *Le cours d'économie politique* (1896), he had formulated, under conditions of pure competition, the general laws of production, distribution, and price. He, and the others who stemmed from Cournot, had given elegance, generality and precision to the traditional value theory analysis. They could, however, find no statistical counterparts for their concepts; nor could they contribute to the analysis and remedy of the economic problems which confronted even the peaceful, relatively self-adjusting world before 1914. For some, the desire to speak relevantly to the statesman, or of his problems, was not immediate. But in 1914 Pareto was thoroughly discouraged with economic investigations of the type represented in *Le cours*. He had turned largely to sociology; and it was as a social scientist in the broadest sense, not as a mathematical economist, that he exercised a profound and enduring influence on Professor Rogers.

The early sections of Pareto's great tract on sociology are devoted to an extensive discussion of the scientific method in the social sciences. There he denies almost bitterly the existence of any objective economic or social laws, insisting that such laws are merely generalizations based on observed uniformities, invested with an artificial and unjustified authority.[2] He believed, in fact, that the absolute pretensions of the physical and natural scientists were little better founded, and was delighted with the unsettling implications of Einstein's work in the field of relativity.

Arising from a quite different intellectual tradition, this attitude towards the social sciences had much in common with that of the American empiricists—Dewey, Veblen, Commons, Walton Hamilton, and Alvin Johnson. Pareto, however, continued to use advanced abstraction beyond the point which most of the American social scientists would have thought it profitable. He never lost entirely his fondness for general constructions and mathematical statement. He lacked, further, any compulsion to deal with current issues or to speak to a wide or popular audience. Pareto regarded himself as a kind of Olympian observer of society as a whole. The pupils of Veblen—like the Fabians in Britain—were deeply concerned with specific problems, and their most practical solution. They desired to convince and to reform.

While under Pareto's influence, Rogers was confirmed in a suspicion of any abstract statement that could not be tested empirically. He did not, however, like many of his contemporaries, reject the possibility of employing fruitfully advanced theoretical concepts and even the mathematical statement of them. He was trained in the use of such methods well beyond the possibility of their practical application; and he was both bold and imaginative in his view of their relevance.

In his attitude towards the social and economic problems of his own day, however, Professor Rogers found himself much closer to the liberal

American economists than to Pareto—and increasingly so as time went on. He had admired Pareto's ability to regard the World War, while it was in progress, as a distant social phenomenon; and he sought to maintain vigilantly a similar objectivity. He avoided broad statements or commitments to general programs. He chose to judge all questions, professional or otherwise, strictly on their own merits, reducing objectives to the most explicit and immediate terms. His vocabulary had a spartan lack of pretension. Yet few academic men have more consistently devoted their professional attention to matters of public concern. Both in his writing and in the class-room he sought to apply to the limit of their usefulness the apparatus of technical thinking and information he had at his command. Pareto's violent prejudice against democracy entered his thinking only in an awareness of its somewhat devious processes and of the need for flexibility in its forms. Pareto's Menckenian scorn of reformers appeared as a quiet caution against grandiose thinking.

When, in 1915, Mr. Rogers returned to the Yale Graduate School he had been vividly confronted with the basic issues which face the social scientist, and his temperament and training had begun to shape their response. His thesis was an exercise in mathematical economics: *A Mathematical Investigation of the Incidence of Taxation*. This essay restated the conventional propositions of public finance, but pretended to no originality beyond the mode of presentation. Two years before, in Chicago, he had urged the superiority of Walras' over Johnson's manner of statement; but he refused to publish his thesis on the grounds that mathematical restatement constituted merely an exercise, not a positive contribution.

On receiving his doctorate in 1916, Mr. Rogers went to the University of Missouri as an instructor. With the United States at war, he served as statistician with the Council of National Defense (1918-9), then returning to Missouri when this work was completed. Except for the years 1920-3, spent as assistant professor at Cornell, he remained there until 1930. When he came at that time to Yale as Sterling Professor, he was an authority on monetary problems of international repute.

It was natural that Professor Rogers should find his way into monetary analysis. It was the branch of economics which most nearly approximated the physical sciences in the refinement of its terms and the opportunities it offered both for empirical verification and application. The work of Walras and Pareto answered few of the questions addressed to the economist by the public. The approach to economic problems from the side of money, however, seemed more promising. It involved the use of considerably less advanced mathematical procedures than the value theory analysis; but it came closer to the terrain of the political economist or, better, arithmetician—to "the art of reasoning by figures, upon things relating to the government."[3]

Professor Rogers had studied monetary theory with Professor Irving Fisher at Yale, and his experience as statistician with the Council of

National Defense had afforded insight into the possibilities of its application. In the post-war years, every day presented new problems. Reparations, war debts, inflation and deflation on the continent, the return to gold, the American depression of 1920-1—all these were susceptible of quantitative analysis in the terms of then current monetary theory.

There were three analytic tools available which especially appealed to Professor Rogers. The least well known were the formulæ worked out by C. A. Phillips and published in *Bank Credit* (1910). These measured the potential expansion (or contraction) of the banking system as a whole caused by an increase (or decrease) in new deposits, under given reserve conditions. They gave concreteness to the familiar concept of credit fluctuation, and clearly exposed its mechanism in a modern banking system. Phillips' formulæ, and Professor Rogers' elaborations and revisions on them, are familiar to all who have taken his courses. Then there were the two equations designed to analyze and to measure changes in the general price level: Professor Fisher's famous "quantity theory" equation, and the so-called "Cambridge equation," deriving from a long verbal tradition, but formulated most accessibly by Mr. Keynes (*A Tract on Monetary Reform*, 1923). Here were "empty boxes" that could be filled. Data on the monetary system were relatively accurate and inclusive. Useful price and output indexes could be constructed. Even though the terms of the equations were not entirely unambiguous, even though measurement had sometimes to be approximate, still the abstractions had verifiable meaning. And their meaning bore directly on the central problems of a post-war world.

Professor Rogers' major publications in the twenties were *Stock Speculation and the Money Market* (1927), *The Process of Inflation in France, 1914-1927* (1929), and *Foreign Markets and Foreign Credits* (1929).[4] In each case a singular gift for interrelating fact and theory is evident: the framework of theory is used to organize the data and to propound the appropriate questions; significant refinement or modification of the theory is then suggested in the light of the previous enquiry.

In *Stock Speculation*, he examined the financing of stock speculation in an effort to evaluate the significance of the distinction often made between "speculative" and "legitimate" business. It had been implied, during the war and in the immediate post-war years, that speculation was barrenly employing funds needed to finance production and commerce. He found that the velocity of circulation of brokers' deposits was highly flexible, and for that reason large increases in speculative activity required no diversion of new credit to the stock exchange. This hypothesis conformed to available statistical evidence and seemed to explain the puzzling co-existence of easy money and "the greatest speculative activity in our history," in 1925. It seemed, further, to throw light on the "riddle of the close correspondence between the short-time movements of V and of T, with no apparent similarity in their secular trends";[5] *i.e.*, speculative activity (and thus the velocity of the circulation of brokers' deposits) could be expected to increase and decrease with general business conditions. Revised versions of Phillips' expansion formula are used to indicate the relation between brokers' deposits and the banking system as a whole; and, finally, certain modifications in the use of the Fisher equation are suggested, stemming from the peculiarities discovered in the velocity of the financial circulation. Although the subject matter and even the terminology of this highly original monograph now appear somewhat dated, it remains a model of applied monetary analysis.

The Process of Inflation in France is the largest and most comprehensive published work of Professor Rogers. It surveys, from a monetary perspective, the movements of the whole French economy in the war and post-war years. The relation between the monetary circulation, the foreign exchanges, interest rates, prices, and output are fully explored. Early sections are devoted to an analysis of the means of financing peculiar to the French system. The interconnections of the Treasury, the Bank of France, the private banks, and the money market are traced; and the inflationary mechanics of the government's borrowing from the Bank of France is examined. Two extremely suggestive chapters summarize the argument successively in terms of the Fisher and of the Cambridge equations. The previous detailed explanation of events is brilliantly compressed and unified. At the same time the unique characteristics of each of the equations are revealed by their application to the same set of data. This method gives a rare sense of the institutional meaning of the abstractions employed. A similar concreteness pervaded Professor Rogers' teaching of monetary theory.

Foreign Markets and Foreign Credits is the third of Professor Rogers' important writings on the monetary problems of the twenties. It marks, as well, his formal entrance into the field of international finance, which was to occupy a large share of his attention in the following decade. In the essay he added to his analytic armory a device which he afterwards exploited, in his writing and teaching, perhaps more fully than anyone else: the balance of payments. This statistical account of the in- and out-payments of a given country appealed to him for the same reasons as the Phillips' formulæ and the Fisher and Cambridge equations: it permitted the quantitative expression of abstract concepts, in this case those of international trade and finance. In his hands it was an extremely flexible technique, which could be used not only to reveal the forces acting on international trade relations, but internally as well.

Foreign Markets and Foreign Credits considers the assumption by the United States, in the post-war years, of the creditor responsibilities acquired in 1914–8. It describes the process by which we continued to export capital and thus finance increasing exports of goods, and places that process in its international setting. The new directions of our financing and our trade are charted and the consequences on our internal financial position evaluated.

The facts are then referred to the theory of international trade. Here Professor Rogers noted that, despite the persistent tendency of gold to flow to the United States, and despite the partially consequent condition of artificially easy money, commodity prices had failed to rise. The principal automatic check of the classical theory was failing to operate; and our high tariffs seemed to offer no opportunity for decreasing the gold flow here. He pointed, moreover, to the fashion in which the attractiveness of the Stock Exchange to foreign capital was beginning to counteract the crucially important effects, for international equilibrium, of our lending abroad. He closed, significantly, by discussing the possibilities inherent in such a situation of a speculative stock exchange boom.

In the light of subsequent events, the analysis seems to have been essentially correct; although, like most of his contemporaries early in 1929, Professor Rogers did not foresee the complete collapse of the international financial structure which followed, in part at least, due to the forces described in *Foreign Markets and Foreign Credits*. He afterwards accounted for his relative optimism in surveying the twenties by reference to the failure of the commodity prices to rise. The baffling lack of this symptom of dangerous inflation made plausible the belief that serious depression was not imminent.

The fact of depression seriously altered the direction and the emphasis of Professor Rogers' interest. The problems, especially of 1929–33, touched intimately on matters of international finance and central banking in which he was expert. He conceived it his primary task to state the positive fruits of his investigations, as they bore on public policy. There stemmed from this desire to alter the disastrous course of events, the need to address a non-professional audience. Both *America Weighs Her Gold* (1931) and *Capitalism in Crisis* (1938) were, relatively, popular expositions. As Professor Rogers studied the reaction of public opinion to economic events, he was struck by the extent to which sometimes irrational social symbols and attitudes stood in the way of what he conceived to be appropriate measures. In putting forward popular analyses, he sought to strike at these shibboleths. The desire to persuade thus led him away from strictly economic issues.

Still another factor tended to alter his position. The depression, in changing the questions the economist was called upon to answer, also wrought changes in the economist's theoretical constructs. The monetary analysis of the twenties—of Fisher, Hawtrey, and the early Keynes— did not seem adequately to reach the problems of the great depression. The tools of the post-war monetary theorist gradually were altered or replaced.

Keynes' *Treatise on Money* and, later, his *General Theory*, the work of the Scandinavian economists, of Hicks, Hansen, Robertson, Haberler and many others tended to end the isolation from the theories of value and capital that monetary theory had enjoyed since, at least, the day of Ricardo. The theory of money gave way to various general theories of employment and business fluctuation. The revolution has been one of vocabulary, of emphasis, of formal structure. It did not, of course, in any sense "disprove" the older theories. It aimed, however, to reshape the familiar concepts in such a way as to make them bear on depression problems, especially on that of chronic unemployment. Distinctively monetary questions—in the sense of the twenties—no longer commanded the stage.

While he followed the new developments closely and taught the new books in his courses, Professor Rogers felt no great sympathy for them. A consistent, widely accepted vocabulary had not yet been built up; and, above all, the structure taking shape seemed to offer few opportunities for quantitative analysis. The ambiguity of the terms and their immeasurability led him for some time to stick closely to less general problems of technique, where the older theoretical framework was still relevant—gold, the foreign exchanges, the balance of payments, central banking policy. And he found much to say.

America Weighs Her Gold, coming fairly early in the depression (1931), employed the analysis of *The Process of Inflation* and *Foreign Markets and Foreign Credits* to treat the anomalous financial position of the United States: our lending had fallen off, our tariffs had just been raised, and we were acquiring gold rapidly while world prices fell and unemployment increased. Professor Rogers was concerned not merely to analyze, but to make recommendations for policy. He felt that, at a time when "our institutions, our policies, and our philosophies are being weighed," the leisurely scientist should draft and present "workable improvements," lest, by default, the formation of policy fall into the hands of the "politically-minded demagogues."[6] Specifically he advocated a reduction in tariffs, a drastic readjustment of war debts, an easy money policy through Federal Reserve action, and, if necessary, an abandonment of the gold standard. This lucid tract was almost certainly an important factor in Professor Rogers' admittance to the circle of Presidential advisers, where he argued modestly and cogently for these lines of action. He was, of course, not alone in his advocacy of such measures. But he contributed largely to their acceptance as public policy. In the vast literature called forth by the depression, aimed to influence the intelligent layman, *America Weighs Her Gold* holds a high place, and will continue to do so. It is in the best tradition of economic pamphleteering: the tradition that stretches continuously back to Ricardo and Tooke and the mercantilists.

In the following years, Professor Rogers was much occupied with the details of monetary recovery measures. From 1933 he was, of course, among the advisers to the administration; and he sat with the Economic Committee of the League of Nations (1933–7). He spoke often to popular audiences, and, in a series of papers, continued to develop the detailed professional analysis which underlay his conclusions for political action:

Foreign Credits and International Trade (1932), *Federal Reserve Policy in World Monetary Chaos* (1933), *The Prospect of Inflation in the United States* (1936), among many others.[7] Even in the austere pages of *Econometrica*, Professor Rogers concluded an article on *The Absorption of Bank Credit* (1933), by urging the necessity for a positive open market policy to ease credit, as well as a lowering of interest rates.[8]

The coming of the recession in 1937, while there were still some ten million unemployed in the United States, explains, more than any other single factor, the final stage of Rogers' career. The failure of government spending and easy money to achieve full recovery was indeed disheartening. And he turned, in *Capitalism in Crisis* (1938), to cataloguing the reasons for that failure, and to sketching the outlines of a second recovery effort.

Monopoly prices, he felt, must be broken, a measure of government spending must be continued, incipient economic state autarchy must be stamped out. Above all he was saddened by the lack of co-operation between business and government. If capitalism were to survive, if democratic forms of government were to be maintained, somehow an understanding must be reached as to the complementary rôles of each in a modern economic system. Almost a fourth of the book is devoted to portraying the terms and the dangers of this barren social conflict. Technically it was necessary for business spending to revive. The reasons for its failure to revive were, however, not strictly economic, but imbedded deep in fears and suspicions, which, justified or not, constituted a central menace to the survival of existing institutions. He wished, somehow, to clear the atmosphere of irrational elements.

Professor Rogers was aware that *Capitalism in Crisis* could add little to his academic status, and that its popular success was problematical. But as an individual he feared profoundly that ineptness and social misunderstanding, in part unnecessary, might lead to some kind of totalitarianism in the United States. For that reason he forsook the fields of his special competence and wrote in the broadest terms he ever allowed himself.

In his last year, as war loomed in Europe, Professor Rogers considered the problem of measuring the concept of economic power, with an eye to the possible leverage that might be applied by the United States, in war or in a troubled peace. A major opportunity was, patently, the possibility of lending, on the basis of our embarrassing gold hoards, to South American states. His decision to spend the summer of 1939 there was largely conditioned by that current interest.

In surveying Pareto's career, Professor Rogers once wrote:[9]

> He divided human activity into two principal branches, that of sentiment and that of experimental research. The first, he contended over and over again, could not be too much emphasized. . . . But the second branch, that of experimental research, though more modest in its claims, is also essential for all societies. "It furnishes the material which the first uses.

We owe to it the knowledge which makes action effective. Centuries have been necessary to secure a separation of these elements; which separation, in our time, has been nearly entirely accomplished for the natural sciences, and has commenced and progressed for the social sciences."[10] And to advance this separation, Pareto devoted the last twenty years of his life.

Professor Rogers was governed by the same large aim. He went, however, beyond the formulation of scientific tools. He used them with a great competence and originality, not only to illuminate past events but to "make action effective." Although he was capable of separating "sentiment" and "experimental research," the former played perhaps a larger rôle in his work than he would have admitted. It never obscured the clarity of his analysis; but it drove him to deal positiviely with the real problems that men faced. He regarded his training and his knowledge as tools. As a teacher, as a professional craftsman, as a servant of the state, few can claim to have used them more constructively.

NOTES

[1.] *Postulates of English Political Economy*, pp. 78–9.

[2.] Rogers delivered in 1924 a little known paper before the International Mathematical Congress at Toronto—*Vilfredo Pareto, The Mathematician of the Social Sciences*. His evaluation of Pareto reveals clearly the manner in which Rogers' thought was affected by contact with him.

[3.] Davenant, *The Use of Political Arithmetic*.

[4.] Chapter XI, *Recent Economic Changes*, Report of the Committee on Recent Economic Changes of the President's Conference on Unemployment (pp. 709–56).

[5.] *Stock Speculation and the Money Market*, p. 69.

[6.] *America Weighs Her Gold*, p. 189.

[7.] A selected bibliography of Professor Rogers' published works will be found on pp. 31–34. ED.

[8.] The bulk of this article is devoted to presenting in final mathematical form Rogers' development and modification of the Phillips' formulæ. The conclusions as to appropriate Federal Reserve action are expressed in terms of the formal development.

[9.] *Vilfredo Pareto, the Mathematician of the Social Sciences*, transcript of the International Mathematical Congress, 1924, p. 972.

[10.] Taken from address of V. Pareto at the University of Lausanne in 1917 on the occasion of a jubilee commemorating the twenty-fifth anniversary of his appointment to the faculty of that university.

─── TWO

The Interrelation of Theory and Economic History (1957)

───

This essay reflects the phase in the 1950s when academics gathered to consider how their areas of specialization related—or might relate—to the analysis of economic growth. It was also a time when neoclassical economics and econometrics began to capture the imagination of a good many young economic historians, yielding in time the rise of a self-conscious field of cliometrics. The upshot was a meeting of the American Economic History Association held in Williamstown, Massachusetts, late in the summer of 1957 devoted to "The Integration of Economic Theory and Economic History." Incidentally, the cliometric trumpet was blown loud and clear by John R. Meyer and Alfred H. Conrad in a paper entitled "Economic Theory, Statistical Inference, and Economic History."

The relation between economic theory and economic history has been a recurrent subject of exploration, debate, and uneasiness since the field of economic history, comfortably at home with theory from David Hume and Adam Smith to the marginalist revolution of 1870, broke away amidst some polemics and began to define itself as a separate discipline in the late nineteenth century. Chapter 4 suggests that the process of uneasy but now civil and reasonably dispassionate dialogue goes on into the late 1980s.

I

I do not much hold with ardent debate about method. A historian's method is as individual—as private—a matter as a novelist's style. There is good reason for reserve—even reticence—on this subject, except insofar as we seek to share each other's unique professional adventures

───────────
This essay was published in the December 1957 issue of *The Journal of Economic History* (vol. 17, no. 4). Reprinted with permission.

and to listen occasionally, in a mood of interest tempered with skepticism, to such general reflections as we each would draw from those adventures.

Moreover, as a practical matter, no good cause is likely to be served by further exhortation to the historian to use more theory or to the theorist to read more history. Progress in this old contentious terrain is made only by meeting a payroll; that is, by demonstrating that something interesting and worth while can be generated by working with historical data within a conscious and orderly theoretical framework, or by adding to the structure of theory through historical generalization. The present paper is thus justified if at all only to the extent that it sets down some tentative and interim personal reflections drawn from practical work; for I take it to be agreed that man has open to him no alternative but to use theoretical concepts in trying to make sense of empirical data, past or present; I take it to be agreed that, as Keynes said in the preface to the blue Cambridge economics handbooks, "The Theory of Economics ... is a method rather than a doctrine, an apparatus of mind, a technique of thinking" rather than "a body of settled conclusions"; in terms of this definition I take it to be agreed that we all wish to bring to bear in our work the most relevant "technique of thinking" available and would be pleased to use the corpus of received economic theory for all it is worth. The real questions are how, if at all, the theoretical structures developed in modern social science can be used by the working historian and how, if at all, the historian should link his insights to the bodies of theory developing in the social sciences which surround him.

My own answers to these questions are directly colored by a pleasant but somewhat bizarre education. As a relatively innocent sophomore student of modern history at Yale in the autumn of 1934, I was first introduced to an important philosophical notion. This event can hardly be ranked as revolutionary, since the notion has been part of the received Western tradition for some twenty-five centuries; namely, that human perception works through arbitrary abstract concepts and therefore the reality of what we call facts is not without a certain ambiguity. If historical narration of the most responsible and professional kind was thus shot through with implicit, arbitrary theory, why not make it explicit; and, since I was then beginning to study economics, why not see what happened if the machinery of economic theory was brought to bear on modern economic history.

This line of reflection soon opened up two quite distinct areas for experiment: the application of modern economic theory to economic history; and the application of the modern social sciences to the interaction among the economic, political, social, and cultural sectors of whole societies. I was drawn to this latter area in part because I was repelled by Marx's economic determinism without, however, finding a satisfactory alternative answer to the question he posed—an omission not yet repaired in Western thought.

In one way or another I have been experimenting ever since with these two issues; that is, with the reciprocal relations of economic theory and dynamic economic data and with the effort to analyze whole societies in motion. They have given a private unity to study ranging from the study of the Great Depression after 1873 to the selection of bombing targets in World War II; from the likely consequences of Stalin's death to the pattern of the British take-off in the 1780's and 1790's; from the historical application of the National Bureau method of cyclical analysis to the formulation of some general hypotheses about economic growth.

What I have to say about the reciprocal relations of theory and history flows directly from these and similar exercises. As befits a working paper of this kind the argument will take the form of a few concrete, arbitrary, possibly useful assertions which aim partially to answer these questions from one arbitrary and personal perspective. The assertions are essentially three: first, the problem is the most useful link between theory and empirical data; second, of the nature of an economic historian's problems he is fated to be mainly a theorist of the Marshallian long period; and third, of the nature of the Marshallian long period, the economic historian can avoid only with great difficulty being something of a general dynamic theorist of whole societies. From these assertions I derive a final proposition; namely, that in our generation the most natural meeting place of theory and history is the study of comparative patterns of dynamic change in different societies, focused around the problems of economic growth.

II

The problem approach to history can have two meanings. It can mean that history is viewed (and rewritten) in the light of contemporary problems of public policy—as, for example, Pigou reviewed the adjustment of the British economy after November 1918 during World War II, or, in the shadow of impending legislation O. M. W. Sprague examined crises under the National Banking Act. Or the problem approach can mean that history is re-examined to throw light on an unresolved intellectual problem of contemporary interest—as, for example, Schumpeter's hypothesis about entrepreneurship in a capitalist society is now being historically tested. The two meanings are generally related because most of the intellectual issues within the social sciences, no matter how antiseptic their scientific form and articulation, are at no great remove from debate over public policy.

Economic history, as a field of academic study, is peculiarly associated with the problem approach in both senses. Thumbing through the files of our journals or the listing of doctoral dissertations one can still detect the series of fighting issues, arrayed in geological layers, out of which we have evolved. There is first the argument over the universal wisdom of free trade in which the German scholars, then Cunningham and

Thorold Rogers evoked historical evidence against the repeal of the tariffs.[1] The debate quickly broadened to embrace the legitimacy of state intervention into the workings of the economy, the legitimacy of social welfare legislation, the legitimacy of labor unions. Then economic history was pushed into narrower and more technical areas by the debate over monetary and trade policy (and theory) in the 1920's and by the concern of the 1930's with the cause and cure for the business cycle. At the same time longer term reflections about the historical evolution and viability of capitalism stirred by the cloudy interwar years—notably those of Schumpeter—opened up the thriving field of entrepreneurial study, bringing *inter alia* a phalanx of economic historians to debate against their naughty muckraking parents (or occasionally against their libertine youth). And it is not too much to say that a good part of the contemporary effort in economic history is directly shaped by the concern with public policy designed to accelerate growth in the underdeveloped regions of the world, which emerged in the decade after World War II.

Although it is no great trick to identify the historical foundations of our respective interests as economic historians, the conventions of academic life tend to conceal our origins in the rude forum of social and political conflict and policy formation. American graduate schools—their methods and their manners—have a peculiar power to denature problem-oriented thought (in either sense) and to tame it to departmentally organized disciplines; for a real problem, involving whole people, rarely if ever breaks down along the lines into which the study of human affairs is professionally fragmented.

In history what begins as an analytic insight of some power and subtlety often ends in the second and third generations as a flow of monographs, high in empirical content, but increasingly divorced from the living problem that opened up the new terrain. Turner's essay on the frontier, for example, has served as the intellectual basis for two further generations' study. The frontier process has now been explored by regions, by states, and occasionally by counties. Few of these empirical exegeses have, however, added anything of analytic importance to Turner's formulation. Despite a massive empirical effort, the great historical watershed of the 1890's—a part (but only a part) of whose meaning Turner sensed—remains still to be dealt with analytically. And it is often true that in general the academic approach to history tends to divest propositions of their analytic content as rapidly as possible and to convert them into respectable, institutionalized specialties within which graduate students can be safely encouraged to write doctoral dissertations, researchable within a year after their general examinations have been completed.

There is, of course, another side to the medal. However much the historian may be (consciously or unconsciously) guided by abstract conceptions, his profession requires that, for a considerable portion of his working life, he pour over data, sort out reliable from unreliable sources, and (whatever the philosophical ambiguities) assemble facts. No man can be a historian unless he has at least a touch of the antiquarian about him, unless he derives some simple-minded satisfaction from knowing how things really were in a part of the past. Whatever his loyalty to the creation of generalized knowledge, he must derive some sly pleasure at the exception to the broad historical rule. Moreover, even if one acknowledges that the economic historian's activity should in the end be related to the solution of general problems, and even if one accepts the duty of economic history to contribute to the formation of a wiser public policy, these higher order activities need not concern the economic historian all the time, nor need they concern every economic historian. There is room for students of every bent and taste within our field over the spectrum from pure theory to statistical compilation.

When all this is said, I would still assert that economic history is a less interesting field than it could be, because we do not remain sufficiently and steadily loyal to the problem approach, which in fact underlies and directs our efforts. Take a favorable case: the studies in the transfer problem and in the balance of payments under inflationary conditions, inspired by Taussig. Here clear issues were posed, capable of orderly empirical examination; the results could be brought directly into the main stream of one of the oldest and most mature branches of economic thought, foreign trade theory; and in the post-1919 world of reparations and inflation the results bore directly on major issues of public policy. It is no accident that Taussig's inspiration yielded four of the best works in economic history ever written by Americans; that is, the balance of payments studies of Williams, Viner, Graham, and White. And if it is objected that we all have not been regularly favored with doctoral students of this quality, the answer in part is that economic history has not regularly posed to its students issues as clearly relevant to major problems of theory and public policy.

Take a case closer to us, the modern study of entrepreneurial and business history. All the returns are by no means in. We cannot firmly judge the net contribution to knowledge of the enormous postwar effort in this area. Several things can, however, be said with confidence. First, there has been a considerable amount of low-order effort, where the authors have lost touch with their problem, where the analytic terms of reference derive mainly from a firm's books and where the results can be meaningfully linked to no generally useful bodies of knowledge. Second, the most interesting efforts have been those which sought actively to overcome the built-in tendency to antiquarianism and to relate conclusions about entrepreneurship to problems within two quite distinct general bodies of knowledge: either to the process of capital formation as a whole; or to the social structure and values of the society and period whose entrepreneurs were examined. Third, the final evaluation of the worth of this effort is likely to be made not in terms of the number of firms studied—or the empirical gaps "closed"—but in terms of the extent and the character of the problems it solves and the general insights it provides or fails to provide into the workings of economic and social processes that transcend but embrace the field of business history.

What I am asserting, then, is that a heightened and more conscious loyalty to the problem could strengthen in several dimensions the relations between theory and history. The problem helps prevent the historian from becoming the prisoner of a received theoretical hypothesis; for by definition he is dealing with a question unresolved in theory, policy, or both. At the same time, by giving the historian a point of departure independent of his data, the problem helps prevent him from accepting in a fit of absent-mindedness the categories and analytic concepts built into his data. And, finally, the problem—if it is well and carefully defined—provides an area of common discourse, of useful, professional communication between the historian and the theorist, where results can be compared, where the historian can learn how the theorist poses the question and the historian can teach the theorist how things really worked. And should the latter statement be regarded as a mere verbal courtesy to our profession, it should be recalled that the classical concept of the movement of the terms of trade in consequence of capital flows never recovered from even moderately systematic historical inquiry, and that Clapham's pointed questions about empty boxes led directly (on one side of the Atlantic) to the upsetting of perfect competition as the theorist's norm. Seriously undertaken—that is, focused around clearly defined problems of common interest—the relationship between theorists and historians can be a two-way street.

III

Having held up the bright vision of theorist and historian solving problems in cheerful, productive collaboration I come to the lion in the path to its attainment: the theorist has generally been uneasy if not awkward if forced to work outside Marshallian short-period assumptions; the historian—like the human beings he writes about—cannot avoid working in a world of changing tastes and institutions, changing population, technology, and capacity.

The difficulty goes deep. The weakness of economic theory derives from its main strength; namely, that it is the most substantial body of useful thought about human behavior that is Newtonian in character. It represents the logical elaboration of a minimum number of basic assumptions that of their nature permit of maximization propositions and thus permit static equilibrium situations to be rigorously defined. Value and distribution theory are essentially an extensive development of one proposition about man, another about his environment; that is, they derive from the laws of diminishing relative marginal utility and from diminishing returns. And these propositions remain essential, even, in modern income analysis, in the elegant world of interacting multiplier and accelerator.[2]

In both major branches—value theory and income analysis—long-period factors must be handled on an extremely restricted basis if the structure of theory is to retain its shape. As Marshall perceived, the independence of demand and supply is lost in the long period and with it the powerful tool of static analysis.[3] For a theorist it is fair enough to say, as Marshall did, that a case of increasing return is "deprived of practical interest by the inapplicability of the Statical Method"; but this is a curiously chill definition of practical interest for a historian. Similarly, in modern income analysis, when efforts are made to introduce changes in population, technology, entrepreneurship, and other long-period factors, they are made on so formal and abstract a basis as to constitute very little change from the older conventional assumption that they were fixed and constant. To Keynes's famous dictum—in the long run we are all dead—the historian is committed by profession flatly to reply, Nonsense; the long run is with us, a powerful active force every day of our lives.

Indeed the long series of debates between classical theorists and their more empirical opponents reduces substantially to a difference between those committed to the primacy of short-period factors and those who held that long-period factors might be dominant over particular short periods of time: so it was between the authors of the Bullion Report and its opponents in explaining the wartime rise in prices; between free traders and the would-be protectors of infant industries; between the opponents and advocates of legal limitation on hours of work; between those who advocated large-scale government intervention to deal with unemployment and those who feared its revolutionary long-run consequences.[4] In one sense this issue is at the core of the ideological race between Indian and Chinese Communist methods for takeoff: will victory go to the system which uses force to constrain consumption and to maximize the short-period volume of investment or to that which creates a long-run setting of human incentives and institutions more conducive to spontaneous self-sustaining growth, designed to yield (through normal plow-backs and a democratically controlled national policy) levels of investment and productivity adequate substantially to outstrip population growth? (I might say parenthetically that whatever the outcome of this competitive historical exercise, the structure of modern income analysis, as applied to economic growth, biases the case unrealistically in favor of the Chinese Communist method.)

Are we to conclude, then, that of the nature of their professions the economic theorist and the economic historian are doomed to work different sides of a street so wide that it is hardly worth shouting across? Should the theorist, equipped with powerful mechanisms for analyzing economies under short-period assumptions, be left to deal with problems where such assumptions are useful and relevant, leaving the historian and other less disciplined but less inhibited investigators to handle the murky world of long-period change? After all, that is roughly the way our textbooks are written and our courses set up; and there is often wisdom in apparently irrational arrangements that persist.

On the whole, I would take the view that such complacent (or pessimistic) conservatism is both inappropriate and unnecessary.

It is inappropriate because whether we look to the underdeveloped areas, caught up in the early stages of the process of growth, or to the industrial societies that have learned to vote themselves chronic full employment, the economic problems of the foreseeable future, both of policy and of intellectual interest, require the systematic understanding and manipulation of long-period factors. This is self-evident in the underdeveloped areas, where new economic institutions must be created, skills and attitudes appropriate to growth imparted, capacity expanded in appropriate balance, the possibilities of external economies examined and exploited. Even the most classically short-period of economic activities—fiscal policy—must, in the underdeveloped areas, be touched with an acute awareness of changing capital—output ratios, with the need to transfer income flows from traditional to modern sectors, and with other long-period considerations which assume a peculiar urgency in the transition to self-sustaining growth. The industrialized societies are only a little less obviously enmeshed in long-period problems: radical shifts in birth rates, with important consequences for the structure of the population and the working force; radical changes in technology and in the sectoral composition of output; the deepening commitment to make an overt political distribution of resources as among security outlays, social overhead capital, and the private sector; and so on.

In short, if the work of the economist is to be relevant, he must work to an important degree outside the theoretical structures that have mainly interested him since, say, J. S. Mill.

There is, however, no need for pessimism if one looks not merely to the formal structure of theory but also to the total capabilities of economists; and if one looks to the whole long tradition of economic thought, not merely to the theorems of greatest interest in the past several generations. Economists, it is true, receive their contemporary training and develop their professional virtuosity mainly by manipulating a relatively narrow range of propositions; but it has long been in the best tradition of economists to go forth into the world as it is, full of long-period forces; to analyze whole problems; and to prescribe for them. Sometimes those analyses and prescriptions have exhibited the bias of a training disproportionately devoted to the manipulation of short-period forces in state equilibrium situations. On the whole, however, the ablest economists transcended the limits of their most refined tools: from Marshall's testimony on the Great Depression to the Paley Commission Report; from D. H. Robertson's study of industrial fluctuations to the contemporary pilgrimage of Western economists to New Delhi.

Once out in the real world, what relation does economic theory bear to the virtues of economists when they perform virtuously? Are they merely smart fellows, handy to have around when considering a tough practical problem; or does the structure of their formal thought have a useful as well as an inhibiting effect? Put another way, what are the uses of economic theory in analyzing problems where long-period factors are important, particularly problems in history?

Theory can be useful in three distinguishable ways. First, in defining the problem. Although the best-developed areas of theory take the form of short-period propositions, economics offers an orderly way of looking at and defining the totality of factors at work in an economic system. Formal economics can help map a problem, even if it has little to suggest by way of a solution. It can help pose the questions and set up empty boxes in fields as remote from the main streams of theoretical effort as population change, the generation of new technology, and the quality of entrepreneurship. Although economists may have done little in modern times to analyze long-period factors, they are well trained in listing exhaustively the factors they are assuming fixed; and this is most helpful.

Second, although the nature of long-period change may make impossible the development of a long-period economic theory—for example, a theory of economic growth—it by no means bars the development of important theoretical propositions about long-period change. For example, income analysis has been successfully adapted as a rough-and-ready but indispensable aggregative framework for the planning of economic growth;[5] the classical analysis of factor proportions in the theory of production has been adapted to throw important light on certain growth problems;[6] and, in general, the familiar technique of isolating one variable or relationship in movement, within a system otherwise held constant, while inappropriate for the general treatment of a whole interacting historical process, can be an extremely fruitful partial technique of analysis.[7] In short, there are many more uses for theory in dealing with long-period problems than have yet been developed. Neo-Marshallian pessimism on this score—a conviction that rigor had to be abandoned when the economist departs from the short-period, that there is no middle ground between geometry and description—can easily be overdone.

There is a third role for economic theory and theorists in history; that is, to contribute actively to the systematic organization of knowledge about the past in terms of analytic categories that permit cross-comparison and generalization. This role requires that economists, in addition to maintaining and developing the Newtonian sectors of their science, begin to take seriously the biological strands in their heritage embedded in the *Wealth of Nations*, evoked in our time by Mitchell's leadership and by Schumpeter's fruitful suggestions. It is only in terms of some such grand conception focused around some clear concrete problems shared between economists and historians that the full possibilities of interrelationship can be developed. And it is to some of its implications—which most obviously bear on the study of economic growth—that I now turn.

IV

In one sense it is distinctly anticlimactic to suggest that the major common task and meeting place of economists and historians is the analysis of economic growth; and that the systematic isolation of similarities and differences among national patterns of growth is likely to be the most productive method jointly to pursue. What, after all, have we been doing in recent years? A high proportion of recent articles in the economic history journals has been designed to translate aspects of national economic history into the more universal language of economic growth; and articles on economic growth—in fact or in name—have hit the economic journals like a biblical plague. Papers prepared for special meetings—such as the 1954 conference on capital formation—indicate not merely a convergence of interest among historians, statisticians, theorists, and functional specialists but the beginnings, at least, of an ability to communicate when a problem as relatively clearcut as capital formation is explored.[8] Moreover, comparative analysis of national growth experiences is increasingly a feature of the landscape from, as it were, our little family difficulty with nineteenth-century France and Germany to the study of Brazil, Japan, and India.[9] Indeed, we need look no farther than to the sessions which have preceded us, over the past several days, reflecting the progress under way in providing a statistical bone structure for comparative growth analysis, and to the subject of tomorrow's meeting.

We have found, it might appear, an optimum focus for our efforts as economic historians: economic growth permits us to use in a shapely way much of the cumulative work of our predecessors; it provides a problem area in both policy and problem senses; in the analysis of growth the Marshallian long period, in whose treatment we historians enjoy a comparative advantage, cannot be ignored; and since by definition growth takes place over long periods of time, the economist must either study history or call us in on a basis of equal partnership at least.

But I would make two final observations before agreeing that the golden age of economic history and of collaboration between theory and history has already arrived.

First, I do not believe that the efforts now going forward, from many technical perspectives, focused around economic growth are going to yield a usable body of biological theory unless a conscious effort is made to develop that theory. I do not believe that the organization, side by side on a country basis of statistical data, industry analyses, entrepreneurial studies, and monographs on technology, with experts in Harrod-Domar models benevolently looking on, is going to yield automatically, by osmosis, the corpus of organized concepts we shall require if the golden age is to come to pass. In the three quarters of a century or so since we created our graduate schools, and the professional study of history and the social sciences, based on German models mixed with native American empiricism, we have managed to create many barren acres of factually accurate volumes, bearing on interesting issues, in which the authors left the problem of intellectual synthesis to someone else. Ironically this persistent philosophical disease—apparently a disease of modesty and intellectual scruple—has left American academic life, by default, particularly vulnerable to the brilliant, casual, and not wholly responsible insights of a Veblen, a Beard, or a Schumpeter who did not fear to generalize.

The disease can be seen in the state of American history as a whole, not excluding economic history, the latter being a peculiarly shapeless affair; it can be seen in the trailing away without adequate issue of the institutionalist school; it can be seen even in one of the most successful of these native empirical exercises, the National Bureau of Economic Research, whose monographs have enormously enriched our knowledge of limited aspects of the past and present, without, however, fulfilling the grand vision of synthesis among theory, history, and statistics that inspired Mitchell and the institution he founded. Only where the special rigors and risks of synthesis were consciously and boldly faced—as in Abramovitz' study of inventory cycles—can one perceive something of what we have all been hoping for.

I would warn, then, on the basis of our common experience and our ingrained national style, against assuming that theoretical synthesis comes about without special, conscious effort.

But to what kind of synthesis should we look? What kind of framework is capable of posing researchable questions for historians that, if answered, permit empirical results to be compared and generalized and also permit easy and useful intercommunication with the theorist?

Each answer to this question will inevitably be shaped by unique interests and experiences; mine is affected in particular by the job of trying to teach coherently the story of the evolution of the world economy over the past two centuries. I have leaned, as some of you know, to a concept of historical stages held together by a bone structure of more conventional dynamic theory. In a recent article I suggested that it may be useful to regard the period, after a relatively static traditional society begins to break up, as divisible into stages of preconditions, takeoff, and sustained growth. And I have been experimenting in my seminar over the past several years with some subdivisions of the sustained growth stage, notably with substages of technological maturity and of dominance by durable consumers goods and services, both of which are, I believe, capable of reasonably precise definition and approximate historical dating for those societies which have experienced them. (It may be that after the age of durable consumers—when diminishing relative marginal utility has set in sharply for the extra car or portable

TV—that babies take over as a leading sector; but it is a bit too soon to lay this down as immutable natural law.) I doubt that stages by themselves in the old German style will serve our purpose; but if we can link them to a modified corpus of conventional economic theory—and especially provide some definitions that are at least conceptually quantitative and permit reasonably accurate dating—we may generate something of intellectual power and utility.

I would certainly not be dogmatic about the forms of synthesis likely to prove most useful; but I would urge with some confidence that, as we gain an increasing knowledge of each other's work, and as the data pile up, we must allocate more time to building and applying a synthesis than we have in the past.

I come now to a final observation. It is quite simply that the explicit analysis of growth is likely to force economic history in somewhat new ways into the analysis of politics, social structure, and culture. A glance at our textbooks indicates that economic historians are not strangers to these fields. Clapham's affectionate and precise evocation of the round of British life at various historical epochs is as good as anything social history affords; and the role of the state in economic life has embedded us all in the study of politics at one time or another. It is, indeed, possible to criticize much of conventional economic history as too political and social and not sufficiently economic. My point is that the systematic treatment of growth will pose some new problems of relationship between economic and other factors and some old problems in new forms.

The comparative study of periods of preconditioning for takeoff must, for example, focus sharply in most cases around two related questions: the formation of an effective, modern central government capable of exercising fiscal power over old regionally based interests; and the emergence of a group (or usually a coalition) with vested interests in the development of an effective national government and the technical talents and motivation to operate the modern sectors of economy. From postmedieval western Europe to contemporary Egypt and India, from Canada to the Argentine, from Japan to Turkey, the political and social patterns that have accompanied the stage of preconditions have, of course, varied, and yet they have been shot through with recognizable common features. The orderly sorting out of both common features and variations, in their relations to more familiar patterns of economic change, will prove, I believe, an essential aspect of the development of a general biological theory of economic growth. (If we move in this direction we should, incidentally, be able to get much assistance from the current generation of political scientists who are increasingly committed to the study of comparative politics in non-Western societies.[10]) Nor will these extraeconomic concerns end when we have seen our respective countries into sustained growth; for social structure, politics, and culture are not the monopoly of economically underdeveloped areas. As time goes on we shall, I suspect, be studying differences in the sociological bases and political consequences of growth stages dominated by heavy as opposed to light engineering industries, not excluding the significance of the differences within Communist societies; we shall be exploring the social and cultural, as well as the economic anatomy of the durable consumers' and service stages, which we entered in the 1920's and the entrance into which of western Europe and Japan constitutes one of the most surprising and revolutionary features of the postwar decade; and we may even learn a little about the dynamic determinants of the birth rate.

In short, in accepting economic growth as a central problem we shall, from one perspective, be forced to become general theorists of whole societies; for the motives of men and the human institutions and activities which bear directly and technically on the rate of increase of output per capita are not narrowly limited. And our loyalty should be to the problem of economic growth, wherever it may take us, not to the bureaucratic confines of economic history or of economics as they are presently consecrated in our graduate schools.

All this talk may seem heady stuff, perhaps appropriate once in a while at an annual meeting, when the members of the club gather away from their desks and filing cards, but not to be taken seriously. By Monday we shall all be back grappling with our familiar piece of the elephant. And in one sense I would agree, recalling my introductory statement that method is not an appropriate subject for serious debate and certainly not for harangue.

In a larger sense, however, the vision of how we should tackle the problem of economic growth, of where economic history fits, and how it should relate to theory are important questions. They are important because, I would guess—as a matter of prediction rather than special pleading—we are in fact going to do something about them over the next generation of work. In many areas of natural and social science the cast of American intellectual life has radically shifted in the past twenty years or so. We are no longer a nation incapable of creating new abstract concepts nor are we as awkward as we once were in dealing with them. The old generalization that Americans derive their basic science and fundamental inventions, intellectual or otherwise, from abroad requires substantial modification. I do not believe that economic history will prove to be exempt from this national process of emergence into intellectual maturity.

The problem of interrelating theory and history around the problem of growth does indeed require for its solution a difficult merger—a merger of our old national gift for the energetic pursuit of fact, with a new sustained and orderly effort to build an intermediate structure of abstraction and generalization. Our still young field of economic history, full of essential knowledge and accumulated wisdom about the way different societies have handled their economic activities, already responding with vigor to the policy and intellectual challenges of the problem of economic growth, can—and I believe will—play a strategic, indeed an indispensable, role in this merger.

NOTES

1. We can, of course, track our ancestry to Adam Smith, in which case we have done briefs for both sides on the issue of free trade, as indeed we (and other historians) have done on most major issues of public policy.

2. The upper turning point in modern business cycle theories, for example, is usually traced back to a short-period rise in saving (reflecting the diminished relative marginal utility of consumption with a rise in income); to supply bottlenecks and cost increases (reflecting short-period diminishing returns); to a short- or long-period exhaustion of avenues for profitable investment adequate to sustain full employment (again reflecting diminishing returns); or to some combination of these factors.

3. For further discussion see the author's *Process of Economic Growth* (London, 1953), pp. 5–6.

4. This case could, of course, be reversed; that is, it could be regarded as a debate between those who held to classic assumptions and those who faced the long-period reality of inflexible money wage rates. Politically, the Keynesians were the men of the short-period; in theory, the Pigovians.

5. See, for example, *The First Indian Five-Year Plan* (New Delhi, 1951), Ch. ii.

6. See R. S. Eckaus, "The Factor Proportion Problem in Underdeveloped Areas", *American Economic Review*, XLV (Sept. 1955), 539–65.

7. See, for example, T. Haavelmo, *A Study in the Theory of Economic Evolution* (Amsterdam, 1954).

8. See *Capital Formation and Economic Growth* (Princeton: Princeton University Press, 1955).

9. S. Kuznets, W. E. Moore, and J. J. Spengler, *Economic Growth: Brazil, India, Japan* (Durham: Duke University Press, 1955).

10. See, notably, D. Rustow, "New Horizons for Comparative Politics," *World Politics*, IX (July 1957), 530–49. See also George McT. Kahin, Guy J. Pauker, and Lucian Pye, "Comparative Politics of non-Western Countries," *American Political Science Review*, XLIX (Dec. 1955), 1022–41.

THREE

Cycles and the Irreducible Complexity of History (1982)

As on several previous occasions M. M. Postan recruited me for a gathering of the International Economic History Association: this time in Budapest in the summer of 1982, where he would have been honored by the association he founded. Active and productive to the end, he died in December 1981 at the age of eighty-two.

The organizers of the conference asked me to write a paper on long cycles in eight pages. They imposed discipline on the contributors by a splendid device: They sent eight sheets only of the special paper from which the essays would be reproduced for use at the conference.

Challenged by their method I wrote a paper on six types of cycles and their interaction with one sheet unused and a homily on method at the end.

The occasion provided an opportunity to learn something about Hungary's economic reforms and reformers from whom China and the Soviet Union were to learn a good deal—an ironic outcome of the grant of economic liberalism made by Khrushchev to Hungary in the wake of the brutal crushing of the rebellion of 1956 in order to minimize the chance of a recurrence.

1. INTRODUCTION

In a recent essay on business cycles, I made this observation (Rostow, 1980): "What we observe historically, then, are dynamic, interacting national economies trying rather clumsily to approximate optimum sectoral paths, tending successively to undershoot and overshoot those paths, making their way through history like a drunk going home on Saturday night. And although it doesn't concern us here, modern socialist economies, with fully developed institutions for central planning, don't do much better." In fact, the path assumed by economic history is even more complex than this observation would suggest; for multiple cycles operate concurrently, interwoven and interacting. The purpose of this paper, therefore, is to define and illustrate the complexity of the cyclical process in history. The argument proceeds by considering the underlying reasons for cycles of differing lengths; some implications of their concurrence and interaction; and some of the ways non-economic factors may determine, damp, or heighten cyclical paths and rhythms.

2. CYCLES AND THEIR CAUSES

At least six kinds of economic cycles have been identified in history.

A. Long Demographic Cycles

Long demographic cycles, spanning centuries, belong, thus far in our experience, to the pre-modern history of societies. They were, essentially, Malthusian; that is, they occurred mainly because, as Hung Liang-chi, China's predecessor to Malthus, concluded (Ping-ti Ho, 1959): "The increase in the means of subsistence and the increase of population are not in direct proportion. The population within a hundred years or so can increase from five-fold to twenty-fold, while the means of subsistence, due to the limitation of the land-area, can increase only from three to five times." Not many long demographic cycles have been firmly identified; but others no doubt occurred. The most famous such demographic sequence was Europe's two and a half cycles beginning with a trough in, say, the eleventh century. A peak occurred in the first half of the fourteenth century, a trough in the first half of the fifteenth. A second phase of expansion peaked about two centuries later, giving way in the seventeenth century to a spectrum of reactions ranging from stagnation in Britain to substantial population decline in Spain. A third upsurge gathered momentum in the second half of the eighteenth century yielding, in the rapidly industrializing countries, a fairly smooth demographic transition rather than population stagnation or decline. In China, however, where a troubled seventeenth century gave way to a doubling of population in the relatively peaceful and prosperous eighteenth century, a Malthusian crisis occurred, with population stagnant in the second half of the nineteenth century—a process Europe might have shared, as Ashton observed, if the industrial revolution had not intervened (Ashton, 1948).

As we shall note later, these long demographic cycles were not simply the product of a periodic clash between population increase and the limits of food supply, followed by crisis, recoil, and rebound. They interwove in complex ways with non-economic factors.

While demographic history in post-take-off economies assumed the more benign form of the demographic transition, marriage, birth, and death rates, as well as rates of emigration and immigration, continued to reflect in less dramatic ways the cyclical paths that sustained economic growth assumed.

B. Short Demographic Cycles

In pre-industrial Sweden, China, and elsewhere, there is evidence of a shorter demographic cycle of 20–30 years (Rostow, 1975). Detailed demographic studies of particular localities suggest that the explanation for this (roughly) generational cyclical tendency may lie in the fact that a demographic crisis (due, say, to war, disastrous harvests, or plague) yielded in its aftermath a surge in the birth rate and an echo about a quarter-century later as those born in the recovery period themselves formed families. The consequent population expansion would then again exert Malthusian pressure on the constrained economic environment rendering it extremely sensitive to war, bad harvests, or disease (Wrigley, 1969).

C. Kondratieff Cycles (or Trend Periods)

There are, of course, two major explanations for the price, wage, and monetary cycles Kondratieff identified but did not definitively explain: Schumpeter's hypothesis centered on the rhythm of clusters of major innovations; and my hypothesis centered on the relative prices of basic versus industrial commodities, reflecting, in turn, periods of relative shortage and abundance of basic commodities. Although differing dates flow from these hypotheses in the period since the mid-1930's, all students who accept the reality of the phenomenon agree that we are examining a somewhat erratic style about 40–50 years in length.

D. Housing Cycles

The rate of housing construction is, basically, related to the rate of family formation, corrected for the rate of urbanization and, where relevant, public policies bearing on housing construction. Like other forms of investment, housing construction has followed a cyclical path. A housing cycle of about twenty years has been identified in (mainly) pre-1914 British and American data; and the rhythm can be detected, even, in British data for the eighteenth century.

E. Major Cycles

These are the cycles in long term investment which, from, say, 1783 to 1914, exhibited an average length of about nine years. It is to the mechanism of this cycle that most business cycle theories of the twentieth century were addressed. The rhythm persisted, more or less, during the pathological interwar years, with cyclical peaks in 1920, 1929, and 1937. The major cycle gave way to more muted, shorter cycles in growth rates in the 1950's and 1960's; wheras the two oil shocks dominate the cyclical path of the 1970's.

F. Inventory Cycles

Inventory cycles of 3–4 years can be traced in the British data as far back as the eighteenth century and persist into the post-1945 years in the advanced industrial economies.

Putting aside demographic cycles, the latter four types delineated were all cycles in investment either over-all or sectoral (e.g. the Kondratieff and housing cycles). Investment assumed a cyclical path for two reasons: because investors made systematic errors in predicting future profitability; and because investment took time.

Systematic error flowed from the fact that investment decisions were mainly determined by current indicators of profitability rather than by rational long-range assessments; these indicators made many investors act in the same direction, without taking into account the total volume of investment in particular sectors that was being induced by current profit expectations; and, beyond these technical characteristics of the investment process, there was, psychologically, a follow-the-leader tendency, as waves of optimism and pessimism about the profits to be earned in particular sectors swept the capital markets and industries where profits were (or were not) being plowed back in the expansion of plant.

Time lags of three types helped reinforce these distortions and determined the length and amplitude of the various cycles: the recognition (or information) lag between the emergence of a profit possibility (or a decline in profit possibility) and the decision to increase or decrease investment in a particular direction; the period of gestation of the investment; and the longevity of the type of investment undertaken. For example, the greater length of a housing than an inventory cycle: it took less time to build up inventories than to build a house; and a house, once built, lasted much longer than stocks in inventory. The lags inherent in the opening up of new sources of basic commodities decreed historically a still longer cycle. Thus, if there were no lags and if investors were perfectly knowledgeable and wise (including knowledge and wisdom about new technological possibilities), investment would have been allocated to each sector (agriculture, energy, housing, particular branches of industry and services, and the like) in ways which exactly met future requirements and kept the marginal rate of return over costs equal in all sectors at each moment of time. Overall growth would have proceeded smoothly as each sector followed its optimum dynamic sectoral path. Systematically imperfect foresight and multiple time lags explain why this didn't happen.

3. CONCURRENCE AND INTERACTION

Again putting demographic cycles aside, modern economic history consists in large part of a process of sustained growth within which investment—the driving variable—assumed the form of four types of cycles operating concurrently. At any given moment, a particular economy, in take-off or at a later stage of growth, felt the impact of Kondratieff, housing, major and inventory cycles; and this impact was also transmitted to pre-take-off economies, which had entered the trading system of the world economy, via the prices and level of demand for their exports and flows of immigration and external capital.

It should be noted that for post-take-off economies the four types of cycles were not symmetrical. Kondratieff cycles had their primary impact on price, wage, and interest rate trends, on the sectoral composition (rather than volume) of investment, and on regional and international income distribution. Housing cycles also related to the sectoral composition of investment. Major and inventory cycles affected the over-all level of production and employment. They cannot, therefore, be added up to form a single curve reflecting the path yielded by their concurrence as Schumpeter once, in a fit of absentmindedness, combined Kondratieff, major (Juglar) and inventory (Kitchin) cycles (Schumpeter, 1939).

For our limited purposes, the first conclusions to be drawn from this line of argument are these: (i) to examine the implications of the concurrence and interaction of cycles of different character, length, and amplitude it is necessary to study the sectoral character of investment as well as its over-all level and the over-all path of real output; (ii) because of the role (in my view) of relative prices in Kondratieff cycles it is necessary to disaggregate the price level; (iii) because of the special role of interest rates in determining the level of investment in housing, it is necessary to examine all the relevant forces at work on that variable, now neglected in the vogue of modern monetarism for an obsessive focus on the money stock.

When the concurrence and interaction of cycles are examined from this perspective, a number of substantive conclusions emerge which, evidently, can only be stated tersely here:

- An inventory cycle could take place without a major (long term investment) cycle; but inventory cycles accompanied and reinforced all major cycles.
- Kondratieff cycles, in both their expansion and contraction phases, altered the character but not the rhythm of major and inventory cycles. Despite the widely held view that unemployment was, on average, more severe in Kondratieff downswings before 1914, that proposition has not been unambiguously demonstrated (Rostow, 1948). Since 1914 we have had both a Kondratieff downswing (1920–

1933) and a Kondratieff upswing (1972–   ) accompanied by abnormal unemployment. What is clear is that Kondratieff cycles shifted the proportion of total investment allocated to basic commodities; and they brought about, through relative price shifts, significant shifts in income distribution as among regions, within economies, and internationally.

- Kondratieff cycles, because of these income shifts and the altered directions of investment they induced, also had a significant impact on the timing and locus of housing cycles. In a Kondratieff upswing, capital and population flowed to areas producing the basic commodities whose relative prices had risen (e.g., pre-1914 Canada and Argentina, contemporary Alaska, Scotland, and Saudi Arabia). Housing booms naturally occurred as a by-product of the process. On the other hand, housing investment was damped in the countries or regions exporting capital and people (e.g., pre-1914 Britain and the contemporary U.S. northeast), a process heightened by the higher interest rates that normally accompanied a Kondratieff upswing.

4. CYCLES AND NON-ECONOMIC FACTORS

There is, finally, a group of non-economic complexities which both leave their impact on the timing, amplitude, and character of cycles and have, additionally, an independent non-cyclical role in shaping economic history: the luck of the harvests, wars, and the responsiveness (or lack of responsiveness) of societies to the economic challenges history places before them.

- In the eighteenth century, for a good deal of the nineteenth century, and, to a lesser degree, in the twentieth century harvests had a significant role in determining the precise timing of major cycles. In the period 1783–1860, for example, good harvests were usually required for a strong expansion to begin; bad harvests often exacerbated other forces operating to bring on a cyclical downturn (Gayer, 1953).
- From, say, 1700 to the recovery of the world economy after the Second World War, housing cycles are intimately connected with wars; that is, the sharp decline in housing construction during wars yielded post-war housing booms which, after running their course, helped set the subsequent rhythm of housing cycles. In addition, of course, wars left their mark on economic history in many other substantial ways, including the rate of family formation.
- Most important of all are the political, social, and psychological factors that enter quite technically into the story. For example, the dominant indigenous theory of China's nine dynastic cycles is not Malthusian: it is a cycle on the waxing and waning of political virtue (Wright, 1957; Rostow, 1971). It seems likely that the kind

of Malthusian sequence to be observed in China from the late seventeenth to the late nineteenth centuries had earlier counterparts; but the non-economic factors on which classical Chinese historians focused were, surely, not a simple function of the degree of population pressure against the technical limits of agricultural production. The economic and non-economic factors interacted intimately.

Similarly, in more modern times, non-economic factors helped determine the response of less advanced societies to the intrusions of the more advanced (e.g., mid-nineteenth century China versus Japan) and, even, the response of different societies to a favorable or unfavorable shift in the terms of trade (e.g., pre-1914 Argentina versus Canada). Nor did strictly economic factors determine the weakness of Western Europe's response to the third (interwar) Kondratieff downswing or the nearly universal inadequacy of the global response to the fifth (post-1972) Kondratieff upswing.

5. CONCLUSION

The concurrence and interaction of cycles combined with the non-economic factors inevitably at work suggest that the question D. H. Robertson gently posed in 1948 should be put now somewhat more sharply (Robertson, 1948): "We must wait with respectful patience while the econometricians decide whether their elaborate methods are really capable of covering such models with flesh and blood. But I confess that to me at least the forces at work seem so complex, the question whether even the few selected parameters can be relied on to stay put through the cycle or between cycles so doubtful, that I wonder whether more truth will not in the end be wrung from interpretative studies of the crude data. . . ."

High powered theories and statistical methods can be exploited to examine limited facets of economic history. But a costly trade-off exists: the fancier the method, the simpler the theory. The exploration of major problems in economic history requires, therefore, that econometrics be transcended by propositions and methods embracing a larger number of variables including, in the end, non-economic variables.

REFERENCES

Ashton, T. S., 1948, *The Industrial Revolution, 1760–1830*, Oxford University Press, London, p. 161.

Gayer, A. D., et al., 1953, *The Growth and Fluctuation of the British Economy, 1790–1850*, Clarendon Press, Oxford, especially pp. 563–565, 792–794, and 854–855.

Ho, Ping-ti, 1959, *Studies on the Population of China, 1368–1953*, Harvard University Press, Cambridge, Mass., pp. 271–272.

Robertson, D. H., 1948, *A Study of Industrial Fluctuations*, No. 8 in Series of Reprints of Scarce Works on Political Economy, London School of Economics, London, p. vii.

Rostow, W. W., 1948, *British Economy of the Nineteenth Century*, Clarendon Press, Oxford, pp. 45–50.

Rostow, W. W., 1971, *Politics and the Stages of Growth*, Cambridge University Press, Cambridge, pp. 35–53.

Rostow, W. W., 1975, *How It All Began*, McGraw-Hill, New York, pp. 2–4 and 229 n. 2.

Rostow, W. W., 1980, "Cycles in the Fifth Kondratieff Upswing," in *The Business Cycle and Public Policy, 1929–80*, Compendium of Papers submitted to the Joint Economic Committee, U. S. Congress, Government Printing Office, Washington, D. C., p. 37.

Schumpeter, J. A., 1939, *Business Cycles*, McGraw-Hill, New York, p. 213.

Wrigley, E. A., 1969, *Population and History*, McGraw-HIll, New York, pp. 68–76.

Wright, M. C., 1957, *The Last Stand of Chinese Conservatism*, Stanford University Press, Stanford, pp. 43–44.

Professor Arrow on Economic Analysis and Economic History (1986)

When Charles P. Kindleberger was president of the American Economic Association in 1984, he and William N. Parker, the distinguished economic historian, organized a session titled "Economic History: A Necessary Though not Sufficient Condition for an Economist" at the annual meeting. This session brought together a distinguished group from both disciplines.

Kindleberger had recruited me for another session—on Japan and the world economy—but when I saw Kenneth Arrow's paper for the economic history session, I got into the act. Parker organized a short book from these raw materials (Economic History and the Modern Economist).

I believe it is fair to say that, as compared to the discussion in 1957 (Chapter 2) a quarter-century earlier, the neoclassical economists were somewhat chastened. But the serious job of re-integrating theory and history, in the tradition of classical political economy, remains before us.

Professor Arrow's thoughtful paper[1] came to rest, as I read it, on the incapacity of modern economic analysis to deal with the full range of variables at work in economic history and on the potentialities for mutual reinforcement by the two disciplines. This note is designed to sharpen the proposition and to draw certain implications for a more appropriate relation of economic theory both to economic history and to problems in the contemporary world economy. Obviously, Professor Arrow is in no way bound by the conclusions drawn here.

This essay was first published as Chapter 7 in William N. Parker (ed.), *Economic History and the Modern Economist* (Oxford and New York: Basil Blackwell, 1986). Reprinted with permission.

Like Professor Arrow, I regret the ignorance of history among most contemporary economists and, even more, among the current products of our major graduate schools of economics. But the problem is more serious than that. The economic theory our students are taught is often so structured that it is capable of dealing satisfactorily with only a narrow range of problems, either historical or contemporary. There is a great deal to be said for the use of mathematical and econometric method if it is treated strictly as one among other tools to illuminate or to solve serious problems. There is nothing to be said for the tendency to regard the mastery of these techniques as an objective in itself or to cut problems down to a size that permits their management with the limited capabilities which currently fashionable methods provide.

This is the root of the problem of relating economic theory to the flow of events in the active world, past or present. Faculty club conversation would, no doubt, be more civilized among economists if they knew more history. But if we are to bring economic analysis and economic history into the regular and fruitful mutual support implied by Professor Arrow's argument, we must try to solve in our time what might be called the Malthus–Ricardo problem.

Working in close communication from 1811 to Ricardo's death in 1823—with evident mutual respect, friendship, and a rare capacity to place the pursuit of truth above their clashing theoretical formulations—they could never resolve their differences.

Each tried to explain the impasse.

Malthus suggested that the difference arose between those who made a "precipitate attempt to simplify and generalize" and "their more practical opponents [who] draw too hasty inferences from a frequent appeal to partial facts . . ."[2] Malthus concluded: "In political economy the desire to simplify has occasioned an unwillingness to acknowledge the operation of more causes than one in the production of particular effects . . . The first business of philosophy is to account for things as they are . . . where unforeseen causes may possibly be in operation . . . an accurate yet comprehensive attention to facts is necessary."

Ricardo isolated "one great cause of our difference in opinion" in somewhat different but quite consistent terms: Malthus's concern with "immediate and temporary effects" as opposed to his effort to fix his "whole attention on the permanent state of things which will result from them." Ricardo concluded: "Perhaps you estimate these temporary effects too highly, whilst I am too much disposed to undervalue them."[3]

The counterpoint runs on to our own times. Take D. H. Robertson in Malthus's mood:[4]

> We must wait with respectful patience while the econometricians decide whether their elaborate methods are really capable of covering such models with flesh and blood. But I confess that to me at least the forces at work seem so complex, the question whether even the few selected parameters can be relied on to stay put through the cycle or between cycles so

doubtful, that I wonder whether more truth will not in the end be wrung from interpretive studies of the crude data of the general type contained in this volume [*A Study of Industrial Fluctuation*], but more intensive, more scrupulously-worded and more expert.

And, Milton Friedman in the spirit of Ricardo:[5] "A hypothesis is important if it 'explains' much by little, that is, if it abstracts the common and crucial elements from the mass of complex and detailed circumstances surrounding the phenomena to be explained and permits valid predictions on the basis of them alone." The problem is, of course, that both Ricardo's and Friedman's simple, powerful hypotheses, standing alone, failed to yield valid predictions.

If we are to make progress with the Malthus–Ricardo problem rather than fruitlessly to harangue each other or even recapture the gracious spirit in which these two great predecessors tried to define the chasm between them, there are different tasks to be undertaken by both the theorist and the historian.

The theorist must be prepared to try to do three things. First, he must acknowledge the profound limitations of present sophisticated mathematical and econometric methods as ways of coming to grips with the active world. Second, he must try to render dynamic in formal theory some of the variables now fixed "for purposes of reasoning" or on grounds of "analytic tractability."[6] Third, he must accept as part of the theorist's fundamental mission that he budget time and energy to acquire "an accurate yet comprehensive" knowledge of the facts. It is not enough for the theorist to take the view that he is prepared to be helpful if only the historian would organise the data in usable form, with all the parameters properly estimated.[7] This stricture implies that the end product is likely to be a good deal less elegant than he would like. The compensation is that he has come closer to accounting "for things as they are"—or were.

The economic historian, too, has some things to do which he is generally not doing. First, he must refuse to accept current mainstream neo-classical economics as a sufficient theoretical framework for his work. It has sufficed for important studies on certain limited problems; e.g. the diffusion of the reaper (cited by Professor Arrow), tariffs and the emergence of the modern American iron industry, the sources of expansion of American cotton textile production before the Civil War. In my view, it was an insufficient framework for the study of the railroads or slavery and would prove grossly inadequate if the cliometricians were to face up, as they should, to a systematic history of the growth and fluctuations of the American economy over the past two centuries. Second, having abandoned his subservience to received theory, the historian must play a more active role in helping the theorist elaborate and dynamize his models to render them more relevant to great problems in economic history. Finally, the historian, working with the theorist, must strain to develop from the data the best approximations for all the relevant variables he and the theorist agree must be taken into account.

Now, how, as a practical matter, can such intense working partnerships between the theorist and the collector and analyst of evidence be brought about? I doubt that methodological exhortation, or even formal concord, can do the trick. What is needed, I believe, is a shared, strong—even passionate—interest in important, relevant contemporary problems. Professor Arrow referred to the vitality formerly exhibited by business cycle history. That vitality came from a determination to understand the business cycle and to alleviate its grave human and social costs. This aspiration led Wesley C. Mitchell, D. H. Robertson, A. C. Pigou, and some of us in the next generation to concern ourselves with the history as well as the theory of business cycles. After the Second World War the problems of growth in the developing regions played a similar catalytic role for both theory and history, and generated linkages between the two domains. Around us and ahead, there are many unsolved problems with an historical dimension, where concerted effort might be fruitful, linking theorists to historians and other scholars who are prepared to pay "comprehensive attention to facts." Here are a few examples:

Technology and Employment: By what mechanisms did major new technologies introduced over the past two centuries, up to and including the present, generate both additional employment and additional unemployment? In the contemporary world this kind of analysis will require breaking out of the tyranny of the Standard Industrial Classifications and working from input–output employment matrices modified for these purposes, taking account *inter alia* of service employment generated by the new technologies.

Increasing and Diminishing Returns: How, over two centuries, was the tendency to diminishing returns held at bay; and what are the prospects for the next 50–75 years when global population moves to a probable peak? In theory, this requires, as Marshall clearly perceived, a facing up to the embarrassment to equilibrium economics presented by the existence of increasing returns.

The Rich Country, Poor Country Problem: The problem confronted by a relatively rich country which stirs by its example an imitative "fermentation" in a poor country was first lucidly formulated and prescribed for by David Hume.[8] It moved off the center of the stage in economic theory with the British take-off of the 1780s. Two centuries later it is back with a vengeance as the US contemplates Japan, Japan contemplates South Korea, Taiwan, and the dynamism of other developing countries in the Pacific Basin and, in time, China and India. How a front runner maintains (or fails to maintain) his place in the inescapable race is, evidently, a central problem for the future of US society, as the state of our balance of payments suggests.

In all these problems—and a good many others any one of us could cite—the relevance of history is authentic; modern economic theory and econometrics are usable but insufficient; and concerted effort to study the problem as a whole is likely to generate both new and significant theoretical propositions and the mobilization of hitherto underutilized historical and other empirical evidence.

There are, of course, theorists and historians who will not be interested in this kind of intensive sustained collaboration centered on the search for solutions to urgent, practical problems. There are even likely to be some in both theory and economic history who regard explicit attention to problems of current policy as beneath the dignity of their disciplines. Debate with those who cherish such notions is not only fruitless, but counter-productive. Our disciplines do and should contain men and women of different interests and tastes. But the brute fact is that both economic theory and economic history have evolved over the past two centuries in response to specific and identifiable problems in the active world. And that is the route we will have to follow if the current process of diminishing returns in both disciplines is to be reversed.

That is, of course, not the only way to look at the matter. Robert Solow once remarked, towards the close of a conference in 1960 embracing both theorists and economic historians:[9] "... perhaps the best thing might be for economic historians and model builders to remain friends, but no more—for the economists to misuse historians' data and for the historians to misunderstand the economists' theories." But a quarter century later the results of an attenuating friendship between the two disciplines cannot be regarded on either side with satisfaction or complacency. I take it Professor Arrow called on us to do better. I agree.

NOTES

1. Kenneth J. Arrow, "Economic History: A Necessary Though Not Sufficient Condition for an Economist. Maine and Texas," *AEA Papers and Proceedings*, vol. 75, no. 2 (May 1985), pp. 320–3.

2. T. R. Malthus, *Principles of Political Economy*, New York: Kelley, reprinted August 1951, extracted from pp. 4–12.

3. Piero Sraffa and M. H. Dobb (eds.), *The Works and Correspondence of David Recardo*, vol. VII, *Letters 1816–1818*, Cambridge: Cambridge University Press, for the Royal Economic Society, 1952, p. 120.

4. D. H. Robertson, *A Study of Industrial Fluctuation* (1915), reprinted by the London School of Economics and Political Science, No. 8 in Series of Reprints of Scarce Works on Political Economy, 1948, p. xvii.

5. Milton Friedman, "The Methodology of Positive Economics," in *Essays in Positive Economics*, Chicago: University of Chicago Press, 1953, p. 14.

6. The full context of the two phrases is as follows: "The classical theory [of international trade] assumes as fixed for purposes of reasoning, the very things which ... should be the chief objective of study" (John Williams, "The Theory of International Trade Reconsidered," *Economic Journal*, vol. 39, no. 154 (June 1929), p. 196). "It should be quite obvious to any careful reader of this book that our analysis so far is based on a very large number of assumptions, some of which can be justified only on the grounds of their analytic tractability

... further work may require some radical reconsideration of the premises underlying the present type of inquiry" (Sukhamoy Chakravarty, *Capital and Development Planning*, Cambridge, MA: M.I.T. Press, 1969, p. 246).

7. See, for example, Robert Solow in W. W. Rostow (ed.), *The Economics of Take-off into Sustained Economic Growth*, London: Macmillan, 1963, pp. 471–2.

8. Istvan Hont, "The Rich County–Poor Country Debate in Scottish Classical Political Economy," in Istvan Hont and Michael Ignatieff (eds.), *Wealth and Virtue: The Shaping of Political Economy in the Scottish Enlightenment*, ch. 11, Cambridge: Cambridge University Press, 1983, pp. 271–315.

9. Robert Solow in W. W. Rostow (ed.), *The Economics of Take-off*, 1963, p. 474.

PART TWO

Issues of Historical Analysis

─── FIVE

Adjustments and Maladjustments After the Napoleonic Wars (1942)

The following essay, which was presented at the Christmas meetings of the American Economic Association in Washington in 1941, was a kind of temporary farewell to academic life. I had joined the Research and Analysis branch of the Office of Strategic Services late in the summer of 1941 and did not begin my post-war teaching at Oxford until the autumn of 1946.

The essay reflects work I had done from 1939 to 1941 on the study of Britain from 1790 to 1850 directed by A. D. Gayer, which was published after the war. My interpretation of the post-war adjustment of the British economy was in real as opposed to monetary terms, a view I still hold despite a redoubtable challenge forty years later from my deeply respected colleague and friend, Charles P. Kindleberger.*

As for the conclusion about post–World War II policy, I would claim no great prescience. My view obviously had been affected by the then common anxiety that we not relapse into deep depression; thus, the call for "postiive action" to achieve "relatively full employment and secular progress." But there is no foreshadowing of the extension a "Malthusian" effective demand policy would require to deal with the post-1945 dollar shortage.

I

Economic readjustment after a major war in a modern economy involves the following factors: (a) the reabsorption of man power; (b)

───────────────
This essay was published in the March 1942 issue of *American Economic Review, Supplement* (vol. 32, no. 1). Reprinted with permission.

*"British Financial Reconstruction, 1815–22 and 1918–25," Charles P. Kindleberger and Guido di Tella (eds.), *Economics in the Long View* (London: Macmillan, 1982), Vol. 3, Chapter 5.

the diversion of physical resources to peacetime production; (c) the achieving of a new international trade and financial balance; (d) the re-establishment of a stable, domestic monetary system.[1]

The British readjustment after the Napoleonic Wars is of analytic interest because each of the aspects of the process was more or less successfully achieved without positive intervention by the state. The conditions which made possible that kind of transition are therefore worth cataloguing because, by inversion, they define the conditions in our own generation which make constructive and prescient planning a prerequisite to a successful postwar adjustment.

It is as true economically as it is in a military sense that no two wars are alike. It is, nevertheless, both useful and inevitable that each generation re-examine history with an analogical eye to its own experience. What might be called the present conventional view of the Napoleonic Wars and the postwar readjustment was derived largely by analogy from the experience of 1914–18 and after. It is a picture of monetary inflation and monetary readjustment. In war policy itself, it was not until the latter stages of the first World War that analysts and governments turned their attention from monetary phenomena to the direct mobilization of real resources. In the early twenties, governments and analysts were occupied overwhelmingly with the adjustment of exchanges and monetary standards. The present state of the history of the Napoleonic Wars clearly reflects this bias.

There are, it is true, other views of the period. It is a part of the sequence known as the Industrial Revolution, and in a broad way the development of the British iron and cotton industries has been linked to the inflationary impulses of the war era. Social historians have found, in the uneasy years immediately after 1815, the seeds of the dissident labor movements that run contrapuntally through the history of the subsequent generation. The agricultural story of expansion and painful stagnation has also been isolated and exhaustively examined. Although the focus of this paper is the transition from war to peace, it is hoped that the analysis put forth is capable of including within it the wider phenomena of the period.

I shall present a somewhat different economic picture of Britain than those now conventional. It would be idle to pretend that it is less affected by current experience than its predecessors. It does, however, permit the incorporation of a larger body of evidence into a single consistent analytic framework, and the resultant picture illuminates, obliquely at least, the postwar problems that we ourselves shall face.

II. THE NAPOLEONIC WARS, 1793–1815

Two factors can be taken as having dominated the British economic position from 1793 to 1815: the denial, in part, of normal continental sources of grain and raw material imports; and the government expenditures in excess of revenue.

The former, combined with chronically inadequate domestic harvests, raised the domestic price of grain and evoked an enormous increase in agricultural investment, thereby creating a major postwar problem long familiar to historians because of its large place in the political controversies of the three decades after Waterloo. Obstructions to overseas supply also contributed substantially to the rise of costs which lifted the level of British import prices, and consequently the British price level as a whole.

The latter—that is, the government's loan-financed expenditure—had a certain direct effect on the limited group of industries which contributed military supplies: woolens, for blankets and uniforms; iron, for ordnance and small arms; shipbuilding, for the navy and the supply of overseas forces. But it was that considerable part of the government's outlay which took the form of loans, subsidies, and military expenditures abroad which most significantly determined the development of the British economy during the war years, and which laid the setting for the difficulties of postwar adjustment.

In economists' terms, Britain's situation from 1793 to 1815 is best understood as a case in increased capital exports. Theoretically, a shift from domestic to foreign investment should result in the following interrelated changes: a rise in the domestic rate of interest, an increase in exports relative to imports, a relative slackening of the rate of domestic investment, a decline, or at least a check on the rate of increase, of real wages. Although capital was sent abroad during the Napoleonic Wars by political decision rather than through the inducements of a superior market rate of return, the case nevertheless stands.

The basic statistical calculations for sums sent abroad both to finance British expeditionary forces and as loans and subsidies to Britain's continental allies, were made by Professor Norman Silberling in his well-known articles on the "Financial and Monetary Policy of Great Britain during the Napoleonic Wars."[2] They reveal two major periods of large-scale payments abroad: 1793–1802 and 1808–15. In the intervening interval of six years, such payments were on a small scale, and, largely in consequence, prices and interest rates were relatively steady, foreign trade was on a diminished scale, and there were evidences of unemployment. The cyclical movement from a trough in 1803 to a peak in 1806 to a terminal trough in 1808 was probably milder in amplitude than any of the six cycles that can be distinguished during the war period.[3]

The large-scale capital exports of the war years served quite directly to finance the increases in foreign trade which dominate both the growth of the British economy during this period and the fluctuations which took place within it. From 1793 to 1815 the average annual percentage rate of increase in domestic exports was 3.8 per cent; for total exports,

	Bills and Specie for British Armies in Europe (a)	Subsidies and Loans (b)	Total (a) + (b)
1793	0.6	0.8	1.4
1794	2.3	3.0	5.3
1795	4.4	5.1	9.5
1796	1.0	3.4	4.4
1797	0.2	1.4	1.6
1798	0.2	0.2	0.4
1799	1.3	2.1	3.4
1800	1.1	3.4	4.5
1801	1.7	2.2	3.9
1802	0.6	0.8	1.4
1803	0.2	0.1	0.3
1904	0.1	0.6	0.7
1805	0.8	1.9	2.7
1806	0.7	1.1	1.8
1807	1.7	0.9	2.6
1808	3.9	2.8	6.7
1809	5.6	2.7	8.3
1810	6.8	2.3	9.1
1811	11.6	2.2	13.8
1812	13.0	1.8	14.8
1813	17.9	8.2	26.1
1814	15.5	6.8	22.3
1815	7.0	4.9	11.9
1816	1.3	1.6	2.9

including re-exports, the extraordinary figure of 4.1 per cent. The two comparable figures for the period 1815 to 1847 are 3.8 percent and 2.8 per cent. The peculiarly important role of the re-export trade in the war years emerges clearly. British expenditures abroad were not transferred in cash, although there were severe bullion drains from the British reserve in these years. They were transferred, preponderantly, in the form of goods and shipping, banking, and insurance services.

The prewar British expansion, running roughly from 1788 to 1792, was a canal boom. Those which reached their peaks in 1796 and 1802 were overwhelmingly export and re-export booms, centered largely in the continental trade with Hamburg. The virtual monopoly enjoyed by Britain in the carrying trade with the Western Hemisphere, especially the West Indies, thus neatly suited her financial policy during the wars.

We have noted that the relative stagnation in foreign trade from 1802 to 1808 coincides, roughly, with a low level of remittances abroad. There are many evidences, in that interval, that idle British capital was seeking an escape. A symptom of the restlessness of idle funds was the abortive joint stock boom of 1807, a development echoing the South Sea Bubble and mildly foreshadowing the bursts of capital formation in the middle of the twenties, thirties, and forties. When the blockade of the Continent by Napoleon became fairly effective in the latter months of 1808, a potentially serious situation arose. It was resolved by the Latin-American expansion which culminated in 1810. This elaborate and fortuitous foreign trade boom served to fill the gap in the British economy created by the continental blockade and thus to frustrate Napoleon.

From 1811 to 1815, with the continental blockade abandoned by Napoleon and British remittances again at a high level, a major expansion in foreign trade occurred much like those which had reached their peaks in 1796 and 1802.

Investment in physical capital at home was almost certainly inhibited to some extent by the government's absorption of savings and its direction of them abroad. This is not to deny, of course, that a great volume of domestic investment took place: in agricultural enclosures, in the construction of new industrial plant, in the extension of mines, in the building of ships and docks. The intense activity in shipping, however, may be regarded largely as a corollary to the increase in British exports of the period. It is precisely the type of investment which one might expect in consequence of a relative shift in the economy toward capital exports.

The other types of what might be called Industrial Revolution investment were financed from the profits made in agriculture, commerce, and industry during the war years. It is possible, however, that the government's demands, through taxation and the sale of securities, with a consequent rise in the domestic interest rate, served somewhat to limit domestic investment. A striking bit of evidence in this direction is the behavior of the brick production series, which Shannon has presented.[4] Although it shows some increase in the cyclical expansions which ended in 1802 and 1810, its level is relatively steady, if not falling, until the end of the wars. From 1816 to 1825 it leaps upward.

There is no annual average rate of growth in brick production from 1793 to 1815; a rate of 2.8 per cent, from 1815 to 1847. In general, there can be little doubt that the rate of increase in Britain's capital stock was more rapid in the decades after 1815 than those before. The only period in which home enterprise dominated the attention of speculative investors was in the boom of 1807. Short- and medium-term investment in foreign trade and long-term investment in government securities were the most typical of the war years. The government, of course, spent the taxes it collected and the funds it borrowed; and the iron, woolen, and shipbuilding industries especially felt directly the consequences of such expenditure; while the export industries, notably cotton, and the re-export traders experienced indirect stimulus from capital exports in the form of loans and subsidies. But on the whole, the financial program of the British government involved a distortion of activity from normal channels, and one which worked to the relative disadvantage of domestic capital formation.

III. THE PERIOD OF TRANSITION, 1815–21

In 1814 a speculative foreign trade expansion, based largely on extravagant hopes concerning the Continent's power to absorb British manufactures and re-exports, collapsed. The boom revived briefly in 1815, as the United States returned to the scene as a major British market, but by the latter months of 1815 prices fell, bankruptcies increased, and the Luddites rioted.

The depression of 1815–16 and cessation of government expenditure abroad brought the exchanges back to par in 1816, but the expansion of the two following years, accompanied by an abnormal boom in imports, weakened them once again and postponed the opportune moment for the resumption of specie payments.

This cyclical expansion of 1817 and 1818 is of interest because it reveals the essential nature of the British transition. Investors, trained during the war to look to the market for government securities, seized eagerly on the foreign government loans which appeared: French, Prussian, Austrian, and Russian. In general, however, the search for new profitable outlets for capital was unsatisfied. Canals and turnpikes, docks and enclosures, had ceased to be sufficient investment channels. The prices of domestic shares on the stock exchange were bid up sharply. In 1818 this brief but revealing expansion ended and the year of the Peterloo Massacre came. Already, however, the new lines of economic activity had been marked out: brick production was on the rise.

The readjustments in particular sectors of the economy clearly reflect what we have defined as the essential nature of the transition. The war had caused an abnormal development in agriculture, shipbuilding, and in the re-export trade. These branches of activity went into severe and chronic depression. Agriculture did not show general recovery until the fifties; shipbuilding, until the forties; and the re-export trade never again played the role it had in the war years.

Those branches of the iron trade which had been heavily engaged in the manufacture of ordnance (in Wales) and small arms (in Birmingham) suffered depression until about 1822.[5] There was perceptible recovery in the iron industry in 1817–18, but not until the expansion, begun in 1820 with sharp increases in textile exports, had evoked an increase in domestic investment could the ironmongers again exhibit any real confidence. From 1822 to 1825 they were fully employed on the expanding range of civilian iron requirements.

The textile manufacturers made perhaps the easiest adjustment of all. Their output remained subject to frequent and occasionally severe fluctuations, especially in the export branches of the trade; but an expanding world population, the rapid exploitation of technological advance, and even a restricted form of free trade made secular advance easy and fairly continuous, especially for the cotton industry. The woolen and worsted trade, more parochial in its markets, awaited the advent of cheap Australian raw wool supplies in the forties.

Adjustments and Maladjustments

The story of monetary adjustment, as a short-period sequence in government and Bank of England policy, has been, of course, elaborately explored. I shall not re-examine it except to state this: in the perspective here presented the question of the return to a bullion standard is strictly secondary. As it had virtually throughout the wars, the Bank of England behaved passively. It did not attempt to initiate inflation; nor can its actions, even indirectly, be held accountable for the depression of 1815-16 or 1819. It was inevitable, in view of the shift in Britain's international balance, that bullion return to the country. And it was the swift accumulation of bullion, after the crisis of 1818, that caused an embarrased Bank to petition for a premature resumption of the bullion standard. It is possible, of course, that Bank policy might have been so directed as to lessen the short-term difficulties of readjustment; but that would have involved a conception of Bank policy and a subtlety of action which the Old Lady of Threadneedle Street had not yet attained even a hundred years later, under not dissimilar circumstances. Neither the tools nor the attitude necessary for a successful compensatory banking policy existed; and the propriety of such a policy is what most criticisms of the Bank of England in these years imply.

The rapid and salutary fall in the level of general prices in the years after the Napoleonic Wars cannot be attributed to the autonomous policy of Bank or government. During the war, blockade had eliminated or limited important grain and raw material sources of supply. Shipping, insurance, and interest rates were exorbitant. Peace meant a true lowering in real costs. In the war years an easy money policy was necessary to finance a high level of activity under the new cost conditions. The Bank acquiesced. Its role was no more positive after the war than in its course.

A brief summary cannot indicate adequately the full extent of the adjustments that necessarily followed the termination of the war. In public finance it involved the end of large government deficits; in the capital markets the withdrawal of a principal channel of new investment; in the money market the return to a gold standard; in foreign markets the loss of the monopoly of the carrying and re-export trades and the appearance of vigorous competitors; for home industry—especially shipbuilding, woolens, and iron—the loss of government orders; in the labor markets the appearance of some 400,000 men discharged from the army and navy; in agriculture the continuation of a violent fall in grain prices begun in 1813, which caused distress so severe that it has strongly colored our view of the following three decades. The resultant situation was such that Professor Clapham once designated the years between 1815 and 1820 as "economically probably the most wretched, difficult, and dangerous in modern English history."

For British agriculture this description is probably correct, and for labor the years 1816 and 1819 were, without doubt, intervals of extremely severe unemployment; moreover, for shipbuilding and for the re-export merchants the times had taken a long turn for the worse. Looked at closely, however, and leaving to one side the bitterness of Peterloo, and of Cobbett, the speed and success of readjustment is impressive. Already in 1817–18 a sharp shift to internal investment can be noted, and an interval of real prosperity was attained, while the expansion which began in 1819 and was climaxed by the Latin-American flotations of 1824–25 saw the completion of readjustment in this limited sense; that a tolerable series of relations had been established among the economic variables which permitted, for several decades, a secular rise in real wages for an expanding population, and an average level of employment, normal by the standards of the nineteenth century.

IV. THE CHARACTER OF THE POSTWAR PERIOD

The period from 1815 to 1850 was dominated by the continued growth of foreign markets and an enlarged volume of domestic investment. There were three major booms, reaching peaks in 1825, 1836, 1845. The nature of the predominant forms of new investment varied, but in each instance the construction of factories, the installation of new machinery, and the expansion of coal and iron mines occurred on a large scale.

Railway construction in Britain commanded increasing amounts of capital in each of the three major booms, playing a small part in the twenties, a major role in the thirties, and virtually dominating the forties.[6] Although accretions to domestic capital were concentrated, for the most part, in the prosperity phase of each major upswing, technical advance continued even in such relatively quiescent periods as 1819–22, 1826–32, and 1839–42. The development of the Scottish iron industry, for example, after the discovery of the hot blast (1828), was remarkably steady through prosperity and depression.

There was, as well, a considerable but varying amount of capital exports: in the twenties Latin-American government bonds and mining shares; in the thirties United States federal and state bonds; in the forties the beginnings of railway financing abroad. It is difficult, indeed, to calculate the absolute volume of capital exports in each case and to weigh their importance. There is, however, no doubt that the British terms of trade improved rapidly in the decades after 1815 and showed a striking upward movement; that is, a worsening only with the appearance of large-scale capital exports in the 1850's.[7] The movement from 1815 to 1847 is typical of a decline in capital exports relative to the total volume of new investment.

The relative shift to domestic investment was, of course, largely responsible for the falling price level of the postwar decades. In Marshallian terms, long-run cost curves were being rapidly shifted downward; in quantity theory terms the increase in T outraced the increase in MV; although it should be noted that no gold shortage or autonomous monetary influence is assumed by the use of the quantity theory vocabulary in this case.

The argument presented here may be summarized as follows: from 1793 to 1815 wartime expenditure, and especially capital exports, produced in Britain an abnormal expansion in exports and the associated shipping industry, while, exclusive of agriculture, internal investment was held at what might be called a subnormal level. Whether total output would have increased more or less rapidly under peacetime conditions is difficult to say; but the direction of production was clearly affected by the direct and indirect consequences of government spending at home and abroad, as were movements of prices, interests rates, and real wages.

From 1815 to 1850 domestic investment, directed towards the expansion of plant and mineral resources, the improvement of machinery, and later the extension of railway transport, dominated the British economy. There were several intervals when capital exports absorbed a considerable part of the investor's savings, but the barter terms of trade would seem to show the net improvement, in the second period, to be expected after a relative decrease in capital exports. This is not to deny the importance of Britain's export markets in the second period but rather to emphasize the relatively greater importance of home investment.

The essence of this hypothesis involves the distinction between the short-run effects of new investment on income and employment and the long-run effects on productivity, or the rate of increase of capital, somehow measured. Similar volumes of new investment for (say) war materials and cotton factories may, within a given period, have precisely the same income and employment multiplier effects, and they may yield precisely the same secondary increases in new investment. But in the first case society is left with a number of cannon, and in the second case with enlarged facilities for production; that is, lower long-run cost curves. The conception of war inflation as a relative stimulus to productivity is based on the assumption that wastage is more than compensated for by continuous full employment;[8] that the secondary investment consequent upon inflation more than outweighs the relative loss due to primary investment in nonproductive war equipment. The judgment made here is that for Britain, during the Napoleonic Wars, this assumption is not valid. War inflation may have yielded slightly greater than normal employment, but, in net, the rate of increase of productivity was, relatively, slowed down.

A similar theoretical distinction can be made between the consequences of domestic investment and capital exports. In the case of capital exports, however, long-run reductions in import prices and permanently enlarged export markets may result, as they did, for instance, in partial consequence of British financing of the transcontinental American railways. It is probable, however, that the long-run effects will be slower in emerging, especially if the capital exports are being used to develop a backward area. But capital exports during the Napoleonic Wars were not, for the most part, used productively in this sense. Their purpose was to supply war materials and consumers goods, not to open new sources of supply or to increase the productivity of continental industry.

Accepting, for the moment, this view of the nature of the transition, its successful consummation depended upon the following factors: (1) the ability of a rising British population to cushion somewhat the necessarily depressed position of agriculture; (2) the availability within Britain of outlets for new investments; (3) the mobility of factors production and especially of labor; (4) a flexible price structure; (5) an expanding, and relatively free, world market, to provide a persistent stimulus to new technical improvement and industrial expansion; (6) as a consequence of these, a stable domestic and international monetary system.

To one of our generation, who has observed the attempts of the American government and institutions to achieve full employment in the past decade, the post-Napoleonic War adjustment seems incredibly easy. The years 1815–50 do not, it is true, have a good name in economic history. The tendency of both agricultural and industrial prices to fall evoked chronic complaint from the most articulate and powerful groups within Britain; while the combination of occasionally severe cyclical unemployment and the social evils of the new urban industrial life have furnished ready polemical materials to the sympathetic historians of labor. Nevertheless, both statistical and qualitative evidence indicate a considerable net improvement in the real wages of labor, and, by the standards of recent years, unemployment, at its worst, was neither severe nor long lived. Both the period of transition and the situation to which that transition led have much to be said for them, both within the context of the nineteenth century and from the perspective of our own experience.

V. CONCLUSION

There are, superficially, few lessons to be drawn for this day from Britain's experience of 1815 to 1821. The United States, it is true, in its lend-lease policy is pursuing a line of action not dissimilar from that of Britain in relation to its continental allies. And it is possible to see about us a case of supercapital exports. There are, however, two basic and striking differences. First, war in 1941 is much more nearly a full-time occupation for the economies concerned; the diversion of resources by action outside the market process must be pursued on an enormous scale. In the Napoleonic Wars, with the exception of man power and grain, the government interceded relatively little in the mechanism of supply. An openhanded monetary policy sufficed. Second, it is evident that neither economic nor political conditions after the present war will permit a modest withdrawal of governments from their present preoccupation with the workings of their economies. Every device at their command will have to be mobilized to redirect the employment of resources, and to ease the whole process of adjustment with a suitably expansionary monetary policy. After 1815, the British government and even the Bank of England could afford to regard themselves as mere atomistic units in the economic system. With a gesture to the farmers in the Corn Laws of 1815 and a self-righteous return to the bullion standard, the government bowed from the scene, after having shaped the pattern of economic development for more than two decades. After a few bitter years, the opportunities for private investment fashioned an adequate answer. It will be, patently, the first function of postwar governments in our generation to create by positive action such conditions of relatively full employment and secular progress.

Ricardo, when he disputed with Malthus in the years after Waterloo, won the day with a program of financial orthodoxy, domestic laissez faire, and international free trade; and there is much in the subsequent history of the nineteenth century that justifies his position. But we are all Malthusians now.

NOTES

1. The materials for this paper are drawn largely from work done by the author on the yet unpublished study of "The Growth and Fluctuations of the British Economy, 1790–1850," directed by Dr. Arthur D. Gayer.

2. *Quarterly Journal of Economics*, Vol. 38, p. 227. (Figures in million pounds)

3. The closest available approximation to monthly cyclical turning points is the following:

	Trough	*Peak*
Circa	1788	1792 (September)
	1794 (June)	1796 (May)
	1797 (September)	1800 (September)
	1801 (October)	1802 (December)
	1804 (March)	1806 (August)
	1808 (May)	1810 (March)
	1811 (September)	1815 (March)
	1816 (September)	1818 (September)
	1819 (September)	1825 (May)

4. H. A. Shannon, "Bricks: A Trade Index, 1785–1849," *Economica*, New Series No. 3, August, 1934, pp. 300–318.

5. That recovery in the iron industry was delayed some two or three years after the beginning of revival (October, 1819) was not abnormal. The typical cyclical sequence in the first half of the nineteenth century called for revival first in the export industries, and only after some interval, recovery in the capital goods trades.

6. Total railway mileage completed was approximately as follows: 1821–30, 100; 1831–40, 1,400; 1841–50, 5,000. (H. G. Lewin, *Early British Railways*, p. 186, and E. Cleveland-Stevens, *The English Railway*, pp. 24–25.)

7. The most significant break in the trend towards improvement occurs in the mid-thirties when capital exports to the United States were on an enormous scale.

8. It might also be argued, in general, that war furnishes a stimulus to invent and apply new industrial techniques. The best instance of this during the Napoleonic Wars was perhaps in the development of the iron industry, denied the Swedish ores on which it had depended. But the historical evidence indicates, if anything, a greater ingenuity and enterprise in the application of industrial techniques after 1815 than before.

SIX

Some Notes on Mr. Hicks and History (1951)

This critique of John R. Hicks's A Contribution to the Theory of the Trade Cycle *(1950) reflects ideas on the relation between economic growth and the business cycle, which had crystallized while I was writing* The Process of Economic Growth *(1952, 1953, 1960).*

When I settled down to teach economic history at MIT in 1950 I felt it necessary, given prevailing neo-Keynesian macro-economic theories of growth and cycles, to elaborate a theoretical structure that could grip the inescapable characteristics of growing economies as a historian confronted them. This required treating as endogenous the demographic transition and the generation and diffusion of inventions and innovations; the treatment of business cycles as the form that growth had historically assumed and Kondratieff cycles as the consequence of the historically long period of gestation that had characterized the opening up and development of new sources of food, raw materials, and energy. All this required, in turn, a more disaggregated, sectoral concept of equilibrium growth than Harrod-Domar models had provided or neoclassical models were to provide from the mid-1950s forward. It also required a more sectoral approach to the upper and lower turning points of business cycles than was conventional in a system whose dynamics were simply the product of interaction between the multiplier and accelerator, with a stochastic "autonomous investment" intervening from off-stage.

All this emerged in short compass and with reasonable clarity when I set down my notes on Hicks's book, which I still regard as about the best one can do with the over-aggregated concepts that continue to dominate conventional macro-economics.

This essay was published in the June 1951 issue of *American Economic Review* (vol. 41, no. 3). Reprinted with permission.

A considerable portion of the current effort of economic theorists is being brought to bear on the relationship between short-run fluctuations in income, output, and employment, on the one hand, and the rate of economic progress, on the other. This effort clearly brings the historian and the theorist closer to a common perspective on the economic process, for the economic historian has hitherto mainly concerned himself with a more or less purposeful description and analysis of the sequence of economic development in various regions. The present note constitutes a few interim observations on the theoretical structure which has thus far emerged. Its purpose is to suggest the possibility of certain refinements and elaborations in the existing models and to focus the attention of historians and other empirical investigators on certain problems of fact whose solution may assist the elaboration of an improved theoretical framework for the understanding of the growth and fluctuations of economies. This note is organized as a series of discrete comments on the model presented by Mr. J. R. Hicks in *A Contribution to the Theory of the Trade Cycle*.[1] As Mr. Hicks has underlined, his study is part of a growing stream of concepts and speculation. Nevertheless, his formulation is a convenient point of departure.

Fluctuations in Mr. Hicks's system reflect levels of total investment which are inappropriate to the long-run rate of increase of output, in a progressive economy. These inappropriate fluctuations in total investment result from the interplay of the multiplier and the accelerator, when their values are taken at certain levels. In his view, it is likely that the levels of investment induced by a rise in income will yield a spiral of investment and income increases which the system will reject as inappropriate. The form of that rejection is an upper turning point and downward spiral in output initiated by the existence of bottlenecks in capacity which throttle the increase in output and, through the accelerator, lower investment, income and, in turn, investment.

To an historian a striking divergence between this model and the life of economies is that the model fails to take account of and to explain a fundamental characteristic of the history of new investment; namely, that investment has varied in its composition over time and that each trade expansion is characterized, and even dominated by, certain leading types of new investment. There is, of course, within the boom a generalized expansion of new investment, despite the fact that certain types of investment, of expected low yield, may be diminished. Nevertheless, a theory relating the business cycle to the course of economic progress should offer some explanation for the tendency of the composition of new investment to alter; for economic progress has consisted, in large part, of leading bursts of investment, in different directions, in the course of successive cycles, and the secondary consequences of such bursts.

Briefly, the sort of model which would better suit the historian is one in which there was not simply a single ceiling of capacity (like Mr. Hicks's F curve); but, related to such a curve, there was a complex of curves, each indicating an optimum course for output and capacity in different sectors of the economy.[2]

The determinants of these sub-curves would be, essentially, two: (a) the level of demand for particular commodities and services as determined by the growth in population and income (adjusted for changes in taste); and (b) the technical potentialities in each branch of economic activity. There are few difficulties in conception with respect to (a). One can envision a level of wheat acreage and production, cotton acreage and production, coal output, and even forms of industrial plant and transport facilities which would be appropriate to the long-run rate of growth at constant levels of techniques. With respect to technical possibilities, however, it seems likely that a theory of progress will have to look at invention and innovation in a somewhat different way than is now usual. Current theory tends to take invention as a factor outside its system of thought. Thus, in Mr. Hicks, the distinction between autonomous and induced investment. Industrial invention, or better, the application to industry of new technical possibilities is better regarded as a flow, the size of which is a function of certain mixed economic and social variables in a society, the direction of which, in substantial part (but not exclusively), is determined by recognizable economic incentives.

The amount of its talent which a society devotes to science and the application of science to industry, and the eagerness of entrepreneurs to seize upon such possibilities and apply them reflect the whole temper of a society at particular periods.[3] It is not difficult to recall countries in which the flow (*e.g.*, British *vis-à-vis* France, from 1815 to 1848)[4] is high relative to other countries at the same time; or to chart within countries alterations in the size of this flow from period to period (*e.g.*, Britain from 1873 to 1896 *vis-à-vis* Britain in the pre-1914 years). The fact that such a flow may not be, strictly speaking, measurable should not discourage the introduction of some such concept. This is only one of the fundamental factors determining the rate of economic development, the roots of which must be found in social factors difficult or impossible to measure. As for the direction which industrial inventiveness takes and the directions in which it is applied, we can look in substantial part, to recognizable economic inducements. There may be in the productive process, within a given industry or within the economy as a whole, a flagrant lack of balance, perhaps, induced by a higher degree of mechanization in one stage of the productive process than another.[5] Such a lack of balance will set up a strong incentive for inventive talent to concentrate on the problem of evening up the level of technique. The eagerness with which entrepreneurs seize upon and apply the new potentialities is also a function of recognizable economic incentives, related among other factors, to the stage and rate of growth of the industry. The incentive may be strong not only at a period of rapid rate of growth; falling prices in agriculture, for example, appear to have induced the application of improved techniques at various stages over the past century. Even public investment, which is treated by Mr. Hicks as autonomous, has, in the past, in large part reflected the demand for basic public utilities and services which were, in turn, largely a function of population and income growth. In short, it seems possible and useful to narrow the range accorded to autonomous investment and to treat the flow of applied technical possibilities as a function of the social and economic state of a society, and its character as mainly related to economic incentives. From the whole potential flow in each cycle, the investors (capital market, agriculture, and industry) select those which appear most profitable.

One is, nevertheless, left with several forms of investment which might be regarded, still, as autonomous; investment in wars; conscious counter-cyclical government investment; investment in technical possibilities opened up by random discoveries not related to clear-cut prior economic inducements; investments in the mining of precious metals, induced by adventitious discoveries.[6]

Long-run equilibrium could thus be represented by an over-all optimum rate of growth in output, with sub-levels indicating the appropriate level of output in different sectors of the economy, with a margin left for distortions and odd events.

What a theory of the trade cycle in relation to this kind of model must take into account is the fact that: (a) investment in these various sectors of the economy has proceeded at irregular and disjointed rates, fluctuating, in effect, above and below the abstract "optima";[7] and (b) that cycles in the past have been characterized, or even dominated, by disproportionate investment in certain directions, as opposed to others. Not only has investment in general been disjointed, which is the basis for Hicks's and other models, but investment has been disproportionate in various sectors of the economy.[8]

The leading directions of new investment in each boom can in large part be related to disequilibria as between the optimum rates of growth in certain sectors and the levels of capacity existing just prior to the boom; for example, the world-wide boom of the 1830's in substantial part (but not exclusively) had as its focus, a falling behind in raw cotton production in relation to the industrial demand for raw cotton. This took the form in the early 'thirties, of a rising price for cotton and falling cotton stocks in the textile manufacturing regions of the world; and it was followed by a massive land boom, with accompanying transport development. The American land boom (induced by forces wider than the cotton price) was the center of world-wide boom, although the forms of investment pursued in its course were more general.

One can find other booms where relative price movements presented inducements to expand wheat acreage, wool production, meat production, coal production, and so forth; and where the character of investment in the boom reflects a prior disequilibrium in one or more particular sectors of the world economy. One can deal similarly with booms where the central phenomenon is investment in a new industry, involving the exploitation of technical potentialities. Here the form of inducement may not be a rising price but the possibility of lower costs in the face of a constant or even falling price.

A second empirical fact which must be introduced into a satisfactory theoretical model is the persistent tendency for the expansion in capacity in the leading sectors to be carried too far, yielding, toward the end of the boom, a conscious prospect of a level of capacity higher than that which would be required in those particular sectors of the economy in terms of the optimum model. To explain this phenomenon one cannot evade an evocation of the institutional setting for new investment.

The major lines of new investment were (over, say, the past 150 years) mainly determined by the actions of individuals and private institutions; but they were not atomistically determined. In the long-term capital markets, and even in the larger industries, those responsible for investment were operating off common information and common stimuli. They received and exchanged (perhaps over lunch) the same rumors and news. They watched and were influenced by the same set of market phenomena, the same kinds of leadership. These determined a common view of the expected level of profitability in certain lines of new investment. Thus, those making investment decisions tended to move together.

And to explain the classical "manias" which characterized many booms one must, in effect, invoke some version of social psychology. For the flagrant characteristic of the latter stages of many business expansions was the expectation of extremely high yields in particular directions; *i.e.*, demands for capital which were high and inelastic, and out of accord with the real possibilities for future yield, given the volume of investment in fact going forward in those lines and the whole optimum course of economic development: *e.g.*, Latin American mining shares (1825); American state bonds and cotton land (1836); British railways (1845); and so on.

A third factor which clearly influenced the extent to which investment distortion proceeded in each boom was the period of gestation of the leading forms of investment. In an inventory cycle in cotton goods exports, for example, the time lags were short and the fluctuations of production about an optimum level were relatively shallow. In a boom directed mainly to domestic industrial expansion one would also expect the true profitability of the current rate of expansion in capacity to reveal itself in a reasonably short period. Excepting war booms, the most powerful and prolonged expansions, marked by a sustained rise in the level of money wages, have been expansions associated with the move into new territory (including the laying of railways and the building of new towns) where the period of gestation was relatively long and high hopes could be sustained for considerable periods of time, even in the face of rising costs (*vide*, expansions reaching peaks, for United Kingdom, in 1836, 1854, 1872).

The introduction of these factors into Mr. Hicks's model may have certain consequences for the theory of the upper turning point of the trade cycle. Mr. Hicks's model is set out in real as opposed to money terms. It is also set out in terms of macro-concepts which do not center on the motivations and the market position of the individual investor. The down-turn comes when a limitation on capacity prevents further rise in output, thus bringing to a halt the expansive operation of the accelerator. This is probably to be translated into the view that a rise in the cost of new investment (including, perhaps rises in interest rates)[9] produces a fall in the expected yield from current investment and thus a decline in the volume of new investment. Alternatively, it could be interpreted as reflecting an absolute decline in new orders to the investment goods industries caused by a failure of total output to expand at its previous rate.[10]

There seems little doubt that rises in costs have played a part in producing a revision of the expected profitability of new investment in the latter stages of booms; and they must be accounted a possible factor in the downturn of new investment. But another factor appears to have operated; namely, a revision in the investors' judgment concerning the appropriateness of further expansions of capacity in the sectors of the economy which have lead the boom. In macro-terms it might be said that in the early stages of the boom the investment market observed a discrepancy between the current level of capacity in certain sectors of the economy and the level that would be appropriate to the expansion of the economy as a whole and its technical possibilities. Toward the latter stages of the boom the investment market begins to observe that discrepancy has narrowed or disappeared, and the danger of relative over-capacity may become real. Time has passed since the new line of investment was undertaken and the scale on which the economy as a whole has entered into this line can now be better observed. Whether or not the investing group includes in its calculations such an over-all view of the investment possibilities, certain direct market phenomena may confront it: the price of securities (or of commodities) in the new lines may cease to rise; news from the gold fields may reflect leaner yields than had been expected; etc. In short, a boom could turn down not only because investment prospects had been dimmed by rising costs or by a falling off of new orders due to the failure of total output to expand at the previous rate, but also because, in the leading lines of new investment, the market had come to appreciate that expansion in certain sectors had proceeded beyond the optimum level, or that decisions already taken would lead to such disproportionate expansion.

These tentative observations on the trade cycle in relation to economic progress must, of course, be subjected to both theoretical and historical scrutiny. They appear to open for exploration, at least, the view that the central phenomenon of the trade cycle is not an inapropriate total level of investment in relation to the rate of economic progress, but an inappropriate balance of investment in relation to the pattern of economic progress and its technical possibilities.

The proposition that it is essentially an inappropriate composition of investment which distinguishes the boom, rather than its scale, must confront the empirical fact that, in the latter stages of many booms total investment is at an extremely high level; and the view of the future taken in many sectors is more optimistic than a reading of the long-term trends would have justified. Could it not be possible that this generalized investment boom was simply a broad response to the fact that, in certain key sectors of the economy, an inappropriately high level of investment was taking place? This limited distortion would take the form of demand curves, in the capital market and in the markets for labor and materials, which were high and inelastic. These could drive the system to inflationary full employment, and hold it there for a time, depending on the period of gestation of the new form of investment or on other (demand) factors which might produce a revised view of its prospects which, by itself, or in conjunction with rising costs, might decree a decline of enterprise in the new directions.

The decline once begun, through familiar re-enforcing processes, might have general consequences for the level of new investment in many directions. What is essential in this perspective is that all forms of investment did not increase, in the course of expansion, to the same extent, in terms of the concept of equilibrium earlier defined. A boom appears to have generally exhausted a line of development in one sector of the economy, as a leading outlet for investment, for a period longer than a single cycle. The same main direction for new enterprise seldom, if ever, dominates successive major (*i.e.*, nine-year) cycles. This may imply that a downturn was "unnecessary" in that all lines of investment had not exceeded their long-period equilibrium level; that the generalized downturn was an indirect product of the legitimate revulsion only from the scale on which the main lines of investment has been previously pursued. Would this not suggest that the problem of controlling the trade cycle was not ony a problem in the appropriate level of outlays (investment plus consumption) but also a problem in achieving an appropriate composition of new investment? Might it not also suggest that the long-term rates of growth we observe for the economy as a whole are lower than the optimum possible; that a continuing appropriate pattern of investment, at the full employment level, would move real income forward at a higher rate than its trend defined *ex post* in terms of a succession of peak positions, or otherwise established by elimination of cyclical movements which have taken place in the past?

Another possiblity of interest—already familiar, but not fully explored—emerges from these notes; namely, that trade cycles of different length are essentially of the same nature, but are to be distinguished mainly with respect to the period of gestation of the leading forms of investment which dominated their course. The inventory cycle would represent a relatively shallow deviation of production from the optimum, associated with investment in stocks of short gestation period. The conventional nine-year cycle would represent the product of more substantial deviations from the optimum, which took longer to appreciate. The upswings of Schumpeter's Kondratieff's, to the extent that they were not the product of war outlays (for example, the expansion up to 1854), would emerge as cases of booms where the leading forms of investment had an extraordinarily long period of gestation, and proved resistant for a longer period, to cost increases and a revised judgment of further prospects than the more typical boom.

NOTES

1. Oxford, 1950.
2. These curves would conform more nearly to a complex of Mr. Harrod's Gn curves than to Mr. Hicks's F line. R. F. Harrod, *Towards a Dynamic Economics* (London, 1948), pp. 87 ff.
3. Similar factors must be invoked to account for the quality of the working force coming forward, changes in birth rates, changes in the political environment of the economy, etc. It would be helpful to much general historical and social research going forward if economists were to define with precision the social vairables they would wish to see investigated, and to leave explicit place for such social variables in the slope and contour of the lines of growth they tend to draw in their models. Similarly, a conscious effort should be made by historians and other social investigators to make their empirical research bear directly on the factors relevant to economic development.
4. In effect, there are two flows here, related but at times useful to distinguish: the flow of new potentialities, issuing from industrial and scientific laboratories and less highly organized men of ingenuity; and the actual flow of such potentialities into economic practice. There may be cases where the propensity to invent is high, the propensity to apply is low, and *vice versa*.
5. See, for classical examples, T. S. Ashton, *The Industrial Revolution, 1760–1830* (London, 1948), pp. 91–92. For short-period variations in the demand for invention in relation to supply compare Ashton's series for the number of British patents with the trade cycle pattern from 1790 to 1830 (Table 1, p. 229, "Some Statistics of the Industrial Revolution in Britain," *The Manchester School*, May 1948).
6. There is some doubt as to whether the latter two forms of investment should be regarded as autonomous; for, although the invention or discovery may not be the result of an accretion of efforts induced by evident economic requirements, their selection for exploitation as opposed to other avenues for investment, is part of the economic process.
7. Further reflection and investigation might well indicate that the optimum complex of growth curves assuming continuous full employment and appropriate investment was higher than the *ex post* trend lines we can draw from the performance of an economic system subject to fluctuations in employment and investment following patterns which are inappropriate in their composition. The "optima" referred to here are empirical, *ex post* optima, rather than the equilibrium "optima" referred to above.

8. In this context the disproportion would consist in higher levels of investment in certain sectors than the proportion decreed by the optimum pattern of development. Appropriate investment need not be proportionate to the percentage net contribution of each sector to the national income.

9. In passing, the author must, reluctantly, deny himself the immortality of a "Rostow paradox" (Hicks, *op. cit.*, p. 154 n.). The author's conclusion that expansions in the Great Depression period (or the period 1815–48) were not cut short by abnormal monetary stringency is not dependent on a comparison of average rates of interest as between the Great Depression and the mid-century decades. It is based, rather, on the view that the character of the booms throughout the nineteenth century was determined primarily by the character of new investment; that is, by factors on the demand rather than the supply side of the market for loanable funds. This would not exclude the possibility of a change in expectations concerning the main lines of new investment affecting simultaneously both supply and demand conditions in the money and capital market. The author's second judgment in this matter is that, of its nature, the decline in prices and interest rates was not the trend result of a succession of abortive expansions, but the consequence of a world-wide structural adjustment. In this perspective, there is no paradox: changes in the character of new enterprise can account for both differences in the nature of the boom and the character of the persisting trends in prices and rates of interest. A close examination of the history of the money market in relation to new investment simply does not appear to justify a very large place for movements on the supply side of the market in determining either the power of booms or the character of trends. It is on this direct reading of the evidence, rather than a *prima facie* argument from a comparison of interest rates in different periods that the author's by no means unchallengeable view is based. The author, would, however, largely agree with Mr. Hicks's evaluation of the permissive, secondary, and re-enforcing rôle of the money market, presented in his Chapter XII. Compare the author's *British Economy of the Nineteenth Century* (Oxford, 1948) pp. 55–57; 59–61; 79; 182–91.

10. For a discussion of this point see A. S. Duesenberry, "Hicks on the Trade Cycle," *Quart. Jour. Econ.*, Vol. LXIV, No. 3 (August, 1950), pp. 468 ff.

SEVEN

From Dependence to Interdependence: A Historian's Perspective (1973)

This essay, published here for the first time, is the text of a talk that was delivered in Austin in April 1973 at a U.S.-Mexican conference organized by the Institute for Latin American Studies of the University of Texas. I tried to put the doctrine of dependencia into a longer and more dynamic perspective than the context in which it is usually articulated. Along the way, I rather enjoyed exploiting Charles Wilson on British attitudes toward the Dutch in the seventeenth century.

In my essay in Pioneers in Development (1984) I made further observations on this theme in response to the editor's (Gerald A. Meier) instruction.

I

Let me begin with a quotation: "The burden of Mexico's tale of complaint was, in brief, that the United States carried away from Mexico little but raw materials and semi-manufactured goods, making large profits in the subsequent stages of manufacture and commerce. The skill of the United States in selling back manufactures, necessities and luxuries to their victim was only the second stage of a process plausibly represented as one of double robbery."

The quotation might have come from Professor Conroy's background paper for our conference. In fact, it is derived from Charles Wilson's study of British-Dutch relations in the seventeenth century, *Profit and Power*.[1] I have merely substituted Mexico for Britain, the United States for the Dutch. It was the British who then felt themselves in a neocolonial position.

In the subsequent century, the British matched the Dutch and more; then, in the last two decades of the eighteenth century, Britain launched the first industrial revolution, the first case of modern growth, the first take-off, if you will. Other nations followed, but their take-offs did not all come at the same time. Although post-take-off growth has not proceeded in all nations at the same rate, the relative degree of technological virtuosity is roughly related to the time of take-off. Therefore, for almost two centuries the less advanced nations have felt the economic (and sometimes the political and military) weight of the more advanced; and the primary force that has diffused modern industrial growth over the face of the globe has been the reaction of the weaker party to the intrusions of those who had modernized at an earlier time. A reactive nationalism rather than the profit motive has been the principal psychological and political engine of modern growth and industrialization.

It was Alexander Hamilton in 1791, contemplating the dangerous dependence of postcolonial United States, who raised this abiding standard of policy for nations confronting more advanced powers: "Not only the wealth but the independence and security of a country appear to be materially connected with the prosperity of manufactures."[2] And his great ideological opponent Thomas Jefferson came in time, and out of hard-won experience as president in a war-torn world, to agree.

And so the Hamiltonian creed came to grip one less advanced nation after another as it confronted or feared the intrusion of the more advanced: Russia notably after its military humiliation in the Crimea in 1854 and its diplomatic humiliation in Berlin in 1878; Japan after its enforced opening to the external world in 1854; Turkey in the face of the harrowing attrition of the Ottoman Empire; Canada after being cast loose by Britain's policy of free trade in the 1840s and then confronting the colossus to the south that was roaring toward industrial maturity after the Civil War; Mexico as it confronted that same colossus in military and then political and economic terms; and, indeed, after 1945 the whole formerly colonial world, as it struggled to convert formal political independence into a status of dignity on an international scene dominated economically and otherwise by nations that had moved into industrialization in the century-and-a-quarter before 1914.

In examining candidly the current problems of U.S.-Mexican economic relations, we are considering, then, a fragment in time and place of the oldest and perhaps most basic international problem posed by the process of modernization.

II

Turning to the contemporary world, it is perhaps worth beginning with a proposition so obvious it is often overlooked: There is no such thing as economic independence—and, I might add, no such thing as political or military independence. No one understands this better, I suspect, than those who bear responsibility in the two apparently most powerful nations of the world: the United States and the Soviet Union. At every point their freedom of action is hedged about by the state of their economies and by dependence on other nations, large and small, in pursuing their policies, including their economic policies. This is and will remain, as far ahead as any of us can peer, a world of intense interdependence. The patterns of growth and communications and weaponry to which the human community has been committed by the diffusion of modern technology permit no nation to be an island unto itself. And that interdependence will increase as we confront the era when policies of uninhibited growth gradually give way to policies of balance, and nations and the global community seek to accommodate man to the limits of his physical environment.

When we talk about the problems of dependence, the objective of our discussions is not to contrive policies of independence, but of dignified, equitable interdependence.

III

The problems of economic dependence—and their solutions—vary now, as they have in the past, with two factors above all: a nation's stage of growth and its size. I shall consider each in turn.

A good deal of the literature on dependence poses the problem in terms of the relation between the advanced industrial world and the world of developing nations. This approach may be useful for certain rhetorical purposes, but it conceals more than it illuminates. The kinds of inequitable dependence felt, say, by pre-industrial Nepal or Yemen are different from those felt, say, by Nigeria or Indonesia on the eve of take-off. The take-off problems of Thailand and South Korea are different from those of, say, Mexico and Iran, nations well along in the drive to technological maturity. The kinds of inequitable dependence that were dramatized in the 1960s by Servan-Schreiber in *Le Défi Americain*, in a Western Europe caught up in high mass-consumption, differ from the inequities of which Washington now justly complains as it contemplates the grotesque Japanese trade surplus; for the imperatives of the search for quality in the United States create problems, too, in a world economy where others have learned the tricks of the previous stage—high mass-consumption.

This is not the occasion to set out in detail the content of the dependency problems of each stage, but it may be useful to evoke some of them briefly.

In the earliest phase of modernization (for Mexico, say, the period from independence down to Porfirio Diaz), the critical problems are likely to be political and military. The nation, even if formally independent, lacks internal cohesion. It has achieved statehood but neither a pervasive sense of nationhood nor an efficient, centralized structure of administration. It is vulnerable to external military and political pressure and internal factional and regional schisms. It lacks the men and organization to develop its own economy. Its exports of raw materials and foodstuffs are likely to be in the hands of foreigners who alone command the necessary capital, technology, managerial skills, and knowledge of foreign markets. In our time, an example of this stage was the Congo in the troubled years of the early 1960s or, less dramatically, Zambia in the first years of its independence.

At a certain point, political stability is attained and a purposeful policy of economic modernization is launched, as in Mexico in the years after 1877. Military intrusion becomes less likely, but new kinds of economic dependence develop. Infrastructure is required and foreign capital is needed to build it. Historically, a good many nations in this stage were willing to permit rather uninhibited foreign ownership and operation of mines as well as railways, electric power plants, telephone companies, and other basic installations. In our time the existence of the World Bank, the regional development banks, and other forms of foreign aid have shielded nations at this stage from most of the distortions associated, say, with the Porfirian period in Mexico and similar periods elsewhere; but even now foreigners are associated with some of the most fundamental economic sectors in the economy: The negotiation of foreign aid, no matter how antiseptically multilateral, is a burdensome exercise in dependence, and large commitments are acquired to repay foreign loans. Meanwhile, new dependencies emerge as the nation seeks to expand its foreign exchange earnings by increasing exports of its foodstuffs and raw materials. It is caught up in the erratic price fluctuations of world markets, which are inadequately smoothed in our time by international commodity agreements and the kind of compensatory borrowing permitted by the International Monetary Fund.

With take-off comes the first sustained phase of industrialization, as in Mexico in the generation after 1940. The leading sector is usually import-substitution for consumers' goods, and, in this sense, dependence is reduced. The relatively low capital intensity of such industries and their familiar technologies generally permit the expanding pool of local entrepreneurs to manage and, even, finance a high proportion of expansion in this sector. In this stage nations also tend to gain control over basic infrastructure sectors created earlier by foreign capital and management, for example, the Mexican Light and Power Company. On the other hand, an increased dependence on capital goods and, often, raw material imports develops.

With the drive to technological maturity, this kind of dependence deepens rapidly. In this stage a nation acquires virtuosity in the great capital-intensive industries: metals and metalworking, chemicals, and the less sophisticated forms of electronics. At this point, we also get into the complex calculus of advantage and disadvantage when permitting entrance of foreign firms, a calculus that lies at the heart of contemporary Mexican-U.S. relations. It is a problem faced also by Brazil and other Latin American countries and by Iran, Turkey, and India, among others. It is mainly with the dependency problems of this stage that I shall deal in the latter part of this chapter.

But the problems of dependency do not end when the drive to technological maturity gives way to high mass-consumption; that is, the time when the automobile, durable consumers' goods, and the life of suburbia are diffused to the bulk of the population. As the first society to move into this stage, the United States enjoyed certain initial foreign trade advantages; when post-war Western Europe moved from recovery to rapid growth, these advantages were translated into a substantial presence in Western Europe of U.S. firms that manufactured automobiles, durable consumers' goods, and related products.

But in the post-war Atlantic world the problems posed by uneven timing in movement through the stages of growth merge with problems posed by differences in the sizes of economies. In the early 1950s, a part of the U.S. advantage, it is true, consisted of longer experience with large-scale operations in the leading sectors of high mass-consumption. But with the passage of time and sustained high rates of growth in Europe, the U.S. advantage came to rest, not in the more efficient exploitation of then familiar technologies, but rather in the larger size of U.S. firms and the larger pools of management, working capital, and, possibly, the research and development these firms commanded.

In earlier stages as well, size has often mattered. In take-off, for example, the larger domestic markets of, say, Mexico or India provided a more spacious framework for the expansion of import-substitution consumers' goods industries than those of, say, Peru, Uruguay, or the nations of Central America. In the drive to technological maturity, Brazil finds it easier to develop efficient steel, metalworking, and chemical plants than does Chile or, even, Argentina. Canada, despite its full attainment of high mass-consumption and its rich natural resources base, still struggles, as it has for more than a century, to keep its dependence on the United States—a country ten times larger—within politically and psychologically (as well as economically) manageable bounds.

But we should exercise some care in evoking the question of size. First, the size of a population does not necessarily represent the size of its effective market: A substantial part of Latin America, let alone India, has only a tenuous link to the market system. The effective market is much smaller than the population, and income per capita can vary greatly even at similar stages of growth, depending on the proportion of population to arable land, natural resource endowments, etc. Second, a purposeful, energetic people with a good educational base, a framework of political stability, and an ample supply of innovating entrepreneurs and public administrators can build a highly sophisticated industrial society on a small population base by exploiting with vigor the possibilities for exports. This is what Sweden and the other Scandinavian nations did; the same thing is happening in South Korea, Taiwan, and, even more remarkably, in Hong Kong and Singapore.

These cases are worth underlining because the degree of inequitable interdependence is clearly a function of the vigor with which economic development and export markets are pursued, as well as a function of relative stages of growth and size.

I conclude this introduction, then, with four observations drawn from history as well as the contemporary scene:

1. A sense of excessive or inequitable dependence is as old as modern history—three centuries old at least.
2. A reactive nationalism that aims to recover dignity in the face of the intrusions of more advanced countries has been the primary engine in spreading industrialization over the face of the globe.
3. Inequitable dependence has arisen inevitably from two major sources: differences in the timing of take-offs, and differences in the sizes of countries and their effective domestic markets. Movement through the stages of growth for the latecomers has involved the emergence of new forms of dependence as problems associated with an earlier stage are solved. But the vigor and purposefulness of a nation's modernization effort can, to a degree, reduce the weight of the successive dependencies inherent in lateness and smallness.
4. Above all, the lesson of history is that there is no such thing as economic independence, only more or less equitable and dignified interdependence; this proposition holds for the most advanced as well as least advanced nations.

IV

All four of these propositions are reflected in the history of Mexico since independence and in the difficult, tangled, but increasingly constructive story of Mexico's relations with the United States.

At the moment the most important—or at least the most discussed—issue in Mexican-U.S. relations is the question of private capital imports. A good deal of the past is embedded, almost clause by clause, in the draft bill "to promote Mexican investment and to regulate foreign investment" that was placed before the Mexican Congress late in 1972 by President Estaban Echeverria.

In Chapter I, Article 3, for example, foreigners who acquire Mexican property cannot invoke the protection of their governments with respect to such property: the reassertion of a sovereignty whose violation and dilution in the past is etched in many Latin American minds and hearts.

In Article 4, in the spirit of 1938, the Mexican government reserves to itself the nation's basic infrastructure, petroleum, basic petrochemicals, and much of the mining industry; it reserves to citizen ownership the radio and television industries as well as those of air and road transport, forestry, and gas distribution.

These articles consolidate a good deal of previous policy and define, after a fashion, a century's progress in Mexico's ability to absorb and manage efficiently a wide range of modern technologies. But the process of absorption is not complete, and Article 5 of the draft bill begins to define some areas where foreign capital is wanted for Mexican progress: automotive components, secondary petrochemicals, and in the exploitation of certain mineral reserves. And in Chapter III, Article 13, the draft bill lists (in a style quite convenient for teachers of development policy) the criteria by which the National Commission on Foreign Investment will decide to act, positively or otherwise, on particular investment propositions.[3] As Under Secretary of Commerce Campillo Sainz tersely summarized present policy, "Foreign investment will be welcome insofar as it contributes to the improvement of our technology, promotes the development of new and dynamic industries, produces goods for export to the entire world and contributes to the achievement of our national goals."[4]

This is a doctrine highly appropriate to a nation about midway through the drive to technological maturity. Mexico, for more than a decade, has been moving beyond the import-substitution for consumers' goods and absorbing efficiently the technologies of metalworking (including heavy engineering and automobile manufacture), chemicals, and electronics, but it still has a considerable distance to go. Mexico still relies heavily on imported capital equipment in some of its most rapidly expanding sectors: for example, petrochemicals, pulp and paper, electric power, and electronics. On the other hand, its virtuosity in the less complex branches of these sectors permits and justifies a major effort to increase its exports of manufactured goods, and this increase in exports is happening.

What does a nation at Mexico's stage of growth demand by way of equity in the contemporary world? Foremost, it demands that its late take-off vis-à-vis the United States (a gap of about a century) permit it to behave in various asymmetrical ways. Mexico claims (and is granted) access to World Bank and IDB capital, including the latter's Fund for Special Operations, although Mexico, as one of the more advanced developing nations, recognizes that it can legitimately draw only small sums from the soft loan windows of the multilateral banks.

But still Mexico faces problems it regards as inequitable. It complains of a variety of limitations on its potential exports to the United States; of its bilateral trade deficit; of the large burden of interest payments and profit remittances from Mexico to the United States. It complains also of the small contribution of multinational corporations to its export drive in manufactures. Mexico faces special problems in the long osmotic border areas, including the problem of salinity in the Colorado River Basin. And (like Canada) it complains of being linked inextricably to a rich and massive nation whose domestic fluctuations have disproportionate consequences on the Mexican economy and that, with the best will in the world, cannot help creating an environment in which Mexicans feel their fate is unfairly beyond their control.

As Octavio Paz has recently put it

> In Northern Mexico, the phrase "the other side" is used to speak of the United States. The "other side" is a geographical reality: the border; a historical reality: another civilization, another language, and, above all, another time (the United States is a modern culture while we are still struggling with our past). It is also a metaphorical otherness, for the United States is the image of everything we are not. It is otherness itself, except that we are doomed to live with that otherness; the other side is the contiguous side. The United States is always present in our midst, even when ignoring or turning its back on us; its shadow falls on the whole continent. It is the shadow of a giant. . . .
> The United States represents the denial of what we were in the sixteenth, seventeenth, and eighteenth centuries; of what we could not be in the nineteenth, and of what many among us wished we were in the twentieth.[5]

Both relative stages of growth and relative size—as well as differences in cultural heritage and a long shared border—are at work in the equation of U.S.-Mexican relations.

Sensitive—at least in our generation—to Mexican complaints and uneasiness, responsible U.S. citizens listen with sympathy to Mexico's problems. And sometimes they join in debate, as, for example, Ambassador Robert McBride did in Acapulco on October 12, 1972. He noted that, despite tendencies to restrict imports in the light of the balance of payments situation, the United States has offered an expanding and accessible market to Mexico, especially for an increasing proportion of manufactured goods; that the United States has accepted an asymmetry regarded as "incongruous" by some of its citizens that permits Mexican textiles to flow to the United States, within limits, while Mexico permits no competition in "either textiles or automobiles"; that despite policies that seek to reduce U.S. capital exports, their flow to developing nations has not been inhibited; that the Mexican trade deficit is significantly offset by the U.S. bilateral tourist deficit; that a balance of payments approach to profit remittances fails to take account of multiplier effects in employment and upgrading of labor; that Mexico's trade deficit with the Common Market is egregious; etc. The debate is familiar to us all.

V

I would not pretend to arbitrate in this debate or to define the just solution to each component in Mexico's agenda of inequitable dependence in its relations with the United States. Finding such solutions should be the subject of continuous, fine-grained professional dialogue between Washington and Mexico City. I would permit myself, however, three general observations.

First, it is clearly essential that Mexico make a maximum effort to press forward its export drive in increasingly sophisticated manufactures.

Mexico—aided by good policy and considerable smuggling—was somewhat less guilty than most other Latin American nations of developing bad, inefficient habits during the era when its leading sectors were in heavily protected consumers' goods that substituted for imports. But it did not generate the export-or-die mentality of, say, Japan, South Korea, or Taiwan. One of the most hopeful features in the world of developing nations is the growing capacity of some among them to acquire the disciplines of efficiency, quality control, and knowledge of external markets that are necessary to sell manufactured goods abroad. Brazil and Iran belong on this list as well as Colombia, El Salvador, and even some of the more enterprising African states. I would not pretend to advise the Mexican National Commission on Foreign Investment; but if I sat on the commission I would surely insist that criterion III of Article 13 be vigorously implemented—namely, that foreign investment have "positive effects on the balance of payments and, especially, on the increase of export trade." U.S. firms in Europe have generally made such a contribution; they should certainly do so in Latin America as well. But Mexico cannot rely on foreign firms to do the job. It must develop a new exporting breed of entrepreneurs of its own.

Second, Mexico must look to world markets, not merely to the United States, in selling its exports. Since 1940, the accessibility of the U.S. market, the ties developed with U.S. firms and the U.S. capital market, the mutual acceptance (despite its occasional frictions, irritations, and costs) of a massive tourist flow from north to south, the gathering maturity and sense of responsible partnership between the Mexican and U.S. governments—all this has permitted Mexico to move through take-off into the drive toward technological maturity in remarkably good order, in comparison with experiences elsewhere in Latin America and on other continents. Mexican-U.S. economic relations will be critical for Mexico for a long time to come, but it is time for Mexico to look to the world beyond. I, for example, would like to see Mexico take more seriously, and assume increased leadership in, the critically important movement toward a Latin American Common Market, embracing also the real but somewhat fragile initiatives represented by the Andean Common Market and the Central American Common Market. We all know the acute problems that are holding up progress in this direction, but there is no other politically as well as economically satisfactory destiny for the smaller nations of the region. And the larger nations—notably Mexico, Brazil, and Argentina—should lead the way. In the short run, they may feel their domestic markets are sufficient to move forward on their own; but a larger and longer view suggests their security and prosperity will hinge on building a spacious regional environment within which the medium and smaller states of Latin America can also absorb efficiently the tricks of technological maturity. Moreover, the lesson of hsitory is that prosperous industrial nations that are rapidly moving forward provide mutually reinforcing markets to one another, despite elements of competition. That is the way it was between, say, pre-1914

Britain and Germany; within Europe and across the Atlantic in the past quarter-century; and in U.S.-Japanese relations since the early 1950s. Therefore, without abandoning its ties to the United States, Mexico should, in my view, expand its economic ties with Latin America and also with Europe, Asia, and Africa. The industrially mature Mexico, which is surely emerging, should become a world trading nation. The setting of that target will help bring it about. And the diversification of economic ties will reduce the sense of undue dependence on the colossus to the north. I would immediately add, however, that this judgment does not relieve the United States and the other rich nations of the world of the urgent responsibility of resolving their monetary, trade, and domestic price policies in ways that will permit increasingly liberal trading terms to the latecomers.

Third, an observation that bears on policy in Mexico and in other developing nations: Be extremely cautious in evoking popular sentiments of aggrieved nationalism when dealing with these problems of capital imports and trade. Despite many real, unresolved problems, progress has been made in devising rules of the game that protect the interests of capital-importing countries while still attracting private investors concerned with profit. A set of asymmetrical trading rules has been created that permit developing countries the time to absorb new technologies, protected from competing imports. In refining these rules, and rendering them more equitable, there is an ample agenda. But nothing is gained and much can be lost by bringing these issues in coarse-grained ways into the political arena. Once there, governments can become prisoners of the nationalism they have helped to inflame.

I once reviewed the problems of foreign investment in Latin America with seven distinguished Latin American colleagues on the Inter-American Committee on the Alliance for Progress (CIAP), including my revered friend Don Roderigo Gomez, who led the Bank of Mexico for so long. None of us was naive about the problems posed by such investment in Latin America nor about what, at its best, foreign investment could contribute by way of technology, management, and training as well as capital itself. We all agreed that serious negotiations between governments could narrow or eliminate the inequities in the private capital flow, but that to present the problems in the black-and-white terms of conventional political debate would be damaging to the interests of the citizens of Latin America. In fact, several examples of such damage were before us as we surveyed the scene, and it is not difficult to find such examples today. The equivalent problem in the United States and other advanced nations is protectionism. It is extremely easy to rouse the protectionist beast in U.S. politics; it takes endless, determined effort to keep it at bay. The economic world that has been created since 1945 is clearly short of perfection, and the number of inequitable burdens borne by the latecomers ought to be removed or reduced. But a good deal has been learned since Britain twice went to war with Holland in the seventeenth century to improve its relative economic position. This is not yet a world where all can operate in dignified interdependence despite differences in stage of growth and size; but it is a lot nearer there than it once was, and it is worth preserving these gains rather than striking out in frustration for an independence that does not exist—a lesson I would apply to the foreign policy of the United States as much as I would to that of Mexico.

VI

There is a special reason for making this point in the context of Mexico's relations with the United States. No reasonably sensitive citizen of the United States can read the history of the relations between the two countries—notably during the period from 1836 to Ambassador Henry Lane Wilson's (and his president's) obsessive interventions in Mexico's domestic affairs in the years before 1917—without realizing that the policy of the United States, to use an understated British phrase, was "no better than it should be." There was little self-restraint as the United States pursued its interests of power, economics, and politics against a weaker neighbor that was struggling to define its nationhood and its destiny in the modern world. Out of that experience, it is not difficult to understand the emergence of a xenophobic strand in Mexican nationalism.

From these unpromising beginnings extraordinary changes evolved, both within postrevolutionary Mexico and in its relations with the United States. Mexico is moving with some vigor through the stages of growth, having gone far to reconcile its immensely rich and complex cultural heritage with the imperatives of modern life. Not unconnected with Mexico's domestic progress, foreign relations with the United States have moved toward balance, mutual respect, and, in some areas, toward authentic partnership.

Looking down the road, it is not difficult to foresee a time when a fully modernized Mexico has achieved technological maturity, has enjoyed (or suffered) its own version of high mass-consumption, and is gripped, like the contemporary United States, with the complex agenda of the search for quality. I would not be dogmatic about timing, but Mexican children born now should see that day. As I said toward the close of *The Stages of Economic Growth*, "the end of all this is not compound interest forever; it is the adventure of seeing what man can and will do when the pressure of scarcity is substantially lifted from him."[6] That era has not yet come for the United States, and it will arrive, probably, a little later for Mexico than for the United States. Moreover, there will remain, after two centuries of uninhibited growth, the agenda of balancing man and his physical environment. But, unless life on earth is destroyed, that will be humanity's common destiny.

I make this point because it is easy to lose perspective on the current state of Mexican-U.S. relations. The problems and frictions are real and deserve attention on both sides of the border. Nothing in the historical framework I have tried to evoke justifies complacency. But both nations have moved a long way in the past half-century toward a dignified interdependence; the forces at work in both societies are capable of moving them farther in that direction in the future; and, with perspective and steady hard work, they will.

NOTES

1. Charles Wilson, *Profit and Power* (London: Longmans, Green, 1957), p. 144.
2. Alexander Hamilton, "Report on manufactures" (1791), in Samuel McKee (ed.), *Alexander Hamilton's Papers on Public Credit Commerce and Finance* (New York: Columbia University Press, 1934), p. 227.
3. Article 13 follows:

"In order to determine the desirability of authorizing foreign investment and to fix the percentages and conditions by which it will be governed, the Commission will take into account the following conditions and characteristics of the investment:

I. To be complementary of domestic investment;
II. Not to displace local companies that are operating satisfactorily, nor to enter fields that are adequately covered by domestic enterprise;
III. Its positive effects on the balance of payments and, especially, on the increase of export trade;
IV. Its effect on the labor force, taking into account the level of employment it generates and the wages it pays;
V. The employment and training of Mexican technicians and personnel;
VI. The incorporation of domestic inputs and components in the manufacture of its products;
VII. The extent to which it finances its operations with resources from abroad;
VIII. The diversification of sources of investment and the need to foster Latin American regional and subregional integration;
IX. Its contribution to the development of the relatively less economically developed zones or regions;
X. Not to occupy monopolistic positions in the domestic market;
XI. The capital structure of the branch of economic activity involved;
XII. Its technological contribution and the role it plays in the country's technological research and development;
XIII. Its effect on price levels and quality of production;
XIV. Its influence on the country's social and cultural values;
XV. The importance of the activity in question in the context of the country's economy;
XVI. The extent of the identification of the foreign investor with the country's interests and his connection with foreign centers of economic decision; and
XVII. In general, the extent to which it helps to achieve the objectives of, and its compliance with, the policy of national development."

4. From speech delivered by Mexican Under Secretary of Commerce Campillo Sainz, October 14, 1972.

5. Octavio Paz, "Eroticism and Gastrosophy," in *How Others See the United States, Daedalus*, Fall 1972, p. 67.

6. W. W. Rostow, *The Stages of Economic Growth* (Cambridge: at the University Press, 1960, 1971), p. 166.

EIGHT

No Random Walk: A Comment on "Why Was England First?" [by N.F.R. Crafts] (1978)

As the text makes clear, Mr. Crafts wrote a lively article in The Economic History Review *(1977) arguing that Britain rather than France was the first to take-off into sustained industrialization as a result of chance rather than of forces at work making such an outcome "inevitable." He viewed British primacy as the outcome of a one-time match between football rivals, not "a large sample of games." I was led to write the following comment whose brevity was appreciated by the editors.*

I should add that I wholly agree with Crafts that most of continental Western Europe (and the North American colonies) shared with Britain a process of political, social, commercial, agricultural, and intellectual transformation—including the Scientific Revolution—that, since the fifteenth century, had slowly prepared the way for the British take-off in the 1780s and all that followed. This general pre-conditioning explains why Belgium, France, Germany, Switzerland, and the United States could follow the British example so promptly. But I would still argue, barring fresh evidence, that there were identifiable characteristics of eighteenth-century Britain relative to France that made for the probability that the former would be first out of the gate.

My book How It All Began *(1975) deals at greater length with this intriguing issue.*

Some thirty years ago I allowed myself the following rather grandiose observation: "On occasion it may be proper to regard the course of

---

This comment was published in the November 1978 issue of *The Economic History Review*, Second Series (vol. 31, no. 4). Reprinted with permission.

Annual Average Patents Granted and Inventions Approved: Great Britain and France in the Eighteenth Century

	Great Britain	France		Great Britain for comparable years
1702–11	2	6		—
1712–21	5	7		—
1722–31	10	10		—
1732–41	5	6		—
1742–51	9	4		—
1752–61	10	—		—
1762–71	23	(1760–9	7	21)
1772–81	31	(1770–1	10	25)
1782–91	54	(1789–92	22	63)
1792–1801	72	(1796–8	8	69)

Source: W. W. Rostow, *How It All Began* (1975), p. 176.

history as inevitable, *ex post*; but not *ex ante*."[1] I was, therefore, pleased to see Mr Crafts try his hand at a stochastic explanation of the coming of the first Industrial Revolution.[2] In exploring this hypothesis, however, he confronted two lions in his path. It is conceivable that further and deeper research might remove them. He chose to ignore them, rendering his essay unsatisfactory.

The first lion is the marked acceleration in the scale of British relative to French inventions from the 1760s onwards. The presently available statistical data are frail, but, taken at face value, make a powerful case.

If these numbers were all we had, I, at least, would not be wholly convinced. But contemporaries and historians, without the benefit of comparative statistics, were fully aware of the marked absolute and relative acceleration in British inventions, not least contemporary French officialdom. It was after 1760 that the French government became most ardent in trying to acquire British technology. The French became conscious that they were falling behind in this particular respect. It was, for example, sixteen years after the founding of Birmingham's famous Lunar Society that the first private organization addressed to this problem was set up in France: "The Free Society of Emulation for the Encouragement of Inventions which Tend to Perfect the Application of the Arts and Trades in Imitation of that of London."

The British advantage in the scale of inventive activity was noted by a Swiss calico printer as early as 1766, in quoting what was already a proverb:[3] ". . . for a thing to be perfect it must be invented in France and worked out in England." This statement reflects an important distinction between an invention incorporating a principle later proved viable, and an invention refined to the point when production on a cost-effective basis can begin. Working out an invention almost always requires many hands and minds. Present evidence suggests that British society diverted more talents to these tasks of invention and refinement than France. A serious case for a stochastic theory of the British Industrial Revolution must address itself, therefore, to the scale of inventive activity not merely to aggregate data of pre-modern economic expansion, or to the allegation that Frenchmen just missed hitting on the spinning-jenny and water frame.

Now the second lion in the path: innovational zeal. The case against the stochastic hypothesis is heightened if one separates sharply invention and innovation, which Mr Crafts fails to do. One must, at least, try to get at the relative vigour of private innovative entrepreneurship in the two countries. Here Mr Crafts is a bit evasive. He uses the work of Shelby McCloy when it appears to fit his thesis but fails to quote McCloy's final conclusion: "Private business of eighteenth-century France thus was more to blame than the government for failure to pursue invention."[4]

In this matter of estimating innovative zeal, one must go beyond Hargreaves's spinning-jenny and Arkwright's water frame. One must look at the full range over which entrepreneurs were seizing on and applying new inventive insights, including agriculture, road and canal building, iron manufacture, and the steam engine, as well as cotton textiles. Here, evidently, we do not have orderly, even imperfect, statistical data. But we do have contemporary judgement and the conclusions of wise and careful scholars. Their universal conclusion that the innovational spirit in the private sector of post-1760 Britain was stronger than in France need not be regarded as sacrosanct. But their cumulative judgement must be altered by equally serious scholarship. It cannot, simply, be ignored.

Nor can the explanation some have offered for this phenomenon be ignored; namely, that, for whatever reasons, English non-conformists and Scotsmen, provided a more congenial setting by their society than their French counterparts, played a grossly disproportionate role in innovation as well as invention. This was, after all, what Hagan (inadequately paraphrased by Mr Crafts) was getting at, on the basis of Ashton's classic analysis.

Was Britain's achievement of the first Industrial Revolution "inevitable"? I would stick with my youthful *obiter dictum* and still say no. But until Mr Crafts (or others) is prepared to cope with these lions in the path, I would conclude that there were, indeed, "factors which made the probability of the onset of the Industrial Revolution" higher in Britain than in France. Until new and serious research upsets the received findings, the evidence is that the levels of inventive and private innovational activity over a wide front were higher in Britain than in France during the critical quarter-century that preceded the coming of the first Industrial Revolution. The test which took place from, say 1760 to 1783 was not a one-time match between Walsall and Arsenal, but "a large sample of games" in which Britain, with a population about a third that of France, generated sustained processes of invention and innovation on a scale the larger nation could not then equal. This was no random walk.

NOTES

1. W. W. Rostow, *British Economy of the Nineteenth Century* (1948), p. 143.
2. N. F. R. Crafts, "Industrial Revolution in England and France: Some Thoughts on the Question, 'Why was England First?'" *Economic History Review*, 2nd ser. xxx (1977), 429–41.
[3]. A. P. Wadsworth and Julia Mann, *The Cotton Trade and Industrial Lancashire, 1600–1780* (1931), p. 413.
[4]. S. T. McCloy, *French Inventions of the Eighteenth Century* (Lexington, Ky. 1952), p. 191.

NINE

Review of Immanuel Wallerstein, The Modern World System II: Mercantilism and the Consolidation of the European World Economy, 1600–1750 *(1981)*

Following is the first of five book reviews scattered about this volume. Like most academics, I believe a certain amount of book reviewing is a professional responsibility; I have, over the years, written a good many. The reviews included here all examine books with which I had quite serious disagreements. On such occasions I always recall what I remember as Charles Ives's Rule.

Ives was editor of the New Haven Journal Courier when I attended New Haven High School and Yale College (1928-1936). He ran an extensive daily array of book reviews in conjunction with the editorial page. His reviewers were mainly Yale students, but I was recruited in my senior year in high school because I edited the weekly newspaper. Ives's initial instruction was memorable, and I never violated it in my five years of writing reviews for him: "Remember, your first duty is to tell the reader what the author was trying to do and how he went about it. Then you can use the final 10 percent of the review to express your view."

I'm afraid I may have extended that austere proportion as time has passed, but I still try to remain loyal to the first part of Ives's charge.

This review provided me with the occasion to set down my view of the inadequacy of the core-periphery framework for the analysis of the period from 1600 to 1750. My reservations on its utility beyond 1750 are

---

This review was published in the July/August 1981 issue of *Transaction/Society* (vol. 18, no. 5). Reprinted with permission.

even more severe and relate to dependencia *doctrine, which is the subject of Chapter 7.*

Immanuel Wallerstein carried forward, in this the second of a projected four-volume series, his analytic history of the world economy. This first volume, published in 1974, focused on the break-up of feudalism in Europe when the expansion which began around 1150 gave way to the Malthusian crisis of, say, 1300–1450. The consequent decline in population and labor supply and falling prices yielded by the sixteenth century an agriculture increasingly based on money payments to labor and for land rental as well as a more diffused ownership of land. In the sixteenth century, of course, Spain and Portugal pioneered the new routes and empires beyond Europe. In that century, also, the balance between population increase and the food supply shifted and prices rose, a process linked in ways still debated to the flow of bullion from Latin America. In Wallerstein's view, capitalism emerged as the solution to problems feudalism could no longer manage from the mid-fourteenth century on; and from 1450 to about 1600 the European economy enjoyed a phase of expansion parallel to that which preceded the crisis of the fourteenth century, but within a new, more resilient and diversified structure stretching beyond Europe.

All this sets the stage for his analysis of the period from 1600 to 1750. Although I have some difficulty with Wallerstein's theoretical framework, to which I shall return, the main lines of the story, as he perceives it, are clear enough:

- There was a setback to agriculture in the seventeenth century in the form of a relative, unfavorable shift in the prices of agricultural products; price inflation slowed; and some indicators of prosperity, difficult to quantify, suggest a loss of momentum if not a setback as compared to the previous century (e.g., rate of population increase). Wallerstein never clearly decides on the extent to which the setback was an economic (or demographic) phenomenon or a product of the endemic civil and international wars of the century. He bypasses the question by implying that it is unimportant because the wars were a product of the economic deceleration.
- The response to this loss of momentum was not, as two centuries earlier, a pervasive crisis, but a consolidation and, even, extension of the capitalist world economy.
- In this setting, the great mercantilist struggles for power and profit occurred, from which the British emerged as dominant by 1783, although they were about to be mightily tested by the French—an episode that evidently belongs to Wallerstein's next volume.

In elaborating the dynamics of the seventeenth and eighteenth centuries, within this broad framework, Wallerstein uses the concept of core states and peripheral areas, a contruct which emerges strongly at the close of his first volume. He also defines an intermediate category of "semi-peripheral" states. The core states command power in all its relevant forms: political, military, industrial, commercial, financial. The peripheral areas export food and raw materials and are, in varying degree, politically weak, dependent on and exploited by the core countries. Wallerstein's fundamental architectural decision in writing this book was to take the core-periphery concept, initially developed to deal with certain relationships generated in the period 1815–1914, and push it backward in time a further two centuries and more. He presumably adopted this method because he proposes to use the concept in a fundamental way in his analysis of later times, making it the grand unifying theme for the whole sweep from the late fifteenth to the late twentieth century.

Applied to the period 1600–1750, Wallerstein's account breaks down as follows:

- A three-way struggle for dominance occurred in the core area of northwest Europe: Dutch hegemony in the seventeenth century gave way to the struggle between Britain and France, with the waning Dutch more or less joined with Britain after 1689. By 1783 Britain emerged well ahead.
- The peripheral areas suffered from weakened export markets and underwent painful internal readjustments mainly at the expense of the least advantaged social groups within them. The regions principally examined are Latin America, the Caribbean, and Eastern Europe.
- He rounds out his analysis with an account of the "semi-peripheries," some of which declined in the face of the challenges of the period (e.g., Spain, Portugal, Flanders) while others gained ground (e.g., Sweden, for a time, Brandenburg-Prussia, and the colonies of New England and the Middle Atlantic). The critical variable determining the outcome is taken to be the strength of the state and the vigor of its policy.

In each case, Wallerstein seeks to relate the social and political changes within each society to its external economic environment and the endemic international struggle among the contending states. His greatest strength in this enterprise is his prodigious knowledge of the literature. The bibliography at the end of the book is not only impressive and useful but is also reflected in the footnoting of each passage. He notes and takes his position on a great many of the large and narrow controversies generated in the specialist literature bearing on the regions and problems he embraces. In fact, his interest and involvement in the controversies keep diverting him from the main lines of his exposition.

Wallerstein's general economic analysis of the century and a half that concerns him and the use of the core-periphery paradigm are a good deal less than satisfactory. His basic economic analysis is confined to some twenty pages in chapter 1. At its core is a partial acceptance, at least, of Simiand's notion of a 250-year price cycle, with expansion in Phase A, contraction in Phase B. His exposition consists of a review of various theoretical perspectives on the period 1600–1750 (viewed as a Phase B), ending with his own judgment that it was a period of consolidation rather than decline.

The first problem, clear from his and everyone else's accounts, is that the fate of the nations and regions varied greatly. For Spain it was a period of sharp decline and limited recovery; for the Dutch, a period of dramatic rise and slow decline; for Brandenburg-Prussia, a period of consolidation and gathering strength; etc. "Consolidation" has, then, a narrow meaning: the emerging international trading system did not collapse after 1600, but in some dimensions (e.g., the emergence of the colonies in North America) even expanded.

The second and even more basic problem is with Wallerstein's view of the economic process which he believes suffused the life of this century and a half. I read his first chapter over a good many times before writing this review. The fault may be mine; but I am still not clear what the critical variables are in Wallerstein's view of the long cycle he perceives from a trough at about 1450, to a peak about 1600, and trough about 1750. I think they are two: the relative prices of agricultural products and the rate of population increase. The problem is not made easier when he evokes as evidence against the notion of a setback in the seventeenth century such diverse phenomena as the rise of strong nation states, a revolution in mores, and incremental improvement in British agronomy. Indeed, the list could be—and ought to be—greatly extended to include, among other creative phenomena, the Newtonian climax to the scientific revolution and the formation of the Royal Society, the French Academy, and similar institutions elsewhere. And, as Wallerstein is uneasily aware, the dazzling performance of the Dutch Republic at the peak of its relative power and the creative competitive strivings it stirred in Britain and Colbert's France do not fit the image evoked by Phase B; nor does the fact that unfavorable terms of trade for agriculture mean rising real wages in the growing towns and cities.

The analytic problem here is that the relations among price (or relative price) movements and production, trade, investment, and income distribution are extremely complex, quite apart from the complexity of the interactions among the economy, social structure, politics, and culture. Wallerstein bypasses most of these economic and societal complexities by his references to other authorities and a rather touching faith in his own version of the Marxist categories. In any case, I have no doubt that the book would have been better, and the reader better served, if Wallerstein's critically important first chapter had been confined to the most lucid and straightforward statement he could muster of his central hypothesis about the period without a single reference to the views of others and no footnotes whatsoever.

As for the core-periphery paradigm, it conceals for the seventeenth century more than it reveals. Latin America and Eastern Europe make rather strange bedfellows among the peripheral regions, Sweden and New England among the "semi-peripheries." Surely, the extraordinary pathology of seventeenth-century Spain, including a 25 percent decline in population in the wake of its great but sterilizing imperial exertions of the previous century, is not significantly illuminated by being tossed in among the "many semi-peripheral areas which lost ground." The fact is that when Wallerstein settles down to state what actually happened in each country and region, his summaries are sometimes excessively terse; but he introduces a good deal of the richness and uniqueness of the story. For just this reason, his larger generalizations fade into the background and lose their grip. Neither Wallerstein's economic categorization of the period nor his core-periphery scheme is capable of fulfilling the unifying tasks assigned to them. They are, simply, too crude an intellectual framework for a passage of history as variegated and complex as the century and a half, on both sides of the Atlantic, with which he has chosen to deal.

His ambitious and serious effort belongs, clearly, with a gathering tendency to break out of narrowly specialized and nationally focused economic history towards larger perspectives embracing the world economy. I have in mind, for example, the work of Paul Bairoch, Fernand Braudel, Carlo Cipollo, W. Arthur Lewis, and Douglass C. North. Volume VII of *The Cambridge Economic History of Europe* and some of my recent writings reflect this widely shared impulse. As we grope to give some shape and order to the story of the world economy, we shall no doubt experiment, as we already have, with a wide range of theoretical perspectives. Each will have its strengths and deficiencies. However one casts up the balance sheet on Wallerstein's second volume, his effort commands respect and justifies interest in the volumes to follow.

… TEN

The Terms of Trade and Development (1982)

It is an amiable—even comforting—tradition in academic life that when we approach a certain age our friends organize collections of essays in tribute to our work and longevity. This essay, in honor of W. Arthur Lewis, is of that character as are those in Chapters 24 and 25.

I have admired Lewis and his work since about 1945. We have shared a number of interests including the study of determinants of the terms of trade, in which we have both sought to go beyond the confining short-period assumptions of the classical theory of international trade. It was natural, therefore, that in this essay I tried to extend my previous analyses of the problem.

INTRODUCTION

This essay* concerns the interacting linkage between movements in the terms of trade and economic development. It argues not only that conventional neo-classical economic theory does not provide tools capable of usefully framing this problem but also that critical variables must be introduced from outside the terrain of economics.

SECTION II

A good deal of Arthur Lewis' work has focused on the connections between the terms of trade and economic development: both the com-

---

This essay was first published as Chapter 9 in T. E. Barker, A. S. Downes, and J. A. Sackey (eds.), *Perspectives on Economic Development, Essays in Honour of W. Arthur Lewis* (Washington, D.C.: University Press of America, 1982). Reprinted with permission.
*I wish to acknowledge with thanks the helpful comments on an earlier draft of this essay by David Kendrick, Charles P. Kindleberger, and Stephen P. Magee.

modity (or net barter) terms of trade and the factoral terms of trade measuring relative physical productivity. His approach and method belong in a long tradition reaching back to Adam Smith and Robert Torrens, carried forward in counterpoint to orthodox foreign trade theory by Keynes, D.H. Robertson, Colin Clark, C.P. Kindleberger, and myself, among others.[1] It is a tradition of dynamic Marshallian long period analysis which takes its start historically with the perception that the course of productivity might differ as between agriculture and raw materials, on the one hand, manufactures, on the other. Thus, Adam Smith contrasts the "necessary rise on the real price of rude materials" with "the natural effect of improvement—to diminish gradually the real price of almost all manufactures."[2] But economic history did not unfold in a simple and elegant way, reflecting the steady operation of diminishing and increasing returns to raw materials and manufactures, respectively. There were, it is true, recurrent fears that the old devil, diminishing returns, was at last, once and for all, about to force an industrializing world, in Stanley Jevons' phrase, "to reduce its motion to rest."[3] But the opening up of new areas and resources, multiple revolutions in transport, and the generation of new technologies relevant to agricultural and raw materials output have managed for two centuries to fend off diminishing returns to the sectors rooted in material resources, excepting timber where substitutes have had to suffice. Now, in the wake of the explosion of grain and energy prices in 1972–1973, it is once again to be proved, as on at least four occasions in the past, that human ingenuity and enterprise can continue to hold diminishing returns at bay.

The unfolding of this drama, since the late eighteenth century, has taken the form of erratic, more or less cyclical phases of relatively abundant and relatively scarce basic commodities yielding periods of relatively low and relatively high prices for Smith's "rude materials." The phases were not only erratic but, of course, the relative prices of such materials did not all move together. Nevertheless, the analytic literature to which much of Lewis' work belongs responded to such phases and, in some cases, looked back over the sweep of history in an effort to give order and sense to the contemporary scene. That was notably true of the period between the two world wars. A great deal of this literature was oriented towards Britain, a massive importer of basic commodites, coal excepted. It was, therefore, natural that analysts of this bent should examine the discomfiture experienced by a highly industrialized nation as it sought to adjust to large, often sudden, shifts in its commodity terms of trade; e.g., Keynes, Robertson, Clark, Alfred Kahn. Lewis belongs to a narrower group of analysts who have been at least equally concerned with the impact of such shifts on nations producing and exporting predominantly basic commodities.

The fact is that the major shifts in the terms of trade over the past two centuries can only be understood if one is prepared to examine the price dynamics of the major commodities entering into world trade; and

CHART 1. British Terms of Trade, 1796–1974 (1913 = 100).

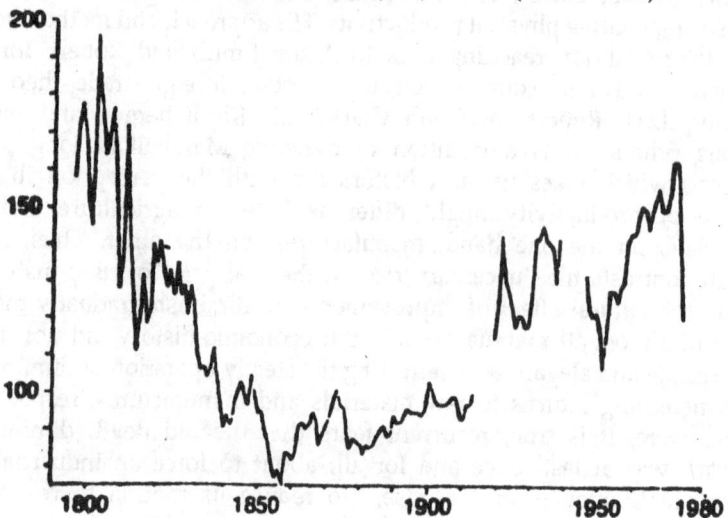

Source: Albert H. Imlah, *Economic Elements in the Pax Britannica,* updated from Board of Trade data (*Statistical Abstract of the United Kingdom*).

then to examine the impact of their special vicissitudes on the terms of trade of particular countries in the light of the changing composition of their imports and exports, as they move—or fail to move—through the stages of economic growth. One must learn a good deal about wheat and cotton, wool and coal, meat and dairy products, timber, coffee, oil, etc. It is interesting, rich, often inelegant, work; but indispensable if one aims to account for the terms of trade movements that have actually occurred. Putting wars and the luck of weather aside, such analyses, however, are not shapeless, empirical exercises. As I have long argued, what we observe in economic history are dynamic, interacting national economies, trying rather clumsily to approximate optimum sectoral equilibrium paths—Allyn Young's "moving equilibrium"—tending successively to undershoot and overshoot these paths, like a drunk making his way home on Saturday night.

Take, for example, the British terms of trade set out in Chart 1 for the period 1796–1974.[4] Putting aside the complexities of the pre-1815 years, much influenced by harvest fluctuations and the relative efficacy of blockades and embargoes, here, tersely summarized, are some of the major forces which determined movements in the British terms of trade.

The Postwar Rise: 1814–1821. Despite a few bad harvest years, the return of peace brings down the prices of basic commodities, notably cotton and wheat, more than export prices. This happened because sources of supply obstructed by war are re-opened, while freight and insurance rates fall sharply.

The Downward Trend: 1821–1840. Down to 1830 this powerful movement is the outcome of an interacting race between the decline of both export and import prices; specifically, between the cheapening of raw cotton, as new areas were opened up, the cotton gin was diffused, and Atlantic freight rates fell, and the cheapening of cotton goods, as the technologies of modern manufacture unfolded. When the differing proportions raw cotton bore to total imports, cotton goods to total exports, and the proportion of raw cotton to total cost of manufacture are taken into account, it emerges that the net downward trend in the British terms of trade up to 1830 is mainly the consequence of the technological revolution in the cotton industry.[5]

Although technological progress in cotton manufacture continued at a decelerating rate beyond 1830, the sharp deterioration of the British terms of trade in the 1830's results from a different set of circumstances than those operating in the 1820's: the catching up of cotton demand with existing acreage by the end of the 1820's; the consequent transatlantic cotton boom down to 1836; and then a sharp decline in British export prices, after the cyclical peak of 1836, unmatched by an equivalent fall in import prices.

Easement in the 1840's. The relative supply of cotton and some other basic commodities generated by investments of the 1830's permits Britain a powerful cyclical expansion, with a double peak in 1845 and 1847, accompanied by a favorable shift in the terms of trade; but the Irish potato famine and parallel troubles on the Continent yield a rise in imported grain prices and a transient terms of trade deterioration in 1845–1847.

The Terms of Trade Collapse of the 1850's. The British terms of trade worsened by 18% between 1848 and 1857. At the heart of this shift was a turning point in the relative price of grain. The international wheat price just about doubled in 1852–1854 and, in the United States, fluctuated thereafter in a relatively high range. The raw cotton price also rose substantially, as demand caught up with the over-supply induced during the boom of the 1830's. These relative price movements led to a major expansion into new wheat and cotton lands in the United States, accompanied by large capital imports (as in the 1830's) and massive immigration. The inflationary forces at work from these causes were heightened by the Crimean War and the Indian Mutiny.

The Quiet 1860's, the Transient Energy Crisis of 1871–1873 and Its Subsidence to 1877. Despite the effect of the American Civil War on the raw cotton price, the British terms of trade oscillated in a higher range during most of the 1860's than in the previous decade: higher prices for textile exports (including wool and linen) and some years of abundant, cheap grain (notably, 1863–1866) countered the quadrupling of the cotton price from 1860 to 1864. In the great boom leading up to 1873, centered in Germany and the United States, the British coal export price doubled, in the face of an intense, transient supply bottleneck, as did the price of pig iron, yielding a sharp peak in the British terms of trade which subsided to a trough in 1877 as the first phase of the Great Depression struck harder at British export than import prices. This happened, in part, because a building boom in Britain was sustained down to 1877, despite the cyclical peak in 1873. Between 1873 and 1877 coal prices fell by more than a half; timber prices by only 14%.

Improvements and Reversal, 1877–1913. After moving irregularly in the phase of acute depression (1878–1879) and the "profitless" expansion of 1880–1881, a new phase begins. From the early 1880's to the famous reversal of price trends in the mid-1890's, powerful supply-side forces, including enlarged U.S. wheat exports from the late 1870's and a rapid fall in freight rates, drove down British import more rapidly than export prices; and in the subsequent boom another major coal shortage, induced in part by shipping requirements during the Boer War, imparted a second-stage booster to the British terms of trade, lifting them to a level 19% higher than their 1881 low. A 6% deterioration followed, down to the eve of the First World War, as the United States reached the end of its frontier and a rise in prices for imported raw materials (notably cotton and wheat) lifted import prices even more rapidly than rather ebullient export prices, the latter responding to rapid expansions in Canada, Australia, Argentina, New Zealand, and other areas producing and exporting foodstuffs and raw materials.

There is an evident parallel between the basic commodity price turnarounds of the mid-1890's and the early 1850's and their aftermaths in enlarged capital exports from Britain to overseas agricultural regions; but the large British coal export position cushioned the impact on the British terms of trade in the latter case.

Inter-war Pathology, 1919–1938. The British terms of trade index was about 25% more favorable in 1920 than in 1913, the product of a brief export boom; but the underlying over-supply of basic commodities, in the face of relatively sluggish European growth, asserted itself with the recession of 1920–1921, maintaining favorable terms of trade for the balance of the decade as compared to the pre-1914 years, although below the 1920 peak. The terms of trade improve 24% between 1929 and 1933 during the deep global depression, but they trend downward thereafter (excepting the sharp recession year 1938) as the demand for raw materials expands and policies of supply constraint in agricultural and raw material production have some success. As we all know, this phase of extraordinarily favorable British terms of trade was largely dissipated by its depressing effects in British overseas markets, compounded by the 1925 return of the pound to its pre-war gold value, leading to chronic high unemployment in British export industries, diminished earnings in shipping, loss of investment income, etc.

Post-1945 Strain and Two Decades of Easement: 1946–1972. The terms of trade in immediate post-war Britain were substantially less favorable than in 1938 as agricultural and raw material production revived less rapidly than industrial output; and the trend continued down to 1951, exacerbated by the effect on raw material prices of the Korean War.

This imposed strain on the British standard of living but rendered possible a rapid expansion of exports to overseas markets and a reduction in the sterling balances built up during the war—a process compensated for, in part, by Marshall Plan aid. From 1951, however, the terms of trade for Britain and other advanced industrial countries improved down to 1972 underpinning the great boom in consumers durables and services of that generation. The improvement decelerated as the 1960's wore on. Unlike the inter-war years, the marked improvement in the terms of trade was not dissipated in unemployment: the proportion of British trade with primary producers was less; and the primary producers were better sustained by their own development efforts, the strength of the boom in the North, and, to a degree, by a flow of inter-governmental loans and grants.

The Inter-war Years in Reverse: 1972- . Foreshadowed in the 1960's by attenuating grain stocks in relation to global consumption and by the peaking out of U.S. oil and natural gas production around 1970, Britain and the advanced industrial countries experienced as sharp an unfavorable shift in the terms of trade in 1972–1973, with the explosions in grain and oil prices, as they did a favorable shift after the First World War. And they have done almost as poor a job in gearing their policies to the new realities in the world economy, notably the high and rising real price of energy—a subject to which we shall return.

This brisk and evidently incomplete summary of the major forces operating over some 180 years on the British terms of trade is meant to drive home a simple point: terms of trade movements reflect an extraordinary melange of forces, including the supply-demand history of particular commodities; industrial, agricultural, and transport innovations; business cycles: wars; in fact, the whole range of factors which have shaped the world economy over the past two centuries. If one is concerned to explain terms of trade movements, there is no way to escape the kind of laborious historical analysis of an erratically expanding world economy the inherent complexity of the problem demands.

SECTION III

In a majestic, parochial *tour de force*, conventional expositions of the theory of international trade, rooted in Ricardo and the more static propositions of Torrens, have managed down to the present day virtually to set aside the variables required to understand movements in the terms of trade. This is all the more remarkable because Frank Taussig induced an impressive array of his inter-war students to test the adequacy of classical foreign trade theory as it related to the role of the terms of trade in the transfer mechanism.[6] The results differed, of course, country by country; but John Williams' conclusion is a fair summary of what these exercises demonstrated:[7] "The classical theory assumes as fixed, for purposes of reasoning, the very things which, in my view, should be the chief objects of study if what we wish to know is the effects and causes of international trade, so broadly regarded that nothing of importance in the facts shall fail to find its place in the analysis."

Nevertheless, in Frank Graham's phrase, mainstream analyses of international trade have "done nothing but tread the same old Mill";[8] although they have done so with refinements of increasing elegance to which diminishing returns have sharply applied.

Put less polemically, the conventional theory of international trade continues to address itself to a set of questions quite different from Williams' "effects and causes of international trade ... broadly regarded. . . ." Those questions are set out lucidly, for example, in Chacholiades' textbook:[9]

"The pure theory of trade ... is mainly concerned with the following three questions:

"1. Which goods are exported or imported . . . ?
"2. Which are the terms of trade . . . ?
"3. Which are the gains from trade . . . ?"

In expositions in this tradition, the terms of trade begin as the factoral terms of trade; that is, they derive from the relation between the quantity of factors of production required to produce a unit of the same commodities in different countries. Conventionally, only two countries and two commodities are assumed to exist. From assumptions relating to relative labor productivity and, later, the relative productivity of the various factors of production, a range is established within which it is of advantage for the two countries to trade with one another. The exact "terms of interchange," within this productivity range, on which trade will take place, is determined by the relative "strength of the demand" of the two countries for the two commodities in question. The possible outcomes are compared, in the fundamental propositions of theory, by assuming constant returns to scale; that is, by rigorously excluding either short or long-period changes in real costs.

This assumption, along with the others within which classical trade doctrine was framed, permitted the transition from a fundamental productivity and real value consideration of international trade to a monetary and, then, income analysis approach which isolated the effects of demand shifts on the scale and composition of trade as well as on the commodity terms of trade. Short-period cost changes and supply as well as demand elasticities were introduced into the structure of classical analysis, but long-period changes were mainly ruled out. As Haberler wrote:[10]

> A reduction of costs of this dynamic and historical nature has no place in our analysis, since it represents a change of data not to be explained by economic theory.

As neo-classical price and, then, growth theory evolved, they were also woven into conventional expositions of trade theory. With respect to price theory, Haberler's dictum continued to apply; that is, radical changes in the supply of basic commodities were excluded from the analysis. The mechanics of indifference and production possibility curves were introduced; but, as noted above, the bulk of the exposition of international trade theory is still conducted within the framework of constant returns to scale, with given factor endowments and technology.[11] It is, essentially, a static theory.

The elaboration of neo-classical growth theory, from its base in the Harrod-Domar model, has led to formal expositions of the effects of economic growth on trade. Those models were controlled by three characteristics which drastically limited their capacity to illuminate terms of trade movements in the real world.

The availability of resource-bearing land for the production of food and raw materials is either aggregated out of such models or implicitly assumed to appear as an automatic function of the level or rate of growth of demand. This casualness about the supply of basic commodities is, perhaps, an understandable reflection of the fact that most such models were designed by economists in the advanced industrial world during a period of falling or relatively low prices of basic commodities (1951–1972).

The two sectors isolated in neo-classical growth models were generally capital goods and consumption goods, produced by varying proportions of capital and labor. Therefore, the problem of relative prices and income distribution emerged as the question of the relative marginal return to capital and labor. There was no awareness that, historically, major shifts in income distribution within nations and among nations were mainly brought about by periods of relative abundance or scarcity of foodstuffs and raw materials, consequent changes in the relative prices of basic commodities, and the movements of capital and people that flowed from them.

Changes in the capital stock were viewed as incremental: no variations in periods of gestation were envisaged, if, indeed, such lags were introduced at all.

The negative outcome was not surprising. Economists working this terrain were not exploring the dynamics of relative price movements. They were, mainly, trying to define the conditions for a dynamic, full-employment equilibrium, assuming a fixed, over-all rate of technological change, with varying capital-labor (and capital-output) ratios.

With a variable for progress in technology inserted, with a stable consumption function, and with entrepreneurs assumed to choose their technologies in ways which kept inventions Harrod-neutral, such models yield a balanced equilibrium path with per capita GNP growing steadily at the rate of technical progress.

Thus, when the apparatus of neo-classical growth models is introduced into international trade theory, a process pioneered by Harry Johnson, it yields outcomes in which shifts in the terms of trade are the result of the growth process for a given country, depending on: (i) whether or not growth is concentrated in the export sector; (ii) the international price elasticity of demand for the export product; (iii) the extent to which growth is shared in the international economy; (iv) the income elasticity of demand for the export product; and (v) whether technical change is neutral, labor-saving, or capital-saving. These manipulations have permitted international trade theorists to elaborate a range of cases, including the paradoxical case of "immiserizing growth" in which excessive export-based growth by a country whose role in the world market is substantial can under certain conditions, so tip the terms of trade against it as to counter the effects of growth, yielding a net decline in real income.[12]

In general, one can say of this literature what Kindleberger said of the behavior of the terms of trade in the case of capital transfer:[13] "Most readers will mop their brows as this point and conclude that one cannot say much about the terms of trade under capital transfer. Sad but true." In both cases—capital transfer and growth—the number of variables determining the upshot for the terms of trade is so great that the results are either indeterminate or can be made determinate only under strong, simplifying assumptions which render the conclusions of interest only to fellow theorists engaged in the same sport.

Basically, what is wrong with the conventional literature on the terms of trade in relation to both the transfer problem and the process of growth is that it treats changes in the terms of trade as a dependent variable. A more useful sequence is to begin with a shift in the terms of trade, with its roots in the dynamics of the world economy, and then examine the impact of that shift on trade, capital movements, population movements, and growth—including, quite possibly, playback effects of the process on the terms of trade themselves.

SECTION IV

Arthur Lewis' analysis of relative price movements in the period 1870–1913 is, in my view, a model of how one must proceed if the intent is to understand and explain the terms of trade movements that actually occur.[14] The problem is, broadly, to explain the shift in the terms of trade against agricultural products down to the mid-1890's, the subsequent improvement down to 1913 and the consequences of this relative price turnaround in both core and periphery. Lewis proceeded at both highly aggregated and disaggregated levels. In a laborious and original statistical exercise he established the aggregate rate of growth of industrial production for the major industrial countries (the core), the major cyclical fluctuations and their intensity, and the rate of population growth. He thus had in hand a rough index of demand for food and raw materials. This index is then applied to the supply of four major commodities moving in international trade—cotton, wool, wheat, and coffee—and equations established to yield estimated prices which can be compared to actual prices. He is then in a position to demonstrate his central proposition: the upward movement in the relative prices of agricultural prices after the mid-1890's is the result of a "decline in the rate of growth of wheat, wool, and cotton, with the price of substitutes acting in sympathy." Lewis was strengthened in this exercise by finding that his method of estimation approximated the actual coffee price which did not follow the U-shaped trend path of the other three commodities.

Putting Lewis' further exposition of his theme aside for a moment, it is clear that a favorable shift in the terms of trade for agricultural products or raw materials will have three probable and one possible effect in the producing country or region.

1. *A direct real income effect.* By permitting a larger quantity of imports to be acquired with a fixed quantum of exports a favorable shift in the terms of trade directly raises real income.

2. *An increase of immigration.* Population is likely to flow to the country or region experiencing the lift in real income brought about by a favorable shift in the terms of trade, a lift heightened with the passage of time, by the forces delineated in elements 3 and 4.

3. *An expansion of investment and acceleration of growth.* The investment rate in the country or region experiencing favorable terms of trade is likely to rise for three distinct reasons: to supply infrastructure and other capital to expand output of the commodities whose relative rise in price has caused the favorable shift in the terms of trade; to supply housing and urban infrastructure for the migrants; and to exploit disproportionately high profit possibilities through increased capital imports.

4. *A possible acceleration of industrialization.* If the society experiencing the expansionary impulses set out in elements 1–3 is otherwise prepared to absorb new technologies efficiently, the forces set in motion by a favorable shift in the terms of trade can yield a surge of industrialization. This happened, for example, in pre-1914 Canada, Australia, and Southern Brazil. It is happening now in some OPEC countries as well as in the western mountain region of the United States. It did not happen in pre-1914 Argentina, nor the tropical countries, which benefitted to a degree from the increased real income provided by their expanding plantation sectors but did not move on, at that time, into sustained industrialization.

Returning to international trade theory, capital imports are, from this perspective, not a cause for the shift in the terms of trade but a consequence. In the 1896–1913 period it is quite clear that accelerated expansion in the peripheral areas had proceeded for some time before large capital imports arrived. This happened, in part, because the financing of the Boer War constrained the London capital market until 1903. Canadian wheat production averaged, for example, 46 million bushels in 1894–1896, 86 million in 1901–1903. Capital exports to Canada, in fact, move up only modestly until 1905 when, after a brief setback, a truly extraordinary expansion begins.[15] The pattern is general. British net investment abroad averaged £40 million per annum for the period 1896–1900; £45 million, 1901–1905; £150 million, 1906–1910; £214 million, 1911–1913.[16] The secondary role of capital imports—reinforcing rather than initiating the process—is suggested by the case of New Zealand. It enjoyed from the mid-1890's to 1913 a period of great expansion, including increased immigration, based on favorable terms of trade and the potentialities of refrigeration, with only a modest increase in capital imports towards the end of the period.[17]

The flow of capital abroad to the prosperous periphery enjoying favorable terms of trade did, of course, have important consequences. It permitted domestic expansion to proceed at a higher rate and/or for longer than if capital imports were not cushioning the balance of payments; and these typically disproportionate booms, backed by capital imports, had the effect of shifting the terms of trade still further in favor of the peripheral country—a kind of second-stage booster effect. This process can also be observed in the United States during the 1830's and 1850's. But a good many cases of increased international (and interregional) capital flows cannot be understood in the first place unless one is prepared to begin where Lewis begins; that is, with the global supply-demand balance for particular commodities.

International capital flows, however, could also be induced by at least two other forces: major technological change and public policy. And the two were sometimes interwoven.

Argentina, Canada, Australia, and New Zealand, for example, imported a good deal of capital from Britain at various intervals during the period of declining basic commodity prices, say, 1873–1896.[18]

The circumstances of each country differed; but their development during an apparently unpropitious period has certain common characteristics.[19] As of 1870 these regions all suffered from transport systems inadequate for the full development of their resources; and their resources were sufficiently productive to justify economic exploitation at current, even falling, prices, given the economies in transport the railroad and the unfolding revolution in ocean shipping, based on steel, could provide. Other technical developments helped: refrigeration, barbed wire, new seed strains, agricultural machinery, and mining techniques to exploit non-agricultural resources the railroads also made accessible. Political changes in Argentina and new public policies in Canada, Australia, and New Zealand converged with these economic possibilities to draw large flows of foreign capital. Their years of golden prosperity and massive immigration come only after the price turnaround of the mid-1890's; but the 1870's and 1880's were creative decades and a necessary prelude; and they saw considerable, if erratic, inflows of foreign capital.

In Australia, railroad mileage open more than doubled in the 1880's, a period when net capital inflow was about half of gross domestic capital formation. This occurred at a time when wool dominated Australian exports, as gold production tapered off. In the 1880's Australia turned to domestic development and found the rather depressed London capital market in a mood to finance its enterprises. There was no immediate expansion of Australian exports. But from 1884 Australian land policy changed in ways to encourage agricultural rather than pastoral activity.

The Argentine case bears a family resemblance to that of Australia. The initiation impulse in this process was political: the consolidation of a firm central government by Julio Roca in 1880. At the time, Argentina, like Australia, was primarily an exporter of wool. The pampas were, however, obviously an area capable of profitable grain exploitation even at low world prices, if immigrants could be attracted and efficient transport provided. A massive inflow of British capital in the late 1880's provided the latter. Unlike the case of Australia, immigrants came to Argentina in large numbers in the 1880's. As the railways moved out over the pampas and barbed wire permitted the segregation of pastoral areas, the immigrants put increased acreage into production. There was a spectacular surge of output and exports in the early 1890's, helping stabilize the Argentine economy after the Baring Crisis in the face of falling export prices which otherwise would have had disastrous consequences; and then the price increase, from the mid-1890's, induced a tripling in output and a period of golden prosperity.

As in the case of Australia and Argentina, a prior period of creative preparation was necessary for Canada fully to exploit the possibilities of the price increase from the mid-1890's. From the Land Act of 1868 and the Homestead Act of 1872, the Dominion government had been trying to bring the western acreage, with its palpable potential for low-cost wheat, effectively into production. But the railroads had to be built, the population expanded by substantial net immigration, the competition of American extension of the frontier overcome. In addition, there was something of a lag in the adoption and full understanding of the dry-farming techniques pioneered in the United States. All this was framed by an acute political awareness that a Free Trade Britain had left Canada to fend for itself in North America and that the dynamism of post–Civil War United States might absorb Canada on north-south lines unless an east-west transport axis could be established and the resources of the country developed. There were surges of immigration and capital imports (in support of railway building) in the early 1870's and 1880's; and some expansion of new homesteads, responding to transient wheat price increases in the early 1880's and a decade later; but only from the mid-1890's did the great expansion in western Canada take hold and net immigration rapidly increase.

After surviving in the 1860's the Maori rebellions and experiencing a brief gold mining boom and bust, the government of New Zealand turned in 1870 to long term policies designed to exploit its "permanent resources":[20] "The great barrier to further progress was the lack of an adequate system of internal transport; settlement was still largely confined to coastal districts, a national system of roads had hardly been begun, and there were less than fifty miles of railway in the whole country." Over 1000 miles of railway line were open for traffic by 1877, almost 2000 by 1893. Roads and ports, telegraph, telephone, and postal communications similarly expanded. The proportion of the working force engaged in industry expanded substantially; modern farm machinery was imported and used on the wheat lands; and, above all, refrigeration was gradually introduced, changing the structure of agriculture and exports. It was in the period 1870-1882 that capital imports played their largest reinforcing role. The decline of the wool proce bore down heavily; but when prices lifted New Zealand was in a position to make the most of it:[21] "After 1895 the years of meagre return for strenuous effort gave way to a period of widely diffused and increasing prosperity . . . solidly based upon the development of the new industries opened up by refrigeration."

The point here is simple enough: international capital movements could be set in motion by cost-cutting new technologies in transport and production—and by public policies designed to exploit them—as well as by relative price movements rendering the exploitation of basic commodities more profitable through the supply-demand dynamics of the world economy.

An international trade theory that excludes technological change and treats the terms of trade as the outcome of a two-country, two-commodity trading world is, thus, of extremely limited relevance.

SECTION.V

We turn, finally, to an aspect of the linkage between the terms of trade and development which transcends economics; that is, the character of the response of a society to the potentialities, for good or ill, of a sharp shift in its terms of trade. Here we are dealing with a distinction I sought to make central in my *Process of Economic Growth* by viewing economic decisions as a result of the interaction of economic yields, representing objective economic potentialities, and a range of propensities, reflecting the effective response of a society to the yields.[22] The propensities incorporated the cultural, social, and political factors that bear on a society's economic decisions and which may dilute or, even, reinforce an outcome calculated simply in terms of profit maximization.

So far as the terms of trade in general are concerned, Kindleberger has dealt with this linkage most explicitly and systematically.[23] His central proposition is that the cost to a society of an adverse shift in its terms of trade (or of any other adverse change in demand or supply from abroad) depends on its "capacity to transform"; that the "reasons for incapacity to adjust are social in developed countries as well as underdeveloped"; and that "economics is able to tell us very little about the conditions under which given societies will respond in one way or another to the same stimulus."[24]

Arthur Lewis deals with this problem in both *Growth and Fluctuations, 1870–1913* and *The Evolution of the International Economic Order*.[25] In the former his central concern is to explain the differential response to favorable terms of trade from the mid-1890's to 1913 of the temperate and tropical peripheral countries. In general, they all experienced the first three consequences of a favorable shift in the terms of trade listed above . . . ; i.e., a rise in real income, increased immigration; and expanded investment, including foreign investment. But only in Canada, Australia, New Zealand, and Southern Brazil was there a movement, on the basis of these stimuli, into sustained modern industrialization.

He prefaces this enquiry with the following observation:[26]

> To explain why some countries do better than others within the same category is a formidable task, which needs to be approached from two directions simultaneously. One approach deals in generalisations, in theories of what stimulates and what retards industrialisation; the other deals in case studies of individual countries. Without simultaneous movement from both directions understanding is impossible. Valid generalisations cannot be formulated without deep knowledge of many (preferably all) individual cases; while the individual case cannot be understood without sound general theory.

This is not the occasion to paraphrase what Lewis had to say about the unique circumstances determining the outcome in each case. The point here is simply that he combines flexibly his basic general analysis of the nature of underdevelopment with social and political factors (including colonial policies, where relevant) to explain particular outcomes. As we all know, his technical explanation for underdevelopment lies in his view of the factoral terms of trade; that is, the low productivity of food production per acre (and, in some cases, per man) relative to Western Europe—a low-level trap sustained and reinforced by acute population pressure. Thus, poor factoral terms of trade and unlimited supplies of labor decree low per capita real income and prevent a large domestic market for manufactures from emerging. The temperate countries of the periphery (including the United States) enjoyed, in general, even higher per man yields in agriculture than Europe and higher per capita real income. Under the stimulus of the favorable terms of trade of the pre-1914 generation, the latter (excepting Argentina) not only expanded their production and exports of basic commodities but also moved into take-off; while the tropical countries (excepting Southern Brazil) moved forward no further than the higher per capita incomes permitted by expanded production and export of tropical plantation products under favorable market circumstances.

Lewis is quite aware that there is more to the story than low productivity in agriculture with all its far-reaching consequences; and so he contrasts the urban politics of Australia with the dominance of the landed aristocracy in Argentina; clashes between the vested interests of entrepreneurs oriented towards the import as well as export trades and those who aimed to produce manufactures for the domestic market; and he examines a spectrum of colonial policies in a discriminating, subtle and dispassionate way. Lewis judges their impact being in general, not directly to frustrate economic development but "to hinder the development of a native modernizing cadre," in part, because of a neglect of education.[27]

Lewis describes his essay in weaving together the economic and non-economic factors as they bore on the response to a phase of favorable terms of trade as a limited effort "to identify contributing factors which were common to many countries."[28] To undertake a definitive analysis would require in each case the kind of well-focused multi-disciplinary approach used for example, in Cyril Black et al., *The Modernization of Japan and Russia*.[29] And, indeed, the comparative approach might work well in exploring, for example, why a pre-1914 coffee boom (plus railroads) in Southern Brazil triggered a quite distinct regional take-off into sustained industrialization whereas the concurrent beef and wheat boom (plus railroads) in Argentina failed to do so.[30]

Moving beyond the period on which Lewis focuses his analysis, there are three final observations to be made.

First, a negative as well as a positive shift in the terms of trade can yield a constructive outcome if a society commands Kindleberger's "capacity to transform" and exercises it. The best known constructive response to an almost catastrophic economic event is, of course, the successful movement of a number of Latin American countries and Turkey into their first sustained phase of industrialization during the 1930's in response to the collapse of their export markets and export prices.

Second, terms of trade shifts, positive and negative (including wartime attenuation in the supply of imports), have played a role in helping bring about a substantial proportion of the take-offs into self-sustained growth that have been analyzed. By way of a rough arbitrary sampling, I took the twenty take-offs dealt with in Part V of *The World Economy: History and Prospect*, plus the three regional take-offs identified (New England, Southern Brazil, and Manchuria). Of these, twenty-three cases, 11 are related to sharp terms of trade movements: 6 to favorable shifts (United States [1850's], Sweden, Canada, Australia, Southern Brazil, Russia); 5 to unfavorable shifts (New England, Argentina, Brazil, Turkey, and Mexico).

In addition, there is the pre-take-off stimulus afforded industrialization in France, Belgium, and elsewhere on the Continent by the restriction of British manufactured imports during the Napoleonic wars and the parallel process in the United States, during the Embargo and War of 1812, until Francis Cabot Lowell's success gave the New England take-off a solid foundation.

It should be noted that the United States take-off from, say, 1843 to 1860 is a rather special case: its first decade was marked by relatively low agricultural prices and unfavorable terms of trade, with investment flowing into the railroadization of the North-east and the build-up of heavy industry in the Middle Atlantic states; its second decade, by relatively high agricultural prices and favorable terms of trade, with investment, including high capital imports, flowing into the railroadization of the Middle West.

The terms of trade in relation to development is, then, a quite serious aspect of the story of how one country after another moved, finally, into sustained industrial growth; but in no case do terms of trade movements constitute a sufficient explanation for the transition; the non-economic elements at work are of critical importance; and, above all, as the early portion of this essay argued, terms of trade movements themselves can only be understood as a by-product of the dynamics of the world economy; that is, a by-product of the development process itself.

Third, the interaction between the terms of trade and development is a subject highly germane to our disconcerting experiences of the 1970's and the challenges ahead in the 1980's.

With relatively few exceptions, the nations which make up the world economy—developed or developing, capitalist, socialist, or mixed—have exhibited a low "capacity to transform" in the face of the massive shift in the relative price of energy, the considerable relative shift in the price of agricultural products.[31]

So far as energy is concerned, the scale and urgency of the problem of creating a new energy base in substitution for expensive and waning oil supplies has not yet been translated into effective policies. For different reasons, both the United States and the Soviet Union, each well endowed with alternative energy resources, have been extremely sluggish in adjusting to the transition ahead: the United States because of political pressures from consumer interests intent on decreeing continued cheap energy and extremist environmental groups intent on sabotaging the generation of additional energy production; in the Soviet Union because of the implication for other resource commitments of the extremely large, long period of gestation investments required to bring alternative energy resources into production. All but a few current oil exporters also confront the need to develop alternative energy resources promptly if they are to maintain the momentum of their development; but they have been content to postpone such decisions, relying implicitly on a continuing rise in the real price of oil to see them through. Meanwhile, in a profligate way, some of these nations are becoming dependent on food imports on a scale which will cost them dearly in the future. In different degree, the oil importing developing nations are being throttled back as the proportion of the foreign exchange they earn allocated to oil imports continues to rise, reaching, in some cases (e.g.,

India and Brazil), close to 50%; while North-South cooperation, which will be required to build a new energy base in the developing regions, is deflected by rather sterile debate about the New International Economic Order. Some of the oil importing developing nations have done relatively well by disciplining inflation at home via explicit or implicit social contracts and pressing successfully to expand exports abroad. And Brazil, at least, is going about the business of generating an oil substitute with the war-production mentality the problem justifies. But the failure "to transform" at a pace and on a scale required to maintain economic and social momentum is endemic. Chronic stagflation in the North and decelerated growth in the developing regions, at a critical juncture in their evolution, have been the predominant method for balancing our energy books.

So far as the themes of this essay are concerned, there are two observations to be made on this rather undistinguished performance. First, in part it stems from the fact that, as compared to the world before 1914, price and investment decisions are much more nearly in the hands of governments and the political process, in the wider sense. With respect to energy, we are simply not getting the prompt diversion of capital flows in the world economy responding to relative price movements that occurred, for example, in the 1830's (cotton), 1850's (wheat and cotton), 1896–1913 (agricultural products generally). (The fact that economic decisions had become more politicized also helps explain the sluggishness of Britain's un-satisfactory response to excessively favorable inter-war terms of trade.)

Second, behind these generally inadequate performances in the face of the challenge posed by the relative rise in the price of energy lie, of course, deeper social forces. All analysts agree that the resources and technologies exist to cope with the transitional period when oil supplies wane while we await the emergence of essentially infinite and hopefully less polluting sources for the longer future; e.g., solar, breeder, fusion. If we went about the task seriously, a ceiling could quite soon be imposed on the OPEC oil price by a sharp reduction in demand for oil imports and the large scale production of alternatives at prices lower than the current OPEC price. Technically and economically, these are quite attainable objectives in a reasonable period of time; say, less than a decade.

Putting exhortation aside, the lesson is, as Charles Kindleberger and Arthur Lewis have emphasized, that the response to challenges posed by shifts in the terms of trade are determined by forces which transcend economics, even when economics is broken out of its neo-classical straight-jacket to embrace the Marshallian long period.

NOTES

1. For a discussion of various approaches to the analysis of the terms of trade, see, for example, W.W. Rostow, "The Terms of Trade in Theory," Chapter

8 in *The Process of Economic Growth*, Oxford: At the Clarendon Press, 1953, 1960.

2. Adam Smith, *The Wealth of Nations*, Book 1, Chapter XI, "Effects of the Progress of Improvement upon the real Price of Manufactures" (p. 196 in Routledge edition, London, 1890).

3. W.S. Jevons, *The Coal Question*, second edition, London: Macmillan, 1866, p. vii.

4. The major movements in the British terms of trade are analyzed in W.W. Rostow, *The World Economy: History and Prospect*, Austin: University of Texas Press (London: Macmillan), 1978, pp. 91–99 and at greater length in the course of Part Three, "Trend Periods."

5. See W.W. Rostow, *Process of Economic Growth*, pp. 201–205.

6. *Ibid.*, pp. 175–181. For an interesting return to the transfer problem, see Thomas Balogh and Andrew Graham, "The Transfer Problem Revisited: Analyses Between the Reparations Payments of the 1920's and the Problems of the OPEC Surpluses," *Oxford Bulletin of Economics and Statistics*, Vol. 41, No. 3, August 1979, pp. 183–191.

7. John H. Williams, "The Theory of International Trade Reconsidered," *Economic Journal*, Vol. 39, 1929, pp. 195–209.

8. Frank D. Graham, *The Theory of International Values*, Princeton: Princeton University Press, 1948, pp. 5–6.

9. Miltiades Chacholiades, *The Pure Theory of International Trade*, Chicago: Aldine, 1973, p. 13. I use Chacholiades' study here as a serious and representative effort to incorporate refinements in neo-classical price and growth theory into the received body of classical international trade theory.

10. G. Haberler, *The Theory of International Trade*, Clifton, New Jersey: Augustus M. Kelley, 1936, p. 202.

11. Occasionally efforts are made to deal with the inherently awkward case of increasing returns to scale. See, for example, M. Chacholiades, *op. cit.*, pp. 170–185, with a selected bibliography on p. 185. He observes (p. 170): "The analysis so far has been based on the assumption of constant returns to scale. When this assumption is dropped, several difficulties arise, in particular, the problems created by the phenomenon of increasing returns to scale.

"Increasing returns to scale are an indisputable fact of life. However, the treatment of increasing returns in the field of international trade theory has been scanty and unsatisfactory, because of the enormous difficulties encountered in incorporating the phenomenon of increasing returns in a general-equilibrium model." Chacholiades' formal resolution of this problem is achieved, as he acknowledges, only at the cost of extreme simplifying assumptions. C.P. Kindleberger, in dealing more pragmatically with this case, argues persuasively that it helps to explain the large scale trade among highly industrialized countries in "like, but not quite identical, goods" induced by specialization (*International Economics*, Homewood, Illinois: Richard D. Irwin, 1953, pp. 91–94). It should be noted that increasing returns through economies of scale are to be distinguished from increasing returns brought about by substantial discontinuities in supply via major innovations or the opening up of new sources for foodstuffs or raw materials. Conventional economic theory has, essentially, failed to deal with the latter problem. For an extended discussion of this failure, see W.W. Rostow, "Technology and the Price System," Chapter 4 in *Why the Poor Get Richer and the Rich Slow Down*, Austin: University of Texas Press, 1980, pp. 154–188. For an interesting effort to introduce one Marshallian long period factor into foreign trade analysis—research and development and the Vernon product cycle—see Stephen P. Magee, *International Trade*, Reading, Mass.: Addison-Wesley, 1980, pp. 28-38.

12. For a good example of Johnson's work in the field, see "Economic Development and International Trade" in Harry G. Johnson, *Money, Trade and Economic Growth*, Cambridge, Mass.: Harvard University Press, 1963, pp. 75-103, including a useful, eclectic bibliographical appendix. For a later analytic review of the propositions emerging from the linking of international trade and neo-classical growth theory, with certain original features, see Jagdish Bhagwati, *Trade, Tariffs, and Growth*, Cambridge, Mass.: M.I.T. Press, 1969, pp. 311-338. The formal literature linking modern growth analysis to foreign trade theory is only rarely related to concrete situations. Richard Caves and Ronald Jones (*World Trade and Payments*, Boston: Little, Brown, 1973, p. 536) do refer to the possibly perverse effects on the Brazilian terms of trade of a bumper coffee crop; but one would have thought analysts interested in this problem would have paused to contemplate the story of the British terms of trade during the cotton textile revolution: a powerful technological advance in industry so increases demand for a basic raw material (cotton) as to induce in the United States a major technological innovation (the cotton gin) and three major phases of acreage expansion (1816-1820, 1828-1836, the 1850's), yielding a trend decline in the raw cotton price which would have tipped the British terms of trade favorably if the proportions cited earlier . . . did not operate. To introduce this case, which is by no means unique (e.g., petroleum production down to 1972) the analyst must, it is true, leave the world of two commodities; but that should prove manageable.

13. *International Economics*, pp. 316-317.

14. W. Arthur Lewis, *Growth and Fluctuations, 1870-1913*, London: George Allen and Unwin, 1978. In dealing with the much debated fluctuations of the pre-1860 cotton price, two dynamic supply-demand exercises have been conducted similar to Lewis'. See Jeffrey G. Williamson, *American Growth and Balance of Payments, 1820-1843*, Chapel Hill: University of North Carolina Press, 1964, pp. 38-43; and Robert William Fogel and Stanley L. Engerman, *Time on the Cross*, Vol. 1, *The Economics of American Negro Slavery*, Boston: Little, Brown, 1974, pp. 86-94.

15. See, for example, A.K. Cairncross, *Home and Foreign Investment, 1870-1913*, Cambridge: At the University Press, 1953, p. 53.

16. C.H. Feinstein, *Statistical Tables of National Income Expenditure, and Output of the U.K., 1855-1964*, Cambridge: Cambridge University Press, 1976, Table 15 T37-38, col. 16.

17. C.G.F. Sinkin, *The Instability of a Dependent Economy, Economic Fluctuations in New Zealand, 1840-1914*, Oxford: Oxford University Press, pp. 40-48, 182-187.

18. I take a different view of this phenomenon than Arthur Lewis who attributes these counter-terms of trade capital flows mainly to "the band-wagon effect" created by large capital flows to the United States in the 1880's (*Growth and Fluctuations, 1870-1913*, pp. 180-181).

19. The cases of Australia, Argentina, and Canada in this period are treated at greater length and documented in W.W. Rostow, *The World Economy: History and Prospect*, pp. 169-172, with further references on pp. 448-455, 456-462, and 466-474.

20. C.G.F. Sinkin, *op. cit.*, pp. 145-146.

21. *Ibid.*, p. 169.
22. On the propensities, see, especially, *The Process of Economic Growth*, Chapters 1–3.
23. See C.P. Kindleberger, *Foreign Trade and the National Economy*, New Haven: Yale University Press, 1962, especially section 7, "Capacity to Transform," pp. 99–115. See also Kindleberger's *The Terms of Trade: A European Case Study*, Cambridge, Mass.: Technology Press, 1966, especially pp. 303–313.
24. *Ibid.*, pp. 109–110 and 115. The final sentence from Kindleberger quoted here is a precise statement of why, in *The Process of Economic Growth*, I insisted on the introduction of the propensities.
25. In *Growth and Fluctuations, 1870–1913*, see, especially, Chapter 8, "Response," pp. 194–224; in *The Evolution of the International Economic Order*, Princeton: Princeton University Press, 1978, see, especially, pp. 10–11.
26. *Growth and Fluctuations, 1870–1913*, p. 195.
27. *Ibid.*, pp. 214–218.
28. *Ibid.*, p. 196.
29. New York: The Free Press, 1975.
30. A clue to the answer runs counter to one of Lewis' generalizations; that is, that importers in developing countries generally opposed local industrialization. In pre-1914 Southern Brazil importers led the way in industrialization. See, notably, Warren Dean, *The Industrialization of Sao Paulo, 1880–1945*, Austin: University of Texas Press, 1969, especially Chapter 11, pp. 19–33.
31. On the latter less familiar phenomenon, see *Economic Report of the President*, Washington, D.C.: G.P.O., January 1981, Chart 6, p. 116 (ratio of implicit price deflator for food to implicit price deflator for all personal consumption expenditures, 1947–1980). Typical of a Kondratieff upswing, this index moves sharply upwards, over a relatively short period of time (1972–1973), and then oscillates in a substantially higher range than that which obtained in most of the prior downswing (1951–1972).

ELEVEN

Review of Robert L. Heilbroner, The Nature and Logic of Capitalism *(1986)*

In this review I carried forward a stance toward Marxism that had been established during my freshman days at Yale (1932–1933) when I wrote a long paper about a figure from the French Revolution. In the course of that exercise I read a good many histories of the French Revolution including studies by various kinds of Marxists, which led me into reading Marx himself. I emerged respectful of the questions he posed, but in profound disagreement with his answers: notably, his view of society as a superstructure determined uniquely by changing technological and property relations and his consequent view of individuals as simply components of social classes or masses.

These judgments are evidently reflected in this review of Heilbroner's 1985 study.

Sixty-five percent of this short book analyzes the nature of capitalism; about 15 percent offers an analytic history of capitalism from 1760 to the present; about 20 percent reflects on the future of capitalism.

My understanding of its argument is as follows:

(1) Societies are to be defined not merely in terms of their economies but their "social orders," which include the molding of individuals to patterns of rule, obedience, and belief. The historical sequence of social orders is: primitive, imperial, feudal, and capitalist.

(2) Capitalism is a social order dominated uniquely by a process of regular reinvestment of its surplus for productive economic purposes which the author evokes with Marx's M-C-M' formula. The right of the

---

This review was published in the June 1986 issue of *The Journal of Economic History* (vol. 46, no. 2). Reprinted with permission.

capitalist to refuse to sell his commodities or to buy labor power is the basis for his social dominance.

(3) The insatiable drive of the capitalist for wealth is heightened by competitive markets, whose pressure leads to an expanding array of goods and services commercially produced in substitution for household activities (for example, clothes washers and vacuum cleaners). Competition also disciplines the capitalist with respect to wages, rents, and interest payments. The environment of competitive struggle for income and wealth suffuses worker as well as capitalist; but the unequal market position of labor leads to the denial to labor of the full value of its product: "the winning of profit in any form represents the successful exercise of a basically political relationship" (p. 76).

(4) Although the coercive powers of the state are formally separated from the private enterprise sector, the basic function of government is to support the interests of the capitalist ruling class by economic and military as well as legal and political means. The public and private realms are intimately intertwined.

(5) In capitalist ideology the individual is viewed as the basic atomic unit on which the social order is built. This hypothesis leads directly to the legitimacy of both private property and political democracy which has never existed in a noncapitalist society. Although there is much convergence between the private economic and political realms, there are also tensions which are pragmatically resolved by a ruling class drawn from both the public and private sectors, each component managed by a small elite.

(6) Capitalist culture is "rich, brilliant, and diverse... least dependent on the regime of capital, the least directly traceable in its origins to economic life" (p. 132). But it regards ideas as commodities and has no religious or moral base other than science: "no vision of art or idea aside from the commodity form in which it is embodied... ideas thrive but morality languishes" (p. 140).

(7) Capitalism has evolved since the eighteenth century in response to a compulsion to substitute fixed capital for labor and an inability to keep the expansion of the various sectors in appropriate balance. This has yielded a sequence of "roughly twenty-five-year-long periods of buoyant expansion, followed by equally protracted periods of sluggish growth" (p. 148). The periods of sluggish growth are dated: 1800–1848; 1873–1893; 1929–1941; 1973–(?). These alleged phases are incorporated in a chart (pp. 150–152) which also attempts to summarize, for four periods, the conclusions of every other dimension of the book under these headings: Structure of the Accumulation Process; Functions of the Economic and Political Realms; Aspects of Ideology; and General Characteristics of the Crisis Period. The four periods thus characterized are: 1760–1848; 1848–1893; 1893–1941; 1941–.

(8) After examining at some length the difficulties of prediction, the book concludes that problems of "the internationalization of capital, its

propensity to inflation, its extreme social and economic vulnerability to technological disruption" might gradually transform "the most politically advanced capitalisms" into constitutional regimes of democratic socialism (p. 203).

The author notes correctly in his preface that, to non-Marxists, "Marx's thought will no doubt appear as the single most pervasive and important influence" on his analysis. This is patently true of both substance and style when dealing with economic matters. The analytic vocabulary, including Surplus Value, the selective quotations from classical economists, the portrayal of capitalism and its rationale, essentially as of the time of the Benthamites, impart a quaint Dickensian character to a good many passages in the text. For whatever reason, Heilbroner feels no need to reexamine or validate his premises. His exposition often brings to mind Alfred Marshall's observation on Surplus Value (*Principles*, p. 587): "this assumption that the whole of this Surplus is the produce of labour, already takes for granted what they ultimately profess to prove by it; they make no attempt to prove it; and it is not true."

On the other hand, in seeking to deal with the linkages between the economy, politics, and culture, the author finds too much to admire and cherish in the modern capitalist order (and too little, in allegedly Marxist social orders) to remain orthodox, whatever that word may now mean. As a result, there is a kind of schizophrenic oscillation between Marxist clichés and sometimes sensitive Hamletian reflections on how things have turned out.

The book deals, however, with a serious subject, which few analysts are willing to confront: the nature of the linkages and interactions among the various sectors of a society as it moves through time. I found its formulation unsatisfactory; but Marxist or not, Heilbroner's analysis deserves a substantive, even if brief, response.

I would identify the following as its major weaknesses.

First, the image of the individual. All the great philosopher-poets of the human condition (for example, Plato, Hume, Freud) recognized that individuals were both unique and social animals. In powerful acts of useful oversimplification, they each emerged with three interacting, often contending dimensions, one of which constituted the link of the individual to society. These links were, respectively, reason, sympathy, the superego. And they recognized that when man operated as a social animal he brought with him his many-sided nature (in Plato's phrase, the state within us) from which the sectors of society derive. Wisdom in politics has been defined over many centuries, in many cultures, in terms of a balance of respect for the uniqueness of the individual and the imperatives of communal life. Thus, neither half of the following critical assertion is factually correct (p. 120): "Whereas in all previous systems one individual alone is considered to be no more than dust of a shattered social organism, in bourgeois societies he or she is imagined to be a self-sufficient cell from which a living social organism is constructed." It is true that Marx, following Hegel, took essentially the former view; and it is, in my assessment, his fatal flaw. Because Heilbroner has not made up his mind how to deal with the individual in relation to society, he vacillates between a sense of the complex interactions among partially independent domains (economic, social, political, cultural)—derived from the inherently complex nature of the individual—and a hungering for a single, overriding principle. Thus, he rejects Daniel Bell's "multi-axial" view of society but is evidently attracted to it (pp. 80–82).

Second, in conformity with Marx, the author builds both the definition and dynamism of capitalism over two centuries on the compulsion to expand fixed capital. In a failure shared with Marx, the author has nothing to say about the Scientific Revolution (or, indeed, the Renaissance and the Reformation) as it relates to the fundamental watershed; that is, the transition from sporadic inventions to invention and innovation as a flow. Here is the basis for modern capitalism. It was mainly by the ploughback of profits induced directly and indirectly by the technologically new sectors that gross investment in Britain rose from, say, 8 percent of GDP in the 1760s to, say, 14 percent in the 1790s (as Feinstein has recently argued). This obsession with the abstraction "fixed capital" also leads to a serious and systematic failure to recognize the importance of capitalism before the first industrial revolution in many parts of the world. After all, Gregory King calculated the British investment rate at 4.7 percent in 1688. It leads also to grossly inadequate references to technology in his summary table, and to a failure to discuss the new technologies of the 1980s whose implications for the character of capital investment, the structure of the working force, the location of economic activity, and many other variables bear significantly on a satisfactory answer to his climactic question about the future.

Third, the quality of the economic history introduced into the text is systematically low. For example, it is odd to find a serious scholar comparing two periods with respect to average levels of unemployment measuring one from cyclical trough to peak, the other from cyclical peak to trough (pp. 148–49)—and without reference to any statistical data. There is too rich a literature on long cycles blandly to accept Ernst Mandel. For example, the analysis of the post-1945 boom and the nature of the post-1972 difficulties in the world economy are thin and impressionistic. It is possible that the author's proportioning of the book did not permit him to do justice to its historical section.

But I conclude that these and other inadequacies of Heilbroner's book do not detract from the importance and legitimacy of its subject. After all, the issues he addresses were at the center of political economy in the century and a half from David Hume to Alfred Marshall. We live at a time when both mainstream economics and economic history have moved away from the great issues towards intense specialization and the primacy of technique over problems. This book reminds us that we have largely withdrawn from the challenge of asking in the large terms of our great predecessors how in the past (and at present) the individual related to society; how the sectors of society relate to each other; where are we heading; and what is to be done?

PART THREE

Elaboration of a Dynamic Theory Including the Take-off Debate

TWELVE

Trends in the Allocation of Resources in Secular Growth (1955)

This essay was prepared for a round table discussion organized by the International Economic Association that was held at Santa Margherita Ligure, Italy, in the summer of 1953. The essay was later published as Chapter 15 in L. H. Dupriez (ed.), Economic Progress, a volume that contains essays by a good many major figures in the evolution of subsequent thought on development: e.g., A. K. Cairncross, Erik Dahmen, Evsey Domar, Alexander Gerschenkron, H. J. Habakkuk, Simon Kuznets, Hans Singer, C. N. Vakil, and Leon Dupriez himself. Among the discussants at the round table were Colin Clark, Milton Friedman, J. R. Hicks, Walther Hoffmann, Carl Iversen, Erik Lindahl, Dennis Robertson, E.A.G. Robinson, and Richard Stone. This round table had been one of the first "round-ups of the usual suspects" in the field of development at a time when the palpable success of Western European recovery had turned many economists toward the great unsolved problems of underdeveloped regions. My colleague at the time at MIT, Max Millikan, presented my essay as other commitments prevented my attendance.

There are three features of the essay thay may be worth noting.

- It had gone beyond The Process of Economic Growth and reflected lines of thought that would later be incorporated in the March 1956 Economic Journal article "The Take-off into Self-sustained Growth" and in my 1958 lectures in Cambridge, which yielded The Stages of Economic Growth. In particular, I was evidently groping in the essay for a way to link the analysis of sectors, where the impact of new technologies was initially felt, to the macro performance of econ-

---

This essay was published as Chapter 15 in L. H. Dupriez (ed.), *Economic Progress* (Louvain: Institut de Recherches Economiques et Sociales, 1955). Reprinted with permission.

omies. I later refined "supplementary growth sectors" by distinguishing backward, lateral, and forward linkages.
- *The disaggregation of sectors into three categories, including "derived growth sectors," was also part of the process of giving more substance and precision to the notion that had been incorporated in* The Process of Economic Growth—*that of dynamic, optimum sectoral (as well as macro-economic) paths that economies overshot and undershot, either systematically or erratically, as they moved through history. Later, in setting the theoretical framework for* The World Economy: History and Prospect (1978), *I elaborated this concept and even tried my hand at a simplified diagrammatic presentation (pp. 103–110) that clearly bears a family relation to the essay presented here.*
- *The final discussion of C. P. Kindleberger's suggestion—that development policy might seek to isolate and exploit strategic points for concentrated effort—echoed an experience the reader may well not identify. Kindleberger and I found ourselves in London during World War II, caught up in target selection for precision bombing attacks. The doctrine we and our colleagues had developed led us toward intense concentration of effort on target systems with maximum direct and indirect effect on enemy military strength in the field. Although independently generated, our doctrine had turned out to be an application, in unprecedented particular circumstances, of the ancient military injunction to bring maximum concentrated force to bear at an enemy's most vulnerable point. There is an echo in this essay of that doctrine applied in more benign circumstances.*

I

This paper probes at the following problem: How shall we go about analysing the relation between economic growth in general and economic growth in particular sectors of an economy. This problem translates itself into a consideration of the relation between the over-all rate of growth in (say) real income, or real income per capita, and the pattern of current and past investment outlays.

The question is of theoretical, practical, and historical interest. In theory it requires piercing the veil of present growth formulations which either segregate autonomous investment from investment via the accelerator, or which proceed by that form of "endogenous" analysis which makes behavior in period Two a function of circumstances given in period One. In practice, it raises the question of how, in some arbitrary, optimum sense, investment resources should be allocated. Since governments and other units in the economy increasingly make investment decisions in a macro- rather than a micro-perspective, the classic (but not necessarily optimum) solution to this problem—let the private capital markets decide—is not available for a wide range of investment outlays in our time. In history this problem suggests that our knowledge of the past would be usefully increased by studying systematically the pattern of the interacting relationship over time of total and sectoral growth.

On this occasion I intend merely to pursue the analysis of this large set of questions a bit beyond the interim point at which I left it in *The Process of Economic Growth*. The argument of that book seeks to establish, among others, the following propositions:

1) The over-all growth of an economy may be usefully regarded as determined by the interplay of a group of Yields and a group of Propensities; the Yields represent the possible rates of return from the exploitation of known natural resources and the available scientific stock; the Propensities represent the effective will of the society to act on the Yields which determine growth, through its various economic, social, and political institutions.

2) With given Yields and Propensities—which may vary in different sectors of the economy—there exist equilibrium levels of total output as well as of capacity and technique for the sectors, of an economy; and there exists an equilibrium composition for new investment as well as an equilibrium level of total investment input.

3) Although the concept of equilibrium in paragraph 2 above may have some useful meaning *ex ante*, for limited forward time periods, it has an evident reality *ex post*; in the sense that, smoothed of cycles and trends, the over-all and sectoral growth patterns of the past follow shapely patterns of deceleration and represent an arbitrary "realistic" optimum;[1] that is, they reflect the interplay of the Yields and Propensities in different societies, as they have in fact operated, when cleared of the errors and distortions which caused business cycles and trend periods.

4) Business cycles are viewed as arising from differences between actual and optimum investment patterns. The primary basis of this distortion is judged to lie, for each boom, in certain key sectors of the economy where capacity is expanded well beyond the point appropriate to the level of output and rate of growth.

5) Trend periods are viewed as arising from differences between actual and optimum investment patterns of a kind more substantial, even, than the distortions that determine normal (nine-year) cycles. The primary historical basis for such trend distortion is judged to lie in wars and periods of extensive agricultural and raw material expansion which yielded movements in relative prices, income distribution, interest rates, and the character of profitable investment opportunities which determined the environment for several consecutive business cycles.

This paper is designed somewhat to extend and refine the argument mainly as it relates to the first three propositions; that is, those concerned with the long-run growth rate.

II

The most cursory examination of the growth patterns of different economies, viewed against a background of general historical information, reveals two simple facts:

1. Growth rates in the various sectors of the economy differ widely, over any given period of time;[2]
2. In some meaningful sense, over-all growth appears to be based, at certain periods, on the direct and indirect consequence of extremely rapid growth in certain particular key sectors.

There may be a symmetry, then, between investment patterns in relation to business cycles and investment patterns in relation to growth. In both cases, there appear to be certain leading lines of investment, whose scale and productivity—including more distant secondary consequences—drive the economy as a whole forward. But, as discussed below . . . , the leading growth sectors and the leading cyclical sectors are not necessarily identical.

In common-sense terms, the notion of leading sectors in economic growth is familiar enough. The role of the cotton industry in sustaining over-all British growth from, say, 1780 to 1840, is one of the stories on which we are all brought up. And, when cotton decelerates, the domestic and foreign rail booms of the 1840s and 1850s lift pig iron. Pig iron gives way to steel as a leading sector by the seventies and eighties; and so on down through the chemical, electrical, and light-engineering industries, the latter being, perhaps the true hero of mid-century Britain, having sustained both the RAF in war and the export drive since 1945.

In American economic history, somewhat more compressed in time, there is also to be observed this classic sequence of leading sectors. But, even more sharply than in the case of Britain, the western railroads of the third quarter of the century (in turn induced by the world wheat demand) is the instrument for launching the American industrial revolution, yielding as it did the creation of a modern centralised iron industry, and then, in the seventies and eighties, a steel industry. Like the other major industrial powers of the twentieth century, the United States then developed the chemical, electrical, and light engineering industries, with a unique role, however, for the automobile and durable consumers' goods in general.

Such stately sequences of growth, carried forward by leading sectors, are to be observed not only in the well-rounded major industrial economies—including, say, Russia, Germany, and France, as well as the United States and the United Kingdom—but also in the more specialized successful economies, for example, New Zealand and Sweden. Simkin's study of New Zealand tracks out with precision how the growth of that economy, generally dependent upon exports, was touched off in the

1860s by gold and was sustained thereafter by wool, wheat, and dairy products. In turn, the exploitation of this sequence of profitable possibilities led, given New Zealand's Propensities, to considerable industrial development. In the case of Sweden, similarly, timber in the sixties and seventies gives way, with Sweden's strong Propensities,[3] to the rapid growth in pulp and paper towards the end of the century; and the extraordinary rise of iron ore exports from the 1890s leads on to the modern Swedish metal and engineering industries of this century. In both cases, too, although notably in Sweden, the development of export commodities, including their parallel transport requirements, help induce a secondary development of domestic industry, partially to meet the demands of new urban populations.

The leading sectors need not, then repeat the classic pattern of Great Britain: cotton, pig iron, steel, engineering, and so on. They may be based on the effective exploitation of natural resources, in relation to the requirements of the world market, as well as on a succession of breakthroughs in the application of science to economic purposes.

Leaving aside the raw material and foodstuff sectors, the growth process of the modern world over the past two centuries appears to have been based on the elaboration of a finite number of major technical innovations on which leading industrial sectors are based: in textiles, metals, engineering, chemicals, and so on. In Britain, notably, but also in the United States and Western Europe, each was more or less fully exploited as it emerged over the horizon of realistic possibilities; although Germany and the United States enjoyed some of the advantages of the relative late-comer. The early stages of application of each of these technical breakthroughs, involving radical change in production functions, yielded a high productivity return from investment input, in real terms; further refinements in technique, after the initial breakthrough, appear to have yielded diminishing returns.

Discounting the other factors affecting relative growth rates—notably, richness of natural resources, and the Propensities[4]—over-all rates of growth have been partially determined by the timing of the application of these major technical possibilities. Japan and Russia, for example, have, in the twentieth century, been exploiting in much closer time sequence than did (say) Britain the accumulated backlog of technical possibilities. And this virtual simultaneity of growth in leading sectors is one explanation for the high over-all rates of growth they have enjoyed. Put another way, the yields available from the pool of applied science have been higher for the late-comers than for those who exploited the flow of possibilities more or less as they became available. The late-comers were in the position of being able to exploit simultaneously the early, high productivity stages of past as well as current technical breakthroughs; whereas the older countries were enjoying the high productivity stage of only the latest technical breakthroughs.[5]

III

Assuming that, at particular periods, different sectors play a strategic role in the determination of the over-all growth rate of economies, how can we go about analysing in tolerable order the inordinately complicated process by which they have their effect?

I should like to suggest, for exploratory purposes, the usefulness of an arbitrary division of the sectors of an economy into three classes:

1. *Primary Growth Sectors* where possibilities for innovation or for the exploitation of newly profitable or hitherto unexplored resources yield a growth rate markedly higher than the average for the economy. The cotton industry of Britain in the decades after 1780 would fall into this category, as would most of the other key sectors cited above.[6]
2. *Supplementary Growth Sectors* where rapid advance occurs in direct response to—or as a requirement of—advance in the primary growth sectors. These sectors may have to be tracked many stages back into the economy, as the Leontief input–output models would suggest. Arbitrarily taking, for example, the Western American railways of the nineteenth century as a primary growth sector, (although mainly ancillary to the opening up of new lands and mines) the rapid growth in the iron, coal, and steel industries might be properly regarded, in the first instance, as further supplementary growth phenomena.
3. *Derived Growth Sectors* where advance occurs in some fairly steady relation to the growth of total real income, population, industrial production or some other over-all, modestly increasing parameter. Food output in relation to population, housing in relation to family formation are classic derived relations of this order. But more complex links which might be allocated to this category exist. After a sector has gone through its rapid growth stage it may well settle down to a reasonably stable relation to over-all growth, as has steel in recent times in the more industrialized countries.

Very roughly speaking, primary and supplementary growth sectors derive their high momentum essentially from the introduction and diffusion of changes in the cost-supply environment (in turn, of course, partially influenced by demand changes); while the derived growth sectors are linked essentially to changes in demand (while subject also to continuing changes in production functions of a less dramatic character).

Even a shallow experience of the process of growth will suggest the arbitrariness of these categories and the complexity of applying them to particular economies at particular time periods.

First, there is the problem of establishing empirically what is "a primary growth sector." If one makes the definition a matter of ultimate, philosophic causality, the problem is insoluble. There is a meaningful sense, for example, which we all would recognize, in which the western American railways of the nineteenth century were a primary growth sector from (say) 1850 to 1885. They, in turn, were induced, in large part, by a rise in the world price of wheat, reflecting in turn, an increase in population in Europe pressing against existing grain capacity. In turn, again, the rise in European population has its own complex history and causal process. While it is extremely important to recognize the complex causal chains that lie behind a given economic development, it is still possible, in a sensible arbitrary way, to isolate for different areas and time periods those sectors where the exploitation of possibilities for innovation or for developing newly profitable or hitherto unexplored resources yields ramified, creative economic results. If we are prepared to be arbitrary with respect to the chain of causation, I am confident that "primary sectors" can usefully be defined, for particular areas and limited time periods.

It should be noted that while one would expect higher than average growth rates in primary sectors, their isolation cannot be established mechanically by a simple examination of growth rates. It is altogether possible, or even likely, that certain of the supplementary sectors will have higher growth rates than primary sectors. It is the qualitative nature of the primary sector and the supplementary consequences of its expansion rather than merely its growth rate which define it.

In addition to the arbitrariness of the primary growth sector concept, there are some puzzling complexities of identification. A given sector may have within it, for example, both primary and derived elements. The modern oil industry reflects in its growth rate both the consequences of exploiting important new technological developments and a high marginal income elasticity of demand. This admixture of demand and supply influences is likely to operate in many cases, as, indeed, it did in the classic among primary sectors, cotton textile manufacture of the early nineteenth century. Not only may dual forces operate on a sector's growth curve, but they may not be independent over time. As Marshall pointed out in Appendix J of *Money, Credit, and Commerce* (with respect to cotton textiles) a fall in price due to cost changes can produce an irreversible shift in the position and slope of its related demand curve. These difficulties would complicate and, in some cases, possibly rule out an exact statistical filling of the empty boxes. They are unlikely, however, to prevent a meaningful identification of leading sectors and an approximate measurement of their impact on supplementary sectors over limited time periods.

There is a further weakness in conception which transcends arbitrariness and complexity; namely, the fundamentally interacting characteristic of the growth process. Wheat lands may lead to railroads, and railroads to iron and steel; but the railroads, having been built, in turn generate an endless series of further developments with a life and vitality of their own. The railroads may force the development of an engineering industry, for example, from which flow many other industrial innovations. A steel industry devoted heavily to the manufacture of rails, in the first instance, may help generate, by its existence, other applications of steel to bridges, ships, machinery, and so on, when the rail demand falls off. Like other forms of history, economic history is a seamless web within which we can only trace out limited chains of causation. I know of no easy formula for coping with the analysis of external economies on a macro-basis; but the successive application of these categories to particular limited time-periods may give us fresh insights into both the process of growth in the past and into the problem of planning wisely future growth, if we are prepared to allow, for each time period examined, a range of external economy effects, almost certainly not derivable, *ex ante*, from the initial data, as well as for changes in the Propensities, which are not wholly endogenous economic phenomena.

Technically, this approach might permit us to unite tools of analysis, independently developed and now proceeding in separate compartments, with little communication. First, there are the historians who have investigated how it came about that major new technological or resource possibilities were brought to application and primary growth sectors were created at particular times and places. An understanding of this phase of the whole growth process cannot evade some concern with scientific and technical history, and the human, institutional, and market environments of particular industries and societies. Second, there are those who are studying the functional relations as among the sectors of economies, with given production functions, above all Professor Leontief and his band of colleagues and students. Their measurements and insights might permit a reasonably precise analysis of the evolution of supplementary growth sectors over limited time periods. Third, this approach might open for empirical investigation a useful version of the accelerator, by developing a body of systematic knowledge on the relation between over-all growth parameters and capacity requirements in the slower-moving sectors of economies. The rapidly evolving method of Leontief and his colleagues is evidently capable of coming to grips with these rate of growth problems which, one hopes, are high on the agenda of the Harvard Research Project on the Structure of the American Economy.

This approach would, then, break into the interacting process of growth at the level of key-sectors. For a succession of limited time-periods—the decade might be a useful unit—it would consider the primary and supplementary consequences of growth in the key sectors; it would then track out the response of sectors to the increase in real income generated in these more rapidly moving sectors, as well as the response to growth forces determined by more remote factors—notably population changes; it would, finally, allow in each period (and carry over as a given into the next period) external economy effects and changes in the Propensities.

IV

I should like now to make a few tentative observations on the possible link between this mode of analysis and three large questions; the business cycle, the capital-output ratio, and the strategy of investment allocation in underdeveloped economies.

It is my general view that the historical succession of business cycles is best regarded as the direct and secondary consequence of surges forward in certain leading lines of investment in the world economy.[7] In each cycle the direction of the leading lines appears rational in that it was determined by profit possibilities created by the pressure of demand on capacity and by the potentialities of available innovations. But the scale of investment in the leading lines is somewhat irrational in the sense that, if the investors had known what the combined effect of their individual decisions would be, they would have invested less in the leading lines. In macro-terms, irrationality thus consists during a boom in a scale of expansion in capacity beyond that appropriate to the level required and made profitable by the existing level of output and its rate of growth. Thus, from cycle to cycle (and, roughly, from decade to decade), the character of the leading lines changes. Over-expansion in the boom appears generally to exhaust the possibility of a sector as a leading line for a period longer than one cycle.

How do the leading lines of investment in business cycles relate to the three categories of sectors defined above for purposes of growth analysis?

It is evident that the leading growth sectors cannot be simply equated with leading cyclical sectors. While, on the average, a high rate of investment may be maintained in a leading growth sector for several cycles running, it is unlikely that this sector will in fact dominate a succession of booms. It has been more normal in cyclical history to see investment shift from a leading industrial growth sector (say, cotton textile manufacture) to a supplementary sector (say, cotton acreage), to an induced sector (say, housing). No such pleasing symmetry of sequence is, of course, to be found in modern economic history. The point is that the leading lines in a cyclical expansion have depended on where profit is believed to lie; profitability may be created in a supplementary growth sector by a prior disproportionate expansion in a primary growth sector; or it may be created in induced sectors by prior disproportionate expansion in the more rapidly growing sectors, yielding increases in total output and real income which, for a time, may make investment in (say) housing, agriculture, or race tracks more profitable than (say) textiles or steel.

There is, thus, no automatic equivalence between profitability as decreed in free markets by cost-price relationships, and the maximum real rate of return, in terms of the full consequences of an act of investment for the rate of growth. This lack of equivalence has long been recognized in economic theory and in the practice of even the most capitalist of societies. Where, for example, railroads and other public improvements promised important secondary advantages, not imputable to the private investor, the government stepped in, even in nineteenth-century United States.[8] More generally, it can be said that the pattern of demand set up by sovereign consumers' tastes does not necessarily result in patterns of profitability, and of private investment outlays, which maximize the rate of growth of output. This does not imply, of course, that the maximum rate of growth is, in any sense, a criterion superior to consumers' tastes, as reflected in free markets. It does suggest, however, that maximization propositions under dynamic growth conditions, when we get around to making a theory of growth, may be something quite different from those under static, or short period assumptions.

The shifting of the structural focus of profitability over time may help to explain why the over-all rates of growth may vary from decade to decade under conditions where the total proportion of income invested appears relatively stable.[9] Investment in different sectors may have differing productivity effects on the level of output. In his recent comparative analysis of Soviet and American growth rates,[10] for example, Norman Kaplan finds that it is probably the direction rather than the scale of Soviet investment which determines its higher industrial growth rate, notably the relative concentration of Soviet investment in heavy industry, with a low capital-output ratio. It is likely that, when the matter is fully investigated, we will find that the discontinuity in the rate of growth of U.S. real income per capita, established by Kuznets,[11] is related to changes in the character and productivity of investment from period to period.[12]

Conceived thus dynamically, the capital-output ratio becomes extremely complex. The time relationship between a given volume of investment input and its consequence for real output must be sorted out with care, taking account of at least three elements:

(a) *The Period of Gestation of the investment.* A shift, on balance, to investment with a longer period of gestation may, over any short period of time examined, impart an illusory increase in the capital-output ratio, which might disappear if a longer time period is allowed in measurement.

(b) *The Time Period over which the Investment Yields its Service.* A shift, on balance, to investment with a longer period of life imparts an increase in the capital-output ratio, assuming that the proportion of capital services to net output is unchanged. Thus, changes in the capital output ratio must be considered both in the light of the changing life of equipment and the changing degree of capital intensity in production functions.

(c) *External Economies.* The secondary and more remote influences of a given act of investment may be decisive to the growth process (and to the rationale for the investment) although virtually incapable of measurement by present tools.

From all of this I would merely suggest that we have hardly begun to organize our knowledge of the relative productivity of various types of investment in such a way as to assist in the analysis of the process of economic growth.

These observations may bear, as well, on the problem of prescribing for economic growth. Professor C.P. Kindleberger has recently suggested that the proper approach to the problem of generating more rapid economic development may lie in the isolation of strategic points of attack[13]—an instinctive conclusion I am inclined to share. The question arises as to whether this sectoral approach to the growth process is likely to help us in defining with any precision the strategic sectors: that is, sectors of an economy where additional units of investment will yield the maximum increase in output, when the full range of its primary and more remote consequences is taken into account.

At this stage of speculation I am not prepared to be dogmatic. It may be worth exploring, however, whether or not it is possible to identify leading growth sectors for particular underdeveloped economies, in the sense in which that concept was earlier defined. It may prove to be the case that a concentration of effort on one or two sectors in a given economy might drag along the supplementary sectors: and that consequent increases in real income may induce the generalized expansion of the slower growing sectors required for balanced growth.

The identification of leading sectors is by no means simple. As noted earlier, what may be a supplementary sector for the world economy (e.g. an industrial raw material) may be a leading sector for a given region or country. Thus, the strategic point of concentration may not lie, in certain regions, in the exploitation of the classic sequence of industrial innovations but rather in the development and progressively more advanced processing of a natural resource.

Moreover, when one pierces deeper into the conditions likely to release the potentialities of a primary growth sector, one may end up with a problem of social and political policy; a problem of increasing the effective strength of the Propensities. It is evident enough that the problem of accelerating economic growth in many areas lies not in a lack of natural resources or of potential innovations, but in too high a birth rate, a shortage of risk capital, a shortage of enterprising management, a shortage of technicians skilled in the application of new techniques, a shortage of competent and skilled labour, political leadership and institutions whose objectives are inappropriate to economic growth.

At first blush it might appear that, when the growth of a sector is obstructed by the Propensities rather than the Yields, concentrated action is inappropriate. The roots of the Propensities lie in the institutions and value systems of societies; and their influence tends to be pervasive.

Nevertheless, there may be a meaningful sense in which a concentration of effort in key sectors may be appropriate to policy designed to shift the Propensities as well as directly to exploit the Yields. It may be important, for example, that the ablest technical and managerial talent be concentrated in the first instance in the key sectors; that resources devoted to labour training not be diffused too far; that applied scientists be induced to concentrate their efforts on certain key problems; and so on. In short, an acute sense of priority, and a sense of the possibilities of exploiting self-reinforcing processes by powerful stimulus to strategic points might well suffuse the politics and sociology of economic growth as well as resource allocation in its more conventional sense.

NOTES

[1.] No peculiar analytic significance is, of course, to be attached to the smoothed sectoral curves. They are, simply, the result of a statistical exercise. If, in fact, investment had proceeded on the "realistic" optimum pattern the over-all and sectoral-result may, in fact, have been quite different from what it turns out to be, *ex post* (see *Process of Economic Growth*, pp. 94–102). Nevertheless, the isolation and measurement of the scale and character of deviations from the smoothed curves is a useful and practical way to isolate certain key aspects of the processes which led in the past to business cycles and trend periods.

[2.] See, for example, A.F. Burns, *Production Trends in the United States Since 1870*, New York, 1934, especially pp. 50–62.

[3.] Since, in this form of analysis, population is partially determined by the Propensities, the use of the phrase "strong Propensities" must immediately be modified in two respects: (a) too strong a Propensity to have children may weaken, not strengthen the process of economic growth; (b) immigration and emigration must be allowed for. From the point of view of the world economy immigration and emigration may be largely explained; and treated endogenously; but for many forms of national economic analysis it may be useful to treat population movements as a given.

[4.] It will be recalled that, *inter alia*, the Propensities help determine the size and rate of growth of population. See [note 3] for the treatment of migration.

[5.] This element in the rapid rate of growth of late-comers is independent of the more familiar partial explanation; namely, that the age composition of capital is lower for late-comers and incorporates, in higher proportion, best current technical practice. This factor would operate even if diminishing returns did not apply—as it apparently does—in the technological evolution of particular countries.

[6.] From the perspective of the world economy one could, however, regard the rapid exploitation of natural resources as supplementary or even derived growth (in the case of foodstuffs).

[7.] For a more complete consideration of the business cycle in these terms, and especially for the role allowed the conventional multiplier-accelerator mechanism, see Chapter 5, *Process of Economic Growth*.

[8.] For an analysis of the types of railroad which required (and received) public financing, see the unpublished thesis of Dr. Paul Cootner, *Transport*

Innovation and Economic Development: The Case of the U.S. Steam Railroads MIT 1953.

[9.] See, for example, the interesting calculations of Jacob Schmookler, "The Changing Efficiency of the American Economy, 1869–1938" *The Review of Economics and Statistics*, August 1952.

[10.] Capital Formation and Allocation," *Soviet Economic Growth*, A. Bergson (ed.), Chapter 2, Evanston, Ill., and White Plains, New York, 1953.

[11.] S. Kuznets, *National Income: A Summary of Findings*, New York 1946.

[12.] The tables organized by Brinley Thomas suggest for exploration at least the possibility that periods of slower U.S. growth may be associated with high levels of investment in residential housing, in turn related to surges of immigration. See, especially, Table VI, p. 238, in "Migration and the Rhythm of Economic Growth," *The Manchester School*, Sept. 1951.

[13.] *Review of Economics and Statistics*, November 1952, pp. 391–94.

THIRTEEN

Some General Reflections on Capital Formation and Economic Growth (1956)

I was asked to provide a final essay of synthesis and reflection for a 1955 conference on "Capital Formation and Economic Growth" that had been organized by the Universities National Bureau Committee for Economic Research. The other essays for the conference had been prepared by Moses Abramovitz, Henry G. Aubrey, Thomas C. Cochran, Raymond W. Goldsmith, Gregory Grossman, Bert F. Hoselitz, Simon Kuznets, Marion J. Levy, Jr., Adolph Lowe, W. Rupert Maclaurin, and Abbot Payson Usher.

Now, reading over my essay and recalling the cast of characters—and what they said—leaves me with a sense of regret, even sadness. Here were theorists and statisticians, economic historians and sociologists, specialists on the Soviet Union, on the history of technology, and on particular developing regions. They had gathered to consider together how their particular insights—their grasp on one piece of the elephant—might be related to others. As I recall, we shared a conviction that the magnitude and many-faceted character of the problem called for synthesis. So we listened to one another on the assumption that we had a good deal to learn.

But in fact, the disciplines did not move closer together in the years that followed. On the contrary, they followed the conventional modern academic pattern of specialization and loss of communication. The neoclassical growth models succeeded the Harrod-Domar version and a good portion of the theorists peeled off to ring the changes on Solow-Swan-Tobin (and, across the Atlantic, on Kaldor-Robinson) until that game

---

This essay was published in *Capital Formation and Economic Growth*. A Report of the National Bureau of Economic Research (Princeton: Princeton University Press, 1956). Reprinted with permission.

was played out, leaving little residue of wisdom or insight. Meanwhile, Kuznets's great statistical exercise also had begun to emerge in the mid-1950s, spawning a series of excellent but discrete historical studies on the one hand and Chenery's cross-sectional analyses on the other. But diminishing returns operated on the statistical morphologists of growth as well as on the aggregate growth theorists. A third ring of the circus was taken up by analysts focused on contemporary development policy, who also elaborated their doctrines and conducted their debates almost wholly in a world of their own.

The 1970s and 1980s were, of course, cross-cut by traumatic problems and events that none of these three approaches had been structured to handle gracefully: oil shocks; gross problems of international debts, deficits, and surpluses; and a great technological revolution of a kind that only historians could recall.

But growth and the problems of growth have not ceased; one can hope that the 1990s will see an agreement among growth analysts to take stock, as we tried to do at the meeting reflected in this essay, and bring together what of value we think we have learned in the four decades since modern growth analysis emerged in the 1950s.

1. THE THEME: ORGANIZED DISAGGREGATION

The relation between capital formation and economic growth is a large part of the total problem of economic growth. Taking the rate of change of output to be a function of the rate of change in the size and quality of the working force and of the capital stock, this conference is analyzing the total growth problem, leaving the working force aside. And even then, in Levy's paper and elsewhere, the relation of capital formation to the size of the population—and even to the size and quality of the working force (Grossman)—has come into the discussion. We have taken on, then, a considerable and ramified set of issues.

Further, these issues are distinctly revolutionary. There appears to be complete unanimity—reflected in the substance of the papers as well as in the program of the conference—that the relation of capital formation to growth cannot be treated by the conventional tools of short-run economics. We appear to agree that, by definition, we are dealing with problems of rates of change over time rather than with short-period equilibrium; and that continuing changes in capacity, technique, and taste—normally treated exogenously in modern economic theory, or in once-over change exercises—must somehow be introduced endogenously. More than that, we all appear to believe that an understanding of the relation between capital formation and economic growth demands that somehow, at some stage of the analysis, we bring to bear on the relevant economic variables social, political, cultural forces which affect their net movement.

Because we agree about the range of the relevant variables, we come at this problem from many directions in academic terms, from many different disciplines. The contributions here range from Lowe's autere theory through a spectrum of generalized but limited insights, based on empirical situations and data, back to that developing branch of social theory represented by Levy's contribution. At the present, early stage of concerted thought on growth, our contributions necessarily must be partial. All the papers presented at the conference discuss one or another of the sub-determinants of the relation between capital formation and economic growth, rather than the relation itself, in its full complexity and grandeur.

We are, then, trying to make diverse bodies of data and diverse social science techniques effectively converge. On this view of our common problem, the present group of papers represent a major stride forward. There is an emergent area of common understanding—sometimes implicit, often explicit—as to how the various pieces of the puzzle fit together. There is more here than mere courteous acknowledgment that each has a right to his private line of approach. Not only is there agreement that we each have hold of a piece of the elephant; a consensus on the elephant's shape is also beginning to emerge. It is evident that we have been reading each other's articles and books. Before this conference I was inclined to the view that little actual work of synthesis had been done, beyond laudable programmatic statements. The noneconomic variables had not been satisfactorily related to the economics of the growth process. I think we can agree that this conference has made important progress toward this kind of synthesis. Although none of the studies presented for this conference pretend to meet the workmanlike vision of orderly growth analysis that Lowe holds up as a goal, a number of them go an important distance toward linking coherently the disparate variables that determine the relation of capital formation to economic growth.

There is, for example, Aubrey's systematic consideration of the manner in which the conventional profit maximization analysis of capital formation must be modified to fit the context of industrial enterprise in underdeveloped countries. This exercise goes well beyond empirical description. Hoselitz's reflections on British and French entrepreneurship since 1700 are explicitly linked to the relative scale of capital formation and overall growth rates in the two countries; and Cochran seeks to make American entrepreneurial history illuminate Kuznets' American growth statistics. These papers are not merely summaries of odd institutional evidence. Similarly, Maclaurin's reflections on innovation pose questions of the first order of importance concerning the productivity of different kinds of investment and innovations. There are many other indications throughout these papers that the concerted study of a commonly understood problem is replacing methodological exhortation.

Under these circumstances the evident function of a commentator is to heighten a little our awareness of the links among the various

Some General Reflections

approaches to growth analysis and to open up for general discussion the question of useful next steps. I shall simplify my task by elaborating a single arbitrary theme: the importance of organized disaggregation in growth analysis. This theme is relevant whether we are primarily concerned with making formal theoretical models of the growth process (Lowe); organizing rigorous statistical measures of historical patterns (Kuznets); examining functionally such sub-determinants of growth as the flows of loanable funds (Goldsmith) or the flows of science, invention, and innovation (Usher, Maclaurin, Cochran, and Hoselitz); defining current growth problems in particular settings (Aubrey, Grossman, and Holzman); or examining systematically the noneconomic motives and institutions which help determine the economic outcome (Levy). In all these tasks we must try increasingly to link the aggregate variables to organized knowledge of the components and sectors of which they are composed.

2. DISAGGREGATION AND GROWTH MODELS

It follows from this central theme that I have found the argument of Lowe generally sympathetic and suggestive. Although couched in the language of growth, the theoretical exercises of Harrod, Domar, Hicks, and Goodwin (and others) have not been concerned with the variables determining differences in the rate and structure of growth. Their primary purpose has been to demonstrate that the growth process is likely to proceed in unstable cycles of unemployment. By introducing a degree of disaggregation and by setting in motion some of the variables usually frozen in growth models, Lowe has linked income analysis to the problems of changing economic structure. He opens for formal examination the relations between over-all growth and the changing levels of sectorial capacity within the economy; and he makes clear the significance of the timing and sequence of structural change for cyclical and other disturbances.

The principal exercises on which Lowe concentrates are a once-over change in labor supply, the relation between changes in the consumption function and the structure of the economy, and the problem of factor displacement in technical change. These are all important cases. They permit Lowe to bring within the scope of rigorous formal treatment those problems in economic growth which are generally dealt with *ad hoc*, if at all.

At the end of his paper Lower speculates on two major issues which belong high on the agenda for further analysis: first, the question of the capital-output ratio,[1] second, the manner in which formal theoretical analysis can be related systematically to psychological, sociological, political, legal, and other variables which shape the growth process in real life.

I am convinced that we require far more extensive empirical analysis of the relation between changes in the capital stock and its total consequences for the level of output than we now have available.[2] An improved understanding of the past and of relative growth rates among contemporary industrialized societies hinges on a clarification of the determinants of the productivity of different kinds of investment at different stages in the growth sequence. Our ability to prescribe appropriate patterns of investment for underdeveloped areas will also depend on the refinement of such knowledge.

We will have to go behind such global estimates of the capital-output ratio as those used by Lowe in his discussion of Singer's estimates. . . . The capital-output ratio as currently used is, after all, a kind of index number. Its level (and especially the interpretation of changes in it, or of differences in its level as among different areas) can only be understood in the light of an understanding of its components. Those who are now attempting to plan the pattern of investment outlays in underdeveloped countries make more or less explicit assumptions not merely about the total capital-output ratio but also about the short- and long-period effects on the level of output of investment in particular sectors; and they take into account not only sectoral differences but the cost of noncapital inputs as well. I would suggest that there is a weaker case for using over-all capital-output ratios than there ever was for focusing attention on over-all price or production indexes.

The lines of thought suggested in Lowe's paper which link savings-consumption balances to the structural problems of growth deserve to be pursued. But without losing touch with the aggregates which make up his (or other possible) growth equations, we might usefully disaggregate our analyses beyond the level of his theoretical structure.

Over any particular period, in any national or regional economy which is growing, the growth process is carried forward by a relatively few major sectors. These may incorporate new technical possibilities, like the early British textile factories; they may reflect fundamental political decisions of the society, like the post-1945 boom in the armament industries of the world; they may reflect a newly indulged taste, as real income rises, like American suburban housing. These leading sectors set in motion behind them a whole train of secondary effective demands as, for example, suburbanization elevates the demand for automobiles and new commercial construction. Historically these leading sectors create external economies which facilitated the development of new leading sectors as the momentum of the old ones decreased. Thus, for example, the textile engineering firms moved into locomotives; and a steel industry built on rails turned easily to machine tools. In the end, the structural categories suggested by old-fashioned capital theory or by the categories of modern income analysis will have to be pierced to the point where the structural characteristics of growth can be examined with an intimacy and particularity Lowe does not attempt.

3. DISAGGREGATION AND STATISTICAL ANALYSES OF GROWTH

My observations on Kuznets' statistical essay relate closely to those I have made on Lowe's theoretical paper. Kuznets' work has produced an orderly body of data on the relation of capital formation to national product. In particular, he makes possible a quantitative assessment of the historical role of international capital movements in modern economic development.

Those who contribute statistical clarity to the murky field of economic growth put us especially in their debt. They have a right as well as a need to work within narrow analytic boundaries. The particular limitation that Kuznets accepts at the present stage is to postpone the measurement of the relation of capital formation to the rate of growth (as opposed to the relation between capital formation and the level of national income). I have no doubt that he has on hand, or ready at hand, systematic information on this central quantitative relationship. In fact, in his equally valuable statistical study, Goldsmith gives us . . . a table of growth rates which might be directly linked to Kuznets' figures on the proportion of national income invested at various stages in the growth process of Western nations. A portion of Kuznets' subject is, of course, narrower and more sharply focused than the over-all relation between capital formation and growth rates. He is concerned to measure roughly the quantitative importance of international capital flows, and to speculate on the meaning of the proportions that emerge.

When, as will surely happen, other analysts exploit this statistical breakthrough, they will have to proceed in terms not merely of the over-all scale (or proportion) of capital flows but of the particular directions in which they are used by the capital-importing nation. The story of international capital investment is tied up with particular stages in the growth of particular economies, and even with the situation in particular sectors. The capital exports from Britain in the 1830's, for example, can be understood substantially in terms of the world cotton market and the extension of cotton lands in the American South which proceeded in response to current and prospective cotton prices. At later stages in Anglo-American history, substantial British flows are intimately associated with wheat and railroads. In the late 1880's the major flows from London result from the emergence of the Argentine into some kind of political stability, which permitted it to bid for resources to finance basic port, railroad, and other facilities. To understand and to interpret fully the aggregate data Kuznets has supplied, we will have to study the components and examine the recognizable process which led to the ebb and flow of international funds.

I would suggest that Kuznets' generalization that "the volume of international capital exports was restricted primarily because the *supply* of savings available was limited" . . . may be modified when the evidence has been examined in the light of his calculations. Although the United States of the 1840's, for example, had immense if not unlimited long-run capital-absorptive capacity, it also had just passed through a land and public works boom in which the British investor lost a substantial part of his shirt. Americans could appear in the City of London in 1840 only at some personal risk; and the British at this stage turned their flows of investment inward to the development of their own railways. The limitation on international capital flows resulted from a changing balance between the attractiveness and the believed degree of risk in various rapidly developing parts of the world, and the attractiveness of home investment. Moreover, the expected (private) rate of return over cost could be high in domestic sectors where demand pressed against capacity, even when no dramatic technological innovations were being introduced or rich new resources were being developed. The determinants of maximum short-run private profitability are not identical with the determinants of a maximum rate of growth.

In the end, of course, the limitation was, as Kuznets says, one of capital supply; for there were usually, in the nineteenth century, claimants on the international capital markets who were turned away. But international capital flows were the result of a somewhat more complex and shifting balance of market incentives and restraints than Kuznets' conclusion might indicate.

Speculating, for a moment, on what would happen if Kuznets' calculations were combined with data (for comparable periods) of the kind presented in Goldsmith's growth rate table, I suspect that we would find significant differences between the proportion of national income invested and the rate of growth, even among advanced countries, as well as differences within countries at different stages in their economic history.[3] Kuznets' pioneering study (1930) on secular movements in production has demonstrated the universality of deceleration in particular sectors of the economy. There seems little doubt that among the forces which determine deceleration in particular industries is a kind of diminishing returns to particular forms of innovation. The capital-output ratio in the British cotton industry in 1790 was almost certainly quite different from that in 1840, 1890, or 1930. The relative long-term stability of the overall capital-output ratio in certain advanced countries may well emerge as the result of the balancing out of differing rates among different industries at the same period of time, some young, others old. It will only be when we have quantitative knowledge of the capital-output ratio in different sectors of an economy, at different historical stages, that we will be able to understand differing over-all levels, or even relative long-term stability in the over-all level.

Turning now to the other contribution of solid statistical substance (that of Goldsmith) I should like to make one comment in passing, strictly as an economic historian. My field has been bedeviled by a tendency to lapse into institutional description leading virtually nowhere from the economist's point of view. There is hardly a textbook in economic history which does not have its chapters or section devoted to the evolution of financial institutions. Occasionally thrown into these sections are brief and inadequate stories of financial crises, odd price data, and random reflections on the business cycle. So far as I know, Goldsmith's is the first effort to treat quantitatively the accumulated mass of data on the historical pattern of financial institutions in various countries, and the first effort to link such institutional analysis with the problem of capital supply and economic growth. Aside from its contribution to growth analysis, Goldsmith's paper is an important essay in economic history.

Like those of Kuznets and any others who deal with growth in orderly quantitative terms, Goldsmith's conclusions are limited by the nature and character of his data and the limited distance that he can go quantitatively in coping with the growth process as a whole. Nevertheless, his fundamentally agnostic interim conclusion . . . conforms closely to the instinctive answer of an economic historian: namely, that men have made their economic purposes effective in an enormous variety of ways, and one would not expect a simple correspondence between particular kinds of institutions for mobilizing savings and the rate of growth. Modern economic history suggests a certain suspicion of firm correlations between particular institutional patterns (political, cultural, and social, as well as economic) and rates of growth.

One further comment on Goldsmith's paper. I am reasonably doubtful that, even after we have pursued the analysis of growth for several further decades, we will emerge with what a modern economic theorist would regard as a theory of economic growth. There are too many variables to be disciplined into forms where the number of equations are equal to the number of unknowns; and, even more important, the kinds of variables we would all wish to see introduced from the side of politics, social structure, and culture do not lend themselves to a Newtonian kind of theory, elaborated from clear, minimum arbitrary hypotheses. However, the technique of comparative morphology, of which Goldsmith's paper is a distinguished example, and for which there are important precedents in certain of the natural sciences, may prove highly appropriate to our problem.

4. INVENTION, INNOVATION AND ENTREPRENEURSHIP

I turn now to four related papers presented to the conference by Usher, Maclaurin, Cochran, and Hoselitz. As Lowe says . . . , "The theory of technical change is still a stepchild of economic analysis." In one part of our minds and in the ritualistic listing of the determinants of the level of investment and of the rate of growth, the state of technology has always had its formal place in economics. Moreover, Schumpeter and others have produced important and stimulating generalized observations on the process which lies between fundamental science and the productivity of investment inputs. What is lacking is a systematic view of invention, innovation, and the diffusion of innovation which might be effectively woven into a total analysis of the scale and productivity of capital investment.

If the Keynesian curve of marginal efficiency of capital has any operative meaning, it has always contained implicit assumptions about these variables. The level of effective demand for investment, in terms of expected rates of return over costs, has always depended not merely on the state of technology in some generalized sense but on the extent to which entrepreneurs were prepared to apply known innovations.[4] Behind the level of capital demand, even in the short-run Keynesian sense, lie processes analyzed by Usher and Maclaurin and the qualities of entrepreneurship treated by Cochran and Hoselitz.

Usher's paper presents, in heightened form, the thesis with which his name has long been associated: namely, that invention is to be regarded as a continuous flow, representing the product of the more or less purposeful investment of a society in that peculiar creative sector, applied science. Against the background of evidence that Usher has amassed over the years, it is no longer tenable to treat invention and technical innovation as an exogenous force striking from time to time against the productive system through the medium of some Hegelian hero. Despite its peculiarities, invention is a normal part of the investment process, directed, like other forms of investment, toward believed areas of high rate of return over cost. Although Usher himself does not discuss this form of investment—the investment of resources in the generation of productive technical possibilities—in terms of a general theory of capital formation, it is time for economists to weave this variable into their analyses in a quite formal way. This demands that they include, among the sectors of the economy, that sector representing the current capacity to produce new technical improvements, and that they examine the order of magnitude of the investment input and its productivity in different societies at different periods.

Maclaurin's further observations on this theme indicate that to treat innovation in any kind of strict relation to capital formation, we must engage, again, in an important degree of disaggregation. Maclaurin has built up, from his examination of the innovation process in particular industries, persuasive evidence both for the changing productivity of innovation at various stages of an industry's history and for differences in the productivity of innovation as among sectors of the economy. His evidence reinforces the view that the capital-output ratio must be examined in terms of sectors of an economy. Maclaurin dramatizes the argument by exploring the prospects for investment productivity in advanced countries, where an increasing proportion of total output, and especially of new investment, goes into service and other nonmanufacturing industries. Here the natural sciences may not help the growth process as much as in periods when the heavy and engineering industries lead the way. Maclaurin's general argument comes to rest on prospects for the housing industry, which, apparently throughout the world, has resisted innovation with remarkable tenacity. He suggests that the maintenance of high investment productivity in advanced countries may depend on the generation and acceptance of housing innovations, to which the social scientist as well as the engineer will have to contribute.

Taken together, Usher's and Maclaurin's arguments add up to a strong case for including the scale and productivity of the flow of innovations as an important determinant of the capital-output ratio, and for alertness to the possibility of variations in that ratio arising from the historical stage of the innovation process in particular industries and sectors of the economy.

The arguments of Cochran and Hoselitz take us a step further. They are concerned to indicate, in the context of three countries (the United States, Britain, and France) the conditions under which men have been willing to undertake the risks of capital formation. While it is convenient and important in many analyses to distinguish the kind of risk-taking which goes into the lending of money from that associated with its borrowing or with the willingness to initiate or diffuse innovations, these various determinants of the scale and productivity of investment outlays tend to merge under certain institutional circumstances. The papers by Cochran and Hoselitz relate to both sides of the market for loanable funds. The early stages of British and American capitalism saw these separable elements in capital formation focused in the same institutions or even in the same persons. This identity remains partially with us in the current role of retained earnings in corporate finance, as well as in the role of governments as both entrepreneur and supplier of loanable funds on a substantial scale.

It is an important virtue of Cochran's essay that this issue and other analytical problems of general interest come clearly through his effort to take stock of the present position of American entrepreneurial study. His paper is heartening for those who have watched the development of the sprawling field of entrepreneurial research. It seemed for a time that we would be confronted by an endless series of histories of firms drawn up in implicit analytical terms derived simply from the firms' own records, without any link to the main body of thought and research on capital formation and economic growth. Although entrepreneurial study received an enormous impetus from the theoretical insights of Schumpeter, its first phase took the form of the amassing of empirical data, with the little attention to its generalization or to its relationship with other bodies of thought. These individual studies varied, of course, in their general interest and quality; but they were characterized by a failure to relate the role of the entrepreneur to the other factors determining the firm's capital formation. The firm's history was often inadequately linked to the region of which it was a part and to more general aspects of the nation's economic history, as reflected in quantitative and other evidence of growth and fluctuations.

It is clear that Cochran is seeking to make this body of historical data illuminate the statistics, such as they are, and help explain changes in rates of capital formation in the United States. The links that are made by Cochran . . . are certainly not as fine as the statisticians would desire or as Cochran would like to make. Nevertheless, it is evident that we have turned a corner in the field of entrepreneurial history. Cochran's paper is an indication that this field has begun to justify itself as a central part of the study of capital formation at its most generalized level.

Much the same kind of intellectual progress is represented in Hoselitz's paper on the comparative economic performances of Britain and France as they related to the character and quality of entrepreneurship since 1700. Again we find a purposeful effort to link the conclusions on entrepreneurship to the over-all rates and patterns of growth. Although the number of entrepreneurial studies available on France is less than on the United States, the influence of the unique social, political, and cultural structure of France as it operated through its entrepreneurs on the growth process has attracted some of the ablest men working in economic history. Hoselitz's extremely interesting effort at synthesis has excellent foundations.

These two essays in entrepreneurship illustrate once again the central theme of this commentary. When we deal with entrepreneurs, we are dealing with men who made decisions within individual firms and allocated the resources of individual firms. Our evidence is, by definition, micro- rather than macroevidence. We are in a Marshallian world of partial equilibrium when we examine the records of a firm, even a highly monopolistic firm. We are examining the supply of loanable funds, demand expectations, and the risks of innovation in the precise but limited settings of particular capital formation decisions. Our generalizations must be built up, therefore, from knowledge of firms to sectors of the economy; and, ultimately, as Cochran and Hoselitz have tried to do, these intermediate generalizations must be linked with over-all evidence on the rates and patterns of national growth. There is, however, an enormous jump from the microdata of the historian to the over-all, long-period growth rates to which Cochran and Hoselitz relate their entrepreneurial findings. As a result, their evidence can at the moment be brought to bear only in the form of broad generalizations and insights concerning the forces determining high or low, accelerating or decelerating, rates of growth. If, however, they had available systematic data on the growth rates of particular sectors of the economy, their evidence on entrepreneurship in particular industries at particular periods could be much more fully used. Qualities of entrepreneurship have always varied widely among the various sectors of an economy, and the data available to the expert on entrepreneurial history could illuminate the stories of sectors much more precisely than they can aggregate national statistics.

Moreover, in order to explore the meaning of aggregate growth statistics, we must, as noted earlier, examine them in the light of the differing growth rates in different sectors of the economy. Since entrepreneurial qualities are not uniform as among the sectors, we must bring our knowledge of entrepreneurial history to focus at the sectorial level. This will not preclude coming back again to the larger issues which Cochran and Hoselitz approach directly. It will mean that they will be able to approach these larger issues having moved up within a more systematic structure of analysis and a more systematic structure of statistical evidence than is now available to them.

5. THE PARTIAL EQUILIBRIUM ANALYSIS OF INVESTMENT

Although Aubrey's paper belongs, in subject matter, with the growing literature on problems of growth in underdeveloped areas, intellectually it stands with the essays of Cochran and Hoselitz. Like them, Aubrey has organized a vast amount of empirical data at an intermediate level of abstraction, thus rendering our knowledge of the facts more accessible and, especially, more susceptible of manipulation. Whereas Cochran and Hoselitz seek to make their data illuminate the relations between entrepreneurial quality and over-all rates of growth in three major countries, Aubrey's contribution is of a more general, theoretical nature. He systematically explains, in terms of a partial equilibrium analytic structure focused on the determinants of individual investment decisions, the differences between the profit maximization model which governs our thought about investment in the Western world and the shape of the investment problem in underdeveloped areas. He demonstrates forcibly the manner in which the context of underdeveloped areas demands a relaxation or change in many of the implicit and explicit assumptions carried over from knowledge of the capital formation process in Western capitalist societies.

Within its narrow limits Aubrey's paper presents an orderly analysis of noneconomic variables. The social, political, cultural, and technical determinants of economic growth are carefully and precisely linked to the strictly economic variables which govern individual investment decisions. In the end we emerge with a heightened understanding of the clash, from the point of view of the individual investor, between profit maximization and security, and of the cross purposes which may develop between the interests of the individual investor and society as a whole.

Nevertheless, a key problem for growth analysis remains. How can Aubrey's evidence and analysis be translated into terms which would bear on the aggregate categories of such theoretical structures as Lowe's or which would illuminate aggregate data on underdeveloped areas of the kind Kuznets has mobilized on more advanced countries? The answer lies, again, I believe, in building up the study of sectors. At the level of a particular industry we can link the wealth of partial equilibrium data available to the aggregates and seize on the full determinants of the scale and productivity of investment. The leap is too great for systematic analysis without the sectorial substructure; and we are likely to shift from one side of the moon to the other, as we now tend to do, assisted merely by intuitive speculation.[5]

6. THE SOVIET CASE

The two papers available on the Soviet Union, like many of the others, help clarify factors which determine the relation between capital formation and economic growth, without directly assaulting that key relationship.

The student of growth within a single economy has important prima-facie advantages over the general theorist or the functional specialist in one or another variable affecting the growth rate. The examination of a given country makes it vastly easier to bring into focus the full range of forces, economic and noneconomic, at work in the growth process. The unity of the area and the society under examination directly facilitates the unification of various strands in the analysis. It is quite natural for Holzman, for example, to weave into his treatment of Soviet inflation . . . the peculiar Soviet organization of the firm, brilliantly depicted in the various studies of Berliner. Although Holzman is concerned with a relatively narrow and clear-cut issue of public finance, he moves easily between his statistical data and the ideological, institutional, and other forces which determined the outcome for the price level.

Similarly, the analyst of a single national economy finds it easy, if not unavoidable, to treat the aggregates determining capital formation and growth in terms of sectors. There is a quality of intimacy in Grossman's analysis of current trends in Soviet capital formation. His insights into the meaning and problems of the Fifth Five-Year Plan, and the aggregate growth rate it incorporates, come alive for the reason that he is, by definition, examining over-all objectives in terms of their principal sectorial components. Capital-intensity ceases to be a remote antiseptic variable in an equation. . . . It is tied in ways that are quantitative in conception—if not exactly measurable—to the position in Soviet agriculture, housing, and even education, as well as to other sectors of the economy about which we can amass useful, if partial, evidence.

It is not accidental that some of the most original current work on capital formation and economic growth has arisen from speculation on the comparative economic performances of the United States and the U.S.S.R. We may or may not, over the years, be able to organize exact statistical evidence on the productivity of different kinds of investment outlays. But we should certainly be able to develop propositions, quan-

Some General Reflections 139

titative in character, which permit us to compare the growth patterns in different economies, and to isolate the reasons for differences among them. In his essay on "Capital Formation and Allocation" this is precisely what Kaplan did; and he concludes: "Thus, if the data can be believed, and if the analysis has been correct, the greater rate of increase of industrial output in the USSR [than in the United States] has been due, basically, *not* to differences in the USSR–United States rates of investment, but rather to differences in the *direction* of investment."[6]

It has been my experience as a historian that neither the business cycle nor trend periods (in prices, interest rates, etc.) could be understood as historical phenomena until changing sectorial patterns of investment in the past had been examined. I am reasonably confident that the same body of data will emerge as central to the historical understanding of long-term growth rates and their determinants.

7. THE CONTRIBUTION OF SOCIOLOGY

We come, finally, to Levy's study of "Some Social Obstacles to Capital Formation in Underdeveloped Areas." This is a remarkable paper in several respects. First, Levy has taken care to clarify the economic determinants of capital formation before bringing to bear on them the insights of social theory. He has entered into the economist's problem, in terms recognizable to the economist. Second, he has chosen to state his preliminary hypotheses mainly in terms of a comparative analysis of two societies, those of Japan and China. In combination these qualities make possible a more detailed linkage of economic theory and social theory than one usually finds in interdisciplinary efforts. There is no quick generalization here, associating particular social systems with the conditions for rapid growth. Levy has begun to examine the components of social systems in relation to components of the economic process.

My sympathy for his approach derives from the agnosticism of the historian. Men have worked hard and imaginatively in the past out of a variety of motives. Economic progress has been achieved by societies as different in structure, institutions, and prevailing value systems as Britain and Japan, the United States and the Soviet Union. Neither Marxist theory nor any other general theory of society now available satisfactorily accounts for the diversities in pattern which societies have exhibited in general, and in their economic performance.

In contrasting the response of Japan and that of China to the challenge of Western industrial and military strength, Levy has chosen good illustrative material. They differ from the West, and they differ from one another. He has demonstrated how diverse the relations can be between the elements in an old culture and the requirements of industrial capital formation. On the whole, the inherited structure of Japan, as of the mid-nineteenth century, lent itself more easily to economic growth than did that of China; but this net conclusion arises from a complicated set of circumstances, not susceptible of easy generalization. Moreover (as Levy suggests . . .), the comparison is incomplete unless we embrace in our analysis unique historical circumstances—e.g. the chronic military pressure on China, which Japan was spared, including the disastrous effects of the Japanese invasion (from 1931) on the social and economic structure of the Nationalist China which began to emerge in the 1920's.

8. COMPARATIVE MORPHOLOGY AND A NON-NEWTONIAN THEORY OF GROWTH

If it is true that we are unlikely to find simple associations between types of social structures (or cultures) and the conditions for economic progress, what becomes of the prospects for a general theory of economic growth? It is, of course, possible that in the fullness of time we shall develop an accepted general theory of society of which economics is one facet. Given the nature of the growth problem, nothing less is implied by the concept of a theory of economic growth. For the foreseeable future, however, our aim might well be more modest: to array the patterns of growth known to us in terms which permit systematic comparison. After all, the number of societies which have passed through the transition to industrialization is limited. It should not be beyond the capacity of the social sciences to array the quantitative information available on them, in roughly uniform categories; and to explore the reasons for similarity and difference of pattern, in the light of the full determinants of economic performance. From such a grand exercise in comparative morphology, higher-order generalizations will surely emerge, relating both to the strict economics of growth and to the general social determinants of economic performance.

I believe that some such intermediate goal is implicit in most of the papers presented to this conference. The method of comparison of national patterns is used explicitly by Kuznets, Goldsmith, Hoselitz, and Levy; on a functional basis, the morphologist's technique is used by Aubrey, Maclaurin, and Usher; and, as indicated earlier, the general significance of the Soviet economic performance is increasingly being examined by means of international comparison.

I have tried in this paper to suggest the importance of sectorial analysis in furthering our understanding of economic growth. I believe it important for the refinement of theory; in the collection and interpretation of statistics; and, especially, as a means of linking systematically bodies of partial empirical evidence to aggregative concepts and data. Finally, meaningful international comparisons of growth patterns and processes require the building up of this intermediate level of analysis. The degree and kind of disaggregation appropriate will vary, as indicated in this paper, with the nature of the problem chosen for analysis and the nature of the data available.

In concluding I would make a further proposal: we might well attempt to codify, in a rough way, the measure of our theoretical agreement. Theory is a way of looking at things. Whether or not our various particular contributions will be susceptible of aggregation and cross comparison depends in part on whether we look at the growth process in similar ways. More technically, the usefulness of national growth studies will depend in part on whether or not we use comparable statistical categories and introduce into our analyses similar bodies of noneconomic data.

I am aware of the attachment that grows up between a social scientist and his private vocabulary, and of the dangers that inhere in the encouragement of abstract discussion in murky fields. Nevertheless, there may be some use in it for us, seeking to understand a many-sided problem, trying to use, in our own work, the results achieved by colleagues whose training, vocabulary, and data are often unfamiliar.

NOTES

1. The imperfections and ambiguities of the capital-output ratio as a general measure of capital productivity are being examined by others and will not be discussed in the present paper.

2. The author developed this theme at length in his paper presented before the 1953 conference of the International Economic Association at Santa Marguerita, Italy, "Trends in the Allocation of Resources in Secular Growth" [Chapter 4 in the present volume].

3. See, for example, Brinley Thomas's discussion "Migration and the Rhythm of Economic Growth," *The Manchester School*, September 1951.

4. For an effort to link growth analysis to the Keynesian analysis of the determination of the level of investment see the present author's *The Process of Economic Growth*, Norton, 1952, pp. 65–69.

5. For pioneering examples of the kind of sectorial analysis I have in mind see Paul G. Clark, "The Telephone Industry: A Study in Private Investment," and Anne P. Grosse, "The Technological Structure of the Cotton Textile Industry," in W. W. Leontief and others, *Studies in the Structure of the American Economy*, Oxford, 1953.

6. In *Soviet Economic Growth*, Abram Bergson, editor, Row, Peterson, 1953, p. 80.

FOURTEEN

Industrialization and Economic Growth (1960)

During the summer of 1960 my mind was "wonderfully concentrated," in Dr. Johnson's famous phrase, not by the sight of the gallows but by John Kennedy's presidential campaign. I had been working closely with Kennedy since February 1958. I was not on the campaign plane that summer but fed in from Cambridge, Massachusetts, a wide range of material, on request from his campaign headquarters or at my own initiative. I followed the course of the campaign from day to day with attention only matched by my concern for the welfare of the New York Giants before they moved from the Polo Grounds to play baseball at Candlestick Park, San Francisco.

But this absorbing summer was cross-cut by two professional conferences in Europe in which my participation, for different reasons, was necessary: one at Stockholm in August to which I came and went rather briskly; the other, at Konstanz, ran a full ten days in September and is the subject of the note to Chapter 15.

The Stockholm gathering was the First International Conference of Economic History. That session was a key part of the process that was to yield the International Economic History Association whose innovating Schumpeterian entrepreneur was Professor M. M. Postan of Cambridge. In the more than forty years that I was privileged to enjoy his friendship, I never found it possible to refuse a request from him. My essay was, at Postan's suggestion, addressed to one of the two unifying themes of the conference: "Industrialization as a Factor in Economic Growth After 1700."

This essay was published in M. M. Postan (ed.), *First International Conference of Economic History: Contributions and Communications* (Paris: Mouton, 1960), pp. 17–34. Reprinted with permission.

Unlike the conference at Konstanz, the Stockholm gathering was quite uncontentious, chiefly marked by the pleasure of economic historians from many countries finding an occasion to gather.

In terms of substance the following essay, prepared in the wake of the publication of The Stages of Economic Growth, *foreshadows two issues that went beyond that book's analysis: (1) How do the stages of economic growth relate to the social and political evolution of societies? (2) What precisely distinguishes traditional from modern societies and how does the transition to modernity come about? These were among the first questions I addressed after having returned to academic life early in 1969. My responses are to be found, respectively, in* Politics and the Stages of Growth *(1971) and* How It All Began *(1975).*

The purpose of this paper is to examine why and how industrialization is essential to sustained economic growth. The argument is developed in three parts. Part I considers why growth processes, before 1700, tended to be abortive in the sense that expansions in population and income gave way, in time, to periods of decline. Part II summarizes the familiar technical and economic characteristics of industrialization which have made it possible for growth to become a self-sustained process. Part III considers in broader terms the interplay between the economic and non-economic dimensions of modernization and the role of industrialization within them.

I

We consider now briefly the process of growth in pre-industrial revolution societies.

Human history offers, of course, an enormous array of experience. For purposes of simplification—to dramatize the fundamental processes at work in traditional societies—it may be useful to consider two primitive models. First, a model of what might be called a small-scale traditional society; second, a model of a traditional empire.

The small-scale traditional society is one whose economic life is bounded quite rigorously by a relatively fixed area of arable or grazing land and by a narrow (or relatively stable) trading environment. It is mainly taken up with producing for local consumption. Its political and social organization is also tied intimately to the region and does not strain to enlarge the area of its political and economic power, although it may be drawn, from time to time, into offensive or defensive military activities. Production functions may change with chance discoveries or the occasional intrusion of knowledge from outside, such as knowledge of a new crop; but these are essentially once-over changes, to which the society adjusts, moving to a new plateau.

The model is, however, not static: the small-scale traditional society does not ride smoothly along its plateaus. Within its existing production functions and acreage, population and income it is likely to exhibit fluctuations of relatively short duration determined by the interplay of the harvests, disease, and war. The pattern that Heckscher was able to present for eighteenth-century Sweden is likely to prove general for small-scale traditional societies; that is, of "Nature auditing her accounts with a red pencil," with a rise in the death rate roughly—and fairly promptly—cancelling a population surge induced by intervals of peace, absence of epidemic, and good harvests.[1] History also offers cases which suggest a somewhat different model, in which larger political and trading units are permitted, the possibility of substantial increase in acreage is envisaged, and the scale of allocations to military activities fluctuate over a much wider range than in the small-scale case, allowing for protracted intervals of peace and for wars yielding, directly and indirectly, greater economic damage than in the model of the small-scale traditional society. Here we are probing at the dynamics of the Asian empires and dynasties and those of the Mediterranean world and Western Europe.[2] Although history offers us no pure cases—not even in the tempting case of the undulating sequence of Chinese dynasties—the most appropriate model appears to be a cycle of greater length than the relatively short compensatory adjustment of the small-scale model.

The abstract cycle of the traditional empire begins with the establishment of political order over a reasonably large area by strong and purposeful administration, which concentrates a high proportion of its energies and resources on the domestic scene. It comes to power at the trough of a previous cycle when war and epidemic has driven down the population, freed acreage, and disrupted trade. In this special sense, idle capacity exists. Within the new framework of peace and order, agriculture revives, the routes for domestic (and sometimes international) trade are opened (or re-opened) and kept open and reliable; and, where appropriate, the irrigation works are built or re-built and maintained. Agricultural output not only expands but shifts in its composition to exploit the possibility of trade with the cities in commodities of higher value than the basic grains. The taxes are collected with tolerable efficiency by the government; and the expanded outlays of a prosperous government, as well as those above the ranks of the peasantry, stimulate various forms of handicraft manufacture. Processing and manufacture—and, in general, high degrees of specialization—are stimulated as well by an increase in inter-regional and, perhaps, international trade. And efforts may be made, not only to repopulate the old acreage, but to bring new lands under cultivation.

As time passes, however, three factors tend to set a limit on economic progress. First, the pressure of population against good land; second, the built-in difficulty of maintaining over long periods of time efficient, honest, and purposeful administration; and third, the likelihood that the state will become embroiled in wars whose cost outweighs their return either in expanded trade or in acquisitions of good land.[3] At some stage, these three factors yield a downturn in the cycle of the traditional empire, whose symptoms might take the form of some combination of grossly uneconomic military operations; bad harvests arising from land pressed too hard; epidemic; peasants' revolts or other forms of civil strife; and the decay of central administration.

After this upper turning point, economic, social, and political life retreats back to narrower limits, in which the society conducts its affairs on a less productive and a more self-sufficient basis, a process usually accompanied by a decline in population.[4]

As I have emphasized elsewhere, the fundamental technical reason for the abortive character of these expansions (in both small-scale and imperial cases) lies in the fact that economic invention and innovation in traditional societies was not a regular feature of their life.[5] For reasons which reach deep into their cultures, their social values, and their view of the physical world, they did not regularly allocate a substantial proportion of their creative talent to the breaking of economic bottlenecks. Nevertheless, the expansion phase of the traditional empire often contains all the preconditions for take-off except a flow of modern industrial technology capable of fending off diminishing returns to land and coping with the Malthusian propensities of the people.

Within limits set by the technological ceiling of traditional societies, the supply of good land, and the rate at which population responds to peace and prosperity, the central dynamic factor in the imperial model is the political process: the ability of the central administration to sustain, generation after generation, its integrity and purpose and to avoid military adventures whose economic cost outweighed their gain leading to excessive taxation or other gross disruptions of the economy. One can speculate as to whether a decline in administrative vigor and integrity was a built-in feature of traditional societies. Perhaps human and institutional frailty decreed, with the passage of time, that the Mandate of Heaven would be lost, as the court and administration were diverted by the blandishments of prosperity, the Buddenbrooks' Dynamics, or Parkinson's Law from their initial vigor, rectitude, and concern with the domestic scene.[6] One can also speculate concerning the relation between pressure to acquire new fertile land and the military conflicts which sometimes marked the latter phases of expansion in traditional societies.[7] Similarly, while subject to many possible exogenous circumstances, the timing and diffusion of epidemic was often determined by war. And certainly to a degree, peasant rebellions (or urban revolt) were often a response to both the pressures and the perception of waning power at the center which marked the process of downturn. But it is clear that however competent and pacific the central rule, population increase, limitation on good land, and a technological ceiling created, when taken together, basic limitations on growth in traditional empires, gathering strains on the administrative apparatus, and a setting within which crisis and downturn might be initiated by a number of forces, endogenous or exogenous.

To understand the role of industrialization in economic growth we must, in short, begin by accepting Postan's famous challenge: "To lay bare the essential processes of a society held in by physical or, if the term is used in broad sense, Malthusian checks."[8] And, from what we know, his tentatively expressed insights have a meaning beyond the later Middle Ages: in the history of traditional empires, we can, indeed, "find explanations of later decline in the conditions of previous growth." It is not only in fourteenth-century Britain that "the honeymoon of high yields was succeeded by long periods of reckoning when the marginal lands, no longer new, punished the men who tilled them with recurrent inundations, desiccations, and dust storms."[9]

When one turns from primitive models and the isolation of strategic factors to the historical data themselves, one finds, of course, all manner of unique and adventitious circumstance. There are no neat imperial cycles. Nevertheless, elements from this model can be discerned: we can observe men and societies from the Roman world to China struggling with differing degrees of purpose and distraction, to overcome the barriers created by the limitations of land and technology, frustrated in the end by some combination of the insistence of human beings that good times be translated into earlier marriages and more children; by the inherent human and institutional difficulties of maintaining effective rule over wide areas for long periods; and by military conflicts, either induced by the pressures to expand trade or acreage; undertaken for sport or power; or imposed by the chance initiative of the outer barbarians.

It is not, however, the intent of this paper to examine the evolution of traditional empires in terms of the various patterns which these variables in fact assumed. The objective is merely to set the stage for a consideration of how industrialization, taken as an ongoing process, removed the limitations on growth which set the terms for traditional societies. The argument is that industrialization not only defeated diminishing returns to land and permitted the absorption of the surge in population that modernization brought with it, as Ashton's eloquent peroration to *The Industrial Revolution* properly asserts;[10] but, in a much wider sense, by various direct and indirect routes, industrialization played a decisive and climactic role in the long, complex, interacting process whereby traditional societies were transformed into working modern organisms.

Before turning to this large theme, however, it is necessary to define more narrowly the essential characteristics and mechanisms of industrialization.

II

I take it that industrialization is the systematic, regular, and progressive application of science and technology to the production of goods and services. It is, thus, an additional factor of production which has the special characteristic that it is, so far as we know, indefinitely expansible. And the organized creativity of the human mind appears thus far to be of a productivity capable of compensating for limitations of land and natural resources.

The technical and economic prerequisites and characteristics of industrialization, as a process capable of fending off (if not for defeating indefinitely) diminishing returns and population pressure, are too familiar to require more than the briefest summary, here presented in five propositions.

1. The most basic change required is, of course, psychological. It is the acceptance of the view that the physical world is capable of being understood and manipulated in terms of a relatively few stable rules which man can master. It is for that reason Newton's concepts represented a watershed in economic history. As with Marx and Freud, it mattered little that few could read and understand Newton. It mattered greatly—as with the other great intellectual revolutionaries—that a new perspective could be vulgarized in the coffee houses and suffuse the life and work of many men. Out of this atmosphere arose, in Ashton's good phrase, "the impulse to contrive," which set men in the West to work more or less systematically and purposefully to break the bottlenecks which constrained the economic process: in fuel supply for iron-making, in spinning, in the inefficiency of steam engines, in the supply of cattle and grain, and so on. More than Newton was, of course, required to set substantial numbers of men on this path; for in some societies the link between the modern scientific thought and economic innovation was weak or non-existent. But the Newtonian outlook was a necessary initial condition and it remains so.

2. The condition for sufficiency is the existence not only of the inventor but also of a new kind of entrepreneur (private or public) willing to engage capital in a business whose risks differed substantially from those of traditional agriculture, commerce, and banking. In industry the relative illiquidity of agriculture is combined with the more mercurial market risks of commerce and banking and with that special risk (and psychological inhibition) that the installation of new techniques occasions. The extent of the innovator's risk has, however, a compensation: if successful his profits are great. And if he is loyal to his initial commitment (and the price elasticity of demand for his product permits), expansion can take place rapidly from the plough-back of profits. Thus, initially small commitments of capital to industry can often suffice to set in motion an ongoing process, whereas a higher threshold has to be overcome before significant volumes of social overhead capital can be accumulated.

3. Once begun, industry, in a modern scientific and technical setting, is infectious: backward, laterally, and forward. Modern industrial activity sets up behind it a demand for inputs of raw materials and machinery which requires, in turn, an extension of the contriving attitudes and methods. Laterally, modern industrial activity surrounds itself with men,

services, and institutions whose existence strengthens the foundations for industrialization as an ongoing process: a disciplined working force organized around the hierarchies decreed by technique; professional men to handle the problems of law and relations to the various markets for input and products; urban overhead capital; banking and commercial services; and so on. Forward, modern industrial activity creates the setting in which new industrial activities may be induced, either by cutting the cost of an input to another industry or by creating a bottleneck whose removal would evidently be profitable and therefore attracts inventive talent and entrepreneurship.

4. While the new fabricating or processing sectors are the hard core of industrialization, the society cannot progressively modernize unless three non-industrial sectors expand in the early stage of development. Agricultural output must expand to feed the enlarging and increasingly urban population, at least until industrialization has so progressed that foreign exchange can be earned economically and massively to finance food imports. Increased imports of industrial equipment or industrial raw materials must be provided for by enlarged exports, based on expanded (and usually improved) exploitation of natural resources and/or on the foreign exchange economies permitted by the development of import substitution industries. Above all the society must mobilize from its own resources (and, where possible, from capital imports) the materials, labor, and skills required for a massive buildup of social overhead capital, notably to provide education, transport, and energy. The proportion of total investment in industry itself is always relatively modern in an ongoing industrial system.

Technically, it is the requirement of expansion in these three non-industrial sectors which makes the role of the political process in the preconditions for take-off so important; for, with few exceptions, the bringing about of a productivity revolution in agriculture, and the generation of a supply of imports adequate for modernization has required important interventions and leadership by national governments.

5. This many-sided process can yield, finally, postponement not merely of Ricardian diminishing returns but of Malthusian population pressure. The rise in real income it grants, altering the old fatalistic expectations about the level of welfare, may induce a new calculus with respect to family size in which the joys of the new baby in the household are foresworn in favor of a better life for those who remain; and this shift is likely to be strengthened by greater net cost of children in urban than in rural life.

Taken all together, these appear to be the five linked elements in the process of industrialization whose existence defines the central technical difference between a traditional and a modern economy. When introduced into the two models of traditional societies presented in Part I, they remove the ceiling and open the way to self-sustained growth.

But how little they really tell us about the travail and the complexity of the process through which traditional societies must pass before industrial growth becomes their normal condition!

III

Embedded within the somewhat antiseptic characterization of the industrial process in Section II are, in fact, a profound set of changes which touch every dimension of the society. The introduction into a traditional society of the Newtonian view of the physical world, and a corps of innovators and effective industrial entrepreneurs; the development of an institutional, social, and psychological setting such that the society reacts positively to the potential spreading effects of modern industrial activity; the changes in both social structure and in politics required before the preconditions for industrial growth are achieved in the key non-industrial sectors—all of this is a way of stating that a profound revolution has occurred. Leaving aside, for a moment, the economics of the transition to modernization, how are these revolutions detonated and how may they be described in an orderly way?[11]

To simplify the analysis, we shall set aside the question of how the British industrial revolution came about;[12] and we shall set aside also a consideration of the transitional process in societies (mainly derived from Britain) which did not have to extricate themselves from a traditional mold.

We shall assume, simply, that some modern industrial societies exist and pose the question: what forces have broken up the other traditional societies of the world?

The simple answer is, of course, that traditional societies were fractured—losing their unity, cohesion, and prestige—by contact with more advanced societies. The impact of more advanced societies has taken three distinguishable forms: physical intrusion, including in many cases, colonial rule; economic example; and the communication of ideas and skills. These intrusions pushed the traditional societies into a transitional process.

In colonial societies, after a certain point in the revolution induced by the metropolitan power, the energies of those who had acquired some modern skills tended to focus around the goal of independence; and this objective helped to unify elements in the society which, in fact, took quite different views of the modernization process and brought to public life quite different motives and objectives. Where the colonial problem did not exist, the transitional process was moved forward, in different degrees and in different directions, by a sense of military inferiority and national danger; by the pressure of the peasants for their own land; by the pressure of the educated *élite* for a chance to exercise their new skills; by the spreading perception that higher standards of welfare were attainable.

But it was also moved forward by a negative fact. The fracture of the traditional society opened the way for men of political ambition—men who enjoyed the exercise of power—to contend for the vacated or weakened places of authority. Transitional societies which did not experience colonial rule—or newly independent ex-colonial states—generally experienced a period of unstable rule in which various individuals and groups sought to seize and consolidate power. These struggles for power were often merely just that: the contention of men for positions of prestige and authority, quite unrelated to movements towards or away from modernization. But, over substantial periods of time (as, for example, in Latin America over the past century), these struggles for power reflected and became suffused with the views and objectives of various specific groups in the society who wished to achieve—or forestall—various aspects of the modernization process. The raw struggle for power in succession to the traditional leaders or the colonial power (or both in combination) thus became in itself an active element in the transitional process.

It is one thing to intrude on a traditional society, introduce within it certain modern elements, and new dynamic trends. It is quite a different matter to achieve a working modern system. Before a modern society can be achieved—before the modern elements within it can become dominant and effective—a profound and positive series of changes must take place at every level.

Psychologically, men must transform the old culture in ways which make it compatible with modern activities and institutions. The face-to-face relations and warm, powerful family ties of a traditional society must give way, in degree, to new, more impersonal systems of evaluation in which men are judged by the way they perform specialized functions in the society. In their links to the nation, to their professional colleagues, to their political parties, men must find a partial alternative for the powerful, long-tested ties and symbols of the traditional life, centered on family, clan, and region. And new hierarchies, based on function, must come to replace those rooted in land ownership and tradition.

The balance of social and political power must thus shift from the village to the city, from the tasks and virtues of agricultural life to those of commerce, industry, and modern administration. Politically, the people must come to accept new forms for the organization and for the transfer of political power. They must begin—in a process with many difficult stages—to judge politics and politicians in terms of policies rather than merely inherited status or even personality; and, if they are to emerge as democracies, they must develop forms for transferring power by registering consent.

To achieve these conditions requires the passage of time: time for the social structure to be altered; time for new political attitudes and institutions to be created and consolidated; time for the skills and habits and institutions on which capital formation depends to be built. Above all time must pass for new generations to succeed one another, each finding the environment, techniques, and goals of modernization a bit more familiar and acceptable.

At every step of the way, moreover, the forces making for modernization confront elements of resistance and of distractions which slow the process of modernization—if indeed, they do not altogether frustrate it. There is nothing which decrees that the forces of modernization will win prompt or automatic victory. It is, in fact, of the very nature of the transitional process that the impulses making for modernization live in active contention with powerful forces tending to retard and to frustrate the transformation of the traditional society into full modernity. The struggle takes place not only as between groups with different interests and aspirations; but it takes place also within the minds of men torn between the attractions of what modernization appears to promise and attachments to values and institutions of the traditional life.

What kind of intellectual order can we establish in this process of contention, where economic, social, political, psychological, and cultural factors interact?

As a first approximation, it is possible to discern certain key characteristics in the process of interaction.

First, it should be noted that, once the traditional society is fractured, three quite distinguishable forces operate more or less steadily to move the society towards modernization: widened contact and communication with more modern societies; the rise of trade and of cities; and the emergence of new generations less committed than their elders to the old ways, born into a world where modern activity is increasingly a fact of life rather than a perceived break with the past. Taken together these mutually reinforcing factors decree that there will be a gradual shift in the society yielding an increasing proportion of persons knowledgeable in modern skills; tending to accept, in part, modern ideas and attitudes; basing their lives increasingly on the cities and on urban points of view. There is, to a degree, then, a kind of automatic slide in the direction of modernization set up by the nature of the forces which have fractured the traditional society.

But the second major feature of the transition is that there are limits to the pace of this slide towards modernization. The rate of training of modern men is dependent on the scale of travel and education abroad and on the creation of modern institutions within the society; the rate of increase of trade and growth of cities have built-in limitations, as well as the possibility of wide variation depending on the particular economic setting in which the transition occurs, notably the degree of population pressure; and the rhythm of human life itself sets limits to the sequence of generations and their perspectives. And beyond these technical damping factors there is the possibility of wide variation in the extent to which different traditional cultures and social structures prove amenable to modernization or resistant to its requirements.

Within, as it were, the floor and the ceiling set by the force of the modernizing elements on the one hand, the power of the constraints on the other, certain particular problems with profound dynamic significance tend to emerge as central at different stages of the modernization sequence. How each of these problems is resolved helps determine the timing and the contours of modernization.

The first of these modernizing problems centers on the nature of the intrusion of more advanced societies and the character of the reaction to them by the traditional society. The early phase of the transitional process is likely to be taken up with this essentially international relationship, and it is likely to yield a coalition united by resentment of the foreign presence or threat, whose goal is national independence or increased power.

In the next phase, the focus of modernization is likely to shift to the domestic scene. Some version of struggle is likely to occur between traditional and modernizing elements focused around this question: who shall control power in the society newly independent or freshly committed to modern goals?

If this struggle results in victory for a group seriously committed to modernization, a third phase is likely to occur in which alternative directions of policy are explored and the technical preconditions for economic growth are completed. Policy—rather than independence or merely the locus of power—becomes central at this phase.

This perspective on the modernization process—in terms of interaction—has a particular meaning for its economic dimension. Economic progress must be regarded as both a result of movement towards modernization in other dimensions and as a force making for further change. Economic progress needs, for example, a minimum group of modern men in the society before a take-off can begin; but the expansion of modern economic activities itself trains more such essential men. Similarly, economic progress usually needs a certain degree of central direction before it can get well under way; for example, with respect to the buildup of social overhead capital; but a central government gains in efficiency, authority, and stability by the very act of taking effective leadership in economic development. In terms of classes and their outlook, economic progress needs effective elements in the *élite* to accept growth as a goal before growth can get well under way. But economic progress itself creates new kinds of professionals, new urban technicians, new attitudes in the working force, which help shift social authority away from traditional attitudes and vested interests.

Viewed in these terms the take-off acquires a considerable importance because of its feedback effects on the rest of the society. These feedback effects may be summarized under the following five headings:

1. As modernization becomes accepted as the society's central piece of business, the range of political controversy tends to narrow. The issue is no longer whether the political structure of the traditional society

should be altered; nor is it the question of the broad directions nationhood should take. The issues become more procedural, more a question of degree: by what specific methods should modernization be pursued; at what pace; how should its costs and its fruits be distributed. Thus, while the take-off requires an initial commitment by the ruling *élite* to modernization, the course of the take-off itself, when it is successful, strengthens that commitment by providing a new, more narrow, and reasonably well structured agenda for the political process.

2. By the nature of the take-off, communications within the society are likely to increase in their intensity and scope, enhancing the sense of nationhood. This phase is also likely to see a sharp increase in literacy which, in the end, is one of the fundamental preconditions for a modern political process.

3. In the agricultural sector, the spread of national communications and of literacy are likely to be reinforced by the increased commercialization of agriculture, binding its fortunes more closely to the urban areas, and by the execution of national policies (e.g. land reform, taxation, technical assistance, etc.) which bring the farmer into closer operational contact with the nation.

4. The take-off is likely also to increase the pace of urbanization, bringing an increased proportion of the population into the essentially modern set of relationships which characterize city life. In the first instance, urbanization brings with it many problems for those drawn from the more secure and still traditional structure of village life; but over a period of time they tend to accept their new functional role in the society, they enter groupings which diminish the human loneliness of urban life, and they begin to organize and to seek to make their interests felt in the political process.

5. So far as politics is concerned, the most immediately felt consequence of the take-off tends to be the radical strengthening of certain elements in the political *élite*. The take-off increases the number and strengthens the confidence and influence of men of commerce and industry, of civil servants, and of technical and professional groups engaged in modern activities. These groups have a vested interest in the enlargement of the modern sectors of the society and a vested interest, as well, in forms of political organization which are both stable and which give them an increased voice in the society's political process.

Thus, although the take-off may occur under the political leadership and control of an oligarchy—and it may even be dominated by a dictator or a succession of dictators—the acceleration of growth brings about changes in the social structure and the social balance which lay the framework for a quite different political stage.

This way of looking at the transitional process raises the question of whether a useful classification is possible among societies which lie somewhere between traditional states and the successful completion of take-off. Any such effort must begin by acknowledging the wide range of variation that history imposes. Some societies enter the transition with a long national history, a considerable sense of nationhood, and relatively strong central institutions of government; others emerge from, virtually, tribal status. Some societies enter the transition with the *élite* strongly committed to democratic political symbols and seriously intent on creating viable democratic institutions; in others the democratic commitment is shallow or non-existent. Some societies enter the transition with land widely distributed and with firm foundations for an independent peasantry; others must disengage from or radically alter a rigid feudal structure in agriculture. Some societies enter the transition with long histories of successful commerce, and with cultures easily adjustable to modern economic activity; others must develop such activity virtually *ab initio*, overcoming deep cultural inhibitions. And this array is, of course, not exhaustive.

Nevertheless, to a degree, a rough classification of underdeveloped areas is possible. The underdeveloped areas past (and present) can be grouped according to the strategic problems that they confronted (or confront) before they can move forward into the next phase of the modernization process. On this operational principle, underdeveloped areas fall into four categories.

Category A.

These are societies still close to the traditional stage. Politically, socially, and psychologically, important influences are still present from the traditional society. Literacy and popular participation in the national life are low; and the economy has been modernized only to a limited degree. The basic problems to be overcome if modernization is to proceed are usually these:

1. The training of men capable of conducting modern economic and political activity.
2. The development of modern administrative institutions both economic and political.
3. The creation of an agricultural framework within which increases in agricultural productivity may become possible.
4. The buildup of a modern transport network, sources of power, and other minimum social overhead capital necessary for commercial and political unification of the nation as well as to provide a foundation for the further modernization of the economy.
5. The accelerated application of modern techniques to some natural resources in order to earn the increased foreign exchange necessary for the further modernization of the economy.
6. A transfer of political power from groups whose interests and outlook are still rooted in the traditional society—and who deal defensively with the gathering forces of modernization—to men actively committed to accept modernization.

Something like this array of crucial problems confronted continental Western Europe at, say, 1815; Russia in 1861; Japan in 1868; and this is, roughly, the contemporary agenda in most of Africa, south of the desert; in the more backward portions of the Middle East; and in certain of the less advanced areas of Latin America.

Category B.

In this category nations have already gone some distance in creating a minimum quantum of modern men and of social overhead capital. Institutions of centralized government exist. An oligarchy is in power committed, in principle, to modernization; but effective modernization is not yet under way. The six initial items on the agenda of Category A countries are likely still to form a legitimate part of the agenda of Category B countries; but sufficient progress has been made in these directions so that a take-off effort is technically feasible with a fairly short period of further technical preparation. The strategic problem is the problem of focusing the existing energy, talents, and resources of the nation around the domestic tasks of modernization, as opposed to the other goals which may engage elements within the *élite*.

Broadly speaking, something like this situation characterized France and Germany in the decade before the revolutions of 1848; Russia and Japan in the 1870's; and now Iran, Iraq, Pakistan, and Indonesia fall within this group and typify its problems.

Category C.

This category would embrace societies in the midst of the take-off. Here the historical dates are familiar. India and China are, of course, the major contemporary examples of underdeveloped areas at this stage of their evolution; although the Philippines, Brazil, Venezuela, and perhaps others belong in this category.

Category D.

These are societies where momentum has been established in the economic and social dimensions of the modernization process; where, in the post-take-off period, significant structural problems may be encountered before growth can be resumed along a wider front than during the take-off; and where an effort is likely to be made to alter political institutions and the distribution of social power to reflect the shifts which the take-off accelerated. Britain in the period 1815–1832 exhibited this mixture of structural problems, as did France and Germany, in the 1870's, and Russia in the decade before the First World War, (although its take-off was still under way).[*] The problems of Argentina and Turkey symbolize this category at the present time.

Broadly speaking, then, the strategic tasks form a sequence in which, successively, the crucial job is the building of the human, institutional, political, and physical foundations of modernization; the effective focusing of these resources on the goals of modernization; the mobilization of a quantity of resources adequate for the take-off; and the political and social, as well as economic consolidation of the modernization process, as momentum is gained and the society commits itself, in one form or another, to extend the tricks of modern technology out beyond the sectors modernized during the take-off.

The intellectual complexity of the process of industrialization arises because industrialization is, for most individuals and groups in the traditional society, not wanted for its own sake: it is a derived demand. What men want, in a society which has been intruded upon by more advanced powers, is one or another result that only industrialization, in its widest sense, can bring. But industrialization has its own imperatives: psychological, technical, institutional, social, political, and economic. What we can observe—in history and on the contemporary scene—are societies in the process of facing those imperatives, with different degrees of conflict and accommodation between the old ways and the new requirements. It is for that reason that the way to modernization is so often led by men and groups who, in one way or another, were disadvantaged or alienated in the traditional society, and who see in modernizing activities new routes to prestige and power.

But, as time passes, and the fractured traditional society ceases to offer to the young men functions and values which give security and fulfillment to their lives, they accept increasingly the new ways. If the transitional society expands its modernizing activities, they commit their working lives to them, with more or less reluctance and inner conflict; if the political, social, and economic leadership fails to offer these new opportunities, pressures to accelerate modernization grow up, often accompanied by civil strife. Thus, gradually, with more or less disruption, the preconditions for take-off are fulfilled. The gap between men's desire for the fruits of modernization and the attitudes and activities necessary to bring it about is narrowed.

The take-off itself not only imparts momentum to the economy, but shifts the whole social, political, and psychological balance of the society in ways which, thereafter, make easier the progressive march of industrialization. The society's problems are, of course, by no means at an end; and the course of industrialization may be slowed, frustrated, or conceivably, for a time, reversed. But, in every sector of the society,

---

[*Later calculations indicate that Russia entered the drive to technological maturity in the period 1905–1914.]

commitments of value and interest are built in which tend to assert themselves and, in the end, in the world of modern communications and political interconnection, to force the application to the society's resources of what the enlarging pool of modern science and technology may offer.[13]

NOTES

1. E. F. HECKSCHER, "Swedish Population Trends before the Industrial Revolution," *Economic History Review*, Second Series, Vol II, No. 3, 1950. The surges in death rates in Sweden of the 1740's, 1770's, and towards the close of the first decade of the nineteenth century suggest the Chinese proverb that "in every thirty years there is a small upheaval . . ." (SSU-YU TENG, *New Light on the History of the Taiping Rebellion*, Cambridge, Mass., 1950, p. 38.)

2. For some fragmentary but suggestive data on income and its fluctuations in traditional empires, see Colin CLARK, *The Conditions of Economic Progress*, Second edition, London, 1951, "Excursus. Economic Comparisons with the Ancient World," pp. 542–567.

[3.] For a suggestive discussion of the relative cost of "protection" in preindustrial societies, see F. C. LANE, "Economic Costs of Organized Violence," *Tasks of Economic History*, vol. XVIII, No. 4, December 1958.

[4.] The dynamics of cycles similar to that described here have been formalized in the study of certain natural phenomena; e.g., fluctuations in the populations of two species of fish, one of which feeds off the other, and in the cyclical interplay between plants and their parasites. See, notably. V. VOLTERRA, *Leçons sur la Théorie Mathematique de la Lutte pour la Vie*, Paris, 1931; and A. J. LOTKA, *Elements of Physical Biology*, Baltimore, 1925.

[5.] *The Stages of Economic Growth*, Cambridge, England, 1960, especially pp. 4–5. Probably the most scholarly and sophisticated exploration of this problem in something like these terms is M. ROSTOVTZEFF, *The Social and Economic History of the Roman Empire*, Oxford, 1926. His cyclical analysis is stated with great clarity in the Preface (pp. viii–xiii); and his case is argued against other hypotheses, pp. 480–487. Up to (say) the end of the first century he presents, in effect, the buildup of all the preconditions for take-off except the foundations for modern industrialization; but momentum was already lost and the wars of the second century begin the decline. Proximately, Rostovtzeff's explanation of the decline centers on the degeneration of urban capitalism, leading to class struggles between an increasingly defensive middle class and an increasingly repressed but assertive mass of citizens. While rejecting a narrowly economic interpretation of decline, he poses as the crucial question (p. 484): "Why was the victorious advance of capitalism stopped? Why was machinery not invented? Why were the business systems not perfected? Why were the primal forces of primitive economy not overcome? They were gradually disappearing; why did they not disappear completely?" Thus, while his analysis is based on subtle interaction among political, social, intellectual, religious, and economic factors, it remains the story of a society which could not break through fundamental technological limitations which set a ceiling on its ability to expand. It then fell into progressive internal conflict in the face of this constraint which, combined with the burdens of war, overwhelmed the institutions and organization which had been erected in the period of progress which the resources and technology available did permit. While Rostovtzeff's crucial question is, in a sense, economic, a satisfactory answer to it would, of course, transcend economic factors.

[6.] The classical Chinese theory of the dynastic cycle was formulated wholly in terms of human and institutional strength and frailty, as for example, in this excellent paraphrase: "A new dynasty at first experiences a period of great energy, and vigorous and able new officials put in order the civil and military affairs of the Empire. In the course of generations the new period of vigor is followed by a golden age. Territories acquired earlier are held, but no new territories are conquered. Learning and the arts flourish in an atmosphere of elegance. Agricultural production and the people's welfare are supported by the maintenance of peace, attention to public works, and limitation of taxes. This golden age, however, carried within it the seeds of its own decay. The governing class loses first the will and then the ability to meet the high standards of Confucian government. Its increasing luxury places a strain on the exchequer. Funds intended for irrigation, flood control, maintenance of public grain reserves, communications, and payment of the army are diverted by graft to private pockets. As morale is undermined, corruption becomes flagrant.

This process of decline may be retarded by the vigorous training of officials and people in the Confucian social philosophy, but the basic direction of events cannot be altered. Sooner or later, the governing class, blind to those reforms which alone can save it, taxes the peasants beyond endurance and fails to attend to the public welfare. Sporadic local rebellions result, necessitating additional taxes and the recruiting of troops from an increasingly disaffected population. Their stake in the existing order gone, the people express their disaffection in a great rebellion. If the rebellion is successful, the swarming bandits become in the eyes of history the righteous forces.

The great rebellion is usually successful. One of its leaders slowly consolidates his power by securing (1) military superiority; (2) support from the literati, to whom he offers a revived Confucian state that they will administer; and (3) support, at least tacit, from the peasantry, to whom he offers peace, land, reduced taxes, and a program of public works to protect the agricultural economy. The new dynasty thus begins where its predecessor began, and its destiny will follow the same pattern." (Mary C. WRIGHT, *The Last Stand of Chinese Conservatism*, Stanford University Press, 1957, pp. 43-44. See footnote on pp. 43-44 for further references to Chinese theories of the dynastic cycle.) China did not lack those who saw a relation between population movements and the dynastic cycle, among them Hung Liang-Chi (1746-1809), known as the Chinese Malthus. Hung's dictum was ". . . during a long reign of peace, Heaven and Earth could not but propagate the human race, yet their resources that can be used for the support of mankind are limited. During a long reign of peace the government could not prevent the people from multiplying themselves, yet its remedies are few" (Quoted, PING-TI HO, *Studies on the Population of China, 1368-1953*, Cambridge, Mass., 1959, p. 272.) For another view of Chinese cyclical theory which focuses primarily on the ebb and flow of population pressure, with a relatively passive role for the quality of government and administration, see SSU-YU TENG, *op. cit.*, pp. 37-38. In his analysis of the setting for the Taiping Rebellion, however, Teng weaves together pressures arising from the growth in population and those derived from the decay of the Manchu dynasty.

[7.] It is, of course, tempting, when constructing a model, to make the climactic military conflicts of the imperial society a function of pressure induced by population increase or the dynamics of trade expansion; as, for example, in

Toynbee's interpretation of the Greek city states. But rulers of traditional (and, indeed, of modern) societies have become embroiled in wars for reasons which had little to do with rational economic interests; and there is often something to be said for the classical Chinese view that costly engagements with the outer barbarians were a sign of the decay of virtue in the dynasty. And in some cases the occasion and timing of conflict can be interpreted without reference to forces operating within the imperial society; as, for example, in Stevens' account of the invasions at the time of Marcus Aurelius (C. E. STEVENS, "Agriculture and Rural Life in the Later Roman Empire," *The Cambridge Economic History*, Cambridge, 1942, p. 112).

[8.] M. M. POSTAN, "Some Economic Evidence of Declining Population in the Later Middle Ages," *Economic History Review*, Second Series, Vol. II, No. 3, 1950, p. 246.

[9.] *Idem*.

[10.] T.S. ASHTON, *The Industrial Revolution, 1760–1830*, London, 1948, p. 161: "The central problem of the age was how to feed and clothe and employ generations of children outnumbering by far those of any earlier time. Ireland was faced by the same problem. Failing to solve it, she lost in the 'forties about a fifth of her people by emigration or starvation and disease. If England has remained a nation of cultivators and craftsmen, she could hardly have escaped the same fate, and, at best, the weight of a growing population must have pressed down the spring of her spirit. She was delivered, not by her rulers, but by those who, seeking no doubt their own narrow ends, had the wit and resource to devise new instruments of production and new methods of administering industry. There are today on the plains of India and China men and women, plague-ridden and hungry, living lives little better, to outward appearance, than those of the cattle that toil with them by day and share their places of sleep by night. Such Asiatic standards, and such unmechanized horrors, are the lot of those who increase their numbers without passing through an industrial revolution."

[11.] What follows in this section is, essentially, a development of the rather terse observations on the preconditions for take-off in *The Stages of Economic Growth*, Cambridge, 1960, pp. 6–7 and 26–31.

[12.] This subject is treated in *Ibid.*, pp. 31–35.

[13.] The theoretical sub-structure of Part III of this paper bears a family relation to that developed by Gunnar MYRDAL in *An American Dilemma*, New York, 1944, Appendix 3, "A Methodological Note on the Principle of Cumulation," and is a further development of my own notions of interaction among the sectors into which societies organize themselves (*British Economy of the Nineteenth Century*, Oxford, 1948, chap. vi; and *The Process of Economic Growth*, New York, 1952, especially chap. ii). Myrdal applies his model to the problem of underdeveloped areas less systematically than in his study of the American Negro in *An International Economy*, New York, 1956, pp. 15–16, 21–24, and more generally, in chap. xii. Myrdal's model and my earlier notions of interaction were concerned primarily to expose how the interconnections within a society may yield a situation where a change in one variable may result in a series of movements which result in a further, reinforced movement of the initiating variable. In short, these analyses were concerned primarily with the direction of movement in an interlocked system. Here the attempt is somewhat more ambitious in two directions. First, an effort is made broadly to specify the nature of the ceiling and the floor which the cumulative process of modernization confronts at each stage; and from this specification flows the classification of four phases in the sequence of modernization up to the post-take-off period. Second, the take-off is introduced as a distinguishable discontinuity in the process of economic development and, therefore, in the process of modernization as a whole.

The difficulty experienced by some of the initial critics of my thesis about stages of growth comes to rest precisely on this point of basic social theory. Those who have argued that the stages of growth analysis is mechanistic have, in fact, appeared simply to miss an identification of one variable as key to the modernization process; e.g., the conflict between classes with diverse economic interests, the emergence of private capitalists and political democracy, etc. An approach to the analysis of societies in terms of interaction would question the legitimacy of such identifications of unique causal factors.

FIFTEEN

The Konstanz Conference: Leading Sectors and the Take-off (1960) and Epilogue (1963)

The Konstanz conference arose from an initiative of Austin Robinson, then president of the International Economic Association (IEA). At Cambridge, early in the Hilary term of 1959, Robinson asked if I would help design and participate in an IEA conference focused on the take-off into self-sustained growth. The concept had been much discussed and debated in the wake of my March 1956 Economic Journal article and attention had heightened as word got around of my Cambridge lectures in the autumn of 1958 on the stages of economic growth. I agreed and helped Robinson rough out a list of possible participants: theorists of various stripes, statisticians, economic historians, and experts on development. We broke the subject into three sections: the concept in general; country perspectives (United States, Britain, France, Germany, Japan, Russia, etc.); and functional issues particularly relevant to the take-off concept (population, technology, agriculture, etc.). Such a variegated group duly assembled at the Insel Hotel on Lake Konstanz, where they listened to summaries of and vigorously debated some sixteen papers that closely followed the design Robinson and I had contrived. Virtually unbroken rain mitigated our sense of loss at not being free to enjoy the lake and the view.

My opening essay, reproduced as the first part of this chapter, focused on the role of leading sectors in the take-off. I chose the theme because the leading-sector approach to technological change most sharply

---

The following two essays were published in W. W. Rostow (ed.), *The Economics of Take-Off into Sustained Growth* (London: Macmillan, 1963). Reprinted with permission.

distinguished my stage scheme from, say, neoclassical growth models (e.g., Solow) and Kuznets's highly aggregated statistical categories, although I never ceased to acknowledge the pioneering role of Kuznets's early Secular Movements in Prices and Production—a disaggregated analysis Kuznets abandoned, in my view, at great cost.

Although each member of the strong-minded crew that had assembled at Konstanz had his say, the occasion had something of the character of an assault by Kuznets and my reply. I was tolerably prepared for such an assault because Kuznets had circularized some of his colleagues before the event, and I had been informed of his intentions by one of them. In any case, I still profoundly believe what I said in the Epilogue; i.e., that the marketplace of ideas should be "ruthlessly competitive." I thoroughly enjoyed the conference to the degree my overriding concern with the presidential campaign permitted. (My academic colleagues regarded my recurrent walks in the rain to a kiosk by the lake to buy the latest Paris Herald Tribune as rather morbid.)

At its core, Kuznets's assault came to these three propositions:

- growth should be analyzed in aggregate not sectoral terms;
- the data then available did not justify the notion of a sharp rise in the investment rate during take-off and, therefore, no clear line could be drawn between the take-off and the pre-conditions for take-off; and
- "the early phase of modern economic growth" was a better phrase than "take-off."

In his Economic Growth of Nations: Total Output and Production Structure (1971), Kuznets radically revised his Konstanz position on all three points. First, in the Summary and Conclusions he suddenly expressed his "frustration" at the failure of his classifications "to reveal the technologically new components." Some thirty pages follow (pp. 314–43) in which Kuznets, for the first time since his Secular Movements, tried to link radical innovation to changes in the structure and over-all performance of economies—an extremely valuable exercise. Second, he accepts from later evidence a rise in the net capital formation proportion from something like 5 to 15 percent, where it levels off at an intermediate point in the process of modern economic growth (pp. 61–70). Third, he supplies (p. 24) a set of dates for "the beginning of modern growth" that closely approximates my original dating of take-off for eight countries (for discussion see my World Economy: History and Prospect, pp. 778–79).

At Konstanz, the discussions had such momentum that there was no time for me to reply in a leisurely and coherent way to the debate as a whole. Robinson suggested, therefore, that I be granted the right of reply in the volume on the conference. That Epilogue is included as the second part of this chapter. As the text notes, several years had passed, and I was at work in the Kennedy administration when the page proofs arrived. The Epilogue was my last purely academic essay until 1969.

LEADING SECTORS AND THE TAKE-OFF

I. INTRODUCTORY

The purpose of this chapter is to clarify the basic economic mechanism which underlies the notion of the take-off—the idea of leading sectors—and to relate the workings of this mechanism to the other conditions required for take-off.

The exposition proceeds as follows: Part I examines the theoretical and empirical foundations for the concept of leading sectors. Part II relates the leading sector mechanism to the take-off. Part III considers how the initial leading sectors link to the other variables which help determine when and how a take-off occurs. Part IV presents certain concluding observations.

II. RETARDATION AND THE THEORY OF PRODUCTION

We begin with a narrow question: Why does the introduction of modern technology tend to assume the form of a series of leading sectors?[1]

The pioneering economic study of how new technology is introduced into a given sector is Kuznets' *Secular Movements in Prices and Production*. This book remains, in my view, a classic whose implications for economic theory in general and the economics of growth in particular remain still to be developed, despite the elaborations of Arthur F. Burns and others.[2] Kuznets demonstrated, in a merging of technological, economic, and statistical analysis, how the introduction of a new production function in a given sector (including new supplies of raw materials) leads to a phase of rapid growth in that sector often accompanied by a decline in the price of its output; and how a set of forces converge to decree that the path of output in that sector will decelerate. The rapid increase in output results from the decrease in costs of production of an old product (or commodity) or the introduction of a new product with high price (or income) elasticity of demand. Kuznets identified four major factors which determined deceleration: the slowing down of technical progress; the damping effect of slower-growing complementary industries; limitations of finance, as the fast-growing industry achieves large-scale operation; and competition from the same industry in a younger country (with, presumably, lower money costs).[3]

In addition, Merton has suggested how these technical and economic factors may be reinforced by a secular decline in the quality of entrepreneurship.[4] The actual path of deceleration may, thus, fall below that which would have occurred if the Kuznets variables alone were operating on the sectoral curve.

The Kuznets hypothesis introduces a powerful element of potential order into the theory of production.[5] It is a commonplace that different sectors will expand or contract at different rates. But most analyses of the production process are conducted as if these distinctions in rate are essentially random; and that it is sufficient to examine by statistical techniques the average performance of the economy as a whole, or certain highly aggregated sectors within it. If, however, we assume that the life of any sector touched by new production functions will follow a more or less systematic path of deceleration, it follows that the sectors of an economy can be distinguished by, as it were, their distance from their technological origin; and, as Kuznets demonstrated, the paths of deceleration may be expressed in the form of equations which specify the properties of the logistic curves which result. It follows also that the average performance of an economy can be held constant only by the introduction of new production functions which will compensate for the deceleration built into the older sectors.

Sustained economic growth becomes dependent, then, on the recurrent coming into the capital stock of new technology and new production functions (including new land or raw material supplies) which, by imparting rapid growth to a limited number of sectors, manage to keep the average level of growth relatively steady against the inevitable erosion imposed by the passage of time on the momentum of individual sectors.

The Kuznets insight gives the theory of production a shapeliness—a degree of organization—which requires a close examination of individual sectors, the links among them, and their economic, technological, and entrepreneurial history if we are to understand average aggregate performance and its fluctuations. The assumption that differences in rate of output in the sectors are random, and capable of meaningful analysis only by means of averaging techniques, at high levels of aggregation, ceases to be permissible.

Spreading Effects:
Backward, Lateral, and Forward

Now we must go beyond the Kuznets analysis of retardation. The effects of a sector touched by new technology and experiencing a rapid growth phase transcend the sector itself.[6] There are three separable consequences of the rapid growth stage of such a sector which give concreteness to our instinctive sense that certain industries play a disproportionate rôle in growth, at various historical intervals, which justifies the notion of a leading sector.

Extending my own previous analysis of this problem (and drawing a bit on Hirschman's vocabulary[7]) I shall call these effects: backward, lateral, and forward.

Backward Effects. Depending on its technological character, the new sector, in its rapid growth phase, will set up requirements for new inputs of raw materials and machinery which require, in turn, an extension of modern contriving attitudes and methods. These inputs may be material as, for example, modern cotton textiles stimulated the fabrication of textile machinery and steam engines, and encouraged, over a broad front, improved metallurgy. But the new induced inputs may be human; as, for example, cotton textiles required new types of factory workers, foremen, and industrial managers. And they may also be institutional: as, for example, the railways stimulated new arrangements for mobilizing long-term capital on a large scale from small savers.[8]

Lateral Effects. In addition the leading sector will induce around it a whole set of changes which tend to reinforce the industrialization process on a wider front. Modern industrial activity surrounded itself with urban men, services, and institutions whose existence strengthened the foundations for industrialization as an ongoing process: a disciplined working force organized around the hierarchies decreed by technique; professional men to handle the problems of law and relations to the various markets for input and products; urban overhead capital; institutions of banking and commerce; and the construction and service industries required to meet the needs of those who manned the new industrial structure. The coming in of a new leading sector thus often transformed the whole region where it took hold; as, for example, the cotton textile revolution transformed Manchester and Boston and the automobile industry transformed Detroit. Wherever they went, the railroads induced the transformation of old urban centres or the creation of new ones, not merely for railroad maintenance but also to handle the marketing and commercial traffic that the railroads made possible and profitable. These lateral effects—symbolized by the acceleration in urbanization during take-off—expanded the proportion of modern folk in the total population and strengthened modern attitudes towards the production process far beyond the narrow impact of the new activity itself and the inputs it directly induced.

Forward Effects. Finally, modern industrial activity created the setting in which new industrial activity was induced, either by cutting the cost of an input to another industry; by providing a new product or service whose existence was a challenge to the enterprising to exploit; or by creating a bottleneck whose removal was evidently profitable and which therefore attracted inventive talent and entrepreneurship. Leading sectors thus set up incentives and open up possibilities for a wide range of new economic activities, sometimes, even, setting the stage for the next major leading sector. The expansion of the cotton textile industry in eighteenth-century Britain directly and powerfully increased incentives to free cotton manufacture from its dependence on water power; and it thus helped create the setting within which Watt, delicately nurtured by Boulton, performed a task whose consequences reached far beyond the cotton textile industry. Even more directly the expansion in cotton textiles increased the incentive to find ways of transporting cotton material and finished products more cheaply between port and factory;

and it thus accelerated the coming of the Manchester-Liverpool and Boston-Lowell lines, whose prompt success led others to launch railway lines on a broader economic front. Similarly the high obsolescence rate of iron rails created a powerful incentive later in the century to solve the problem of cheap steel which, once available, in turn created an incentive to improve shipbuilding, construction, and machine-building techniques. Leading sectors have had forward effects not only on technology but also on raw material supply. Railroads thrown out into new territories to exploit the possibility of rising grain prices have, along the way, found it possible to link with rich mineral resources whose availability, in turn, set in motion long chains of sectoral expansion.

It is the combination of these three types of spreading effects from rapidly growing sectors infused by new production functions which justifies empirically the notion of leading sectors in economic growth.

III. LEADING SECTORS AND THE DATING OF TAKE-OFF

We come now to the following question: when, along a Kuznets path of deceleration, is it proper to regard a rapidly growing sector as a leading sector? The problem arises because deceleration normally begins virtually from the moment a new production function takes hold.[9] An annual series for railroad mileage opened in a new country might, for example, look like this: 0, 100, 500, 1500, 2000, etc. With the rate of increase under steady decline it is evident that the correct criterion cannot be, simply, the interval of maximum rate of growth of the sector itself.

The interval when a new sector can be regarded as an effective leading sector is a compound of two related elements: first, the interval when it attains not merely high momentum but a certain substantial scale; second, when its backward and lateral spreading effects pervade the economy over a wide front.

Growth must be viewed, then, not merely in terms of a series of decelerating individual sectors, but in terms of clusters of sectors, linked backward by the Leontief chain, which have further lateral and diffuse consequences for growth. In conception, both backward and lateral effects are quantitative, although difficult to measure with precision, especially in the early stages of national growth when data are likely to be scanty. But it does not appear beyond the range of research and calculation to investigate this matter systematically.

Thus far, working with historical data, I have sought to use the full range of quantitative and non-quantitative materials available to form an approximate judgment as to when the rate and scale of a leading sector's growth has been such as to induce substantial further expansion in the economy, also of high momentum, via its backward and lateral linkages. The take-off dates I have tentatively offered on other occasions are the product of such investigations of the total impact of the initial group of leading sectors in the industrialization process of particular economies. It is the coming in of the first leading sector (or sectors), on a scale and with a momentum to induce substantial spreading effects, which creates the *saltum* economies sometimes execute.

Now a major *proviso*. It cannot be too strongly emphasized that the secondary effects of rapid growth in a sector suffused with new technology are not automatic. They are potential effects which require active exploitation by a society's men and institutions. In fact, one measure of a society's ability to move into sustained economic growth is its ability to seize upon and to exploit with vigour all three types of potentiality which flow from a leading sector.

The pre-1914 railroads, for example, had enormous and widespread effect in stimulating growth in Britain, the United States, France, Germany, Sweden, Japan, Canada, and Russia. But their effects were narrow, not merely in colonial India, but in China, whose political and social leadership were not deeply committed to the modernization process; and also in relatively comfortable Argentina, content until the 1930's to enjoy the comparative advantage of production and trade in foodstuffs. Growth is, thus, only an automatic process if one can assume that a society will respond actively and effectively to the potentials for growth available to it.

In the light of this argument the take-off must be defined in two steps: first, it is the period in the life of an economy when, for the first time, one or more modern industrial sectors take hold, with high rates of growth, bringing in not merely new production functions but backward and lateral spreading effects on a substantial scale; second, for a take-off to be said to have occurred, the economy must demonstrate the capacity to exploit the forward linkages as well,[10] so that new leading sectors emerge as the older ones decelerate. It is this demonstration of the capacity to shift from one set of leading sectors to another which distinguished abortive industrial surges of the transition period from a true take-off. This functional requirement has determined that the take-off be defined as embracing, say, a 20-year interval. Some such substantial period is necessary to demonstrate that a society is capable of overcoming the structural crisis which the initial surge of growth is likely to bring and is capable of introducing the changing flow of technology upon which sustained growth depends.

IV. HOW SELF-SUSTAINED IS SELF-SUSTAINED GROWTH?

This latter condition relates to a larger issue which has been posed in discussions of the stages of growth as a whole: How self-sustained is sustained growth? To what extent is growth truly automatic after the take-off?

In one sense, it follows directly from the fact of deceleration that growth is not automatic. If, on this view, a society is to sustain a high average rate of growth, it must engage in an endless struggle against deceleration; for while the flow of modern science and technology may offer the potentiality of fending off Ricardian diminishing returns indefinitely, a society which wishes to exploit this potentiality must repeat the creative pain of actually introducing new production functions as the old leading sectors decelerate; and it must demonstrate the capacity to exploit with vigour its potential spreading effects. In this sense sustained growth requires the repetition of the take-off process.[11] It requires the organization around new technology of new and vigorous management; new types of workers; new types of financing and marketing arrangements. It requires struggle not against the constraints of the traditional society—whose economic bonds are decisively broken in the take-off—but against constraints created in the previous generation or two, around the peculiar imperatives of an older set of leading sectors now no longer capable of carrying the economy forward at its old pace.

These transitions from one set of leading sectors to another are neither trivial nor abstruse phenomena. We can identify their consequences in the sweep of modern economic history and on the contemporary scene. I am inclined to think, for example, that when we have fully examined the 1880's, we shall find the widespread deceleration in that decade related in part to the process of disengagement from the railroad era and to the process of catching hold fully of the potentialities implicit in the new leading sectors: steel, electricity, and chemicals. I am reasonably certain that, as time passes, we shall interpret a significant element in the interwar sluggishness of Western Europe as due to the process of disengagement from the old leading sectors of the pre-1914[12] and wartime years and to the rather slow preparation for the age of high mass consumption which in the 1950's at last fully seized Western Europe, as the old men of steel and electricity and heavy chemicals have been superseded by the bright young men of automobiles and plastics, electronics, and aeronautics. Indeed, Belgium can be regarded still as a nation which was permitted by a series of accidental circumstances to prolong its stay, in reasonable comfort, in the pre-1914 set of leading sectors and which must re-engage in new directions if it is to maintain its status and momentum. And it may not be unhelpful to view the present sluggishness of the American economy as an interim between the time when the automobile and all its works has lost the capacity to serve as a leading sector and the time when new leading sectors take hold.[13]

There is, then, nothing automatic and easy about the inner mechanics—the logistics, as it were—of sustained growth.

But in a larger sense, the experience of take-off may, when we have a longer time perspective, prove to be a definitive transition, like the loss of innocence. The reason for this judgment is that behind the whole industrial process lies the acceptance of the Newtonian outlook, the acceptance of the world of modern science and technology. Phases of difficulty and even relative stagnation after the take-off may, of course, occur; and they may be protracted. For example, interwar Europe was trapped by a world economic environment, by its own political and social attitudes, and by its own economic policies in such a phase of relative stagnation; but beneath the surface, even in Britain (as Sayers has demonstrated[14]), the technological and entrepreneurial basis for new leading sectors and for the new phase of growth which flowered in the 1950's were being created. Similarly, in Spain, we have observed since the end of the Civil War a quite purposeful effort to forestall the further march of the stages of economic growth. But Spain had come far enough forward in the process of modernization, at least in the North, for this effort to fail, notably in the world of modern communications; that is, there is reason for confidence that, over the next decade, we shall see a clearly marked resumption in Spanish economic growth.

In short, on present historical evidence, it appears fair to say that the larger psychological, social, technological, and institutional changes required for a take-off are such as to make it unlikely that we shall see a true lapsing back. Men in societies must continue to struggle to keep growth moving forward; and one of the purposes of this mode of analysis, rooted in leading sectors, is to specify the nature of that struggle. But the deeper fundamentals required for an effective take-off appear, on present evidence, sufficiently powerful to make growth an ongoing process, on long term. Nevertheless, we still have much to learn about the longer spans of the industrialization process.

V. LINKAGES BETWEEN LEADING SECTORS AND OTHER FACTORS

Having sought to clarify the rôle of leading sectors in the take-off, it is necessary now to relate this mechanism to the other economic variables which determine whether, when, and how sustained growth becomes a more or less regular feature of a society's performance.

I shall proceed by considering, in brief notes, some of the linkages which exist or do not exist between the leading sectors of the take-off and certain functional dimensions of growth which are dealt with elsewhere in this book: population; agriculture; technology; capital formation (including social overhead capital); and foreign exchange.

(i) *Population*

The rate of population increase is only obliquely linked to the leading sectors of take-off; and it is not linked in any simple or systematic way. This judgment can be illustrated with respect to the three directions in which population increase influences the growth process; i.e. via the population-resource balance, the industrial labour supply, and the level of effective demand.

With respect to the population-resource balance, a very high rate of population increase in a setting where good agricultural land is limited may require excessive diversion of domestic resources and foreign exchange into food supply and may thus delay or damp the build-up of social overhead capital, the acquisition of foreign exchange for industrial purposes, and the coming of momentum in modern industrial sectors. But it does not follow that ample supplies of good land automatically accelerated the coming in of industrial sectors of high momentum. As the early history of the United States, Canada, and Argentina suggest, a highly favourable population-resource balance, even when accompanied by high rates of population increase, may make so attractive a continued concentration on food and raw material production that industrialization may be delayed. Moreover, we can observe in cases of both weak and strong population pressure on resources (e.g. the United States of the 1850's and Russia of the 1890's) that the installation of a large-scale railway net can trigger the expansion of a cluster of industrial sectors, if the society is otherwise prepared to respond positively to the potential stimulating impulses railways provide.

Population pressure also relates, of course, to the problem of labour supply to industry. Francis Cabot Lowell's most difficult problem in creating a viable factory system in the Boston area, was to recruit a working force under circumstances where the alternative of good land was available to virtually all who wished to farm; and some part of the low growth rate of France after 1848 relative to Germany, is to be explained by the relatively light pressure on land caused by a damped population increase, and the consequently lesser flow of rural men to the cities. In most cases, however, the problem of recruiting an adequate industrial work force has not been a decisive variable in determining when industrialization takes hold. In none of the historical cases examined in this book—excepting perhaps the regional case of New England—did the lack of labour supply present a direct inhibition on the emergence of leading sectors.

The most general proposition would appear to be that ample supplies of cheap labour provide a basis for effective competition with more advanced economies, once the other conditions for an industrial surge have been established, notably the emergence of industrial entrepreneurs, an adequate mastery of existing industrial technology, and an ability to organize the minimum training required to create an industrial working force.

The rate of population increase enters into still another dimension of the growth process through its effects on the size of the domestic market and the rate of increase of domestic demand. In a setting such as Britain in the second half of the eighteenth century, where increased social overhead capital was being created and an increase in agricultural productivity was maintaining or improving the level of food supply, a rising population can be an important stimulus from the side of demand to the development of industries with high income elasticity of demand, at low income levels; e.g. beer brewing and textile manufacture. And even when income per head is not rising, the price elasticity of demand (perhaps made effective by protective tariffs) can provide a market basis for industrialization, under conditions of rapid population increase. But, once again, the outcome depends on the relation between population increase and other variables: there is, evidently, no automatic market connexion between population increase and the emergence of leading sectors rooted in an expanding effective domestic demand.

(ii) *Agriculture*

An increase in agricultural production and productivity plays a multiple rôle in economic development which can hardly be overestimated.[15]

(a) The income above minimum consumption levels incorporated in land rents, and usually sterilized or used at low productivity in traditional or transitional societies, must be diverted into the modern sector and become part of the basis for building social overhead capital or (less frequently) for expanding directly modern industry.

(b) Increased domestic food supplies are needed to meet the increase in population and accelerated urbanization, which are almost universal characteristics of the pre-take-off period, without causing an excessive drain on foreign exchange. And in cases where resource endowments permit an agricultural surplus, an increase in agricultural productivity can earn the increased foreign exchange which economic modernization as a whole demands.

(c) Increased agricultural productivity may be required to provide a basis of increased income per head in order to provide either an enlarged domestic market for consumer goods or increased popular taxation without a repression of rural living standards.

More narrowly, developments in agriculture may relate quite directly to the emergence of leading industrial sectors, in one of the three following ways.

Agriculture as an Input to a Leading Sector. The gathering momentum of the British cotton textile industry in the 1780's set up a requirement for an enlarged and cheapened supply of raw cotton, to which the cotton gin and the spread of the plantation system in the American South was a direct response. This new source of cheap supply helped permit the British cotton textile industry to exploit the high price and income elasticity of textile demand on a world basis and thus to attain the scale and spreading effects within Britain, which justify its status as the leading sector in the British take-off.

Agriculture and the Foreign Balance. Agriculture has served as an indirect input to leading sectors by earning foreign exchange for industrialization, and by providing a basis on which foreign loans could be persuasively negotiated, which permitted, in turn, the rapid construction of railway systems which served as leading sectors in take-off. American cotton and wheat, Japanese silk, and Russian wheat played this rôle in the respective take-offs of the three countries.

Leading Sectors as Inputs to Agriculture. There is a sense in which the second and decisive decade of the American take-off (the 1850's) and the pre-1914 Russian take-off were triggered by the transport requirements for exploiting the grain fields of both countries. The first phase of accelerated industrialization was, to a degree, a by-product of an agricultural revolution. The rising world grain prices of the 1850's and the late 1890's made the massive laying of rail lines attractive; and the direct and indirect consequences of railroadization, pushed both nations into take-off. Railroadization was well under way in the United States in the 1840's and in Russia in the 1880's; and it was the industrial rather than the agricultural consequences of railroadization that created the take-off in each case. Nevertheless, the timing of these industrial surges related directly to the world grain market position and to the existence of hitherto unexploited possibilities for increasing agricultural production.

On a lesser scale and in a less decisive way, agriculture has contributed to industrialization by inducing new manufactured inputs; e.g. with respect to the German chemical fertilizer industry and the American farm machinery industry, which achieved an early precocity in a setting of abundant land and scarce labour.

(iii) *Technology*

The potential spreading effects which may flow from the achievement of high momentum in a given industrial sector evidently have something to do with the technology required in that sector. For example, cotton textile factories require a different kind of input with wider potential ramifications in introducing industrial know-how than, say, breweries; railways, than meat-packing plants.[16] But the lesson of economic history appears to be that the response of the society to the potentials of a new sector using modern technology is probably a more important variable than the nature of the technology itself. In the fourth quarter of the nineteenth century strong impulses towards industrialization flowed from the introduction of the steam saw and cream separator in Sweden, where the will and ability to exploit the potential spreading effects was strong; while the Argentine response to extensive railroadization before 1914 was weak. As Lockwood emphasizes, the organization after 1868 of marketing and quality control in the Japanese silk industry—with low modern technological content—had significant general effects in modernizing the economy;[17] whereas in China in the early twentieth century, the development of quite modern cotton textile mills in a few cities had only a damped effect.

It is, of course, difficult sharply to separate those spreading effects which result from the scale and momentum of a sector from those attributable to the responsiveness of a society to the potential backward and forward linkages. Nevertheless, wherever power-driven machinery is involved, the potential exists to learn a wide range of the fundamental tricks of an industrial society. The incentive to learn will be greater if the modern industry is substantial, profitable, and rapidly expanding. But the wide range of leading sectors which have proved consistent with a take-off suggests that the technology involved is not, in itself, a decisive variable.

(iv) *Capital Formation: Industry and Social Overhead Capital*

The sources of capital required for the early stage of industrialization are familiar enough. . . . As economic history has come to be re-examined in the same terms as the problems of contemporary underdeveloped areas, we have come increasingly to accept these three propositions. First, a very high proportion of total capital investment in the preconditions and take-off period must go into social overhead capital; and this fact lays a heavy burden on the rôle of the state in the early stages of industrialization. Second, in most but not all of the early industrialization processes the initial supply of capital is not a crucial bottleneck. The able and willing industrial entrepreneur can usually scrape up enough to start, if technology permits a beginning in a small way. And if rapid increases in output are attained, a high rate of marginal saving can provide the basis for expansion. Third, the emergence of a rate of net investment sufficient to outstrip the rate of increase in population and to yield a substantial and positive net rate of growth is at least as much the result of prior growth as a cause of growth.

Both historical and contemporary experience would suggest that we must look at the investment process in these early stages not in terms of a once-over shift in the proportion of resources allocated to investment, at the expense of consumption, but as a dynamic process in which developments in agriculture, social overhead capital, the foreign balance, and industry interact to produce a rise in total output under institutional circumstances (including fiscal policy) which also yield a high marginal rate of savings.[18]

In this process of interaction, there is a certain evident priority in time for investment in the build-up of social overhead capital, including that form which yields men with modern technical training and outlook.

In the eighteenth century education, in this broad sense, involved neither large resource outlays nor conscious policy: although Adam Smith, among others, was aware that the character of the educational system was a significant variable in the growth process. In pre-1868 Japan, the quiet sending of men abroad proved a significant and, in the end, essential and productive form of investment, although trivial in resource terms. In the American North the spread of public primary education in the first half of the nineteenth century was a quite massive factor in the society's modernization; and the engineering bias of training at the United States Military Academy provided a highly useful corps of men who played a strategic rôle in the construction of the American transport network. In Germany, the technical schools represented a wider and more conscious effort to provide the human capital for industrialization. In short, the educational process, formal or informal, consciously created or casually introduced, represents an essential primary investment required for industrialization.

Similarly, take-off has been preceded, virtually without exception, by a substantial build-up of transport and other forms of social overhead capital. The most important functions of such investment have been, of course, to reduce transport costs within the economy, to permit resources to be cheaply and efficiently combined, to enlarge the domestic market, and to make possible the efficient conduct of foreign trade. It is in such a market setting that the initial leading sectors are likely to emerge.

The problem of capital supply directly to the leading sectors depends, of course, on what those sectors turn out to be. Where railways have served as a leading sector government has usually played an important rôle: as the guarantor of a minimum rate of return; via subsidies; or by directly financing and managing the construction and operation of the lines. Broadly speaking, the degree of government intervention has depended on the length of the lines and especially on when a rapid increase in traffic could be expected.[19] Where lines were laid into new areas, which required a considerable period of development, government intervention or subsidy on a large scale was generally required to cover this time interval. Where railway lines linked existing and proximate commercial and industrial centres, private enterprise has been able to carry a higher proportion of the load.

On the other hand, when the leading sectors have been in, say, textiles or import substitution industries the initial sums required could usually be privately raised, and subsequent expansion financed by plough-back of profits. It was the entrepreneur rather than the initial pool of capital that was crucial.

One dynamic consequence of the take-off for the capital formation process deserves notice. Quite aside from the increase in investment in the take-off industries themselves and in the industries stimulated by backward linkages, the lateral effects of take-off eased the problem of capital formation by enlarging urban areas and shifting the structural balance of the society. In the rural areas of a traditional or transitional society income above minimum levels of consumption tended to flow to landowners who often sterilized a substantial proportion of the surplus in high living or in investment of low productivity. This tendency, at least as much as pressure from the peasantry, justified land reform schemes. The saving habits of urban populations (and the greater ease of taxing them) made the expansion of the cities an important element in raising the rate of investment in modern activities. Thus the lateral as well as the backward linkages which accompany take-off may assist the raising of the marginal rate of saving and increase the resources accessible to the modern sector of the economy.

(v) Foreign Exchange

As the analysis thus far has already suggested, foreign trade can relate to the take-off process in four distinct ways.

First, an increase in exports may be essential to acquire the resources (including the security for capital imports) required for the build-up of social overhead capital.

Second, an increase in exports may be essential to acquire the equipment and industrial raw materials necessary to build and operate the first group of industrial sectors; and, more generally, to permit the economy to acquire the resources which industrialization demands but which neither its existing industrial skill nor its natural resources can immediately and economically provide.

Third, an increase in exports may be essential to provide economically a margin of food supplies to feed a growing and increasingly urban population.

Fourth, an expansion of exports in commodities with high price or income elasticity of demand may provide the foundation for rapid growth in the leading take-off sector (as in the case of Britain[20]) or in agricultural or raw material sectors which, in turn, help set in motion the industrialization process (the United States, Russia, Sweden).

The relative importance of these functions has varied with the situation of each nation, notably with the scale of transport investment required to create an effective domestic market, with its endowment of agricultural and raw material resources, and with the size of its domestic market.

The rôle of import-substitution industries (generally shielded by tariffs) deserves a special word. In New England the regional take-off was based on the emergence of an economical cotton textile industry, capable of competing in the American market with certain mass consumption grades of British textile manufactures; and the Japanese take-off was based, less exclusively, on this kind of development. In France, Germany, and Russia the emergence of such import-substitution sectors played a substantial but lesser rôle in the take-off. In later cases of the twentieth century, take-offs have been based on import substitution not primarily in textiles but in an expanding range of metal-fabricated products, for both consumption and capital formation (e.g. Argentina, Mexico, India).

Such cases of leading sectors rooted in import-substitution do not contravene the argument that the expansion of foreign trade is an essential condition for industrialization, in its early stages; for new import requirements are created as the leading sectors take hold, even if the leading sectors lie in the range of import-substitution industries. The consequences for Argentina of Peron's policy towards agricultural exports and the scale of assistance required to India, during its take-off, at a time when its existing exports are not capable of radical expansion, underline from recent experience how and why the take-off is likely to increase sharply the total import requirement. Nevertheless, the case of take-off based on import substitution leading sectors deserves special analysis; for take-offs have been triggered not merely by the vigorous exploitation of expanding markets for exports, but by a creative reaction to a crisis in the foreign balance.

VI. SOME CONCLUSIONS

What conclusions emerge from this exploration of linkages?

1. It is clear that, by one route or another, each of the variables on our agenda bears on the development process in general and can help determine what kinds of leading sectors are appropriate to a given economy's take-off, and when they emerge. The rate of population increase, the population resource balance, the rate of increase in agricultural output and in agricultural productivity, the character of technology brought to bear in the leading sectors, the availability of capital and, notably, capital for social overhead outlays, and the evolution of foreign trade are, evidently, all relevant variables in examining the early stage of economic development. They belong to any system of "organized complexity" addressed to the process of economic growth.

2. How these variables relate to one another—the patterns they may form—can vary greatly. There is no single set of linkages that logic or historical experience decrees as universal. Like biologists we are examining differing arrangements of the building blocks of growth.

3. The outcome for an economy of any particular set of initial technical relationships—in the population resource balance, agricultural resources, etc.—appears greatly to depend on the institutional and human response to them. In the vocabulary of *The Process of Economic Growth*, the propensities appear more important than the yields; that is, an active response to an unpromising technical economic setting may produce a better result than a sluggish or complacent response to a more promising setting. No serious analysis of growth can be confined to its economic elements.

4. Although we are dealing with a system inherently interacting, there does appear to be a certain rough sequence in the development process, certain bottlenecks or thresholds which must be overcome before growth can proceed. The initial requirement appears to be the emergence of a minimum cadre of modern men; that is, men who, for one reason or another, are willing to initiate modern economic activity and trained to do so. Second, there must begin a set of changes in agriculture which fulfil the three basic functions [required for take-off], . . . notably the transfer of some part of the rent flow into the supply of capital for the creation of social overhead capital. Third, the internal market must be restructured and the bases prepared for efficient foreign trade by the

build-up of social overhead capital; and this has required, in varying degrees, the leadership (or acquiescence) of the state and thus required important changes in the substance of politics and political objective. Fourth, there must emerge increased capacity to earn foreign exchange. Fifth, in a setting framed by these developments, entrepreneurs must emerge willing and able to manage the leading sectors and to respond to the potential spreading effects they set in motion. This sequence—and notably the sequence of the second, third, and fourth elements—can be logically defended; but, in historical cases they sometimes tumbled together in ways difficult to disentangle. The initiating rôle of modern men and the climactic rôle of an adequately large and responsive cadre of industrial entrepreneurs are easier to discern in the historical cases.

5. As the leading sectors take hold and their potential spreading effects are exploited, the other elements in the growth process remain important. A growing society requires an expanding flow of modern men, agricultural products, social overhead capital, and foreign exchange—not merely an initial stock. But the key to continuing growth—as to its initiation—is the spreading out to more and more sectors of the best relevant technology that the existing world pool can provide, and the endless expansion of the pool itself.

As I have argued elsewhere, the fundamental distinction between the economy of a traditional or transitional society and a modern growing economy lies in whether industrial innovation has or has not become a more or less regular flow.[21] Traditional societies were, evidently, capable of phases of growth in population, income, and, almost certainly in income per head; but their expansion phases came to a halt, and generally gave way to a self-reinforcing process of decline. These growth phases were marked by the emergence of men concerned with and capable of handling complex production and trade processes; by improvements in agriculture and the extension of acreage; by the expansion of social overhead capital and of both domestic and foreign trade. Although the proximate cause of the down-turns has varied widely, the fundamental cause appears an inability to break through the ceiling in productivity imposed by pre-Newtonian science and technology. The story of some traditional societies contains all the preconditions for take-off except a flow of modern industrial technology into their capital stock sufficient to fend off Ricardian diminishing returns to land and to cope with the Malthusian propensities of the people. Industrialization and modern economic growth can be viewed, therefore, as depending in the end on the systematic and progressive application of modern science and technology to the economy. Although a vast series of technical and societal changes must occur before this capacity becomes built into a society's outlook, habits, and institutions, the take-off is the interval when these deeper changes yield their result; and the emergence of leading sectors is the form this result assumes.

NOTES

1. For an analysis of the sectors of the economy, under the headings of primary growth (leading) sectors, supplementary growth sectors, and derived growth sectors, see chapter xi, *Process of Economic Growth*, Second Edition, Oxford, 1960.

2. S. S. Kuznets, *Secular Movements in Production and Prices*, Boston and New York, 1930. Also, A. F. Burns, *Production Trends in the United States since 1870*, New York, 1934. Although my own introduction to sectoral analysis and the economics of retardation came via Kuznets' work, W. G. Hoffmann developed similar ideas, in parallel, in the 1930's. See notably, *The Growth of Industrial Economies* (tr. W. O. Henderson and W. H. Chaloner) Manchester, 1958, a revised and expanded version of his 1931 *Stadiern und Typen der Industrialisierung*; and *British Industry, 1700-1950* (tr. W. O. Henderson and W. H. Chaloner) Oxford 1955, an expanded version of the 1939 German edition.

[3.] Kuznets, *op. cit.* chapter 1, pp. 1-58. For further discussion of the range of forces which determine retardation and references to other analyses, see the author's *Process of Economic Growth*, Second Edition, Oxford, 1960, pp. 96-108. The most complete single analysis of the various dimensions of retardation is, probably, that of A. F. Burns, *op. cit.* chapter iv, "Retardation in the Growth of Industries," pp. 96-173; but see also, W. G. Hoffmann, *British Industry 1700-1950*, Part B, III and Part D, III.

[4.] R. K. Merton, "Fluctuations in the Rate of Industrial Invention," *Quarterly Journal of Economics (1934-5)*, pp. 465-8.

[5.] The distinctions I have in mind here are closely related to those drawn by Warren Weaver in his essay, "A Quarter Century in the Natural Sciences," *President's Review, Annual Report of the Rockefeller Foundation*, New York, 1958, pp. 7-27. Weaver distinguishes, in the history of modern science, "problems of simplicity," in which, "under a significant range of circumstances, the first quantity depends wholly upon the second quantity, and not upon a large number of other factors"; "problems of disorganized complexity . . . in which the number of variables is very large, and . . . in which each of the many variables has a behaviour which is individually erratic, and may be totally unknown. But in spite of this helter-skelter or unknown behaviour of all the individual variables, the system as a whole possesses certain orderly and analyzeable average properties"; and "problems of organized complexity . . . which involve dealing simultaneously with a sizeable number of factors which are interrelated into an organic whole." A good deal of formal economic theory consists in "problems of simplicity"; the bulk of statistical analysis of whole economies or major segments of them consists in "problems of disorganized complexity," where an identification of persistent average behaviour is regarded as sufficient; the concept of take-off and stages-of-growth analysis represents an effort to get on to the middle ground of "organized complexity," in much the way we have succeeded in doing in business cycle analysis. See, for example, the author's "Some General Reflections on Capital Formation and Economic Growth" [Chapter 13 in this book], a chapter in *Capital Formation and Economic Growth, A Conference*, A Report of the National Bureau of Economic Research (Princeton, N.J.: Princeton University Press, 1956), where the case is made for "organized disaggregation" in growth analysis.

The Konstanz Conference

[6.] Although Kuznets did not analyze the spreading effects of leading sectors, his language at certain points implies a transcendent rôle for key sectors in their rapid growth phase (*op. cit.* pp. 3-4, 5, and 10):

"The picture of economic development suffers a curious change as we examine it first in a rather wide sphere, then in a narrower one. If we take the world from the end of the eighteenth century, there unrolls before us a process of uninterrupted and seemingly unslackened growth. We observe a ceaseless expansion of production and trade, a constant growth in the volume of power used, in the extraction of raw materials, in the quality and quantity of finished products.

"But if we single out the various nations or the separate branches of industry, the picture becomes less uniform. Some nations seem to have led the world at one time, others at another. Some industries were developing most rapidly at the beginning of the century, others at the end. Within single countries or within single branches of industries (on a world scale) there has not been uniform, unretarded growth. Great Britain has relinquished the lead in the economic world because its own growth, so vigorous through the period 1780-1850, has slackened. She has been overtaken by rapidly developing Germany and the United States. The textile industries which had so spectacular a rise toward the close of the eighteenth and the beginning of the nineteenth century ceded first place to pig iron, then to steel, while in turn the electrical industries assumed the leadership in the '80s and '90s.

"The view becomes further variegated if we distinguish the different industries in their national units. The rapid development of the English textiles came much earlier than that of the American. The Belgian coal output had reached nearly stable levels in the beginning of the twentieth century when American and German coal production were still showing substantial growth. Industries within the limits of one country frequently show a retardation of development as compared either with the national industry as a whole or with the same industry on a world-wide scale. . . .

"As we observe the various industries within a given national system, we see that the lead in development shifts from one branch to another. The main reason for this shift seems to be that a rapidly developing industry does not continue its vigorous growth indefinitely, but slackens its pace after a time, and is overtaken by industries whose period of rapid development comes later. Within any country we observe a succession of different branches of activity leading the process of development, and in each mature industry we notice a conspicuous slackening in the rate of increase. For example, the vigorous development of copper mining during the years 1880-1900 in the United States did not continue unabated, nor did that of steel after 1870-1900, nor railroad construction after 1830-1880. . . .

"In many industries there comes a time when the basic technical conditions are revolutionized. When such a fundamental change takes place, a new era begins. In the manufacturing industries it is frequently the period when the machine process first supplants hand labour to a substantial extent. In the extractive industries, it is either the moment when the sources and use of a commodity are discovered (petroleum) or when a new and wide application is found for a commodity hitherto but little used. As concrete examples of such periods, one may mention the decade 1780-90 for the cotton industry and pig iron production in Great Britain, the decade 1860-70 for steel, the decade of the '80s for the copper industry, the decade of the '30s for anthracite, and of the '40s for bituminous coal in the United States, the first and second decades of the nineteenth century for zinc smelting (Belgium-Saxony), the '60s for petroleum (United States), and the decade of the '70s for lead (United States). In all these cases we observe a revolutionary invention or discovery applied to the industrial process which becomes the chief method of production. Our generation has been the eye-witness of such changes in the automobile and radio industries." Similarly Hoffmann's analyses of growth, while not focused on the indirect consequences of rapid expansion of particular sectors, is often couched in language which suggests a transcendent rôle for particular industries and industrial complexes at particular stages of national growth.

[7.] A. O. Hirschman, *The Strategy of Economic Development*, New Haven, 1958, especially Chapter 6, "Interdependence and Industrialization," pp. 98–119.

[8.] A few examples may illuminate the rôle of backward linkages. In John Lord's partial compilation of the industrial distribution of steam horse-power in the period 1775–1800, the proportion installed in cotton mills increased as follows: 1775–85, .7 per cent; 1785–95, 37 per cent; 1795–1800, 49 per cent (*Capital and Steam Power, 1750–1800*, London, 1923, p. 175. For further evidence on the early installation of steam engines in cotton mills, see A. E. Musson and E. Robinson, "The Early Growth of Steam Power," *Economic History Review*, April 1959).

With respect to the American railways, Paul Cootner concludes: "In 1849, locomotives accounted for 435,000 horsepower or 35 per cent of the [steam horsepower] total. In the course of the next decade, the railroads acquired almost 75 per cent of the additional output, and its total rose to 1,943,000 horse-power or 60 per cent of the total. In a very real sense the American engineering industry was a product of the growth of the railroad . . ." (P. H. Cootner, *Transport Innovation and Economic Development: The Case of the U.S. Steam Railroads*, unpublished doctoral dissertation, 1953, M.I.T., Cambridge, Mass., chapter iv, derived from C. D. Daugherty, "An Index of the Installation of Machinery in the United States since 1850," *Harvard Business Review*, vi, 1927–8, pp. 283–4.) Between 1850 and 1860, rails rose from 8 per cent of pig iron production in the United States to 22 per cent; and, by 1881, rails were absorbing 76 per cent of steel output, and 34 per cent of total pig iron output. (J. H. Swank, *History of the Manufacture of Iron in All Ages*, Phila., 1890, pp. 316, 324, 387, 388.) In the twentieth century, the automobile has provided the most striking example of backward linkages. For example, by 1938 the automobile industry in the United States was the largest single consumer of the output of the following industries, absorbing the indicated percentages of their output:

	%		%		%
strip steel	51	alloy steel	54	plate glass	69
bars	34	steel in all forms	17	nickel	29
sheets	41	gasoline	90	lead	35
malleable iron	53	rubber	80	mohair	40

(*Automobile Facts and Figures*, New York, 1939, p. 39. For only slightly lower proportions for 1958 and contemporary scale of plastics consumption in automobiles, see *Automobile Facts and Figures*, Detroit, 1959, p. 60.)

[9.] Where a radically new production function is introduced into an existing industry—as in the case of the cotton industry of the eighteenth century—a

The Konstanz Conference 181

phase of increasing rate of increase may occur, before retardation sets in. See, for example, rate of increase of raw cotton imports, 1741–1831, E. Baines, *History of Cotton Manufactures*, London, 1835, p. 348.

[10.] Theoretically—and in fact—the basis for the subsequent leading sectors need not lie only in forward linkages generated by the initial leading sectors; although historically such technological and market connexions have been extremely important. The new leading sectors might arise from the application of technology generated independently of the first leading sectors or from the rapid expansion of output in sectors stimulated by high income elasticity of demand, as incomes rise.

[11.] If I may quote from the original take-off article (*Economic Journal*, March 1956, p. 44): "At any period of time it appears to be true even in a mature and growing economy that forward momentum is maintained as the result of rapid expansion in a limited number of primary sectors, whose expansion has significant external economy and other secondary effects. From this perspective the behaviour of sectors during the take-off is merely a special version of the growth process in general; or, put another way, growth proceeds by repeating endlessly, in different patterns, with different leading sectors, the experience of the take-off. Like the take-off, long-term growth requires that the society not only generate vast quantities of capital for depreciation and maintenance, for housing and for a balanced complement of utilities and other overheads, but also a sequence of highly productive primary sectors, growing rapidly, based on new production functions. Only thus has the aggregate marginal capital-output ratio been kept low."

[12.] The statistical evidence on rates and patterns of growth for Germany, Great Britain, and the United States suggest that the pre-1914 leading sectors may have begun to lose their capacity to sustain the rate of growth towards the close of the pre-1914 decade.

[13.] See the author's "The Problem of Achieving and Maintaining a High Rate of Economic Growth: An Historian's View," *American Economic Review*, May 1960, pp. 106–18.

[14.] R. S. Sayers, "The Springs of Technical Progress in Britain, 1919–39," *Economic Journal*, June 1950.

[15.] See *Stages of Economic Growth*, pp. 21–4.

[16.] For example, a recent study of the economic history of Argentina suggests that the acceleration in industrialization from the mid-1930's was due, in part, to the fact that wider spreading effects flowed from the import-substitution industries that then took hold than from the earlier phase of industrialization, closely linked to the handling and processing of agricultural products. G. Di Tella, *The Economic History of Argentina, 1914–1933* and M. Zymelman, *The Economic History of Argentina, 1933–1952*, unpublished doctoral dissertations, 1959 and 1958, respectively, M.I.T., Cambridge, Mass.

[17.] W. W. Lockwood, *The Economic Development of Japan*, Princeton, 1954, pp. 338–9.

[18.] This dynamic view of the manner in which the rate of capital formation increases bears on the question of the likely course of living standards during the take-off. Two sector growth models—like Marx's and those derived from Keynesian income analysis—lend themselves to the hypothesis that living standards are likely to fall as industrialization begins; that is, there is a tendency to slip into some version of the notion that what is involved is a kind of once-over shift in the proportion of income invested, bound to bear harshly on the level of consumption. In fact, the outcome for living standards during the take-off depends heavily on what happens in the agricultural sector, for an exceedingly high proportion of consumption at likely take-off levels of income consists of food and fibres. In some cases, an increase in agricultural output faster than the rate of population increase will depend on large social overhead outlays of long gestation period; e.g. where massive irrigation projects are involved. Since increased food and fibre consumption is an important component of such investment, a conflict must exist between investment and consumption. In general, however, increases in agricultural productivity have hinged on widespread changes in method, where the investment involved is of short gestation period and highly productive. It is to the detailed economics of the agricultural sector that one must look to weigh the likely upshot for living standards during the take-off, not merely to the large aggregates; and both theory and history suggest that many current formulations are excessively pessimistic. More than that, leaving the social overhead problem aside, a rise in domestic income (which in most poor societies implies a rise in agricultural productivity and retained income) is an essential market foundation for the spread of industrialization, unless leading sectors are to be built around the requirements for military expansion. This issue arises directly in Prof. Tsuru's treatment of Japan, Chapter 8.

[19.] For the relative rôle of government in financing various American railways of differing length, gestation period, and period of production, see P. H. Cootner, *op. cit.*, especially Chapters II and IV.

[20.] For a cogent argument of this point see K. Berrill, "International Trade and the Rate of Economic Growth," *Economic History Review*, April 1960.

[21.] *The Stages of Economic Growth*, Cambridge and New York, 1960, pp. 4-6; and "Industrialization and Economic Growth," paper prepared for the First International Congress of Economic History, Stockholm, August 1960. In this context industrialization includes, of course, the application of techniques, rooted in modern technology, to agricultural and raw material production and processing, as well as to industrial fabrication, in the narrow sense.

EPILOGUE

Special pressures and distractions, at play first on Professor Hague and then on myself, confront me with the task of writing this reply to the debate a little more than two years after it took place at Konstanz. There may be some virtue in this lapse of time. It may permit a detachment that mitigates the chivalrous irregularity of the Association's invitation to one contentious participant to provide an introduction to this book. This procedure was judged at the time more appropriate than my taking the time of the conference to reply to Professor Landes' summing up at the ninth session and to Professor Solow's, at the final session.

I

Re-reading the papers and Professor Hague's summary of the discussion I believe that in this volume the conference speaks well for itself. The

Association succeeded in bringing together a distinguished group of historians, specializing on particular nations; statisticians; theorists; and experts on functional aspects of growth. They answered, each from his own perspective, the question: Is the concept of take-off useful, misleading, or wrong? In so doing they laid on the table their latest reflections on the process of economic growth and, either implicitly or explicitly, their own analytic approaches to the problem. Those contributions are, evidently, the principal justification for the volume.

As for the take-off, it will have to look after itself. Each reader will make his own assessment of the debate. Like all intellectual constructs it will survive only if it meets the hard pragmatic test of usefulness to others—if it illuminates problems that deeply concern them. No market is—or should be—more ruthlessly competitive than the market-place of ideas, even though, as the record of this conference suggests, it is an oligopolistic market; that is, the coming in of a new idea is felt by the other producers to involve a potential shift in the shape of the demand curve that confronts their own products, and they react appropriately. As I remarked at one point in the debate, the introduction of a new concept—especially a new term—is an act of aggression against respected colleagues and friends. Both at the time—and in retrospect—I found the debate instructive.

Taking stock of the papers and the discussion at this distance I shall use this occasion to do two things. First, I shall reply more spaciously than the discussion permitted to Professor Kuznets' criticism of the take-off. His approach was not only more frontal, but also embraced many of the issues raised by others. Beyond Professor Kuznets' four grand questions, the summary of the discussion contains, by and large, what I would still wish to say about the other papers, with one exception—Professor Solow's final statement. My second purpose will be, therefore, to respond briefly to his interesting challenge to re-formulate the take-off concept in terms an economic theorist is likely to find more comprehensible.

II

The first of Professor Kuznets' questions is whether there is a sharp rise in the investment rate during take-off and a sharp rise in the rate of growth of total national product.

He begins with an "implicit" conclusion; namely, that the take-off should see a sharp rise in total national product. In fact, a rise in the rate of investment need not yield an equivalent acceleration in national product. The magnitudes are not rigorously related in the short period; and even over the long period capital-output ratios may vary. Moreover, forces may be operating during the take-off which yield stagnation or even decline in certain massive sectors of the economy (for example, within agriculture, in agricultural surplus areas); and these could damp or even overwhelm the effects on real product of the rise in the rate of investment in social overhead capital and industry.

In the general case, I am confident that the data—if we had them—would exhibit an acceleration in national product during the take-off years; but I shall confine my observations here to the movement of the investment rate during take-off.

In presenting the notion of the take-off, I pointed out the following factors which might alter what we might call "pure Arthur Lewis" (or 5–10 per cent) behaviour of the investment rate during the take-off.

(1) Variations as among nations in the rate of population increase.
(2) Variations in the level of investment required for social overhead capital (mainly transport) in the pre-take-off and take-off decades.
(3) Variations in the capital-output ratio.
(4) The enclave case; that is, a high rate of investment in a narrow region or export sector, with very damped effect—if any—on the economy as a whole.

In addition, I noted a difficulty which has evidently not been remedied and may prove beyond remedy; that is, we do not have reliable investment data for the pre-take-off decades in most societies.

The reader may also recall that I referred to the rise in the investment rate during take-off as a "necessary but not sufficient condition for the take-off"; and in the summary of the stages of economic growth (*Economic History Review*), I referred to the achievement of a sustained rate of net investment of the order of 10 per cent as an "essentially tautological" way of defining take-off.

What is the point here? The point is that within normal ranges of population increase and of the capital-output ratio, a regular and substantial increase in national product per head requires, by definition, a net investment rate of something like 10 per cent. We can find cases where such rates persisted in pre-take-off decades, usually because of heavy outlays for long-distance transport or because of limited enclaves of modern economic activity. There is nothing in the take-off analysis as a whole to make a shift in the investment rate itself a crucial test of the take-off.

On the other hand, I am confident that a rise in the investment rate will prove to be a normal take-off phenomenon, when more evidence is available. Of its nature, the take-off process is likely to bring about a rise in the investment rate for three reasons. The rise will come about in part through the plough-back of profits in the rapidly industrializing sectors; that is, in the leading sectors themselves and those directly linked to them, where a high marginal rate of saving is likely to prevail.

It will come about also from the more widespread expansion of investment in modern sectors that the acceleration of urbanization (and the probable rise in *per capita* income) during take-off are likely to bring about.

And the usually substantial rôle of governments during the take-off—notably in mobilizing social overhead capital—is likely to reinforce the other two tendencies.

I submit that a careful scrutiny of both contemporary and historical data—where they exist—including the data on Great Britain, Germany, Sweden, and Japan in this volume are consistent with this view: the investment rate is likely to rise during take-off; the extent of the rise will vary with specific factors, notably the scale of social overhead requirements; but a rise in the investment rate is not the sole relevant criterion for take-off.

Behind this argument lies my disagreement with the following passage from Professor Kuznets' paper: "All that is claimed here is that aggregative data for a number of countries do not support Professor Rostow's distinction and characterization of the "take-off" stage. On the other hand, the fact that the evidence is confined to aggregative data does not limit their bearing. Economic growth is an aggregative process; sectoral changes are interrelated with aggregative changes, and can be properly weighted only after they have been incorporated into the aggregative framework; and the absence of required aggregative changes severely limits the likelihood of the implicit strategic sectoral changes."

With this I disagree. Modern economic growth is essentially a sectoral process. It is rooted in the progressive diffusion of the production functions modern technology can provide. These changes in technique and organization can only be studied sectorally. The sectors are, of course, intimately interrelated; and changes in income flows play a rôle; but the aggregates—like any other index number—merely sum up the performance of the sectors. Put another way—of course growth is, in one sense and on one definition, an aggregative concept; that is, it consists in a regular expansion of output per head. But without sectoral analysis we cannot explain why growth occurs. I would not, of course, abandon the aggregates. But to confine growth analysis to them is to play the piano while wearing mittens.

III

Professor Kuznets' second point follows from his first: "There is no clear distinction between the 'pre-conditions' and the 'take-off' stages."

In presenting the concept of take-off, I sought to make clear that it flowed directly from the form of sectoral analysis I developed in *The Process of Economic Growth* and, in particular, it derived from the notion of leading sectors in growth analysis elaborated from *The Process* and first presented at the IEA Conference at Santa Marguerita in 1955.

Contrast, if you will, these two passages. First from Professor Kuznets' "Notes" (p. 28): "But a review of the empirical evidence on this point [that is, on leading sectors] holds little interest if I am correct in assuming that the major distinctive characteristic of the 'take-off' is a marked rise in the rate of growth of *per capita* and hence of total income." Second, from the conclusion of the take-off article in the *Economic Journal* (1956):

> This hypothesis is, then, a return to a rather old-fashioned way of looking at economic development. The take-off is defined as an industrial revolution, tied directly to radical changes in methods of production, having their decisive consequence over a relatively short period of time.... What this argument asserts is that the rapid growth of one or more new manufacturing sectors is a powerful and essential engine of economic transformation. Its power derives from the multiplicity of its forms of impact, when a society is prepared to respond positively to this impact. Growth in such sectors, with new production functions of high productivity, in itself tends to raise output per head; it places incomes in the hands of men who will not merely save a high proportion of an expanding income but who will plough it into highly productive investment; it sets up a chain of effective demand for other manufactured products; it sets up a requirement for enlarged urban areas, whose capital costs may be high, but whose population and market organization help to make industrialization an on-going process; and, finally, it opens up a range of external economy effects which, in the end, help to produce new leading sectors when the initial impulse of the take-off's leading sectors begins to wane.

This is the central proposition. I believe the national product and investment aggregates will normally reflect this complex sectoral process. But we must look directly at the take-off process in the sectors, not at the aggregates alone.

It is possible that we have all been so deeply committed by the Keynesian revolution (and by Marx' economic analysis) to think in terms of two-sector models—in which output is broken down into consumption and capital goods; income, into spending and saving—that there is a perhaps unconscious resistance to overcome before we are prepared to enter deeply into sectoral analysis. Both theoretical and statistical analysts would, evidently, prefer to stay with the large aggregates.

The point takes on a certain drama because, in my own education, I derived much from the early work of Professor Kuznets on secular trends in prices and production. As my paper for this conference suggests, I moved on from his analysis of deceleration in individual sectors to examine the various spreading effects which flow from them. When this is done systematically, the over-all sequence of growth becomes not merely a matter of movement in the aggregates; it becomes a succession of surges, in clustered sectors, linked in turn to the sequence of leading sectors which mark the story of modern economic history.

This is the view, I submit, which is implicit or explicit in the work of most economic historians of particular nations; this is the view which, in the end, underlies the most pertinent generalized insights in the work of Schumpeter and Walther Hoffmann; and this is the view which once caught the imagination of Professor Kuznets himself, as the long footnote quotation [in Note [6] of "Leading Sectors and the Take-Off" in this chapter] will indicate.

In a quite technical and literal sense, the stages of growth analysis is in part—on the supply side—an elaboration of Kuznets' early judgment that: "As we observe the various industries within a given national system, we see that the lead in development shifts from one branch to another."

Let me relate this argument to the distinction in time between the take-off and the pre-conditions periods. How were the take-off dates set? As I say in the paper submitted to the conference:

> ... working with historical data, I have sought to use the full range of quantitative and nonquantitative materials available to form an approximate judgment as to when the rate and scale of a leading sector's growth has been such as to induce substantial further expansion in the economy, also of high momentum, via its backward and lateral linkages. The take-off dates I have tentatively offered on other occasions are the product of such investigations of the total impact of the initial group of leading sectors in the industrialization process of particular economies. It is the coming in of the first leading sector (or sectors), on a scale and with a momentum to induce substantial spreading effects which creates the *saltum* economies sometimes execute.
>
> Now a major *proviso*. It cannot be too strongly emphasized that the secondary effects of rapid growth in a sector suffused with new technology are not automatic. They are potential effects which require active exploitation by a society's men and institutions. In fact, one measure of a society's ability to move into sustained economic growth is its ability to seize upon and to exploit with vigour all three types of potentiality which flow from a leading sector.
>
> ... Growth is, thus, only an automatic process if one can assume that a society will respond actively and effectively to the potentials for growth available to it.
>
> In the light of this argument, the take-off must be defined in two steps: first, it is the period in the life of an economy when, for the first time, one or more modern industrial sectors take hold, with high rates of growth, bringing in not merely new production functions but backward and lateral spreading effects on a substantial scale; second, for a take-off to be said to have occurred, the economy must demonstrate the capacity to exploit the forward linkages as well, so that new leading sectors emerge as the older ones decelerate. It is this demonstration of the capacity to shift from one set of leading sectors to another which distinguished abortive industrial surges of the transition period from a true take-off. This functional requirement has determined that the take-off be defined as embracing, say, a 20-year interval. Some such substantial period is necessary to demonstrate that a society is capable of overcoming the structural crisis which the initial surge of growth is likely to bring and is capable of introducing the changing flow of technology upon which sustained growth depends.

I would be gratified—and I am sure Professor Kuznets would be easier in mind—if I could offer a straightforward statistical test; for example, the period of maximum rate of growth in a designated leading sector. But the problem is not that easy. First, the maximum rate of growth for a new industry is likely to come at a time when its scale is not significant enough to induce the spreading effects which are key to the take-off analysis. Second, the spreading effects themselves are difficult to trace with statistical precision, notably what I call the lateral and forward effects.

Nevertheless the spreading effects are key to the notion of leading sectors. Professor Kuznets' mathematical illustration (pp. 29–30) of the limited impact of one or two high growth sectors on the industrial production index misses this point. The industrial growth directly and indirectly induced by the surge in British cotton production in the last two decades of the eighteenth century or induced by the railway surge in the United States in the two decades before the Civil War cannot be estimated by looking at cotton or railway statistics alone.

In the present state of knowledge, then, the estimate of when a take-off occurs cannot be a simple statistical exercise, although it requires the use of all the statistical data available. One must examine the whole performance of an economy to satisfy oneself that it is responding actively to the potential spreading effects which derive from the leading sectors. It follows from this fact that there is a margin of legitimate debate about when a take-off should be dated.

In presenting the take-off, I referred explicitly to two problems, both of which bear on Professor Kuznets' feeling that the line between preconditioning and take-off may be fuzzy.

One is the case of an abortive industrial surge which does not lead on to self-sustained growth. Many nations have experienced such surges; the United States during the Napoleonic Wars, for example; India in the last decade of the nineteenth and the early twentieth century; Brazil in the period 1901–12; Argentina and China during the First World War. The subsequent periods of stagnation or relapse are so clear in such cases that they do not present great difficulty.

The more difficult problem is what one might call the problem of the decade preceding take-off—a problem referred to in the original take-off article. The surges of industrial growth which marked the take-off did not, of course, arise out of the blue. The take-off, in my view, is a recognizable discontinuity in the stream of history; but it is not a process without a history.

The pre-take-off decades are, generally, dominated by changes in the economy and in the society as a whole which are essential for later growth. These changes are likely to involve the training of new men; alterations in agricultural institutions and techniques; an expansion of trade at home and abroad, an expansion of cities; and in many cases there are important political changes as well in the pre-take-off decades which are necessary before take-off can begin. But, of course, there is likely also to be some expansion in industrial output.

In Britain the years of war with the United States ease the problem; that is, there is, despite much industrial ferment, not much basis for including the 1770's in the take-off. But what about the 1830's for the United States; the 1840's for Germany; the 1860's for Sweden; the 1880's for Russia?

These are all, in my view, debatable cases on my sectoral definition of take-off. I have examined the evidence and weighed it. I have concluded that, on balance, the scale of the leading sectors and the extent of their spreading effects in these preceding decades do not justify their inclusion in the take-off; and that the activities dominating the economy in these intervals were primarily non-industrial, typical of the pre-conditioning process rather than the take-off. But I do not regard my assessments of each case as final or beyond challenge.

Of its nature, this is a problem that can only be dealt with case by case; and the country papers included in this book provide an opportunity to do so. What I would say here is, simply, that the quite tractable problem of "the preceding decade" is the only problem I perceive in distinguishing, in particular cases, the pre-conditions from the take-off.

IV

Professor Kuznets' third point is the following: "The analysis of the take-off and pre-conditions stage neglects the effect of historical heritage, time of entry into the process of modern economic growth, degree of backwardness, and other relevant factors on the characteristics of the early phases of modern economic growth in the different traditional countries."

I would not agree that I have neglected these factors, if by neglect is meant a failure to consider them, to refer to them, and to make certain prelilminary observations about them. The problem may arise from the fact that Professor Kuznets focused his attention on the take-off article published in *The Economic Journal* in 1956 rather than on Chapter III in *The Stages of Economic Growth*. Moreover he did not have available the paper focused directly on the dynamics of traditional societies I presented to the Stockholm Conference of 1960, nor the still more ambitious communal effort to order the preconditioning process, to which I contributed: *The Emerging Nations* (Boston, 1961, ed. M. F. Millikan and D. L. M. Blackmer).

If by neglect Professor Kuznets means that there is much more to be done in trying to make order of the interval between the first modern intrusion on a traditional society and the period of take-off, I wholeheartedly agree.

The key economic problems of the pre-conditions are, I believe, fairly straightforward and familiar. I list them as a sequence [in] my paper for this conference. They appear in different form in each nation, of course, depending on its prior economic history, population-resource balance, etc. But I do not believe the strict economics of the pre-conditions period will present us with great difficulties, if we choose to do systematic cross-comparisons of national experiences.

The great challenge in the analysis of the pre-conditioning process will lie, I believe, in its non-economic dimensions: the psychological, social, and political processes which interact with each other and with economic change, to move societies from their own particular version of a traditional society to their own particular version of a growing society. Here, I would simply agree that, although I have had somewhat more to say about the range of problems than Professor Kuznets' stricture would imply, we all have more work to do.

V

Professor Kuznets' fourth point, concerns the question of how self-sustained growth really is. Here I shall simply quote the most relevant passage from my paper for this conference which attempts to deal with this important and wholly legitimate query:

> ... To what extent is growth truly automatic after the take-off? In one sense, it follows directly from the fact of deceleration that growth is not automatic. If, on this view, a society is to sustain a high average rate of growth, it must engage in an endless struggle against deceleration; for while the flow of modern science and technology may offer the potentiality of fending off Ricardian diminishing returns indefinitely, a society which wishes to exploit this potentiality must repeat the creative pain of actually introducing new production functions as the old leading sectors decelerate; and it must demonstrate the capacity to exploit with vigour their potential spreading effects. In this sense sustained growth requires the repetition of the take-off process. (A point made in the original take-off article.) It requires the organization around new technology of new and vigorous management; new types of workers; new types of financing and marketing arrangements. It requires struggle not against the constraints of the traditional society—whose economic bonds are decisively broken in the take-off—but against constraints created in the previous generation or two, around the peculiar imperatives of an older set of leading sectors now no longer capable of carrying the economy forward at its old pace.
>
> There is, then, nothing automatic and easy about the inner mechanics—the logistics, as it were—of sustained growth.
>
> But in a larger sense, the experience of take-off may, when we have a longer time perspective, prove to be a definitive transition, like the loss of innocence. The reason for this judgment is that behind the whole industrial process lies the acceptance of the Newtonian outlook, the acceptance of the world of modern science and technology. Phases of difficulty and even relative stagnation after the take-off may, of course, occur; and they may be protracted.

In short, on present historical evidence, it appears fair to say that the larger psychological, social, technical, and institutional changes required for a take-off are such as to make it unlikely that we shall see a true lapsing back. Men in societies must continue to struggle to keep growth moving forward; and one of the purposes of this mode of analysis, rooted in leading sectors, is to specify the nature of that struggle. But the deeper fundamentals required for an effective take-off appear, on present evidence, sufficiently powerful to make growth an ongoing process, on long term. Nevertheless, we still have much to learn about the longer spans of the industrialization process.

VI

In the end, Professor Kuznets suggests that we substitute the notion of the "early modern growth stage" for the take-off. This is, evidently, a matter which each of us will decide for himself. I can understand how a concentration on aggregative evidence might lead to this view; and, as I said in the original take-off article: "from the perspective of the economic historian the isolation of a take-off period is a distinctly arbitrary process." A part of my mind and of my training is wholly sympathetic to the notion that economic history—like other forms of history—is a seamless web.

To understand why, on balance, I find the notion of take-off proper and essential, one must go back to what it is that distinguishes a modern society from a traditional society. Here Professor Kuznets and I substantially agree. He says: "Behind all this is the increasing stock of useful knowledge derived from modern science, and the capacity of society, under the spur of modern ideology, to evolve institutions that permit a greater exploitation of the growth potential provided by that increasing stock of knowledge."

The history of traditional societies offers us many cases of growth, including cases of significant changes in production functions. What is lacking is a more or less regular flow of innovation on a scale capable of defeating Ricardian diminishing returns and the Malthusian propensities of the people. On this view of what modern growth is about, the take-off has a particular meaning that transcends the aggregates and the sectors; it is the phase when a society demonstrates the capacity not only to mount an accelerated industrial surge, but to move on to absorb and apply new production functions—progressively spreading the techniques that modern technology can offer, as deceleration operates on the initial leading sectors.

In that sense, the take-off is a definitive watershed in a society's history: the innovational process has ceased to be sporadic and is a more or less regular institutionalized part of the society's life. The demonstration of that capacity gives the take-off a fundamental historical meaning.

The basic problem that the counterpoint between Professor Kuznets' and my position poses is this: how shall we relate aggregative to sectoral analysis; or in the term I derived from Warren Weaver and used in my paper for the conference, how shall we make growth analysis a system of "organized complexity"? We must come to understand how the sectoral forces we know to be both relevant and interrelated link to each other and to the growth process as a whole.

In a sense our task is to relate and to make order of the insights of the early and the later work of Professor Kuznets. The later Kuznets moves from the austere world of reputable statistics, of a high order of aggregation, to the grand qualitative vision of the diffusion over the face of the globe of modern science and technology. The heart of the growth process lies in between, in the interwoven life of the sectors.

VII

Now, briefly, a word in reply to Professor Solow. He asks: how can one translate all this fuzzy talk about take-off into something which an economic theorist can understand and grapple with; what are the initial conditions, parameters, and changes in rules of behaviour which distinguish a take-off from earlier periods?

In one sense, the problem may not be soluble. Economic growth is the result of an interacting process involving the economic, social, and political sectors of a society, including the emergence of a corps of entrepreneurs who are psychologically motivated and technically prepared regularly to lead the way in introducing new production functions into the economy.

Economic theory has been, in Warren Weaver's phrase, a world of "problems of simplicity"; and from this fact it has derived its great power, over a limited range. It may not be able to function in the world of "organized complexity," which growth analysis, at its best, is bound to be. Growth analysts cannot and should not cut their labours down to the level of simplification, aggregation, and abstraction which the tools of economic theory require, any more than they should restrict themselves to the consideration of those variables only for which reputable statistical measures exist.

On the other hand, formal economic theory has already contributed some substantial insights to growth analysis (e.g. the Harrod-Domar model and Professor Solow's work on production functions and "the residual"); and the effort at communication should be pressed from both sides.

Can the take-off concept be expressed, then, in terms of initial conditions, changes in rules of behaviour, and parameters?

First, the parameters. As a first approximation one can describe these as three: the rate of population increase, the state of existing technology, and the availability of known natural resources. In fact, all are subject to change out of inter-action with the growth process itself; but no great violence is done by assuming them fixed for purposes of formally examining what a take-off is about.

As Professor Solow points out we require a definition. For these purposes we define the take-off as the period when a society begins regularly to absorb new production functions in a setting where the direct and indirect consequences of this new mode of behaviour yield a more or less regular increase in output *per capita*.

Second, the initial conditions. The whole process of the pre-conditioning is, in a sense, a statement of the initial conditions. For a society to absorb new production functions in ways which generate the spreading effects on which the take-off depends requires massive prior change away from the pattern of the traditional society. Technically this pre-conditioning embraces a build-up of transport sufficient to begin to make the markets of the economy interact quickly and efficiently and to make domestic raw materials available at tolerable economic cost; an initial minimum quantum of literate and technically trained personnel in the working force; an initial minimum quantum of power resources, and other overhead capital. In addition, for take-off to proceed successfully, the bases must be laid during the pre-conditions period for the generation of increased flows of agricultural products and, usually, of imports. These are required both to feed the inevitably expanding urban population and to meet fixed and working capital requirements which the economy, at its assumed stage, cannot itself generate.

This whole set of changes in the economy's infra-structure, working force, its agriculture, and foreign exchange earning (or borrowing) capacity can be generalized in the proposition that before take-off can occur there must be, in the widest sense, a certain minimum prior build-up of social overhead capital if the necessary spreading effects from the take-off's leading sectors are, in fact, to occur or if the take-off is not to be distorted or actually aborted by the lack of adequate flows of working (and fixed) capital in the form of agricultural products and imports. The scale of this prior minimum build-up will vary from one economy to another depending on its prior history, geography, natural resources, etc. Both history (pre-1914 Russia) and the contemporary scene (post-1958 Communist China) indicate that nations have begun take-off without a balanced stock of pre-conditioning capital, and these structural flaws raised serious problems for them during the take-off years.

Third, changes in rules of behaviour. The prior build-up of social overhead capital, in the special generalized sense used above, is a necessary but not sufficient condition for take-off. There must also emerge a minimum initial group of entrepreneurs prepared, in the assumed environment, to launch the take-off's leading sectors and to react positively, in the sectors linked backward and laterally to the leading sectors, to the potentials for profit which the momentum of the leading sectors provide. Their central differentiating characteristic resides in their willingness and ability to introduce new production functions. They can be either public servants or private entrepreneurs; but the innovations required in the social overhead sectors (including, for these purposes, agriculture and the generation of adequate flows of foreign exchange) has usually decreed that entrepreneurs, as here defined, emerge in both.

Technically, it is the inescapable rôle of the state in these social overhead functions that justifies the proposition, stated in *The Stages of Economic Growth*, that the most important pre-condition for take-off is often political.

Thus, one can say to Professor Solow that take-off requires by way of initial conditions the prior build-up of a certain minimum quantum of social overhead capital, to provide the technical conditions for the requisite spreading effects; and it requires a change in rules of behavior such that new production functions available are actually brought to bear in the capital stock, within the initial leading sectors and those linked backward and laterally to them.

The resulting path of change in output per head will be determined by the parameters, as well as by the scale and efficiency of the entrepreneurial corps, in the public and private sectors—efficiency being measured by the rate at which they close the gap between existing relevant technology and pre-take-off technology in the economy. At this stage, as Professor Solow properly reminds us, the path of growth will be affected by the consumption function and conventional income analysis comes into its own.

I am not clear whether this abstracted reformulation will permit economic theorists to grip the take-off analysis in ways interesting for them; but Professor Solow's brilliant final statement justifies the effort.

PART FOUR

Issues of Current Policy

SIXTEEN

The Problem of Achieving and Maintaining a High Rate of Economic Growth: A Historian's View (1960)

This essay, which was presented at the Christmas meetings of the American Economic Association in 1959, may, at first reading, seem more appropriate to the late 1980s than the late 1950s: for example, its emphasis on the challenge to the U.S. status as the global economic front-runner; the critical role of a productivity increase along a broad front; the need for more innovative entrepreneurship in many sectors of the U.S. economy; the shortfall in investment in infrastructure; the importance of lowering abroad "outdated barriers to dollar imports"; and a relaxed attitude toward Soviet growth rates.

But in fact, the analysis was a product of its time as well as of my work of that period. It is sometimes forgotten that the late 1950s was a rather awkward period in the U.S. economy and in U.S. society. Dwight D. Eisenhower's memoir discusses this interval under the heading "A Sputtering Economy." Within the framework of the Bretton Woods system, balance-of-payments pressures resulted in some gold drain; those pressures arose in turn from the increased virtuosity of Western Europe and Japan in exporting manufactures to the United States from their revived and re-equipped industries. Meanwhile, in the United States wage increases began to outstrip the rate of productivity increase in important sectors, imparting a strand of cost-push inflation to the economy and rendering the dollar's fixed exchange rate overvalued. The result was that the United States began to fall into something like the post-war British

This essay was first published in the March 1960 issue of the *American Economic Review* (vol. 50, no. 1), pp. 106–118. Reprinted with permission.

pattern of stop-and-go policies with recessions imposed by balance-of-payments constraints. In this setting, anxiety also increased in a number of other directions, some triggered or enhanced by the Soviet launching of the first space satellite in October 1957: the pace of the U.S. missile and space programs, the adequacy of the U.S. educational system and infrastructure investment in general, the need for increased attention in U.S. policy to economic growth in the developing regions. There was a widespread, bipartisan consensus that a revival of energy and definition of new goals were required (e.g., the Rockefeller Brothers Fund panel reports). All these conditions lay behind John Kennedy's adoption of the campaign slogans "Let's get this country moving again" and "The New Frontier."

My work during this period made it natural that I should get caught up in the movement Kennedy captured and led, including the formulation of its slogans. The elaboration of the stages of economic growth in the Cambridge lectures during the autumn of 1958 drove home the reality that the diffusion of the mass automobile, durable customers' goods, and a home in suburbia could not serve much longer as the leading sectors in American growth. The need to define and pursue new frontiers had appeared three different times in those lectures.

This perception of the need for a new pattern of growth also converged with another line of work. From 1955 to 1958 I had directed a project at the MIT Center for International Studies on the interplay of American society and U.S foreign policy. That project yielded, among other studies, my The United States in the World Arena (1960). One of its concluding themes was the need for the nation to transcend a strong, historically rooted aspect of the national style: a tendency to innovate incrementally and to await acute crisis before radically changing course.

In any case, this essay accurately reflects the underlying analysis that shaped my recommendations to Kennedy between 1959 and 1961 on the domestic economy, notably those relating to the more vigorous application of new technologies, accelerated industrial re-equipment, and wage-price guideposts.

The title of this session, as it was first transmitted to me, was the lofty scientific phrase: "The Conditions of Economic Progress." But a few months later it was transmuted to a more pragmatic, more typically American, theme: "The Problem of Achieving and Maintaining a High Rate of Economic Growth." This change is, I believe, significant of more than the national style; for what brings us here is not merely scientific interest in the wealth of nations but also a concern with quite specific and urgent issues of public policy.

Nevertheless, I shall begin by considering the question of growth—and American growth in particular—in its formal, academic setting; and I shall consider only in the latter part of my paper the sense in which American growth and its future is a problem.

In dealing with the prospects and problems of American growth, I shall apply a method of analysis which seeks to relate the history of sectors to the aggregate performance of economies.

Homerically simplified, my proposition comes to this: Within the framework set by the consumption function and the rate of increase in the working force, the rate of growth of an economy at any period is decisively affected by the momentum (or lack of momentum) in certain leading sectors. These leading sectors derive their high momentum from the entrance into the economy and the subsequent diffusion of new cost reducing production functions and/or from the rapid increase in output of products which enjoy high income elasticity of demand.[1] The leading sectors have certain direct effects on other sectors by setting up a powerful effective demand for new inputs; and they provide to the economy a wide range of external economic effects which, as it were, spill over outside the directly affected sectors.

These leading growth sectors sometimes also serve as leading sectors in business cycle expansions; that is, effective demand is sharply increased by the direct and multiplier effects of bringing new production functions into the capital stock. But in some booms the leading sectors are predominantly associated with lateral expansion in the economy, with no marked long-run effects on productivity; e.g., housing. The implication of this distinction between the effects of a sector's expansion on effective demand as against productivity is examined below; and it is fundamental to this paper.

But so far as growth is concerned, retardation,[2] and the complex set of forces which impose it, lies at the basis of this view—a view which makes economic history, at its hard core, the story of a succession of leading sectors, at an early high-momentum stage of their evolution, carrying growth forward as the old leaders flag, by imparting to the economy as a whole a wide ranging set of direct and indirect impulses to expansion.

From this perspective, I have analyzed over the years a good many of the world's economies, emerging with the notion that the path from traditional societies to the era of high mass consumption can be broken up usefully into stages, each of which is dominated by a phase of high momentum in a definable group of leading sectors.[3]

On this view, the economic history of the United States since about 1910 assumes a quite particular shape. At about 1910 there was a waning of the impulses stemming from what we might broadly call the steel revolution, which had carried growth forward after the railways ceased to dominate growth in the 1880's.

The phase of growth which then emerged has been dominated down to very recent years by the diffusion to the American population of new patterns of consumption, a new way of life built on the mass automobile and the single family house in the suburbs. It has embraced a succession of electric- and gas-powered household gadgets; new types and qualities of food; new types and qualities of clothing; new habits in the consumption of tobacco and drink; new patterns of expenditure on leisure activities, including various new forms of mass communication; and the vast outlays on construction required to mount and to tidy up this persistent inner migration.

Technically, this revolution was made possible not merely by the level which American income had attained at the period when the new pattern took hold (in, say, the twenties); but it has depended for its continued momentum (as has the continued rise in real income) on a group of technological revolutions in electricity, light engineering, petroleum, rubber, and chemicals. In terms of timing, the process of diffusion occurred in two great surges: the boom of the twenties, and the sustained decade of expansion after the second World War.[4]

The question arises as to whether the statistical evidence now available supports this view of the sectoral foundations for recent American growth. It is not easy to array data in their existing form so as to test this hypothesis rigorously. There are two basic reasons for this difficulty. As I emphasized in introducing the concept of leading, secondary, and derived sectors, the conventional grouping of production and productivity statistics cut across these analytic categories and make their exact statistical identification difficult.[5] Second, certain of the impulses which derive from a leading sector are difficult to trace, taking us as they do into increasing returns and external economies.

Nevertheless, the data available tend to suggest, at least, that the hypothesis is not inconsistent with the facts already established. For example, Kendrick's rank order array of thirty-three American industries with respect to productivity increase is led by those most intimately connected with these new dimensions in consumption: electric and gas utilities, rubber production, tobacco manufactures, transport equipment, crude petroleum, chemicals, printing. And his array of industries ranked in order of percentage increase in output is similar in its implication.[6]

My confidence in this hypothesis has been strengthened by the pattern of development in Western Europe in the past decade where a similar revolution in consumption patterns has palpably been under way, associated with high momentum in a similar group of leading sectors within the Western European economies.[7]

In terms of the view that phases of growth can be usefully related to leading sectors, what can we say about the present position and prospects of the American economy?

Essentially these large features of the situation stand out:

1. The diffusion to so high a proportion of the total population of the single-family house, the automobile, and the standard mix of household gadgets makes it unlikely that growth can depend as much as it did in either the twenties or the first postwar decade on the further diffusion of this pattern of life and of consumption to increasing proportions of the American population.

2. Without pretending to explain the phenomenon, it can nevertheless be said that in postwar years Americans behaved as if they preferred, at the margin, an enlargement of families to additional increments of income taken in the forms which have become conventional since the twenties. In a sense, diminishing relative marginal utility appears to have set in for real income itself, when conventionally defined. One consequence is that the United States faces the requirement of a massive lateral enlargement of the nation's economic base: social overhead capital; capacity to produce and to provide private services; and in the total level of consumption itself.

3. The backlogs in social overhead capital built up in the postwar decade, combined with increased social overhead requirements to serve the enlarging population, make it likely that such outlays may play a relatively larger role in the coming decade than they have in the first postwar decade. The continued rise in public construction during the recent recession suggests that such a shift in the balance of outlays is already under way.[8]

4. Thus, the income elasticity of demand revealed by Americans at present high-income ranges—with its heavy emphasis on babies and services—has weakened, in a sense, the historic link between the expansion in consumption and the key developments of industrial technology which has existed for about two generations. Put another way, we do not lack leading sectors capable of creating an expansion in effective demand; but, to a degree, we must look elsewhere for the maintenance of the rate of increase of productivity.

5. But a potential Jack Dalton exists. American society is in the midst of a quite remarkable process of scientific and technological development, reflected in radical increases in research and development outlays, which for some time appear to have been expanding at a rate of something like 10 per cent per annum in real terms.[9] On the other hand, the continued shift of activity away from manufactures to trade, services, and construction (as well as the shift to "nonproductive workers," other than those in research and development, within manufactures) might be expected to damp the rate of productivity increase, despite some increase of productivity in services and certain branches of construction. Nevertheless, a society endowed and motivated as we are, with scientists, engineers, and industrial research and development departments, need have no prima facie cause for despair, even though it no longer appears to have leading growth sectors tied intimately to the areas of high income elasticity of demand.

Thus, if our only concern was with the "conditions of economic progress" as applied to, say, the next decade of the American economy, we might conclude that our society had found, out of its own dynamics—notably in the rise of the birth rate and in the acceleration of applied science and technology—a basis for leading sectors in both effective demand and productivity; that the precise outcome for consumption per head was likely to vary marginally depending on a number of factors unpredictable at the present time; but that Americans would continue to face the relatively happy choice of distributing as among leisure, private goods and services, and public services a fairly regular increment in consumption, concerning themselves increasingly with the quality of American life rather than with conventional aggregate measures of production of goods and services.

But whenever this picture is drawn of the cheerful implications for American society of the onward march of compound interest, ghosts rise up to haunt the enterprise. Historians will find, for example, much significant in the counterpoint between the triumphant text and troubled footnotes of the CED's February, 1958, statement on *Economic Growth in the United States;* and in the contrast between the majestic patterns of growth and productivity presented to the Joint Economic Committee last April and the worried questions of the Committee's members.

It is clear, in short, that the future of American growth is now regarded by many Americans as a serious problem.

There are, in fact, six separable problems which evidently concern large numbers of Americans and which relate (or are believed to relate) in one way or another to the prospects for American growth. These may be stated as follows:

First, is the long-run rate of Russian growth, relative to that of the United States, a menace to American interests? Second, is the United States allocating sufficient resources to deter Communist aggression in the form of major or minor military excursions? Third, is the United States supplying sufficient capital to the underdeveloped areas to maximize the chance that they will be able to maintain their independence and to hold open the possibility of a democratic evolution of their societies? Fourth, is the United States allocating sufficient resources to social overhead capital? Fifth, is the United States in its international economic position moving towards a situation of protracted dollar weakness which would require a contraction of outlays abroad and/or increased protectionist policies? Sixth, does control of inflation require in our democratic society a damping of the rate of growth?

In one way or another, these six issues are the underlying substance of the dialogue between those economists concerned with the growth of the American economy and those concerned with public policy.

With respect to the first, I shall not enter here into the increasingly widespread international sport of comparing the rates and patterns of Russian and American growth.[10] I would merely state flatly this much: For the next decade at least there is nothing in the relative prospects for growth as between Russia and the United States that justifies making this matter, in itself, an issue of public policy.

The second, third, and fourth problems cited—those pertaining to the scale of allocations for military, foreign aid, and social overhead purposes—are, however, real enough. But to what extent do these problems of allocation relate to the rate of growth?

Their root cause does not, in my view, lie in the rate of growth but in certain American habits of mind, carried over from earlier phases of our history, and in the workings of the political process, as they affect the allocation of resources. This interplay of intellectual conception and conventional politics conspires to make it difficult for Americans to increase the scale of public outlays except at moments of acute crisis. Here lies an authentic danger to the national interest and a threat to the quality of American society.

Specifically, the working concepts of modern economics encourage the view that public outlays should be accommodated to the natural ebb and flow of the private sector, perhaps to be expanded at times of recession but certainly to be restrained when the private sectors exhibit high momentum.[11] This perspective, carried over inappropriately from an era of depression and peace to a time of chronic cold war and secular expansion, constitutes a powerful deterrent to outlays in the public sector, especially at a time of chronic prosperity; for it renders difficult a rational choice between marginal outlays in the public and private sectors, without extraordinary exertions of political leadership which have not been forthcoming. Without such efforts, the calculation takes the form of a crude clash between the total claims of the state as against the individual family budget, in which the latter enjoys an evident prima facie advantage. The existing level of taxation acquires a degree of acceptability as citizens accommodate themselves to its burdens. Familiarity breeds not contempt but stoicism. Lacking a concerted effort of political leadership to dramatize the meaning of marginal shifts from the private to the public sector, it is difficult to generate the political base for tax increases or other forms of restraint on private outlays; e.g., checks on installment spending. This leads politicians, except under acute crisis circumstances, to work out the pattern of public outlays within ceilings determined by what the existing tax schedules—the arbitrary product of the last acute crisis—will yield at existing levels of income, if indeed it does not lead to inappropriate tax reductions.

It is essentially these two features of the American scene—one intellectual, the other political—which have made our response to the changing directions of challenge in the cold war so sluggish on the one hand and convulsive on the other. Neither our concepts of political economy nor our notions of politics have made it possible to deal with threats to the national interest in a forehanded flexible way. We have shifted erratically from the moods and political economy of peace to those of war. In the interval between, say, mid-1948 and the attack in Korea, for example, men in responsibility came to believe that a military budget beyond 15 billion dollars was a threat to the American way of life. After the convulsive reaction to the Korean war had lifted military outlays more than threefold, this new range became again accepted as a line to be defended with a quite irrational ideological fervor. And this new upper limit exerted a restraint on social overhead outlays by the federal government which, if the marginal public-private calculus were differently presented, a majority of Americans might well have rejected.

The heart of the Soviet challenge lies, then, in presenting us with a situation where our interests may be eroded away, without palpable crisis, to a point where a traditional convulsive American response will no longer suffice. Our conceptions and methods of allocation to the public sector are inappropriate to a world caught up in a technological arms race and a slow grinding struggle for power and ideological conception in the underdeveloped areas. It is not the Soviet growth rate we need fear but a mode of American allocation which tends to imprison us at a level of public outlays determined by our arbitrary response to the last major crisis.

Nevertheless, the rate of growth—and especially the rate of growth in productivity—does bear on the problem of allocation, as Report IV of the Rockfeller's Fund Special Studies Project dramatized;[12] for a high rate of growth in gross national product makes it possible to enlarge both private income per head and public outlays, at existing tax rates. Put another way, the higher the growth rate, the less the potential clash between the claims of the two sectors. But a high rate of growth, in itself, does not guarantee that the public sector will be adequately supplied with resources; for the American allocation system does not automatically maintain constant fixed percentage allocations to various purposes (assuming for a moment that such a system would yield increases adequate to the national interest at high rates of growth in GNP). Without purposeful efforts the natural tendency of the American system is for public outlays to decline as a percentage of total resources, except at intervals of acknowledged crisis. In fact, as a rough approximation, it is not wholly unfair to define the Soviet advantage over the United States as consisting in a more stable percentage allocation to military and foreign policy sectors, starting from a high initial base, at a time of rapid increase in Soviet GNP.

I conclude, therefore, that at least three of the major worries that have generated recent discussions of the American growth rate are rooted in our concepts and method for allocating resources; and that these problems might be eased but they would not be solved by achieving a higher rate of growth.

Something of the same may be said about the problem presented by recent pressures on the American foreign balance. The existing level of American military and foreign aid expenditures has come under pressure because of two striking developments of the fifties. First, in general, the rate of expansion of world trade, under circumstances where gold production in the free world is expanding at a lesser rate, has forced the dollar to bear an increasing burden as a reserve currency.[13] Second, the emergence of Western Europe and Japan into the age of high mass consumption has induced a scale and technological virtuosity in those industries in which the United States has hitherto enjoyed a relative advantage such that the European share of certain exports has increased and, moreover, these new dynamic leading sectors in Europe have attracted substantial flows of American capital. The reserve problem now confronted by the United States and the free world will, thus, not be automatically solved by a higher rate of increase in GNP. It requires a sober reappraisal of the international reserve problem as a whole, a lowering of barriers to dollar imports, and a more equitable sharing of the free world's military and aid responsibilities. In the light of such a reappraisal and the international actions that might then be taken, some revisions in American payments and trade policy may or may not prove justified. If they are justified, they should be made in ways which minimize damage to our military security, our alliances, and the prospects for independence and democracy in the underdeveloped areas. Without such a direct and forehanded approach there is an active danger that we shall chip away at the reserve problem piecemeal, cutting outlays and altering policies in terms of domestic political opportunism and damaging American interests in ways that are quite unnecessary.

Nevertheless, one of the components of an American policy designed to deal with the reserve problem might well be a concerted public and private effort to accelerate the rise in American productivity, which, if directed to the appropriate sectors, might sustain the American export position at a time when the march of the stages of growth has tended to narrow certain earlier American advantages. Like other more advanced nations (and more advanced regions, like New England) the American balance-of-payments position requires that new sectors of comparative advantage be developed and sustained, as the diffusion of technology proceeds, and that productivity be increased in the older, sluggish sectors of the economy.

Now briefly the inflation problem and the rate of growth. In my view the inflation problem of the fifties is only superficially to be analyzed as the product of a peculilar wage-push or effective demand-pull. More fundamentally it arises from a historical change in the institutional methods and attitudes brought to bear in setting industrial and farm prices on the one hand and wages on the other.[14] These changes have two distinct effects. First, they render it difficult to pass along productivity increases in lower prices. The common expectation is, therefore, that prices will rise; and money wage negotiations must bear the full brunt of achieving a rise in real wages. Wage negotiations are thus complicated because business negotiators must try to discount the effect of probable wage increases; and labor negotiators must try to discount the effect on real wages of probable price increases. In trying to hedge against the inflation they assume, they perpetuate inflation at the expense of the public interest. The existence of a strong price floor is compounded by a second and even more fundamental institutional fact: Money wage bargains are struck in a setting largely divorced from price policy—and from the course of average productivity—where the negotiators feel little responsibility except a short-run responsibility to their immediate constituents.

The challenge confronting our democratic system is not to achieve sufficient restraint in total effective demand to prevent a chronic increase in wages and prices; for even if that were to prove politically and socially acceptable, on the scale of restraint required, it would yield a growth environment likely to make difficult the pattern of allocations most likely to protect the nation's interest and the quality of the society. Again, it is not the lower rate of growth that, in itself, would cause the difficulty, but the problem of making adequate allocations to the public sectors, at a time of stagnation or slow rise in GNP.

The challenge confronting our democracy is to fashion price and wage policies under chronic high-employment conditions which are judged equitable and which allocate increases in real income by means other than money wage rates disproportionate to the average productivity increase. There appears to be no way of achieving this result via conventional fiscal and monetary policy without also bringing about changes in price policy which would permit some part of the increase in real wages to assume the form of price decreases made possible by higher productivity and changes in wage policy which would roughly accommodate the rise in average real wages to the average rate of increase in productivity.

But again, as with the foreign balance, the rate of growth, and especially the rate of growth of productivity, becomes a strategic variable; for the possibility of fashioning and operating successfully a regime of steady (or very slowly rising) money wages hinges partly on whether real incomes are palpably rising. In this connection, it is an often forgotten lesson of economic history that periods of relative peace in labor relations have tended also to be periods of declining trend in living costs.

A historian is quite comfortable with this prospect, and it is time for economists to shake off the images of the inter-war years and the assumption that, somehow, in all circumstances declining price trends must always be linked to severe unemployment.

Given its partial but strategic role in the solution of this whole range of problems, it is worth, even in a brief survey of this kind, considering at somewhat greater length the prospects for productivity over, say, the coming decade. All of us, I assume, are duly impressed with the two most obvious encouraging facts in our situation. First, the extraordinary increase in the scale of science and technology and in the number of scientists and technologists in our society. These institutional and human facts give meaning to the burgeoning and increasingly fashionable research and development activities within the economy. Second, I assume we are all impressed with the rapidly unfolding possibilities of certain particular, relatively recent scientific breakthroughs—notably in atomic energy, electronics, and certain fields of chemistry. Over the reasonably long future, it is difficult not to assume that the potentials for the increase in productivity will be very great.[15]

On the other hand, in the more immediate future, there is some reason for caution in counting too much on these factors to lift from us the burdens of hard choice in making public policy. First, in both scale and apparent effectiveness, industrial research and development have historically been concentrated in a relatively few sectors closely linked in their origins to modern science: aeronautics, chemicals, and electricity. And a great deal of contemporary research and development within these sectors is directed to fields of military interest from which the civilian economy benefits only in indirect ways. Second, the levels of income now enjoyed in American society appear to be associated with high-income elasticity demand for services, including government services, rather than with manufacturing industry. With all due respect to electronic office equipment and road-building equipment, the trends in new technology and in patterns of American consumption do not appear automatically to converge. Third, as Kuznets emphasizes, the introduction of certain major innovations has tended historically to be accompanied by massive construction requirements which, for a time, elevate the incremental capital-output ratio.

Taken together, these factors might limit, at least, the consequences for productivity of the constructive impulses which are operating.

In my view it would be wholesome, therefore, to place the issue of productivity high on the national agenda. It might be useful, for example, for private and public authorities jointly and systematically to examine the productivity potentials in the various sectors of the American economy with two objectives in mind. First, to see whether it might not be in the common interest to allocate increased research and development talent of the first order to those older and less glamorous fields where deceleration or decline has long since set in but where very substantial proportions of the nation's resources are consumed; e.g., housing, steel, textiles, and even automobiles. The objective would be to correct a little the natural tendency, familiar to economic historians, for the new, rapidly expanding fields to absorb a disproportionate percentage of first-class talent.[16] In my view, we must now create a policy of productivity advance along a much wider front than in the past. Second, we might systematically examine the extent to which entrepreneurship in the various sectors is or is not effectively bringing to bear the potentials which already exist for increased productivity;[17] and we might consider what tax incentives or subsidies might be created to bring average levels of productivity closer to best-proved standards, in sectors peculiarly touched by the public interest.

Among the particular sectors that deserve close examination is what might broadly be called staff work, both within government and in the private economy. Some of us hold the view that we Americans have carried over into staff work criteria of specialization derived historically from notions of scientific management which originated in the problems of running a railroad system, an army in peacetime, and a machine shop.[18] This leads to overmanned staffs, with tremendous inertia built into them, consuming their energies in maintaining the *status quo*, obscuring the locus of responsibility in endless committees, radically damping the pace of innovation. The increasing role of government in all our lives as well as the increasing role of staff work in the private sector, absorbing as they do so high a proportion of first-rate human capital, may justify a serious examination of this prejudice.

In any case, it would be a mistake to assume that even a powerful upward movement in the aggregate sums devoted to research and development will automatically yield those changes in the rate of productivity (and in its sectoral composition) which are, in fact, needed to minimize the inevitable strains within American society over the next decade, as we confront our domestic and international challenges.

It may seem odd to commend productivity teams to a nation which still leads the world in productivity and which, for so long, has been able to count on high productivity as an almost automatic by-product of its evolution. But we must bear in mind that high productivity is not enough; it is the pace of increase that will help determine how easy or difficult it will be to meet our domestic and international challenges. And we should also bear in mind that the stage of growth which the United States has attained has altered the old connection between areas of high income elasticity of demand and high technological momentum. History appears to have decreed that, in order to remain a front runner, we shall have to continue to pioneer—in this case to pioneer in bringing about productivity increases along a broad front. And in facing this challenge we should not complain; for the grand lesson of economic history is surely this: a front runner's status is never automatically sustained. It must be constantly renewed.

My argument comes, then, to this:

1. Viewed from the perspective of a historian's concern with leading sectors, the potentials in the United for high levels of effective demand and for high rates of productivity increase over the next decade appear excellent. Unlike the situation during the past two generations, however, there does not appear to be a close link between sectors of high income elasticity of demand and high technological momentum.

2. Now and foreseeably the United States is faced with challenges to both its position on the world scene and to the quality of its society. These challenges require increased allocations to public sectors. In addition, the United States faces the task of dealing with its foreign balance without an isolationist retreat and with inflation by means other than a radical damping in the rate of growth.

3. These challenges, which lie behind the present intense concern with American growth, must be dealt with by a revision in attitudes towards the allocation process which would make the marginal choice

between public and private sectors more rational than it now is; by a direct approach to the problem of economizing international reserves as well as by lowering of outdated barriers to dollar imports; and by a revision in attitudes towards and procedures for setting both prices and wages.

4. While these problems will not be solved by an accelerated increase in GNP, they could all be substantially eased by an increase in productivity along a broader front than in the past. After a study of the potentialities in the various sectors, such an increase might be achieved by tax incentives or subsidies designed to increase productivity in sectors of particular importance to the public interest; by a more purposeful disposition of research and development efforts; by an improvement in the average level of entrepreneurship, notably in the older sectors of relatively sluggish technological advance; and by alterations in American staff work which would yield higher rates of innovation.

NOTES

1. See the author's *Process of Economic Growth* (New York, 1952), especially Chap. iv, v, and "Trends in the Allocation of Resources in Secular Growth," *Economic Progress*, ed. Leon H. Dupriez with the assistance of Douglas C. Hague (Louvain, 1955).

2. See the author's summary of the factors determining retardation in the book, *The Process of Economic Growth* (ibid.), pp. 99–102, and the source citations in footnotes 25, p. 97, and 35, p. 101.

3. For a summary of this argument see the author's article, "The Stages of Growth," *Econ. Hist. Rev.*, Aug., 1959, Vol. 12, No. 1. The theme will be fully developed in the forthcoming *Stages of Economic Growth* (Cambridge Univ. Press, 1960).

4. This view of American growth suggests a particular explanation for the length of the depression of the thirties, stemming from the character of the new leading sectors. See "Rostow on Growth," *The Economist*, Aug. 15, 1959, p. 415, and the fuller discussion in *The Stages of Economic Growth*.

5. "Trends in the Allocation of Resources in Secular Growth," op. cit., pp. 374–76.

6. J. W. Kendrick, "Productivity Trends in the United States" (1959, mimeographed), Chap. VII; and S. Fabricant, op. cit., pp. 340–41. Also S. Fabricant, *The Output of Manufacturing Industries 1899–1937* (New York, 1940), especially Chap. IV.

7. United Nations, "Consumption Trends in Western Europe," *Economic Survey of Europe in 1958*, Chap. V (Geneva, 1959); and Milton Gilbert and Associates, *Comparative National Production and Price Levels* (OEEC, Paris, 1958). Discussions in the spring of 1959 with those concerned with fifteen-year plans in Eastern Europe also suggested the connection between relatively high levels of mass consumption and disproportionately rapid growth in the sectors of high momentum in the United States between 1919 and 1956 and in Western Europe of the fifties.

8. *Economic Report of the President*, transmitted to Congress, Jan., 1959 (G. P. O., 1959), p. 176.

9. R. H. Ewell, "The Role of Research in Economic Growth," *Chem. Eng. News*, July 18, 1955, p. 2981.

10. The author's views on this subject are contained in a statement released by the Joint Economic Committee, Nov. 16, 1959, and in testimony of Nov. 20, 1959.

11. For example: "It is true that federal spending increased much less rapidly than did the nation's total expenditure after 1954. It may justly be held, however, that there was a need for special restraint on the government's part at a time when the rest of the economy was displaying extreme exuberance." See A. F. Burns, *Prosperity Without Inflation* (New York, 1957), p. 40.

12. Rockefeller Brothers Fund, *The Challenge to America: Its Economic and Social Aspects*, Report of Panel IV of the Special Studies Project, "American at Mid-Century Series" (New York, 1958).

13. See notably, R. Triffen, *The Return to Convertibility: 1926–1931 and 1958–?*, No. 48, Mar., 1959, and *Tomorrow's Convertibility: Aims and Means of the International Monetary Policy*, No. 49, June, 1959 (both reprinted from *Banca Nazionale del Lavoro Quarterly Review*, Rome).

14. Some of the complexities inherent in this problem, which cannot be explored here, are exposed with clarity in *Wages, Prices, Profits, and Productivity*, ed., Charles A. Myers (The American Assembly, Columbia Univ., June, 1959), esp. Chap. 3–6, by James S. Duesenberry, Clark Kerr, Lloyd G. Reynolds, and John T. Dunlop, respectively.

15. See notably the discussion of Simon Kuznets, "Capital in the American Economy: Its Formation and Financing," Chap. X (NBER, May, 1959, mimeographed).

16. See, for example, the author's *The Process of Economic Growth*, *op. cit.*, pp. 100–01.

17. I have in mind here the systematic application of the kind of technique developed by Mrs. A. P. Carter, of Harvard, for measuring the range of technique and of productivity in the particular sectors.

18. See, for example, E. E. Morison, ed., *The American Style* (New York, 1958), chapters by George F. Kennan and W. W. Rostow and the commentary of Richard M. Bissell, Jr.

SEVENTEEN

The Bankruptcy of Neo-Keynesian Economics (1976)

A Reluctant Keynesian, a Reply by Abba P. Lerner (1976)

A Rejoinder (1976)

The following exchange with A. P. Lerner (who was at that time Visiting Distinguished Professor of Economics at Queens College, of the City University of New York) took place in an extremely worthy but somewhat obscure journal: the Intermountain Economic Review, *the first student-edited journal in economics. (It is now, unfortunately, defunct despite the support some of us tried to provide.)*

My essay was stimulated by articles in the Fall 1975 issue on stagflation by Paul Samuelson and Lerner, which the editors had called to my attention, inviting comment. Using conventional macro-economic, neo-Keynesian tools, they failed, in my view, to come to grips with the supply-side factors, in particular sectors, that had accounted for the price explosion of 1972–1975 as well as with the technological and sectoral price movements that had largely driven the remarkable boom in the advanced industrial world of the previous two decades. The essay reproduced in Chapter 19 is in much the same vein. My frustration with macro-economic analyses—monetarist as well as neo-Keynesian—that led

"The Bankruptcy of Neo-Keynesian Economics" was published in the Spring 1976 issue of the *Intermountain Economic Review* (vol. 7, no. 1); "A Reluctant Keynesian, a Reply by Abba P. Lerner" and "A Rejoinder" were published in the Fall 1976 issue of the *Intermountain Economic Review* (vol. 7, no. 2). Reprinted with permission.

to poor public policy later yielded The Barbaric Counter-Revolution: Cause and Cure (1983).

I might add that this exchange in the Intermountain Economic Review later resulted in a pleasant occasion in the spring of 1977. The School of Business at Austin invited Samuelson and me to debate the question "Is Keynesian Economics Bankrupt?" We decided a reflective discussion rather than dogmatic confrontation was more appropriate to our mood. The large student audience may have been mildly disappointed by the lack of confrontation; but the occasion permitted us to resume an old tennis rivalry.

THE BANKRUPTCY OF NEO-KEYNESIAN ECONOMICS

I

The special issue on Stagflation of the *Intermountain Economic Review* (Fall 1975, Vol. VI, No. 2) was, at once, depressing and heartening. Two of the most distinguished neo-Keynesian economists of the older generation implicitly declared their methods bankrupt[1]; but the younger writers were having none of it. With varying degrees of success, they struggled to pierce the veil of stagflation with models which aimed both to illuminate its causes and to suggest remedy. I hope this paper cheers the younger economists on.

I shall indicate briefly why I regard Professor Lerner's and Professor Samuelson's papers as statements of bankruptcy; present my own view of the causes of current stagflation; outline the kind of policies I would commend; and suggest, finally, the character of the dynamic, disaggregated theory of production and prices required both to understand where we are and where we ought to go.

II

I chose the title for this paper because their neo-Keynesian analytic structure prevents Professor Lerner and Professor Samuelson from offering:

1. a credible explanation for the sharp rise in unemployment in 1974–75 and the mediocre prospects for the cyclical expansion now under way;
2. a credible policy for returning to the relatively stable, high rates of growth and low unemployment of the period, say, 1948–74; or
3. a credible policy for bringing inflation under control.

In the macro-world of neo-Keynesian income analysis there is no formal place for oil or wheat or meat. They are inconvenient micro-objects, their peregrinations strictly exogenous and, hopefully, mutually frustrating. It is necessary for neo-Keynesians, therefore, to convert the nameless horrors that occurred in food and energy markets in 1972-74 into something familiar and manageable. Professor Lerner does it by assuming that some exogenous force has set up expectations of accelerated price increases which lead to accelerated wage increases. Full employment equilibrium then requires that spending be accelerated to match the two-stage inflationary rocket. United States fiscal and monetary policy has failed to do so. Therefore, we have and shall continue to have rather severe unemployment until some exogenous event alters expectations or until we liberalize monetary and fiscal policy. If expectations are not knocked flat by large harvests or benign Arabs, we shall continue to experience inflation until we introduce some form of incomes policy.

Professor Samuelson's exposition is a bit more complex. There are explicit references to Asian and African droughts and a passing reference to the possibility that the OPEC oil price might not be easily reversed. There is even, for a moment, a glimmer of light when he notes that "Microeconomic commodity inflation . . . refuses to remain microeconomic." [17; p. 9] But, in the end, there is even less of an explanation for the high levels of unemployment in the OECD world than Professor Lerner's unmatched expectations. With respect to policy, Professor Samuelson merely refers to the recurrence of the "relevant debate" about the Phillips curve trade-off. [17; p. 15] As for inflation, he argues for its inevitability and, in effect, for its passive acceptance. He closes with a few pious words about stagflation being our Achilles heel and "the continuing challenge to professionals in economic science."

There really has not been much progress in the neo-Keynesian world since the same author urged President-elect Kennedy to postpone action on wage-price guidelines and concentrate on expanding effective demand, noting, however, that "if recovery means a reopening of the cost-push problem, then we have no choice but to move closer to the day when that problem has to be successfully grappled with." [16; p. 28] President Kennedy, over-ruling the advice of the neo-Keynesians, took wage-push inflation seriously when a 6-7 per cent unemployment rate was associated with a 1 per cent rate of inflation. He proceeded to make wage-price arrangements, in a rough and ready way, so that inflation was contained until 1966. And, in my view, he was right thus to free his hands, at the pit of recession, for an expansionary fiscal and monetary policy. And now, if the experts and their computerized models of our economy are to be believed, we live with a Phillips curve passing through a point where, say, a 7+ per cent unemployment rate will be associated in 1976 with a 6 per cent rate of inflation, despite stagnant or falling food and raw material prices for the past two years and only a slight rise (if any) in the money price of oil. Notwithstanding this cooling in the price environment and high unemployment, the effective money wage rate rose 8.6 per cent in 1975, unit labor costs were rising at 5.6

per cent in the fourth quarter. Neither variable is expected to move substantially in a more wholesome way in 1976. As we all know, a 7 per cent average unemployment rate is now associated with an 18 per cent rate for those 16–19 years old, about 12.5 per cent for non-whites. The projected prospects for 1977 are for only slightly lower unemployment and a slightly higher inflation rate. We are staring at the likelihood, then, of at least four consecutive years of stagflation (1974–77).

The Council of Economic Advisers accepts this prospect as the best that can be devised without risking even higher rates of inflation. [4; p. 19] Professor Walter Heller marginally disagrees and gives the neo-Keynesian position concreteness. He wishes to see a budget for fiscal year 1977 perhaps $20 billion higher than the President proposes. [6; p. 18] He also suggests some gentle government jawboning to keep wage-settlements in "a pattern of moderation" in 1976. Professor Gardner Ackley finds the projected rates of prolonged unemployment "simply intolerable," but he argues only for "a somewhat more stimulative fiscal policy" which would involve "negligible costs in increased inflation." [1]

What's wrong with these humane neo-Keynesian prescriptions? First, no likely increase in the federal budget deficit (e.g., $20 billion) is going to close rapidly the gap between current GNP (about $1600 billion) and its level at, say, 5 per cent unemployment (about $1725 billion). Second, in effect, the neo-Keynesians (as well as the Council of Economic Advisers) have just about given up on the control of inflation.

It is time to contemplate the possibility that the modes of economic analysis and policy which have served us reasonably well for almost forty years have, to a significant degree, run out their string. We may have come to a time when "the profession can no longer evade anomalies that subvert the existing tradition of scientific practice," and we must begin "the extraordinary investigations that lead the profession at last to a new set of commitments, a new basis for the practice of science." [8; p. 6]

III

Technically, what's wrong with neo-Keynesian analysis is, of course, that it is set up under Marshallian short-period assumptions. It cannot, therefore, deal with long-period supply changes in the system and must focus obsessively on the aggregate level of effective demand and its manipulation. And when the effort is made to deal with growth, via the Harrod-Domar model, long-period factors appear in highly abstract and over-aggregated form. The short-run Keynesian model is merely tilted upwards with variables inserted for the rate of working force and average productivity increase. When Marshallian long-period forces are seriously introduced into economic analysis, one is immediately forced to disaggregate. This is the case because technological change develops neither evenly nor incrementally throughout the economy: it is both lumpy and uneven as among the sectors. One cannot conduct a useful analysis of a real economy by throwing in a variable (as does Professor Lerner) for the over-all increment in output per man. [9; p. 1] Moreover, the income elasticity of demand has significant sectoral consequences which require specification.

With those general observations in mind, here is a terse account of where current stagflation came from and where it fits in the sweep of history.

1. The great boom in the OECD world from 1948 to 1974 had two main sectoral pillars: the diffusion of the automobile, durable consumer goods and the life of suburbia, with all their attendant technologies, backward and lateral linkages; and a sharp rise in real outlays for certain public and private services with high income elasticities of demand in rich countries (notably, higher education, health services and travel).

2. From 1951 to the closing months of 1972 the boom was conducted in a supportive environment of relatively declining prices of foodstuffs and raw materials (including energy); although the relative decline tended to cease as the 1960s wore on. In that decade the rate of increase of global demand for grain outpaced that of supply; this led to an enlargement of the numbers of grain deficit countries, a concentration of surpluses in the United States, Canada and Australia, as well as a drawing down of world grain reserves as a proportion of consumption. All this rendered the world market exceedingly vulnerable to a bad harvest year like 1972, and the exercise by the Soviet Union of its oligopsonistic powers. Similarly, the rate of increase of U.S. demand for oil outpaced the rate of increase in U.S. supply, leading to an increased dependence on oil imports from the Middle East and an end to the illusion that the United States was a reserve energy supplier: oil production began its absolute decline in 1970-71. The process was exacerbated by U.S. natural gas policy, which blithely ignored the rapid decline in reserves. All this rendered the world market exceedingly vulnerable to the exercise by OPEC countries of their virtually monopolistic powers in the international oil market. There were particular unique aspects to the events of 1972-74; but there is no way to understand what has happened without examining the dynamic rise in tension between grain and oil supply and demand in the 1960s, a form of analysis which has no place in either conventional macro- or micro-theory.[2] (Mr. Caceres is right about import prices and the inadequacy of the Phillips curve trade-off; but he needs a different model to get at the factors he lists on p. 27.) [2] The accompanying charts show how the price explosion worked itself through the American economy through December 1975, exacerbated (as Professor Lerner correctly points out) by labor's efforts to fend off its consequences for living costs by higher rates of increase in money wages.

3. These price increases struck at the sectoral pillars of growth in the OECD world in multiple ways. The rise in energy prices caused

increased consumer outlays for energy (despite some economies) and reduced outlays for other goods and services. This effect was compounded by the policies of fiscal and monetary restraint induced by the radically unfavorable shift in the terms of trade, accompanied by reduced export sales to other oil importers which was not fully compensated for by increased sales to oil producers. The upshot was a sharp decline in outlays for houses, automobiles and durable consumer goods which quickly reduced investment levels. The consequent recession was intensified by increased caution both among businessmen and consumers. Overall, the OECD suffered declines in GNP about twice the level that can be directly attributed to the rise in oil prices. Against this background of relative price and real income movements, the second pillar of the great postwar boom (increased public and private outlays for certain services) was also weakened. Travel was constrained, for example, as were public outlays for education and other welfare services. In some cases, the latter may have been approaching a natural phase of deceleration after two decades of disproportionate expansion. But, in addition, as private real incomes stagnated or declined, a political revolt swept the OECD world against increased public outlays at the old rate. Without the built-in income stabilizers of the past forty years, a dangerously acute world depression might well have been set in motion.

4. This is the fifth time in the past two hundred years that such a shift in relative prices has occurred; and on each of the other four occasions it has been accompanied by exactly the same manifestations we have experienced since 1972: an accelerated general inflation, an extremely high range of interest rates, pressure on the real wages of industrial labor, pressure on those with relatively fixed incomes and shifts of income and terms of trade favorable to producers of food as well as energy.[3] The other four occasions occurred in the 1790s, the early 1850s, the second half of the 1890s and the late 1930s. On each occasion, food and raw material prices then fluctuated in a relatively high range for about a quarter-century. Approximately another quarter-century followed in which the trends reversed. Each of these periods was, in an important sense, unique and the trends did not unfold smoothly; but the fact is that the world economy for almost two centuries has been subject to a rough and irregular pattern of long cycles in which periods of about 20 to 25 years of high relative prices for food and raw materials gave way to approximately equal phases of relatively cheap food and raw materials. (This is, somewhat over-simplified, my view of what lies at the heart of the Kondratieff cycle.) The last downswing ran from 1951 to 1972. I am not wedded to the notion that these cycles will continue in the future. But I would guess that the inexorable pressure of excessive population increase in the developing world, the tendency of the poor to spend increases in income disproportionately on food, the rising demand for grain-expensive proteins among the rich and the high marginal cost of expanding the non-OPEC energy supply will persist for some time. Given these powerful and sustained forces operating

Figure I
The Price Revolution of 1972-75: U.S. Wholesale Prices, Monthly (1967 = 100)

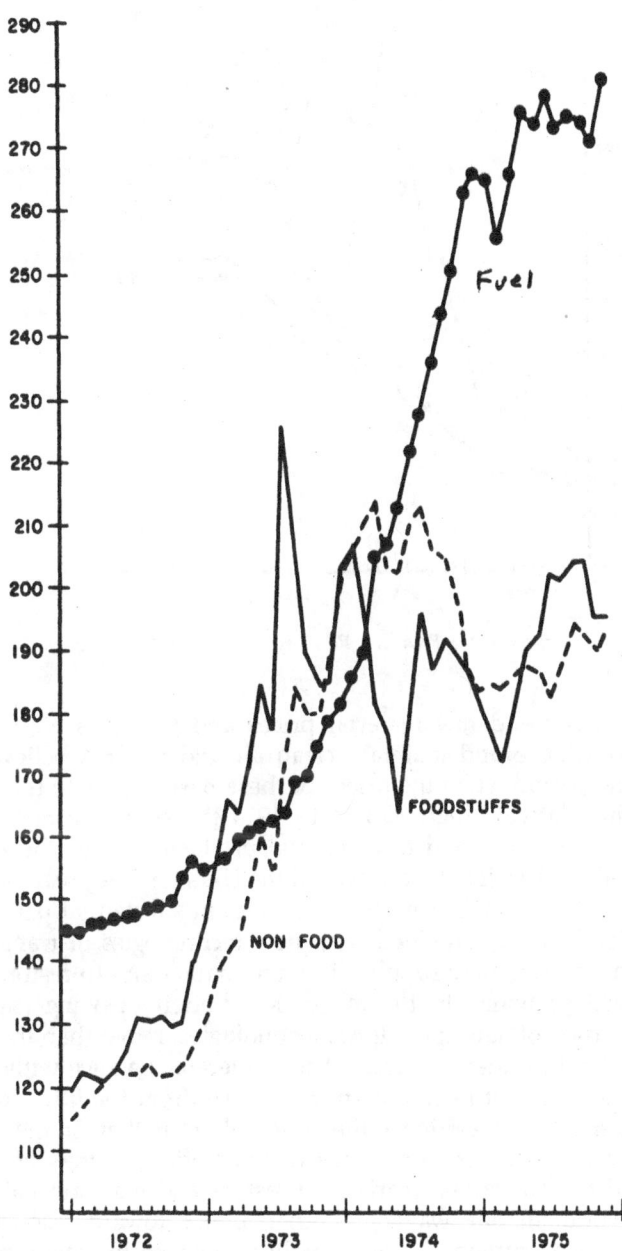

Source: *Economic Report of the President*, February 1975, pp. 301-2; January 1976, pp. 227-8.

Figure II

The Price Revolution of 1972-75: U.S. Wholesale Prices, Monthly (1967 = 100)

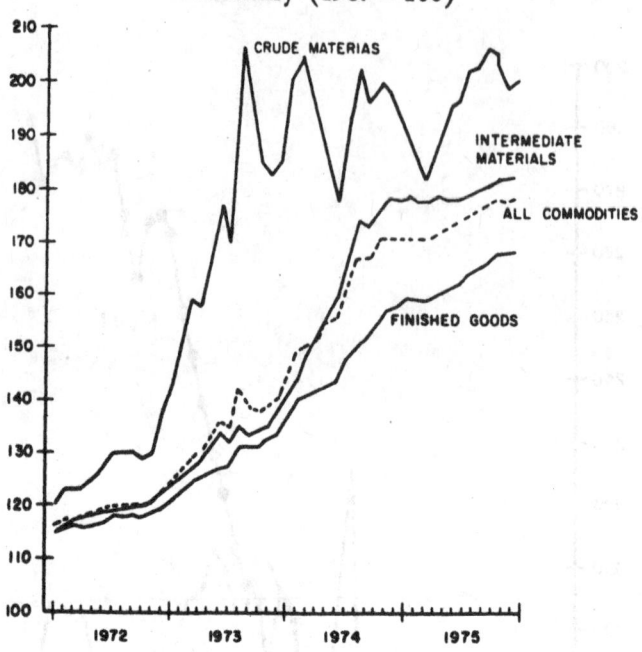

Source: *Economic Report of the President*, February 1975, pp. 301-2; January 1976, pp. 227-8.

on food, energy and raw material prices and the costs we shall have to incur to achieve and maintain clean air and water, I believe we are in for a long period when the prices of these basic inputs to the economy will remain relatively high. Down to 1914 the classic response was to open new agricultural and raw material producing areas: the American West, Canada, Australia, Argentina and the Ukraine. The great movements of international capital during this era were, in substantial part, induced by the price system, combined with new technologies of transport and production, to bring new supplies into the market and to restore balance in the world economy. In the fourth Kondratieff upswing (say, 1936-51), the diffusion of new agricultural technologies, rather than the opening of new physical frontiers, reestablished a tolerable balance without much conscious government intervention. But we confront the fifth Kondratieff upswing period in a setting quite different from that of the past. We cannot rely to the same extent on the automatic workings of the price system and private capital markets to restore and maintain balance. All over the world, in one way or another, policy toward resources is in the hands of governments or is strongly influenced by governments. At every stage in the effort to restore balance, therefore, public policy will be involved, seeking, if we are wise, to supplement—and in some cases to control—the incentives and constraints set up by the price system.

5. In the short run, we also face a new problem of trying to get back to full employment. The rise in the relative price of energy has rendered a return to full employment in the sectoral pattern of the past quarter-century difficult, as well as somewhat irrational. One can, of course, conceive of some increased level of consumer income induced by extravagantly lowered taxes and an extravagantly unbalanced federal budget that would permit rapid increases in automobile production and use, expanded sales of energy-intensive durable consumer goods and a general overriding of high energy prices. But its retribution would swiftly come, involving a rapid increase in oil imports and severe balance of payments difficulties. Besides, we know instinctively that such a policy doesn't make sense and, for good reasons, it is politically unrealistic. This is what Gilbert Gould seems to be saying when he urges us to attack the cause rather than the symptom of illness. [5; p. 44]

IV

What, then, are the policy implications of this way of looking at things? First, the route back to full employment, in general, is also the route to re-establishing balance in the American and world economies. Following the pattern of the four other Kondratieff upswings, we must, in Mr. Gould's phrase, "concentrate on the supply sector." [5; p. 44] That means we must mount programs of rapidly expanded investment in areas such as these: energy, energy conservation, mass transit, insulated housing, programs to clean the air and water, to preserve the viability of our agricultural base and to radically expand research and development over a wide front. The private sector cannot do the job wholly on its own and the government should not try to do it all by itself. We have entered a phase, which I believe will be protracted, in which, if we act intelligently, we must generate a new partnership (and sense of partnership) between the public and private sectors. We require systematic, selective, sectoral planning. Some of the things required of government do not involve large increases in public expenditure; e.g., a settlement of energy price policy and of the environmental-energy trade-off that would permit increased private investment in energy production. On the other hand, the public role in cleaning the air and water, in certain energy projects too large for the private sectors to undertake, in expanding research and development and perhaps in solving the front-end financing problem with solar energy, could (among other things) demand substantially increased federal outlays. We ought to move toward an explicit investment component in the federal budget and create a federal bank like the old RFC.

This line of thought could, of course, be greatly elaborated; but for these purposes, I trust it is adequately clear. As opposed to the neo-

Keynesians, I argue that we should seek not a slightly greater deficit in the federal budget but greatly enlarged levels of investment in specific sectors through public/private collaboration.

Now inflation. If we in the United States and the OECD world in general could agree that the route back to full employment was through a shift of resources toward expanded investment in the specific inputs required to balance and sustain industrial civilization, I suspect our inflationary problem could well be confined to wage-push inflation. We would be acting purposefully on the supply side in ways that ought to contain inflationary forces from that direction. Moreover, against the background of that kind of purposefulness, a serious OECD-OPEC settlement ought to prove possible, given the inherent potential strains within OPEC.

I do not underestimate the difficulties that democratic societies face in bringing wage-push inflation under control. As long ago as 1953 I wrote that the problem of controlling inflation "lies implicit in the acceptance by peoples and political parties of the proposition that unemployment is no longer to be regarded as an act of God"; and it would involve "changes no less profound than that wrought by the Keynesian revolution . . ." [14; pp. 237, 259] Moreover, I know that the economic history of the past thirty years is littered with efforts by democratic governments to implement incomes policies that worked, at best, for relatively short periods of time. I understand, therefore, Professor Samuelson's caution against cheap optimism in this field. On the other hand, I am not prepared to settle for his defeatism. First, we know that there is a deep anxiety in democratic societies concerning inflation. It is usually judged as a problem of higher priority than unemployment in public opinion polls. There is a political base for dealing with inflation if we can generate the political statesmanship. Second, I am convinced that labor leaders would be prepared for a sustained incomes policy if we could find credible ways to guarantee two conditions: (1) that no labor leader lose or gain significantly relative to any other and (2) that wage discipline not result in a disproportionate increase in distributed profits. Given the institutional structure of our unions and political life, these are not easy criteria to meet; but they are by no means impossible. Required is a formula to be worked out between labor and business that is backed by the full commitment of the Executive Branch and Congress; a program designed to last at least five years. We need a period of this length to allow an initial phase of equity adjustment of wage rates negotiated at different times in the past and, after that, a long enough period to alter expectations along the lines argued by Professors Keller and Gray as well as by Professor Lerner. [7], [9]

I believe, moreover, that a good setting in which to try to come to grips again with wage-push inflation is a time in which, in any case, we as a national and international community ought to be co-operating to deal with problems of energy, food, population and environment which have marched so disconcertingly to the center of the stage.

I happen to believe that the best formula for an incomes policy would be fixed money wages with falling prices as productivity increases. Although I did not derive the idea from Keynes, it is generally forgotten that this formula is sympathetically examined in his *General Theory* (pp. 269–71). I shall not burden you with this view, which my colleagues tend to regard as extreme; I would settle for less. But I would note that, on the basis of both logic and economic history, it is the optimum resolution for labor; the focus on productivity changes it would require in relation to prices and profits, in particular industries, could lead to the increased attention to monopoly Mr. Diemer and Professor McKean advocate. [3]

In the context of this paper as a whole, what I would underline is that a serious approach to an incomes policy requires not only the supplementing of economics with institutional and political analysis, but also, once again, disaggregation. Disaggregation is essential if we are to understand the problems as among various unions and their leaders in achieving stable equity; and it would be equally necessary in monitoring a new long-term set of wage-price guidelines with respect to productivity, profits and prices.

V

Now, finally, what kind of theoretical structure is needed if it is agreed that something like my analysis of the cause and cure for stagflation is correct?[4] I have for long been convinced that we need a dynamic, disaggregated theory of production and prices which would link the analysis of national income and its large components to the life of the sectors, bringing within its orbit: population change, invention, innovation and the sectoral allocation of investment.[5] I was driven to this view because an economic historian must live in a world where the Marshallian long period is moving every day and the important movements occur in particular sectors—sometimes even in a particular plant or workshop. Theories which screen out the Marshallian long period or deal with it in a highly aggregated way are of limited use.

Evidently, I cannot elaborate here my view of an appropriate dynamic disaggregated theory of production and prices. But perhaps I can suggest its character.

Take it on faith, for a moment, that population change, the generation of scientific knowledge, invention and innovation can be rendered significantly endogenous. Assume also a given consumption function and set of tastes, including the income elasticity of demand. It is then possible to conceive of a dynamic equilibrium path for a peaceful, closed economy and all its sectors. These overall and sectoral optimum paths imply that investment resources are allocated to the sectors in a changing pattern without error or lag, taking into account changes in technology as well as in consumers' and inter-industry demand. We can thus formulate abstractly a disaggregated moving, rather than static, equilibrium; a kind of truly dynamic, optimal input-output table.

In fact, of course, the economies we study in history were not closed; they were often at war or affected by war and investment was subject to systematic errors and lags. Moreover, the coming of new technologies often took the form of large discontinuous changes in the economy and its structure. Also, even in the most capitalist of societies, the economic role of government was significant. What an economic historian observes, then, are dynamic interacting national economies, trying rather clumsily to approximate optimum sectoral equilibrium paths, tending successively to undershoot and overshoot those paths.

If these various economies had the entrepreneurial capacity more or less regularly to absorb, in the appropriate sectors, the technologies cumulatively generated by the world's investment in science and invention, then they grew; that is, with many irregularities and vicissitudes, their income per capita tended to rise. That process of growth, accompanied as it regularly was by increased urbanization, education and other social changes, underlies the demographic transition, as well as the rising quality of the work force. Where investment lags were particularly long, as they have historically tended to be in expanding output from new sources of foodstuffs and raw materials, the dynamics of growth yielded trend periods (or Kondratieff cycles) generally marked by rather massive undershooting and overshooting of optimum sectoral paths with widespread impact on the price level, terms of trade, interest rates, income distribution, as well as the structure of world trade and patterns of investment. When the lags were shorter, and investment errors more quickly corrected, we had nine-year business cycles and (still shorter) inventory cycles. When national growth is analyzed with special attention to the effective absorption of the lumpy sequence of major technologies and all of their spreading effects, the stages of economic growth emerge.

It is this dynamic disaggregated theory of production and prices which equally determines my emphasis on the sectoral character of the great post-World War II boom, the sectoral character of stagnation and on the changed directions of investment required both for regaining momentum in the world economy and recapturing a structural balance which eroded in the 1960s and has been lost since the end of 1972. And if the control of wage-push inflation emerges as an essentially political and negotiating task, conducted within bounds which respect certain key economic parameters, this is not the first time in the history of our profession that we have had to accept the inherent inelegance of political economy if we are to fulfill our highest mission.

The phrase is not a rhetorical flourish; for chronic stagflation is serious business, indeed. It threatens to corrode the social and political life of North America, Western Europe and Japan; it has already sharply decelerated the rate of economic progress in Latin America, Africa and Asia, except for OPEC countries; moreover, it threatens to enfeeble the capacity of the United States and others to deal with a world poised, in a rather fragile way, between movements toward peace and increased chaos and violence. The character of American economic policy could tip the balance.

Every economist should re-read from time to time D. E. Moggridge's *The Return to Gold, 1925*. [10] It tells how serious and able men—politicians, civil servants and economists—controlled by memories and models that had served them well for all their mature lives, failed to understand the underlying problems at work in the British and world economy and made an unfortunate decision, which was off by 10 per cent. A British exchange rate 10 per cent less than $4.86 would not have solved all its interwar-economic problems, but the decision of 1925 did palpably contribute to the enfeeblement of British economic, social and political life down to 1931. And when Britain began to recover, the Japanese militarists were already on the march and Hitler was in the offing.

It would be sad if a generation of economists who treasure their linkage to Keynes—one of the two major figures who opposed the 1925 decision—should, a half century later, at a critical moment in their own time, play out the role of Montagu Norman and Otto Niemeyer.

BIBLIOGRAPHY

1. Ackley, G., Statement before the Joint Committee, U. S. Congress, *Hearings on the Economic Report of the President*, Feb. 5, 1976.
2. Caceres, L. R., "Stagflation: An Open Economy Analysis," *Intermountain Econ. Rev.*, 6, no. 2, Fall 1975, pp. 16–28.
3. Diemer, J. A. and J. R. McKean, "An Oracular and Pretentious Comment on an Old Prescription to Alleviate Stagflation," *Intermountain Econ. Rev.*, 6, no. 2, Fall 1975, pp. 55–59.
4. *Economic Report of the President*, Washington, D.C., G.P.O., Jan. 1976.
5. Gould, G., "The Possibility of Continued Inflation Without Recovery as a Result of Expansionary Monetary or Fiscal Policy in the Mid-Seventies," *Intermountain Econ. Rev.*, 6, no. 2, Fall 1975, pp. 32–44.
6. Heller, W., "Ford's Budget and the Economy," *Wall Street Journal*, February 5, 1976.
7. Keller, R. R. and S. L. Gray, "A Neo-Classical Argument for Wage-Price Controls," *Intermountain Econ. Rev.*, 6, no. 2, Fall 1975, pp. 46–53.
8. Kuhn, T. S., *The Structure of Scientific Revolutions* (2nd ed.), Chicago 1970.
9. Lerner, A. P., "Stagflation," *Intermountain Econ. Rev.*, 6, no. 2, Fall 1975, pp. 1–7.
10. Moggridge, D. E., *The Return to Gold, 1925*, Cambridge 1969.
11. Rostow, W. W., "Technology and the Price System," *Science and Ceremony: The Institutional Economics of C. E. Ayres*, (W. Breit and W. P. Culbertson, Jr., eds.), Chapter 5 (forthcoming).
12. Rostow, W. W., "Kondratieff, Schumpeter, and Kuznets: Trend Periods Revisited," *J. Econ. Hist.*, 35, no. 4, December 1975, pp. 719–53.
13. Rostow, W. W., *The World Economy: History and Prospect*, (forthcoming).

14. Rostow, W. W., *The Process of Economic Growth*, Oxford 1953 and 1961.
15. Rostow, W. W., *The Stages of Economic Growth* (1971 ed.), Cambridge.
16. Samuelson, P. A., *New Frontiers of the Kennedy Administration, The Texts of the Task Force Reports Prepared for the President*, Washington, D.C., 1961.
17. Samuelson, P. A., "Worldwide Stagflation," *Intermountain Econ. Rev.*, 6, no. 2, Fall 1975, pp. 8–15.

NOTES

1. I refer to Professors Lerner and Samuelson as neo-Keynesians because it is evident, on the basis of his intellectual life, that Keynes would have not gone on, frozen to models and policy positions rendered significantly irrelevant by the course of events. In fact, he was exceedingly sensitive to the consequences of the kind of shift in the relative prices of foodstuffs and raw materials versus manufactured goods which has brought on the current phase of stagflation. He took most seriously, for example, the unfavorable pre-1914 shift in the terms of trade against industrial Europe. That shift strongly affected his views at Versailles and in *The Economic Consequences of the Peace*. Then, suddenly, in 1920–21 the terms of trade shifted so radically in Britain's favor as to weaken its export markets and export industries. Keynes, promptly recognizing the meaning of the phenomenon, created a new terms of trade definition (embracing the volume of exports as well as relative export-import prices) and turned his mind to how Britain might break out of a structural problem which was, in many ways, the precise obverse of that now faced by the industrialized world. This story is briefly traced out in [14; pp. 184–88].

2. The gathering tension in key commodity markets during the 1960s is, incidentally, much like that which preceded the general price explosions of 1798–1800, 1852–54 and 1898–1900, as well as the famous 57 per cent rise in the cotton price between 1831 and 1835.

3. This case of the early 1970s is unique in its association of the price explosion with a subsequent recession and increased unemployment. But there is an historical analogy to current stagflation. In the period 1790–1850, bad British harvests often contributed to a cyclical downturn and rising unemployment. The mechanism was quite similar to the dual effect of high oil prices on monetary policy and real incomes. Bad British harvests required enlarged outlays for grain imports (thus raising interest rates and tightening capital markets) and, more directly, it brought on recession through higher food prices, reduced consumer expenditure on non-food items not fully compensated for by higher expenditures of some domestic farmers who profited, on balance, from reduced output and higher prices.

4. I was struck, in reading the *Stagflation* issue, with the fact that Messrs. Caceres and Gould concluded their papers by calling for more complex, supply-oriented dynamic models [2; p. 27] and [5; p. 44] and, I daresay, Messrs. Keller and Gray, Diemer and McKean would agree that their arguments could be buttressed and rendered more realistic if less simple models were used.

5. The basic exposition of this structure is in [14]. Elaborations of it are also to be found in: [15; pp. 12–16 and Appendix B], [12; pp. 750–53] and [11; Ch. 5]. My forthcoming book, [13] is, in effect, a sustained exercise in the application of this structure.

A RELUCTANT KEYNESIAN, A REPLY
BY ABBA P. LERNER

Dr. Rostow's article is one of a series of recent attacks on Keynesianism (and on various hyphen-Keynesianisms). [2] Before commenting on this article I would like to sketch the background of these attacks.

The essence of the Keynesian revolution is the rejection of the "classical" axiom that by order of the Law of Supply and Demand, unemployment would cause wages (the average nominal wage) to fall, and thereby to equate supply and demand in a full employment equilibrium. The Keynesian policy conclusion is that since the wage does not automatically adjust itself to the level of spending, it is the responsibility of the government to maintain prosperity by adjusting the level of spending, in accordance with full-employment equilibrium.

Keynes made it very clear that a sufficiently *low* wage would make *any* level of spending (and the corresponding quantity of money) adequate for full employment. His point was that the policy of depending on unemployment to adjust is far too costly; it could only induce *falling* wages which, unlike sufficiently *low* wages, would make things much worse before it made them any better. Further, such a policy would be abandoned long before full employment was achieved.

In the 1930s it was reasonable for Keynes to limit himself to the problem of depression and the failure of wages to fall far enough and fast enough to yield full-employment equilibrium. If the government would only adjust the level of spending to wages, all would be well. There was no need to worry about the behavior of the wage. If it refused to budge, prices would fall as productivity increased, and we would have a rate of price deflation in which pensioners and the like would get their share of the economic progress. Even if wages rose proportionately with overall productivity the convenience of a stable price level would be maintained. Only much later did faster escalation of wages come to plague us.

In his attempt to discourage classical economists from applying the inappropriate micro-economic Law of Supply and Demand to wages, Keynes showed why labor could not be treated like a normal commodity in micro-economics. A lowering of the price of labor could not be assumed to leave other prices, aggregate money income and the demand curve virtually unaffected. The automatic full-employment theory could be saved only by substituting a much more sophisticated argument. Wages would have to fall far enough—or rather I should say would have to *have fallen* far enough and then remained stable—to make goods cheap enough, to make the value (purchasing power) of money high enough, to make liquidity easy enough and the rate of interest low enough, to make investment large enough, to make income big enough to make the demand for goods and services great enough to bring about full employment!

This "correction" of the classical model turned it into a "Keynesian Classical" model whose sarcastic function was to show how unreasonable were the assumptions required to validate the theory of automatic full employment. But some enterprising classical economists wrapped the argument in sufficiently abstruse mathematics and complicated geometry, in the course of which the sarcasm dropped out of sight. The complete list of "enoughs"—sarcasm and all—was swallowed whole. The Keynesian Classical *Model*, which showed *why* wages *would not* adjust to the level of spending was transmogrified into an alleged Neo-Classical *Synthesis* of Keynesian and Classical thought to show *how* unemployment *would* adjust wages to yield automatic full employment.

This "synthesis" is indeed Keynesian inasmuch as it incorporates Keynes' spelling out of the missing assumptions required for automatic full employment. It leaves out only the sarcasm and the essence of the Keynesian revolution: the recognition that wages do not adjust to the level of money spending.

As if to balance this attempted kidnapping of Keynes by the "pre-Keynesian" Classical right, there is a symmetrical plot by some "post-Keynesians" on the left. The neo-classical "synthesis" embraces Keynes as a *conservative* classical economist who put some finishing touches on the theory of automatic full employment. The left-wing kidnappers claim that Keynes was basically a communist who did not believe that a capitalist society could ever be made to provide stable high employment. Joan Robinson, Minsky, Davidson, Hotson and many others denounce as "Bastard Keynesianism," not the neo-classical "synthesis" (for which the expression would be most apt), but the view that capitalist countries, by appropriate monetary and fiscal policy, can maintain adequate spending for stable high employment.

This view would clearly seem to be one held by John Maynard Keynes himself, and is what Rostow calls "Neo-Keynesian." Keynes' main purpose in writing *The General Theory of Employment Interest and Money*, and indeed the chief aim of his life, would seem clearly enough to persuade the governments of the western world to adopt his theory and the corresponding policies. But that gives little pause to the kidnappers from the left. Joan Robinson even quotes Keynes' own statement that "provided governments make sure that there is enough investment to maintain full employment . . ." and "provided that there is enough production, there is no objection to be raised against the classical analysis." But she dismisses this as "an ill considered remark" which nevertheless presents "the Bastard Keynesian theory in its purest form."[1] Was Keynes also his own illegitimate son?

Such shenanigans, right and left, can only thrive when there is a general state of confusion. A state of confusion has indeed existed since the emergence of simultaneous rising prices and high unemployment—Stagflation.

The rising prices are due *not* to excess demand but to wages rising faster than productivity. This makes costs rise. For continued production, prices must also rise. But there is not excess demand to contradict the deficiency of demand which is the immediate cause of the depression. Indeed, it is precisely the increase in costs and prices that is behind the insufficiency of demand. The authorities, hypnotized by an identification of inflation with excess demand, fail to provide the increased money spending needed to maintain a prosperity at the higher wages, costs and prices. But those to whom rising prices constitute irrefutable evidence of excess demand, see in stagflation too much spending and too little spending at the same time. Their mind naturally rebels, and they look for some new (presumably mindless) way of thinking—a new "paradigm."

The confusion was further complicated by another pair of distortions. First was the widespread identification of Keynes' *general* theory of employment interest and money with "deficit financing," the *special* policies he pressed on a world in the depths of severe depression. The second distortion corresponds to the supposition that deficit financing, the natural remedy for inadequate demand when prices were falling, could not also act as the natural remedy for inadequate demand when prices are rising. In the confusion, Keynesian thought is declared a failure, or bankrupt, in a flight not so much from Keynesianism as from economics.

Professor Rostow's article falls into this category. He promises an alternative explanation of stagflation. But when it comes to fulfilling the promise he is forced at every point to fall back on the Keynesian explanation of depression as caused from insufficient spending. He is similarly forced to explain the continuing inflation as a consequence of the escalation of wages and to urge the necessity of an incomes policy to hold them down.

Rostow's "dynamic disaggregated theory of production and prices" boils down to a scepticism concerning the ability of price changes to induce adjustments to changing demand or supply conditions. But all of his examples consist of cases where for reasons good or bad, the appropriate price changes were not permitted. His account of my own explanation is eminently fair, except for the suggestion that my "force" that "set up expectations of accelerated price and wage increases" is inherently mysterious. He does not seem to disagree with my view that barring serendipitous accidents we shall, as he puts it, continue to experience inflation until we introduce some form of incomes policy;" and all that he can do is to provide some plausible adhocery to explain the onset of the inflationary expectations and to make a number of useful suggestions about how an incomes policy might be made acceptable.

I agree that a $20 billion deficit cannot fill a $125 billion income gap. But I do not see, in this over-modest arithmetic, any "anomalies that subvert the existing tradition of scientific practices." Unlike Kuhn, I do not believe in the emergence of new ways of thought other than the uncovering of errors in logic or in observation. The appeal to a new "paradigm" (Rostow wisely avoids the word) is nothing more than an excuse for failing to show what the alleged errors are in the "old way of thinking."

It does not help to bring in other problems, no matter how serious they are—such as the long-run world-population problem, or how sudden they are—such as the establishment of oil monopoly. Nor is it true that the free market system cannot deal with changes as great as the recent changes in the price of oil or in the supply or demand for meat or wheat. Much larger changes—war mobilization and demobilization—were realized without having to call in new ways of thinking.

Rostow sees "the obvious" error in Keynesian analysis in its being "short period," so that it cannot deal with "long run" problems. But it is even more obvious that we are always living in the short period—namely *now*. Depression is always due to insufficient demand in the short period—*now*; inflation is always due either to too much demand *now*, or wages being raised *now*. These problems can be alleviated, or prevented, only by measures that affect these forces *now*—in the short period.

I do not mean to deny that long-period consideration can, with wisdom and with luck, lead to measures that will make the world a better place in the more distant future. And Rostow gives many important examples. But these are not the Keynesian problems of general depression and inflation. Depression and inflation will not be prevented by any long-run planning, unless good luck makes up completely for our unfortunate lack of omniscience.

"Enlarged investment in specific sectors through public-private collaboration" may be good or bad for future generations. But it depends on how wise and how lucky such investments will be rather than on who does them. "The route back to full employment" is not "through a shift of resources" for any such long-run objectives; it is only through the shift of resources from unemployment to employment. Indeed, to emphasize the essential independence of the two issues, Keynes shocked his readers by pointing out the benefits for employment and for the output of consumer goods, or even completely wasteful "investment" of digging holes in the ground and filling them up again.

In any case it is not true that long-period analysis forces disaggregation. The world is very complicated and a closer look always calls for disaggregation, long period or short period. But the closer look is not always necessary, and in general, it is *less* essential for long-run policy than for short-run adjustments. In the long run one can make adjustments (short-run adjustments!) in plans; also there is more of an automatic adjustment of supplies to demands and vice versa. The unavoidable simplification of our complex world by aggregation, without which nothing can be understood by a finite brain, are less damaging in long-run analysis than in short-run analysis. But the world does not wait. We must always act in the short run, otherwise we will have no opportunity to give consideration to any long-run issues. If we do not keep the ship on course, it matters little which harbour we prefer to reach.

The most interesting part, to me, of Rostow's article is his reminder that a number of Kondratieff-type fluctuations in economic prosperity may have been the result of swings in the terms of trade between agriculture and industry. The shifts in favor of agriculture enriched the agriculturists and landlords, leading to decreased spending and increased wage demands by impoverished industrial workers. Rostow suggests that with increasing pressure on population and food, and with increasing scarcity of fuel, we may expect the forces inducing stagflation to be stronger and more persistent than ever. I find this long-run projection extremely plausible. But even if it should turn out to be absolutely correct, we will still need "short-run" adjustments in total spending to prevent demand inflation from short-run excess demand and to prevent depression from short-run deficiencies in demand, as well as an incomes policy, operating in the short run, to check escalation of wages.

Disaggregation naturally draws attention to the existing ratios between different economic activities and tends to make these seem "natural" for the long period. This is what I see in the concept of "re-establishing balance" and in the sensing of a "tension" when a change in supply or demand calls for a change in price. Strangely enough, Rostow's call for "systematic, selective, sectoral planning" for the purpose of "re-establishing balance" comes immediately after his demonstration that a return to the sectoral patterns of the past quarter-century is "difficult, ... irrational ... doesn't make sense ... and is politically unrealistic."

All these are backslidings from general economics, micro more than macro. With perfect Keynesian orthodoxy, Rostow explains that the depression was caused by "reduced outlays" for other goods and services as a result of the rise in energy prices, "compounded by fiscal and monetary restraint" and "constrained ... public outlays for education and other welfare services." At the same time he recognizes the importance and difficulties of "bringing wage-push inflation under control" and makes some very useful suggestions toward achieving this. But this is just what Keynes would have fought for if he had been faced by wages that were rising rapidly instead of wages falling and thereby intensifying a severe depression.

Rostow concludes with a warning to "economists who treasure their linkage to Keynes" against playing out the (depression-aggravating) role of Montagu Normand and Otto Niemeyer. The warning seems to be intended for "Neo-Keynesians." If so, it is wrongly addressed. The dangers to prosperity, and indeed to free society, come not from those who advocate adequate spending and an incomes policy, even if they have to confess that they have not yet been able to devise a satisfactory and acceptable incomes policy. The warning should rather be delivered to the would-be kidnappers of Keynes and to the detractors of Keynesianism.

Rostow seems to want to be considered among the latter, but he really has no quarrel with either Keynesianism or Neo-Keynesianism. He seems to be unnerved by the great dangers to civilization from the failure of Keynesians to persuade authorities to adopt Keynesian policies, dismayed by the excessive modesty with which some more politically-minded Keynesians hope to overcome this political resistance, disturbed by Keynesian confessions of failing to devise an acceptable and effective incomes policy, and distracted by other important social problems which it would be wonderful to solve at the same time—forgetting that the better can be the greatest enemy of the good.

Rostow's warning should, in the first place, go to the touters of a "synthesis" that suggests waiting for full employment to return automatically in its own good time. It is they who are responsible for the pathological patience of the U.S. Government with its four-year plan for a gradual return to a somewhat milder depression. Another warning should go to the kidnappers on the left who would not start from here, perhaps hoping for things to get worse before something could be done about changing "the whole system." This utopianism is the kind that evoked Karl Marx's most extreme scorn. But yet another warning is needed for those who read only the titles of articles like Rostow's and believe that the texts validate the titles.

BIBLIOGRAPHY

1. Robinson, J., "The Age of Growth," *Challenge*, May–June 1976.
2. Rostow, W. W., "The Bankruptcy of Neo-Keynesian Economics," *Intermountain Economic Review*, Spring 1976, 7, no. 1, 1–11.

NOTES

1. See [1; p. 9]. There seems to be some confusion here between the notion of an illegitimate son and the notion of a pretended heir.

A REJOINDER

Professor Lerner's reply [4] to my "Bankruptcy of Neo-Keynesian Economics" [5] is so lucid that our differences in theoretical structure, analysis of the contemporary scene and prescription for policy can be made quite clear.

THEORY

We differ in two related respects. First, Professor Lerner believes, in effect, that the kind of disaggregated sectoral analysis I commend as a necessary supplement to Keynesian income analysis is beyond the grasp of "a finite brain." Therefore, we must retreat to the "unavoidable simplification of our complex world by aggregation." Over some three decades I have published disaggregated theories of growth, cycles and trends (Kondratieff cycles), closely related to the economic history of the past two centuries. [1] Professor Lerner is, of course, quite free to take issue with those analyses; but scholarly debate is not much advanced by ignoring the fact that some have regarded the degree of aggregation commended by Professor Lerner as "avoidable" and have made their case at length. The reason for accepting and working with the key sectors, as well as the income aggregates, relates to our second theoretical difference: the role of the short and the long period. As Professor Lerner well knows, the short period refers not to time, but to the factors screened out of the analysis for purposes of simplification, e.g., changes in technology, industrial capacity, food and raw materials supply, population, etc. In this sense, Keynes was quite wrong. We are not dead in the long period; the long period is with us every day of our lives. Even if we confine ourselves to the problem of business cycles (let alone growth or trend periods), no real cycle can be understood without piercing the veil of aggregates and identifying particular forms of investment or stimulus to consumption which characterized the period of expansion; the particular sectoral increases in costs, bottlenecks or changed profit expectations that brought about the upper turning point and the downswing. Highly aggregated multiplier-accelerator models are good sport; but no serious historian or responsible public servant working on counter-cyclical policy could regard them as an adequate theoretical framework. We must study the long-period factors and disaggregate, then, to understand even the most purely Keynesian problem; that is, fluctuations in the level of employment over relatively short periods of time. This is the case, fundamentally, because the business cycle (as well as trend period) is a systematic distortion in the process of growth, not fully to be understood outside that context.

What is Professor Lerner's reply to this line of argument? It is, essentially, that in a regime of competitive markets for goods and services and profit-maximizing private capital markets, long-term structural adjustments will take care of themselves in time, so long as public authorities maintain an appropriate level of effective demand. This is not a satisfactory answer for an economic historian, because over the long sweep of modern history, public authorities did no such thing. The economic historian must deal with growth, cycles and trends as they have actually occurred, not by imposing some stylized Harrod-Domar or neo-classical growth model held in full-employment equilibrium by such grossly unrealistic assumptions as constant returns to scale, neutral inventions, an absence of lags and constant income distribution. Moreover, even if the growth of the world economy had unfolded in that serendipitous way, a historian, by the nature of his profession, would have insisted on probing beneath the surface of the broad aggregates. Professor Lerner's criticism that a coherent, general disaggregated theory which systematically takes into account growth, trends and cycles is "a flight not so much from Keynesianism as from economics," is the oddest statement in his reply. There is much more to economics, as Keynes would have insisted in the 1970s, than the manipulation of effective aggregate demand.

The Contemporary Scene. These differences in theoretical perspective explain directly our differences in analyzing the contemporary scene. When I evoke the supply-demand forces at work in the 1960s (notably in agriculture and energy markets) which set the stage for the price explosion of 1972–74, they are, to Professor Lerner, "plausible ad-hoccery." To an analyst of trend periods, they are an essential part of the disaggregated analysis of inputs to the industrial system required to understand Kondratieff cycles. Indeed, what happened in the 1960s was quite similar to phases of market tension which preceded the other four Kondratieff upswings. Thus, Professor Lerner finds it difficult to acknowledge that there was a powerful element of raw-materials push as well as wage-push inflation at work in this period: he says that, "The rising prices are due not to excess demand but to wages rising faster than productivity." The raw-materials push in fact made a double contribution to inflation: a substantial direct contribution; also an important indirect contribution by stimulating higher money wage demands in a sterile effort to avoid the decline in real wages. I daresay Professor Lerner also would put, in the same *ad hoc* category, my observation regarding the sectoral pillars of the OECD boom of 1948–74. He regards the particular sources of effective demand which yielded the chronically high levels of employment (and mild cycles in growth rates) of that period as analytically irrelevant. I regard the changing pattern of demand and changing distribution of investment to be essential not only for a serious understanding of that unique boom, but also for dealing with the recession and unsatisfactory recovery that followed 1974.

Our most interesting (even amusing) analytic difference, however, relates to the state of the world price system. At one point Professor Lerner remarks: "Rostow's 'dynamic disaggregated theory of production and prices' boils down to a scepticism concerning the ability of the price changes to induce adjustments to changing demand or supply conditions. But all of his examples consist of cases where, for reasons good or bad, the appropriate price changes were not permitted." Professor Lerner is quite wrong about the content of my theory of production and prices, but he is quite right about my view of the world price system in basic commodities. OPEC is an inter-governmental monopoly seeking to maximize its Ricardian rents; every phase of energy policy, including price policy, in the United States is subject to law; in the non-OPEC world, energy-investment policy, as well as environmental policy, is largely shaped by governments; much the same can be said for raw materials, research and development, and agriculture where governments in the developing world will have to alter radically their investment allocations if the populations scheduled to be born over the next quarter-century are to be fed.

What makes our difference amusing is that Professor Lerner begins by describing the Keynesian revolution as flowing from Keynes' perception about the stickiness of wages in the face of declining effective demand. One would have thought that Professor Lerner would take more seriously the brutal fact that, for good or ill, food, energy, raw material and environmental policies are now so greatly influenced by governments. Commodity markets have departed from the classical model about as much as the inter-war labor market. In any case, my policy prescriptions—not my disaggregated theory of production and prices—flow from a perception that governments will have to think and act their way through the Fifth Kondratieff upswing, unlike the four previous parallel experiences which were surmounted more or less through the workings of the price system and changing directions of private capital flows.

Prescription. Against this background of theoretical and analytical contention, our differences in prescription are obvious. Professor Lerner does not much care, as a pure neo-Keynesian, what forms the increase in effective demand take, so long as we go back to full employment. Guided by my disaggregated, dynamic theory of production and prices, I am concerned that we go back to full employment through changed patterns of investment which would yield the supplies of food, energy, raw materials, air, water and new technologies we need for the continued viability of industrial civilization; and I believe those new investment patterns will require public-private collaboration.

Now, a final word about Professor Lerner's title. I am not a reluctant Keynesian. My first exercise in economic history (in 1934) was to try to apply Keynes' *A Treatise on Money* [3] to the inflation during the Napoleonic Wars. It didn't work. The factors operating on the supply side proved paramount and could not be taken into account. A few years later, I found *The General Theory* [2] to be an inadequate framework for analyzing the great price decline from 1873 to 1896. Thereby I did not reject the Keynesian insights, as Professor Lerner correctly perceives. Taken by themselves, I have simply regarded them as unsatisfactory to deal with growth, cycles and trends. However, I have always insisted that the kind of disaggregated, dynamic analysis I elaborated over the years be linked, ultimately, to the Keynesian aggregates.

When Keynes opposed the 1925 decision on the return to gold, he did not reject the whole received corpus of theory bearing on international trade and finance. He merely tried to persuade his colleagues that a lower exchange rate would yield a higher level of British employment while avoiding a potentially tragic effort to lower British money wage rates.

In now opposing those who argue that an expansionary fiscal and monetary policy alone can bring us out of stagflation, I am not rejecting the whole valuable corpus of income analysis generated by the Keynesian revolution. I am trying to persuade my colleagues that the required expansion of effective demand ought to come not merely from the manipulation of fiscal and monetary mechanisms, but also from an expansion of investment in certain sectors which only public policy can bring about. Rigid Keynesian prescriptions could lead to results as dangerous as the 1925 decision.

Professor Lerner is quite right in judging that I even more strongly oppose those who would try to contain inflation by slowing the pace of recovery and maintaining relatively high levels of unemployment, while not facing up to the difficulties of an incomes policy. But I end where I began in 1934: Keynesianism is not enough. After all, bankruptcy is not a state where assets have been reduced to zero; they simply fail to match liabilities.

REFERENCES

1. Rostow, W. W., *Essays on the British Economy of the Nineteenth Century*, Oxford 1948., Gayer, A. D., W. W. Rostow and A. J. Schwartz, *Growth and Fluctuation of the British Economy, 1790–1850*, Oxford 1953, 1975., Rostow, W. W., *The Process of Economic Growth*, Oxford 1953, 1960., Rostow, W. W., *The Stages of Economic Growth*, Cambridge 1960, 1971.
2. Keynes, J. M., *The General Theory of Employment, Interest and Money*, New York 1936.
3. Keynes, J. M., *A Treatise on Money*, New York 1930.
4. Lerner, A. P., "A Reluctant Keynesian," *Intermountain Econ. Rev.*, Fall 1976, 7, no. 2.
5. Rostow, W. W., "The Bankruptcy of Neo-Keynesian Economics," *Intermountain Econ. Rev.*, Spring 1976, 7, no. 1.

EIGHTEEN

Review of Ernest Mandel, Late Capitalism (1979)

Ernest Mandel is, by his own designation, a Trotskyite. Because Trotsky was intimately involved in the debate on long cycles, the subject—including Kondratieff's views—is no longer forbidden territory as it was until quite recently in the Soviet Union. In Late Capitalism Mandel applied his view of the Kondratieff cycle to the fate of capitalism.

Late Capitalism. By Ernest Mandel. Translated by Joris De Pres. London: NLB (Verso Edition), 1978; distributed in the USA and Canada by Schocken Books. Pp. 618. $9.95.

This volume seeks to explain in unadulterated Marxist terms the main features of modern economic history. It especially focusses on the post-1945 boom in the advanced industrial countries of the non-communist world, and the reasons "it would be followed by another long wave of increasing social and economic crisis for world capitalism, characterized by a far lower rate of overall growth" (p. 7).

In deploying the cumbersome Marxist apparatus, the heart of Mandel's analysis is his interpretation of the Kondratieff cycle—a variation on Schumpeter's hypothesis in *Business Cycles*. Capitalism is seen as having evolved on the basis of four technological revolutions: textiles, based on handicraft machines, coming to a close about 1848; the railroad, steel, and machine tool revolution, based on the production of machines by machines, coming to a close in the 1890s; the electricity and internal combustion engine revolution, coming to a close in the 1930s; and the electronic and nuclear power revolution whose deceleration marks the end of the fourth Kondratieff upswing in the second half of the 1960s.

This review was published in the September 1979 issue of *The Journal of Economic History* (vol. 39, no. 3). Reprinted with permission.

As in Schumpeter, each cycle has a phase of increased profits "when production sites have first to be created" (p. 121); and then a phase of rapid diffusion, when profit rates fall and the overall growth rate slows down. These phases of deceleration are dated 1824–1847, 1874–1893, 1914–1939, and 1966–.

The bulk of the analysis, however, is devoted to the evolution of the world economy since the 1930s; that is, the emergence of late capitalism. Mandel argues that multiple forces are tending to reduce the rate of profit; these are compounded by the pressure of wage demands in excess of productivity increases which can only be contained by incomes policies which he counsels labor to resist. He further argues that the inner contradictions of late capitalism will force the bourgeoisie into armed violence to protect surplus-value. To emancipate world society from these contradictions requires "the conquest of political power and the demolition of the bourgeois State apparatus, by the associated producers" (p. 499). A socialist world state will then emerge; for, true to his Trotskyite heritage, Mandel is as profoundly opposed to socialism in one country as he is to capitalism in one country (pp. 514 ff.).

Putting aside Mandel's political pamphleteering, the structural weakness of his system is that it is a two-sector model which (like neoclassical growth models) fails to take into account fluctuations in the relative abundance or scarcity, relative prices and profitability of investment in agricultural products, raw materials, and energy. They are embedded in Mandel's system somewhere in Department 1 (capital goods). He misses, therefore, a good deal that is central to his long cycle upswings; misses the dynamics of the 1830s and the late 1880s which run counter to his first and second downswings; misses the role of the shift in relative prices from the 1930s to 1951; misses the critical role of declining relative prices for basic commodities in the boom of the 1950s and 1960s; fails to introduce adequately in this 1978 edition the meaning of the price revolution of 1972–1978.

This failure bears significantly on his assessment of the prospects for democratic capitalist societies. There are ample opportunities and need for productive investment in the generation ahead in resource-related fields, e.g., energy production and conservation, the control of pollution, agricultural output to match the population bulge in the developing regions, raw material development, research and development over a wide front. For our times, investments of this kind are the equivalent, say, of those required to open up the American West in the third quarter of the nineteenth century, and Canada, Australia, and Argentina in the pre-1914 generation. Although, as in other such periods, the rate of growth of urban real income may be less than in the 1950s and 1960s (when the terms of trade shifted favorably by about 25 percent for the OECD world), it need be neither a period of stagnating real income nor of chronic unemployment.

Mandel's thesis falls, then, in the general category of those of Shuman and Rosenau, Forrester, Heilbroner and the other pessimists who echo the secular stagnation hypothesis of the 1930s. The text is heavy going and somewhat turgid; but the main lines of Mandel's argument are clear enough.

NINETEEN

Comment from a Not Quite Empty Box (1982)

This essay was stirred by a sophisticated, low-key debate between Keynesians and monetarists in the March 1981 issue of The Economic Journal. *As the text indicates, James Meade had constructed for the occasion a rather complex diagram exhibiting various combinations of the two gospels with an empty box for lost souls, if any.*

Still troubled by the gross inadequacy of both forms of macroeconomics (or combinations of them) to deal effectively with the forces at work in the world economy, I formulated—as in Chapter 17—a protest.

The papers on monetarism in the first fifty-seven pages of the March 1981 issue of this JOURNAL are so decorous, temperate, and occasionally elegant that one hesitates to intrude on so stylish an occasion. But the issues of theory and policy not gripped by the debate are too important to ignore and I have, therefore, decided to intervene.

I shall define myself initially as a non-Keynesian and non-monetarist for whom James Meade provided only a questionable empty box. I have long since concluded that both theoretical frameworks are grossly insufficient for the serious analysis of historical and contemporary problems.

My general proposition, as stated elsewhere, is this:[1]

> ... both neo-Keynesian and monetarist analyses of prices and output are conducted essentially within a Marshallian short-period framework or with the long-period factors exogenously determined and treated as fixed trends.
> This is not only an unsatisfactory way to go about the analysis of the pre-1914 world; it is also a grossly insufficient way to deal with the world economy of the 1970s and 1980s where radical shifts in relative prices have occurred and are likely to continue to occur, where many major

---

This essay was published in the March 1982 issue of *The Economic Journal* (vol. 92, no. 365). Reprinted with permission.

Table 1
Variables Bearing on Inflation: The United States, 1968–1981 II

	Average unemployment (%) (1)	Output per hour (%) (2)	Compensation per hour (%) (3)	Unit labour cost (%) (4)	Consumer price index (%) (5)
1968	3·6	3·3	7·4	3·9	4·2
1969	3·5	−0·3	6·5	6·8	5·4
1970	4·9	0·3	7·0	6·6	5·9
1971	5·9	3·3	6·6	3·1	4·3
1972	5·6	3·7	6·7	2·8	3·3
1973	4·9	2·5	7·6	4·9	6·2
1974	5·6	−2·4	9·4	12·1	11·0
1975	8·5	2·1	9·6	7·4	9·1
1976	7·7	3·2	8·1	4·7	5·8
1977	7·0	2·0	7·6	5·5	6·5
1978	6·0	−0·2	8·5	8·7	7·7
1979	5·8	−0·7	9·7	10·4	11·3
1980	7·1*	−0·3	9·9	10·3	13·5
1981 I	7·3	4·3	11·6	7·0	0·8
1981 II	7·4	−0·9	9·6	10·6	0·6

* Estimated annual figure.
Source: *Economic Report of the President, January 1981*, Washington, D.C.: G.P.O., pp. 267, 277, 293. 1981 revised quarterly figures, Council of Economic Advisers.

Note: Cyclical troughs and peaks were as follows:

Trough	Peak
Oct. 1967	June 1969
Nov. 1970	Oct. 1973
June 1975	June 1979

economies have experienced deceleration in the rate of productivity increase, and where radical changes in the direction of investment will be required to reachieve structural balance and resumed rapid growth.

In this compressed comment I shall merely illustrate this proposition with four observations and draw a conclusion.

(1) *None of the contestants deals with the short-run behaviour of productivity in relation to the rate of inflation.* As Table 1 and Fig. 1 demonstrate, for the United States at least, the systematic counter-cyclical behaviour of productivity, set against the stickiness (or counter-cyclical behaviour) of money wages, has rendered each of the three US exercises in purposeful monetary restraint (1969–70, 1974–5, and 1979–80) counterproductive. Unit costs and the inflation rate rose in response to recessions induced by monetary policy;[2] and the sequence of recessions induced a decelerating trend in the rate of productivity increase.

(2) *None of the contestants deals with the role of trend movements (or even short period movements) in the relative prices of basic commodities and their implications for output, real income, and prices.* One would think that even monetarists, but especially Keynesians,[3] would, at least, note that the great boom of the 1950s and 1960s was accompanied by (and, in my view, was made possible by) a systematic if decelerating favourable

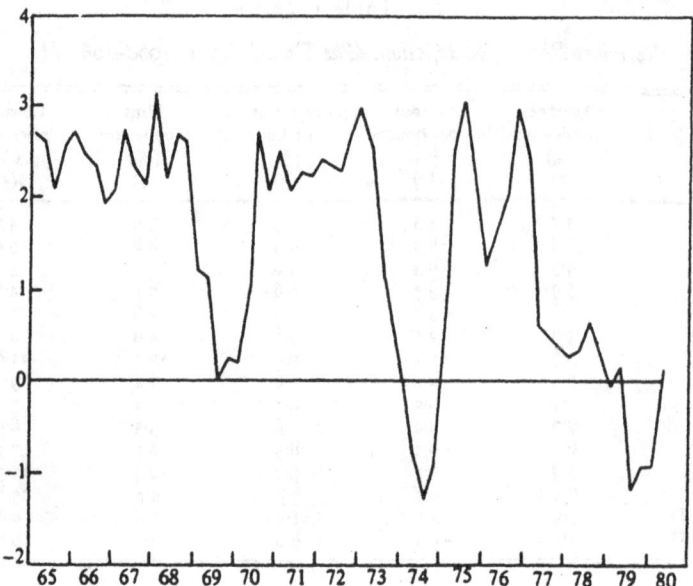

Fig. 1. Cyclically adjusted productivity – percentage change from four quarters ago. Source: Council of Economic Advisers estimates (cyclical adjustment based on percentage changes in the GNP gap for the current and three prior quarters, with a dummy variable set at 1 for quarters after 1973: 1. Productivity is output per hour of all persons in the private nonfarm business sector).

shift in the terms of trade for advanced industrial countries of about 25% between 1951 and 1972; that a radical unfavourable shift of about the same order of magnitude occurred in 1974–5, playing a large role in the process we call stagflation; and that the price and output performances of our economies have, since 1975, been greatly affected by subsequent fluctuations in the terms of trade, influenced notably, of course, by the real international oil price.

More narrowly, Keynesians and monetarists equally ignore the role of the absolute decline of raw material prices in damping the over-all inflation rate in the 1950s and helping lift the inflation rate in the course of the 1960s as decline ceased and gave way to slow increase. Between 1951 and the trough in 1964 the US price index for crude materials fell at an annual average rate of 2.4%; the consumer price index rose at an annual average rate of only 1.4%. Between 1964 and 1970 (before President Nixon's price and wage controls intervened), the two indexes rose at annual average rates of 3.6 and 3.8%, respectively. Evidently, forces other than crude material prices help determine the consumers price index; but the change in direction of those prices after 1964 removed a significant damping factor on the rate of inflation.

An irony of the present situation in the United States is that a phase of falling real prices for oil and, perhaps, of good world harvests—both of which have no legitimate place in monetary analysis of the price level—are the major hope of the nominally monetarist Reagan administration for damping the inflation rate at a time when money wage settlements are still running at about 10% and the rate of productivity increase is low, although rising with the uncertain course of recovery.

(3) *The macro character of both monetary and Keynesian theory denies to their practitioners essential regional and sectoral insights.* Take a few simple examples stemming from shifts in the relative price of energy in the United States. What is the meaning for both analysis and policy of a national average level of unemployment for 1980 of, say, 7.1% when it is made up of a spectrum ranging from 12.6% in Michigan to 3.9% in Wyoming which is enjoying an energy-based boom like most of the Mountain States? Of a national average real growth rate of 1.6% for the period 1973–8 and a population growth rate in the 1970s of 0.9% when these figures may range from negative to Texas' 5.8% rate of growth in gross state product, 2% in population?

How useful is it to know that in 1980 dollars business investment as a share of GNP in the United States in 1978–81 was just about what it was in 1966–9 (11.3%) without also knowing that the proportion of outlays for energy within that total has risen at least from 16 to 31% and that this variable is critical for the rate of decline of oil imports with all that implies for the macro performance of the economy, and greatly affected by public policy?

The point is, of course, that without sectoral and regional disaggregation, we quite literally may not know what we are talking about; and we may, therefore, not pose the right questions in formulating policy proposals. There is, for example, a good case for viewing the key economic problem of the United States as a problem of certain regions linked to a few sluggish sectors (notably the portions of the Northeast and industrial Middle West linked to steel and automobiles) in somewhat the way Britain's interwar problem came to rest on coal, the export industries, and the regions linked to them.

(4) *The commentators skirt and treat as peripheral a point which should be central and dealt with systematically and professionally; that is, the problem of controlling inflation in the post-1945 world is essentially political and social.* What we call the Keynesian Revolution ended an era when citizens more or less regarded recurrent periods of severe unemployment as an act of God rather than man. It wasn't quite true, as the concurrence of phases of political and social unrest with deep depressions and the punishment meted out to incumbent politicians at such times indicate. Nevertheless, quite aside from built-in stabilisers which emerged from social policies introduced into the postwar world, the expectation was established that periods of deep and protracted unemployment would not be permitted by the political process; and in the United States this proposition was written into law in 1946. The exacerbated inflation rates of the post-1972 world economy are forcing us all to think again. As several commentators pointed out, the monetarist approach, in both its

gradualist (Thatcher) or more Wagnerian versions (Hayek), is essentially an exercise in political economy designed radically to alter expectations and lead the working force to accept wage rate increases approximating the average increase in productivity. So, of course, are various versions of incomes policies, including the partially implicit incomes policies which have shielded, say, Japan, the Federal Republic of Germany, Switzerland, and Austria rather well in recent years. My point here is that economists should deal with this problem head-on, professionally, as a matter of social science analysis in its widest sense. To understand the inflation performance of different societies requires, in each case, careful historical, social, institutional, and political analyses. It is not enough for economists to provide *ad hoc* observations while searching for some economically elegant substitute for their rather romantic image of how the disciplines of the gold standard actually worked in the pre-1914 world.

Incidentally, despite their speeches on formal occasions, there is no group that better understands the limitations of the monetary instrument and the need for a total societal approach to the control of inflation than central bankers—an approach embracing fiscal, monetary, and incomes policies as well as the most effective unifying political leadership the society can muster.

The examples could, of course, be extended; and I have elaborated elsewhere more fully and systematically the argument underpinning them.

But the fact is that the great boom of the 1950s and 1960s cannot be understood without taking into account the great unapplied backlog of technologies available to Western Europe and Japan in 1945 as well as the favourable shift in the terms of trade after 1951. Surely, macroeconomic demand policy, fiscal and monetary, played a role; but its apparent success depended on factors neither monetarists nor Keynesians took into account; and the failure to understand the structure of the boom accounts in good part for the defensive discomfiture since 1972 of the Keynesians who enjoyed intellectual primacy in the course of it. Similarly, the dramatic shift in relative prices after 1972 rendered growth on the pattern of the previous generation impossible through the operation of the price-elasticity of demand in key energy-related sectors as well as the impact of changes in the terms of trade on the rate of growth of real income. Palpably, we require—and are slowly moving toward— new patterns of investment. But the composition of investment is outside the framework of both monetarist and Keynesian thought. The former— at least Professor Friedman—falls back explicitly on Walrasian equilibrium as the ultimate foundation of the system. But Walrasian equilibrium is inherently static and does not provide a credible mechanism for dealing with the lags and frictions of Marshallian long period change. Therefore, in an economy of rapidly altering technologies and acute sectoral problems, the prescription of free competitive markets either does not suffice; or it is, as a matter of simple fact, unrealistic because key sectors are in the firm grip of public policies.

The argument becomes clearer if we turn from our intensely parochial debates within the profession and examine a world economy confronted by the massive challenge of making an interim transition from oil to other energy sources while simultaneously preparing a longer run transition to wholly new energy sources; where something like $680 billion (1980), by World Bank estimates, will have to be invested in the developing regions in the 1980s to provide them with an energy base consistent with minimum necessary growth rates; where a marked acceleration (to, say, 4% per annum) will be required in agricultural production in the developing regions to feed decently the populations scheduled to be born; where the fecklessness of policy in the advanced industrial world is imposing through stagflation heavy burdens on the developing world as well as painful frustrations on the peoples of the industrial North. In such circumstances, it is a bit odd to observe a high proportion of our most talented economists debating alternative formulations of macroeconomic theory and policy which are, to put it mildly, only partially relevant to the challenges of the active world.

In the end, the not quite empty box I occupy should be designated Keynesian-Monetarist-Plus. The Plus is no more or less than the linking of macro-analysis to the systematic treatment of the Marshallian long period, increasing returns and all. As Marshall was acutely aware, once that step is taken there is no stopping place short of dealing, in his phrases, with "the high theme of economic progress" and "society as an organism." For the generation ahead, no lesser intellectual framework will permit us usefully to serve our societies and end the costly repetition of the interwar irrelevance of mainstream economics that has marked the past decade.

NOTES

1. W. W. Rostow, *Why the Poor Get Richer and the Rich Slow Down* (London: Macmillan, 1980), p. 256.

2. Professor Friedman and I shared with others in different parts of the United States a radio discussion in the wake of President Reagan's Inaugural Address on 20 January 1981. When I made this point Professor Friedman promptly responded that now we had a president of character who would, he implied, have the courage and persistence to impose a sufficiently protracted monetary discipline to break back the rate of increase in money wages. He was immediately reminded by a third party in the discussion that in the rhythm of American politics time was short. The new administration would soon be thinking of the elections ahead.

[3.] Keynes was extremely sensitive to the meaning for Britain and Europe of movements in the relative prices of basic commodities versus industrial products and would certainly have taken this element into account in an analysis of the 1970s and 1980s. I examine the evolution of the terms of trade strand in Keynes's analysis in *The Process of Economic Growth*, (Oxford: Clarendon Press, 1953, 1960), pp. 184-9.

TWENTY

Review of P. T. Bauer, Equality, the Third World, and Economic Delusion *(1982)*

In this review I squared off against a colleague from what is conventionally regarded as the Right, although I have difficulty making relevant sense of the old French Revolution terms when applied to a time two centuries farther down the road.

My disagreement with Bauer is still real on a number of important matters, but I share his assessment of some of his favorite targets and believe he has made important contributions to the debate on development policy that is now four decades old. In short, the first sentence of my review is seriously meant.

If P. T. Bauer did not exist it would have been useful to invent him. For a quarter century now he has been an ardent and articulate critic of most forms of economic assistance to developing countries, of what he took to be the prevailing economic doctrines underlying such assistance, and of a good deal of the political analysis and rhetoric that surrounded the subject. Surely, issues as inherently complex as economic growth theory and policy, ramified in their linkages to politics and highly emotionally charged, needed a devil's advocate. For those like myself who have since the 1950s supported certain policies of development assistance, it has been helpful to have Bauer on the scene to assure we had thought through, to our own satisfaction at least, the issues he raised so provocatively.

The present volume is a kind of Bauer sampler. It consists of fifteen chapters covering the major issues with which he has been professionally

---

This review was published in the December 1982 issue of *Transaction/Society* (vol. 20, no. 1). Reprinted with permission.

concerned. Most were published as articles in the 1970s, one written with Hla Myint, two with A. A. Walters, one with Basil Yamey, who has been for many years a close collaborator of Bauer's, notably in his work on Africa. Despite its episodic character, this book captures well Bauer's contribution to the protracted debate on development policy and North-South relations in general.

It is structured in three parts. Part one consists of two essays on equality. The first argues that equality of income is a chimera and that policies of income redistribution are most unlikely, on balance, to benefit the poor. The second argues that the British class structure has been and remains notably dynamic and flexible, contrary to the image it sometimes projects.

Part two, the heart of the book, contains nine rather disparate chapters, touching on the theme "The West and the Third World." They range from a fairly technical critique of schemes of commodity stabilization to an impassioned attack on Ali Mazrui's 1979 Reith lectures; from an extended argument that foreign aid can do little good but much harm to a defense of British economic policies in colonial Africa, except for their final phase of increasingly direct state control over export commodities.

Part three, on "The State of Economics," includes lively assaults on theorists of the dollar problem, on John Hick's foray into economic history, and on economists who overemphasize the role of investment in economic growth and the role of mathematics in the formulation and teaching of economic theory.

Bauer is to be understood as both a polemicist and a social scientist of a particular theoretical bent. The two roles are related but distinguishable. In the former role the target of his polemics is clear enough: it is his image of what might be called the international liberal establishment. He is against those who believe that the North should accept a burden of historical guilt in dealing with the South; against those who look on foreign aid as a device for income redistribution in favor of poorer nations; against those who believe intervention in the free market process (even with respect to policies of family limitation) is justified. In conducting his polemics, Bauer isolates his targets by name, if possible, and goes after them hammer and tongs, using, where available, selected quotations which incorporate the offending views in their most egregious and assailable form. Bauer has a gallery of favorite villains: Kwame Nkrumah (for his feckless and wastrel economic policies); Julius Nyerere (for his creation of a low productivity collectivized agriculture); Professor Mahalanobis and the Indian Second Five Year Plan (for its emphasis on expansion of the capital goods industries); perhaps above all, the designers and supporters of the New International Economic Order, which incorporates just about all the major economic and political doctrines and attitudes which Bauer despises. I should note that among his villains are the "MIT development economists," of whom I was one in the 1950s; but he does not devote much time or space to our views beyond a few quotations taken out of context. He is, nevertheless, correct in his judgment that our image of the development process and development policy differed radically from his.

Bauer's views as a social scientist must be deduced largely from the character of his criticism of others and his observations on particular cases; e.g., on Hong Kong. He does not provide a systematic, positive exposition of his doctrines. But, in fact, they are clear enough. In first approximation, he can evidently be classified as a neoclassical economist of a rather pure kind who believes the market mechanism should be permitted to work its will to the limit and that the individual thrives best in an environment where the power of the state is minimized. His most basic criticism of foreign aid is, in fact, that it has, in his view, strengthened the power of governments in the developing regions. Bauer belongs, in good part, with the Lionel Robbins-Friedrich Hayek tradition at the London School of Economics and the Milton Friedman tradition at the University of Chicago.

There is more to his perception of the world, however, than the austere and rather sterile paradigm incorporated in those traditions. In his critique of John Hicks on economic history and of the current tyranny of mathematical formulations in economic theory, Bauer exhibits, for example, an awareness of two kinds of complexity: the complexity of interactions within the economic system; and the complexity of interactions among the economic, social, and political sectors of society. There are asides which reflect an awareness of the power of tribe, race, caste, and culture in economic arrangements, notably in dealing with Africa and India. His knowledge of the other developing regions appears thin.

Bauer's weakness as a social scientist and analyst of development is that he has never organized his more subtle perceptions about societies as a whole and related them systematically to the economic process. There is a gap between the market economist and the wider but somewhat casual commentator on the human condition. In the end, Bauer is most comfortable as the neoclassical gadfly on the rump of the international liberal establishment.

Many of his critical judgments are shrewd, and I share some of his prejudices—for example, against foreign aid as a device for income redistribution; against the rhetoric, agenda, and global negotiating technique of the New International Economic Order; against the Nkrumahs and Sukarnos of the Third World. I do not believe Bauer is correct in his assertion that, without foreign aid, the market process would be stronger, the governments weaker in the developing world. I would guess foreign exchange limitations would have driven many developing countries into even more centralized, autarchical policies than they have, in fact, pursued. But I believe that, as in advanced industrial societies, government bureaucracies are subject to the temptation of self-aggrandizement and, as the quality of private entrepreneurship improves, a good many functions could and should be pruned out and allocated to the private sector. The competitive market process can accomplish a good deal; but the conditions for its viability are more complex than Bauer would allow.

A review of this kind is not an appropriate occasion to restate at length my own positive approach to development. My basic difference from Bauer lies in the appropriate point of departure. Development is a process involving every dimension of a society; and economic development policy must respect that fact. Modernization is painful and inherently revolutionary. It is driven forward, against powerful and understandable resistance, not by the profit motive but by the perception that nations cannot stand with dignity on the world scene—resistant to humiliating intrusion—unless they modernize. But modernization takes time. It requires a succession of generations trained and motivated for the essential tasks, some of which lie in the private sector, some in the public sector. Hong Kong is a remarkable case; but the marriage of a British administrative system with a corps of overachieving private entrepreneurs and a highly educated work force in a city-state largely freed of the task of modernizing a large low-productivity agricultural sector is not a model capable of wide emulation.

In attacking Mazrui or the promulgators of the New International Economic Order or their various Western sympathizers, Bauer is not dealing with the serious actors in the drama of modernization. Those who attend United Nations meetings on development are foreign-office officials who have little or nothing to do with development policy at home. The serious actors are those who carry forward the modernization process, day by day, on farms and in factories, in schools and laboratories, and in offices in the public as well as the private sector. Economically, their objective is not an international redistribution of income but the achievement and maintenance of sustained growth accompanied by the progressive absorption of increasingly sophisticated technologies in their nations' economies.

They accomplished a good deal over the past generation. The average growth performance of the developing regions in the 1960s and 1970s fell in the range of 4.5–5.5 percent per annum, yielding an average increase in GNP per capita of 1.6 percent for low-income countries, 3.8 percent for those in the World Bank's middle-income range. The former figure approximated the nineteenth-century performance of the presently advanced industrial countries during take-off (1.7 percent); the latter substantially exceeded the earlier performance during the drive to technological maturity (2.1 percent). These aggregate growth rates were strongly reflected in such basic social indicators as length of life and level of education: by World Bank calculations life expectancy increased from 42 to 57 years of age in low-income countries between 1960 and 1979, from 53 to 61 in middle-income countries; population per physician more than halved in both categories; adult literacy rose from 27 to 43 percent in low-income countries between 1960 and 1976, from 53 to 72 percent in middle-income countries; the numbers enrolled in secondary schools and institutions of higher education about doubled in both categories. There is still a long way to go; but sustained economic growth in the third quarter of the twentieth century was neither a statistical artifact nor a process insulated from the life of the average citizen.

Those who brought about these historic changes hardly appear in Bauer's book. He seems, in fact, unaware of their existence. But these are the men and women with whom the World Bank, the regional development banks, and the national aid administrations work. Indeed, it was the MIT doctrine in the 1950s that a central function of foreign aid was to strengthen their hand and to elevate their influence as they helped move their societies forward in a process of modernization which would fulfill their nations' ardent nationalist aspirations in as constructive a way as possible. There were, evidently, failures and setbacks and distortions; but I, at least, have no doubt that, aside from providing a useful if modest margin of external resources, foreign aid accomplished this large purpose and, in so doing, rendered an inherently explosive world somewhat less dangerous than it otherwise would have been.

In his debate with Mazrui, Bauer makes the following observation: "Professor Mazrui writes well. He moves easily between vivid, pertinent episodes and wide political issues. He presents thought-provoking information on various matters. . . . The merits of the book are, however, peripheral. They do not affect the fundamental flaws of the argument." I come to much the same conclusion with respect to Bauer's latest volume.

TWENTY-ONE

Technology and Unemployment in the Western World (1982)

This lecture was delivered in the spacious, old Schools building on the High Street, Oxford, almost exactly thirty-six years after I delivered, in the same place, my Inaugural Lecture as Harmsworth Professor. The later lecture was altogether a rather nostalgic occasion. I had come to Oxford in November to receive the first copies of a festschrift organized by two old friends, Charles Kindleberger and Guido di Tella; our thoughts were much of Munia Postan who wrote a biographical essay for that enterprise but who had died late in 1981. And, in an engaging coincidence, a friend since our Rhodes Scholar days, Gordon Craig, had been booked to deliver a lecture in his field (modern Germany) at exactly the same time in the same building. The Warden of St. Anthony's, Raymond Carr, fully gowned, served as a rather elegant traffic cop in the lobby, directing the arrivals to the appropriate lecture room.

As the text makes clear, I decided to try to answer the question posed by Postan in our last conversation—a question with resonance back to the post-1815 debate between Ricardo and Malthus: Would the current technological revolution yield high chronic technological unemployment? My tentative and exploratory answer in 1982 was: There are no objective economic reasons this should happen. Now, as the 1980s draw to a close, I would assert that proposition somewhat more confidently.

Superficially, the evidence in the advanced industrial world is mixed: Japan and the United States have enjoyed (or moved to) relatively low levels of unemployment; unemployment has persisted at uncomfortably high levels in Western Europe. On the whole, however, I would suggest that this has occurred because of Europe's somewhat slower pace in absorbing the new technologies, various rigidities in the labor market, fear of inflationary overheating of the economy, inadequate infrastructure and pollution control investment, etc.

Put another way, the introduction of the new technologies appears to generate a great many more jobs, at various levels of skill, than some initial assessments had suggested; however, a good deal of physical mobility and job retraining is necessary to exploit that fact.

I

My theme this afternoon derives from the last talk I had with Sir Michael Postan. The Postans and I had dinner in London on Sunday, September 20, 1981—a few months before his death. As always, we plunged into what was then most on our minds. His concern, widely shared in the advanced industrial world, was that we were moving into a time of chronic high unemployment. He was not talking about the kind of unemployment that can be induced by stringent monetary policies designed to reduce the rate of inflation. What he sensed was that the character of the new technologies coming forward, combined with the erosion of the older manufacturing industries, would render a significant margin of the working force unemployable. We did not explore whether such unemployment might happen because of the capital intensity of the new sectors; or because of a possible mismatch of training and skills; or because real wage rates would not justify the employment of the less skilled in other sectors; or because a part of the working force might prefer unemployment and its emoluments to work on the kinds of jobs that might be available; or because the macro-economic policies pursued by our governments would keep us in a state of chronic underemployment. But Postan had evidently been giving more thought to the problem than I had, and he was troubled about the societal consequences of a substantial body of more or less permanently unemployed men and women. Postan's capacity to get to the heart of the matter was so sure that I took his point very seriously, indeed.

I reminded him, quite unnecessarily, that we economic historians had been vicariously living with such anxieties ever since, in years of acute cyclical depression, the hand-loom weavers went about breaking up the new textile machines in the factories. And, to be sure, the succession of technologies over the past two centuries has forced important changes in the structure of the working force that have been often accompanied by painful human and regional adjustments. But, by and large, these changes have proved to be transitional. Chronic technological unemployment has not been a significant feature of modern economic history. Putting aside the rhythm of business cycles, the peculiar pathology of the inter-war years, and our current incapacity to reconcile control over inflation with sustained growth, the labor market has more or less cleared despite considerable problems of immobility, friction, and stickiness.

Despite this temperately optimistic professional bias, I had no firm response last September to the question Postan posed. I have, in fact, no dogmatic answer to provide now, a year later. And I do recognize that some things happen for the first time. But I thought it somehow appropriate that I should, on this occasion, try to make a tentative contribution at least to the analysis of the problem Postan raised, which I shall rephrase: Given the pace and character of technological change, are there likely to be demands for labor in the generation ahead in skill categories that are attainable and in industries sufficiently profitable to employ fully the working forces of the advanced industrial economies at then existing real wage levels.?

I shall begin by considering the implications for investment and employment of two major dynamic forces at work in the world economy—what I have come to call the Fifth Kondratieff Upswing and the Fourth Industrial Revolution.[1] I shall then move on to the prospects for the older basic industries, the possibilities for enlarged exports to the developing regions, and the employment implications of reversing the erosion of infrastructure in at least some of the advanced industrial countries. Finally, I shall address the policy implications of the perspective that emerges.

II

Now, the Fifth Kondratieff Upswing. I have taken the view that, with some foreshadowing in the second half of the 1960s, the world economy moved at the close of 1972 into the fifth protracted period of relatively high prices for basic commodities after some twenty years of absolute or relative decline in those commodities, starting in 1951. These intervals of relative shortage or abundance of basic commodities are, I believe, at the core of the phenomena that Kondratieff sought to explain; a sequence of erratic long cycles in price levels, interest rates, and money wages, reaching back to about 1790. There are, of course, a variety of long-cycle theories; but I have found no other hypothesis that can consistently explain this pattern, which can now be traced back over two centuries. Cycles in innovations, wars, and gold discoveries, or cycles in overall growth rates, do not do the job when subjected to close analysis.

I would underline that the cycles Kondratieff identified were by no means smooth sine curves. There are, even, elements of uniformity in their irregularity. Before 1914, for example, the cycles began with a sharp, initial rise that lasted a few years. Of the trend rise in British prices in the First Kondratieff Upswing, 66 percent occurred between 1798 and 1801; in the second, 71 percent occurred between 1852 and 1854; in the third, 57 percent came between 1898 and 1900.[2] The world economy experienced such a convulsive rise in 1973–1975.

There was also a second, fairly consistent irregularity. The upswings and downswings usually exhibited an interval or cycle in which the trend movement abated or reversed and then asserted itself again. In the British case, for example, the cycles of 1803–1808, 1832–1837, 1862–

1868, 1886–1894, and 1904–1908 all, to a significant degree, ran against the trend. I shall raise the question later as to whether we are now experiencing such an interval.

For our purposes, the central phenomenon of a Kondratieff upswing is a shift in the direction of investment toward the expansion of supplies of (or substitutes for) high-priced commodities that are in relatively short supply. On the downswing, with some interesting explicable exceptions such as the opening of the Argentine pampas in the late 1880s, investment shifts toward industrial sectors, urban infrastructure, and service sectors where the relative profitability of investment would then be favorable. Such a shift happened between 1951 and 1972.

The Fifth Kondratieff Upswing began at the close of 1972 with an explosion of grain prices that was followed by a quadrupling of oil prices the next year. In both cases exogenous events played a role: respectively, the poor harvests of 1972–1973 and the Middle East war of October 1973. But a deeper examination makes clear that strong endogenous forces were at work in the late 1960s that decreed, in time, a reversal of post-1951 relative price trends.[3] In the United States, the absolute decline in basic commodity prices ended in 1964; there was a marked decline in the proportion of world grain stocks to annual consumption, rendering the markets increasingly vulnerable to a bad harvest year; a rapid increase in global oil consumption in the 1960s was accompanied in the United States by rising requirements for oil imports at just the time when U.S. oil and natural gas production was peaking out—an event that happened in 1970–1971. Spot oil prices began to rise and the staff of OPEC, well trained in Western universities, calculated correctly that strong monopoly leverage on the oil market was possible if discipline within the organization was maintained.

Despite various government efforts to suppress or mitigate the impact of the energy price on consumers, the Kondratieff upswing process worked to a degree: Energy-related investment sharply increased. In the United States, for example, conventional energy investment rose from 1.8 percent of GNP in the mid-1960s to about 3.5 percent in 1981. (This excludes large investments in energy conservation, which may have amounted to 3 percent of all capital outlays in 1981.[4])

At the moment, of course, energy, food, and raw-materials prices are soft as compared to their levels, say, two or three years ago; it is wholly appropriate to ask if the Fifth Kondratieff Downswing has begun after a much shorter upswing than in the past. After all, the length of the upswings was often determined in the pre-1914 world by the time it took to open up new territories and bring them into large-scale, efficient production. In fact, thirty years ago, when writing of such cycles and the process of expanding agricultural production, I observed: "Now further development of this type . . . would consist less in the opening of new territories than in the improvement of productivity in existing territories, with less likelihood of substantial overshooting."[5]

On the other hand, it may well be that we have another transient break in the trend and the Fifth Kondratieff Upswing will reassert itself. Consider, for example, the following:

- In diminishing degree, geared to income elasticities of demand, the softening of raw materials, energy, and agricultural prices has been caused by the current severe recession.
- Even so, near the bottom of recession (September 1982), crude-materials prices (1967 = 100) in the United States stood at 317; total finished-goods prices at 283. The U.S. terms of trade, which had deteriorated relative to 1972 by 26 percent in the first quarter of 1980, were still 15 percent less favorable in the second quarter of 1982 than they had been a decade earlier, despite an artificially strong dollar. A revival in the world economy is likely to reverse, in some degree, the recent relative price shift in basic commodities.
- As for the future of the world oil price, no one's crystal ball is clear. There are those, for example, who would argue that OPEC is about to self-destruct. But this judgment, I would suggest, is a bit premature despite the evident tensions that exist within OPEC. If the world economy revives, a little-noted aspect of the pattern of world energy consumption is likely to reassert itself: namely, that much higher rates of increase in energy consumption take place in the developing regions than in the advanced industrial world. For example, primary energy consumption increased in the United States and Canada, between 1971 and 1981, at the rate of 0.8 percent per annum; in Western Europe at 1.0 percent; but in Latin America, the Middle East, Africa, and Asia at between 5.1 percent and 6.6 percent.[6] The proportion of world energy that is consumed in the developing regions will rapidly rise. History, in fact, is not linear, but a quarter-century from now primary energy consumption in the developing regions would exceed that in both Western Europe and North America combined if the differential expansion rates of the 1970s persist. The reasons for the higher energy growth rates in the developing regions include: higher real growth rates at this stage of their history than the growth rates of the advanced industrial countries; high rates of population expansion in energy-intensive cities; the rapid absorption of energy-intensive technologies such as steel, metalworking, and chemicals; and high rates of expansion in motor vehicle use.
- Question marks hang over the probable future rates of production of certain great oilfields in the United States and the Soviet Union; the best geologists I know tell me it is unlikely that new finds, which will certainly be made, will match the run-down of existing established oil reserves.
- Finally, the oil-producing region of the Middle East is not particularly stable.

With respect to agriculture, the inescapable population increase in the developing regions that is due to age structures, despite current declines in birth rates, may add something like 2 billion human beings to the planet in the next generation. Overall, the rate of increase in agricultural production in developing regions does not yet match the rate of increase in the demand for food, thereby inducing an annual rate of growth in grain imports of more than 3 percent per annum. In addition, there is the apparently intractable pathology of agriculture in most of the communist states.

As for raw materials, there is evidence of underinvestment in recent years and of distorted patterns of investment. In Latin America, for example, the tension between an understandable nationalist desire to control fully natural resources and foreign investors' understandable desire for stable and reasonable terms for their outlays has often resulted in reduced rates of raw-materials development. If the world economy revives we may encounter raw-materials bottlenecks.[7]

I am inclined to believe, on balance, and without dogmatic confidence, that the Fifth Kondratieff Upswing is not over if the world economy revives in the 1980s.

For our purposes—reverting to Postan's question—this conclusion means that very large additional investments in energy, agriculture, and raw materials must take place within the world economy if growth is to go forward at normal rates and still rapidly enlarging population is to be accommodated with adequate food supplies.

We do not have the data required to estimate firmly the diversion of investment to these resource sectors that would be necessary to maintain a viable world economy. Where calculations have been made, the numbers are large. For example, a World Bank estimate suggested that energy production investment requirements in the developing regions would approximate $683 billion (in 1980 U.S. dollars), with an annual investment growth rate of 12.3 percent, lifting the proportion of investment allocated to this purpose from 2.3 percent of GNP in 1980 to 3.2 percent in 1990.[8] A good deal of this capital would have to come from abroad.

For Latin America alone, the Inter-American Development Bank estimated that in the course of the 1980s something of the order of $300 billion (in 1980 U.S. dollars) would be required for investment in energy production, about 45 percent of which would have to come from abroad.[9] The proportion of GNP allocated to energy investment would, on these calculations, rise from something like 3 percent to 4 percent.

For the United States, my colleagues and I at the University of Texas estimated a few years ago that to render the United States a marginal net energy exporter, by full exploitation of coal and synthetics, would require a rise in the proportion of energy production investment to GNP from 3.5 percent to at least 4.2 percent.[10]

As in the other Kondratieff upswings, a part of the increased investment in resources will occur in the relatively advanced industrial countries, depending on their resource endowments; a part in what we call developing regions. Depending on how North-South relations evolve or are organized—a subject to which I shall return—a substantial expansion of employment opportunities should emerge in industries, both old and new, in the advanced industrial countries.

If, by appropriate investment patterns and the introduction of new technologies, we succeed in inducing the Fifth Kondratieff Downswing over, say, the next decade, the consequent sustained relative decline of basic commodity prices and improved terms of trade would, of course, accelerate the rise of real incomes in the advanced industrial countries. We would return, in a sense, to the pattern of the 1950s and 1960s. The income elasticity of demand might express itself in somewhat different ways than it did then, but thus far, at least, our peoples have not experienced difficulty in finding ways to spend higher real incomes, although the proportion of income saved might rise. Perhaps the easiest of all human adjustments is to move up in the world.

III

I turn now to the Fourth Industrial Revolution. For this analysis we are in the world of Schumpeter's theory of the Kondratieff cycle rather than mine; although contemporary Schumpeterians, unlike the master, forget that Schumpeter was trying to explain the price, interest rate, and money wage data on which Kondratieff initially focused. Instead, they seek to associate innovational surges with periods of high growth rates and periods of growth deceleration with a relative lack of new, innovational industries.

I would immediately pose the question of whether innovations, in fact, come in clusters. If so, why? What is the nature of the clusters? And if such clusters do occur, are we in the midst of the Third, Fourth, or Fifth cluster?

First, to start at the less glamorous end of the spectrum, a great deal of important invention and innovation has consisted of incremental improvements in existing technologies since the 1780s. Some of these incremental improvements find their way into patent records; many do not. The rates of productivity increase that we observe in history have been significantly determined by this kind of endemic, incremental invention and innovation. Following Julius Wolff's Law, enunciated in 1912, the path of this kind of refinement by small steps is probably subject to diminishing returns as particular technologies age and potentialities for improvement decline. But, overall, such learning by doing is unlikely to yield bunching on a grand scale, although, if we knew enough about the flow of incremental invention and innovation, shorter, positive cyclical patterns might emerge.

Second, innovations of varying significance that create new industries, large and small, are initiated (in modern times) over a wide front; and they are by no means all related to each other. Svennilson, for example, lists selectively 17 substantial innovations, rooted in technologies and processes known before 1914, that played an important part in the interwar years. They range from aircraft to ball bearings to more efficient office machinery and canning methods.[11]

A more recent and extremely valuable study headed by Christopher Freeman at the University of Sussex, using data generated by John Jewkes and his colleagues, lists 62 innovations between 1920 and 1970.[12] They range from the zip fastener, the ballpoint pen, and cinerama to electronic digital computers, DDT, and synthetic fibers. Each is dated with respect to time of invention and time when significant commercial production began. (As Freeman points out, nuclear reactors and other important innovations are not included.) The question is: When undifferentiated data of this kind are aggregated, do they yield clusters? Gerhard Mensch has argued that clusters do emerge, and that they typically occur in periods of acute depression and provide the basis for the next expansion.[13] In contrast, Freeman and his team argue that, using such data and other innovation indicators on a more refined basis, some clusters do, indeed, emerge; but that they are not systematically related to any particular cyclical phase. On this matter, I vote with Freeman.

Third, we have Schumpeter pure. Without trying to enumerate inventions and innovations, as did Svennilson, Jewkes, and their successors, he grandly asserted that there had been three giant innovational clusters: factory manufactured textiles, Cort's method for making iron from coke, and Watt's steam engine, all of which came on-stage in a substantial way in Britain of the 1780s; the railroads, which made considerable commercial headway in the 1830s and then generated substantial booms in Britain, the U.S. northeast, and Germany in the 1840s; and finally, electricity, a new batch of chemicals, and the internal combustion engine, which all became significant around the opening of the twentieth century. This grouping of innovational giants, which conformed to the way economic historians had conventionally told their stories, has still a good deal to commend it, although it is, of course, highly oversimplified.

Fourth, there is Freeman's elaboration of the Schumpeterian insight, in the form of "new technology systems."[14] Freeman and his colleagues focused, particularly, on synthetic fibers and plastics and on electronics. In Freeman's view, these inventions both constituted important components in his (not my) "Fourth Long Wave" and illustrated vividly the dynamics of innovation, its clustering, and its evolution over time. Freeman's study deals almost exclusively with the period between 1955 and 1975; although the study notes the earlier origins of the innovations on which it focuses.

Freeman's general, neo-Schumpeterian theory is the following: An innovative entrepreneur demonstrates that large profits can be made by applying a new technology. A "swarming" of less heroic entrepreneurs then occurs in the new sector. Output and employment rise rapidly in the new industry and in those related to it. Simultaneously, scientific, inventive, and innovative talent moves in to improve processes and break bottlenecks, yielding a cluster of innovations related to the initial breakthrough. But strong forces operating on both demand and supply sides impose a path of deceleration. As the curve of growth flattens out, not only will the rate of increase in employment decline but forces will also converge to reduce the relation of employment to output. A Freeman-type Kondratieff downswing ensues.

Freeman's view is that the innovational cluster that had carried growth forward in the advanced industrial world in the 1950s and 1960s began to flatten out after 1965 and brought us into the Kondratieff downswing (as he interprets it) of the 1970s and early 1980s.

Governments collect statistical data in response to clearly defined, inescapable problems of public policy or, occasionally, in response to the conventional wisdom of the mainstream economics of the day. Neither of these forces has operated on the field of invention and innovation in relation to investment and employment. Therefore, none of us now commands the orderly, reliable time series with which to test Freeman's hypothesis, although he has worked hard to find data that relate to his argument. Nevertheless, I have no doubt that his general theory of entrepreneurial swarming, innovational bunching, deceleration, and a decline in the labor force–production ratio is broadly correct. This theory closely approximates the dynamics of leading-sector complexes as I have elaborated that notion.

And I would add two points not usually dealt with in the literature. First, in history, the particular major innovations that define each of Schumpeter's three grand waves proved to be closely related. Watt's steam engine was essential for Cort's puddling process and also permitted the cotton factories to move beyond the waterfalls. The high obsolescence rate of iron rails set up a premium on producing cheap steel, to which inventors and innovators responded. Indeed, in its first phase the modern steel industry was overwhelmingly a supplier of rails. The automobile required not only light electrical gear but also important help from evolving industrial chemistry in the form of refined gasoline and vulcanized rubber. It also depended on refinements in steel manufacture and metalworking that followed the initial concentration in the steel industry on supplying the railroads. To close the circle, the chemical industry was highly dependent on increasingly cheap supplies of electricity. In short, there have been systematic, subtle interactions within each grand innovational cluster.

Second, I would note that Kondratieff cycles, as I interpret them, and the sequence of industrial revolutions are not wholly independent phenomena. Both historically and at present, relative resource scarcities and industrial innovation have interacted in complex patterns. The steam engine, after all, emerged in Britain to get the water out of the mines and provide enlarged mineral supplies. The relative rise in the price of timber in eighteenth-century Britain set up a powerful incentive to solve the problem of making cheap, high quality iron from coke. The cotton gin expanded and cheapened remarkably the raw-material supplies for the great industrial leading sector of its time. The railroad (as Clapham said of France) produced a greater agricultural revolution than all the peasant uprisings of previous centuries and permitted the efficient transport of large new supplies of both industrial raw materials and agricultural products. The motor vehicle, when converted to farm machinery, and the chemicals of the Third Industrial Revolution together yielded a massive rise in agricultural productivity. The Fourth Industrial Revolution, via genetics and now synthetic materials, is already yielding promising results in agricultural production and in substitutes for raw materials that might otherwise rise in relative price in the generation ahead; it may also contribute in various ways to the transition in energy sources away from reliance on oil.

Turning back to Freeman's study, I would differ somewhat with his interpretation of the post-1945 era in two respects. First, he does not take fully into account the extent to which the great boom of the 1950s and 1960s—rooted in the rapid diffusion of the automobile and durable consumer goods—had been based on an extension (and refinement) of old, rather than new, technologies. While recognizing, of course, that significant innovations were introduced in the 1950s and 1960s, I am more inclined to regard those decades as the rounding out of Schumpeter's third innovational wave than as a true fourth. I would not argue the point, given the inadequacy of appropriate data and the impressionistic character of all human judgments, except that it directly relates to future employment prospects, to which I shall return.

Second, Freeman does not deal with the Fourth Kondratieff Downswing, as I define it; that is, he ignores the role of relatively falling basic commodity prices in the 1950s and 1960s (and a 25 percent favorable shift in the terms of trade for advanced industrial countries) in driving the expansion forward via rapidly increasing real incomes. Nor does he relate stagflation in the period since 1973 to the price and income elasticity effects of the rise in energy prices and the marked deterioration in the terms of trade for most advanced industrial economies. Some significant portion of the chronic high unemployment of recent years is surely a product of the failure of our societies and their policies to adjust to what I call the Fifth Kondratieff Upswing, rather than a simple result of the waning of Freeman's Fourth Long Wave of innovations.

You will also note that Freeman's unemployment differs from the unemployment that concerned Postan. Freeman focuses on deceleration in now aging sectors; Postan was troubled by the possible employment implications of the new, emerging innovational sectors. This difference is why a case exists for distinguishing rather sharply what went on innovationally in the 1950s and 1960s from what should happen in the 1980s and 1990s.

In dealing with electronics, Freeman is aware that its prospects differ from synthetic fibers and plastics. At one point, for example, he provides a diagram that shows an "extension of life cycle" for a given innovational breakthrough, with deceleration giving way to a new phase of acceleration as a major innovational refinement is achieved.[15] It is that kind of process I have in mind, for example, in extending Schumpeter's chemicals of the third innovational cluster down to synthetic fibers and plastics. Freeman applies this kind of extension to electronics, where he perceives many still unfolding breakthroughs and applications.[16]

Recognizing the arbitrariness of all this, I am inclined to define the Fourth Industrial Revolution, now in its early stage, as embracing innovations in microelectronics, communications, the offshoots of genetics, the laser, robots, and new synthetic materials. Before it runs its course, the Fourth Industrial Revolution may yield breakthroughs in photovoltaic cells, hydrogen, and more economical ways of producing synthetic oil. Fusion, as I understand from my friends in plasma physics, is farther down the line.

This is the batch of unfolding or potential technologies whose implications for future labor demand concerned Postan. There are four questions to pose and try to answer.

- How big will the new industries become?
- How many will they employ and unemploy?
- What mix of skills will they require?
- And, above all, are other likely or possible demands for labor in the advanced industrial economies capable of keeping the workforce, over the whole spectrum of skills, fully employed?

In writing this lecture I tried to find in the current literature approximate answers to the first two questions, with rather thin results. Part of the problem is that we cannot even measure the size and employment characteristics of an old innovational complex. We are victimized, in this matter, by our Standard Industrial Classifications, which are fiendishly designed to conceal a great deal of what we wish to know. What we need are data on all the output of goods and services and all the employment generated by a given industrial complex. The U.S. automobile industry is the best documented case we have.[17] As of 1972 this industry, broadly but still incompletely defined, employed over 5 million people in the United States. Of those, only 16 percent helped manufacture motor vehicles; 2 percent were in petroleum refining; 11 percent in wholesaling; 32 percent in retailing; 8 percent in repair and other services; 27 percent in transportation. These calculations do not include employment in producing steel and other components for motor vehicle manufacture. Overall, in 1972 something like 18 percent of GNP was generated by this complex.

It is unlikely that the innovations of the Fourth Industrial Revolution will generate quite so impressive a range and scale, although one set of calculations for the United States estimates total employment in 1990 of 2.45 million in the following high technology sectors: robot production; laser processing; handling of new synthetic materials; genetic engineering; bionic medical electronics; laser, holographic, and optical maintenance.[18] I cite this figure simply to suggest that, because the new technologies are likely to suffuse a wide range of sectors, employment within them could become quite large over the next generation or so, depending on the rate at which the technologies are diffused.

For our purposes, however, I would underline two narrower points.

- First, as the motor vehicle sectoral complex suggests, manufacturing employment is only a modest proportion of total employment generated by an innovational industry. All manner of workers—not merely Ph.D.'s and engineers—can find employment in innovational complexes when these complexes move from the laboratory into the economy. A recent pamphlet of the U.S. Department of Labor contains an article on employment prospects in the computer industry that captures this point in a brisk summary in the table of contents, with a vivid, if rather odd, analogy: "Computers—key weapons in the Post-Industrial Revolution—need an army-sized workforce to keep them aimed, loaded, and firing. The duties of these troops are so varied that almost anyone can find a place in their ranks."[19] Moreover, the evidence thus far is that the introduction of computers into business and government offices will not reduce the demand for clerical workers. To some degree a change in skills is required, but this does not appear to have posed formidable problems.[20]
- Second, a point memorably made by Adam Smith's homily on pin manufacture and vindicated by more than two centuries of economic history down to a highly efficient electronics plant in the Watts section of Los Angeles: Large-scale production permits not only specialization of function but also the productive employment of relatively unskilled labor. (I remember well how, during World War II, the head of the Courtauld Art Institute in London converted the institution into a round-the-clock producer of tools and gauges of the highest precision for the Royal Navy, employing former secretaries, hairdressers and other women without prior factory experience. The proud artisans in that field were amazed and somewhat discomfited.)

From what we now know, I find it difficult to believe that the computer revolution, in most of its applications, will generate serious problems of chronic technological unemployment. Robots are a different matter, and I suspect they are the component in the Fourth Industrial Revolution that lies at the heart of a great deal of the anxiety about technology and future employment prospects.

After all, robots are instruments that directly replace men and women in the manufacturing industry, a sorely beset component of the advanced industrial economies of the West. At an outer limit, a Carnegie-Mellon study suggests that, over a period of twenty years, nonservo-controlled robots could replace up to 1 million workers in the United States while servo-controlled robots could replace up to 3 million, out of a total of about 8 million operative workers in manufacturing.[21] The automotive, electrical equipment, machinery, and fabricating metals industries are the most likely candidates for this process.

Replacement, of course, does not mean displacement. Robots require not only operators but also manufacture, programming, and maintenance. No satisfactory estimates appear to exist on the numerical balance of jobs replaced and created. What seems to emerge is that retraining for robot operation is not a difficult process; maintenance requires considerably higher skill levels; and manufacture and programming require quite advanced engineering abilities and computer virtuosity. On balance, the most likely outcome of the diffusion of the robot is the net displacement of unskilled workers or workers so near to retirement that firms may not be willing to invest in retraining them. Robot diffusion will also generate a heightened demand for engineers and computer programmers. Depending on the pace at which robot diffusion proceeds, the scale of the problem posed by the net displacement of less skilled or unrestrained workers could be substantial.

My tentative response to the first three questions I posed is, then:

- The new industries could get to be quite large by historical standards because the technologies they incorporate are potentially ubiquitous; but the flimsy evidence available does not permit confident prediction about the pace of diffusion and the ultimate scale of the new industries.
- Therefore, we simply do not know how many members of the workforce the new industries will employ and unemploy.
- But the mix of skills required in the innovational complexes as a whole is likely to be wide and, with large-scale production, the skill requirements in manufacture are likely to diminish.

If these tentative judgments prove true, the expansion of these new industries is unlikely to be impeded for long by skilled labor bottlenecks. Certain types of engineers and technicians may, for a time, be in short supply; but a large-scale, rapid diffusion of the robot may, indeed, pose an employment problem for the less skilled—a problem whose scale we cannot measure.

IV

I turn, therefore, to my fourth question, which I would rephrase as follows: Given the uncertain rate of expansion, employment, and skill requirements of the new innovational industries, the potential offloading of unskilled workers into the labor market by robots, and the possible further loss of employment in older industries, is a return to full employment feasible in the advanced industrial countries? In this question we are dealing with very large issues, indeed; and I shall have to be both cryptic and more dogmatic than I prefer.

First, I do not believe that the older industries of the Atlantic world are doomed to disappear without a trace and be supplanted by imports from Japan and the emerging industrial countries of the developing world. Present low levels of output in those older industries are the product not only of foreign competition but also of high interest rates and a deep U.S. recession. As for Japan, the automobile industry in the West could retrieve a part of the lost market, without corrosive protectionist devices, by introducing new technologies and management practices; and the steel industry could do the same. Moreover, the relative rise of real wages in Japan is likely to mitigate a part of Japan's current comparative advantage if the United States and Western Europe come to match Japanese technology and efficiency—a process not beyond their reach.

As for the emerging industrial powers of the developing world, only a few are likely to command the domestic markets required to generate efficient automobile and steel production. They can and should compete internationally. But if those industries in the advanced industrial world take advantage of new, emerging technologies (for example, robots and new industrial materials), they should remain viable at, probably, lower levels than their historical production peaks but much higher levels than at present. These industries are not likely, of course, to resume the high growth rates of the 1950s and 1960s.

Looking ahead, the decisive competitive battle in the advanced industrial world is likely to be over the technologies of the Fourth Industrial Revolution rather than those of the Third. But I do not believe the older industries are automatically destined for oblivion, if steady growth is resumed in the advanced industrial world and if entrepreneurship of a reasonably high order is exercised in those industries, including the application of some of the new technologies.

Second, coming back to the Fifth Kondratieff Upswing, the possibility and need exist for a new North-South partnership centered on the key resource sectors of which I spoke earlier; and that partnership could generate greatly expanded employment in export industries as well as capital movements from North to South. The Brandt Commission Report could have driven this point home but failed because of a discontinuity in its analysis. A good deal of that report dramatized, correctly in my view, the need for expanded investment and production in the South in the fields of agriculture, energy, and raw materials. It also touched on the need for investments to prevent or reverse gross environmental degradation. Instead of then recommending that the new North-South partnership be built on recognition of common interest in the solution to those sectoral resource problems, the report switched to a quite different theme: a plea for a massive transfer of resources from North to South justified, on economic grounds, by an alleged lack of investment and employment opportunities in the North. There is a distinct strand of secular stagnation theory in the Brandt Report, which I believe is no more correct now than when it was evoked during the inter-war years. In any case, the report's overriding plea for a gross, undifferentiated increase in resource transfers to the South was rejected and, I suspect, will continue to be rejected.

The proper course, in my view, is to bring the North and South together to assure flows of private and public investment to the key resource sectors on a scale that will avoid the deceleration or strangulation of growth in the South that might otherwise occur. Incidentally, I believe the bulk of this work is likely to be best conducted on a regional basis centered, perhaps, around the Inter-American, African, and Asian development banks, but with the full participation of the World Bank as well as the United States, Western Europe, and Japan in each region. Once begun successfully, such North-South collaboration is likely to extend to embrace practical work on other North-South issues.

The case for an effective North-South partnership of this kind rests on an assumption that should be made explicit: I believe that the large political, strategic, and economic interests of the North require that we do what we can to assure high and steady growth rates in the South. Among other things, the proportion of total trade of the advanced industrial countries with developing countries has been rising and, under reasonably normal circumstances in the world economy, should continue to grow as a matter of historical trend. In the case of the United States, for example, the portion of exports flowing to the developing regions rose from about 29 percent in 1973 to 38 percent in 1981, and the shift in proportion was by no means confined to members of OPEC.

In addition, there is another source of employment of a kind capable of engaging unskilled as well as skilled labor: the backlog of investment that has developed in basic infrastructure—roads, highways, bridges, water supply, sewerage, pollution control, etc. On this issue I can speak confidently only of the United States. Under the pressure of slow growth on public revenues and of high interest rates, public authorities have cut back such infrastructure outlays over the past decade. In that sense, the United States has been living off capital. The result is a backlog that may amount to some $2.5 trillion (1982) if previous infrastructure standards are to be regained. Even for a $3 trillion economy, and even if spread out over 10 or 15 years, this is a formidable increment of required investment with large implications for employment prospects over a wide range of skills. My casual impression is that such backlogs exist for both Western Europe and Japan, but they are, relatively, less substantial.

V

Taken all together, the potentialities and imperatives of the Fifth Kondratieff Upswing, the Fourth Industrial Revolution, the need to modernize the older industries, the common interest in sustained high growth in the developing regions with its implications for expanded exports to the South, and the infrastructure backlog decree that what we might call the objective marginal efficiency of capital curve for the advanced industrial countries is high; and, if exploited by a return to low real interest rates and appropriate public policies, this situation should provide ample employment opportunities over the foreseeable future for the workforces, skilled and unskilled, of the advanced industrial countries.

But, evidently, a lion stands in our path—our common incapacity to reconcile high growth rates with effective control over inflation. If we continue, as we have since 1973, with stop-and-go policies and low average growth rates, low investment rates, and much idle capacity, the diffusion of the new technologies will be slowed, among other things, by the resistance of the unions; the decline of the old basic industries will continue; the will to deal creatively with the South will be feeble; and the erosion of our physical and social infrastructure will be progressive. High levels of unemployment could, indeed, then become chronic. To avoid this outcome, we shall, evidently, have to find ways to control inflation by means other than monetary restraint and high real interest rates, and the discipline of chronic unemployment, idle capacity, and low investment rates that these policies impose.

It is not difficult, as a historian, to explain why policies like those of, say, Prime Minister Margaret Thatcher and President Ronald Reagan have emerged. Between 1950 and 1973 the annual average rate of real growth in output per capita in the advanced industrial countries approximated 3.8 percent.[22] This rate was unique—about three times the average level for the period from 1820–1950 or for any sub-period within it. This interval of economic exuberance happened because of an accidental convergence of the favorable terms of trade of the Fourth Kondratieff Downswing with a time when Western Europe and Japan had achieved, with post-war recovery, levels of real income per capita that rendered possible the mass diffusion of the automobile and durable consumer goods that, in turn, carried with them a backlog of familiar technologies hitherto fully diffused only in North America. In addition, plastics, synthetic fibers, television, and other new technologies emerged and were rapidly diffused. Real income and productivity lifted in an extraordinary way. This surge in affluence led to highly commendable outlays for social services at rates higher than the rates of growth of real GNP. At some stage, deceleration was obviously required if these outlays for social services were not to absorb unmanageable proportions of GNP. But when growth rates and private real incomes suddenly stagnated or declined, strong political pressures to reduce the flow of resources to public authorities emerged in virtually all the Western countries. Thus, even existing levels of social services have been endangered. The maintenance of those levels—let alone their expansion—will clearly require a resumption of steady, reasonably high growth rates.

Meanwhile, our macro-economists, with some notable exceptions, tended to believe the glories of the 1950s and 1960s were the result of the New Economics, which did, indeed, play an ancillary role. But, by and large, the mainstream economists and the political leaders they served failed to understand the structural and inherently transient character of the expansionary forces at work. Some, at least, encouraged the popular belief that affluence was now automatically assured, and suggested that men and women in advanced industrial societies could turn wholeheartedly to refining the quality of life. Sustained high employment also provided leverage of a kind never before experienced in the history of industrial societies to the labor unions, which the unions exploited in explicable but sometimes counterproductive ways; and expectations of full capacity utilization led to labor-hoarding by firms. And so, as societies, we were highly vulnerable to the change in fortunes that we experienced with the coming of the Fifth Kondratieff Upswing at the end of 1972. In one sense, we have since done as badly adjusting to a gross unfavorable shift in the terms of trade as our predecessors did with the gross favorable shift in the terms of trade after 1920.

It is not surprising, then, that democratic political life has generated a rather barbaric Hegelian (or Friedmanesque) antithesis to the benign but somewhat ephemeral thesis of the 1950s and 1960s. It is now, I suggest, time to strive for a civilized synthesis.

In conventional economic terms, one basic component of the synthesis is simple enough to state. Evidently, we require long-term incomes policies that would discipline the average rate of increase in money wages to the average rate of productivity increase. (My own rather eccentric view is that the appropriate formula, at a time of such high employment in the public sector, is fixed average money wages with prices falling with the rate of productivity increase—a policy advocated by E.F.M. Durbin in the 1930s and examined respectfully by Keynes in *The General Theory*.) With a firm incomes policy, the instruments of macro-economic policy can perform the balancing role for which they were designed.

But, as I have argued recently in *The Economic Journal*, the creation and maintenance of an effective incomes policy is not a matter of conventional economic policy.[23] It is a problem of generating and institutionalizing a working consensus on a critical issue in societies otherwise dedicated to vigorous competitive contention. It is, essentially, a constitutional problem and should be approached as such, with appropriate gravity. In democratic societies we maintain minimum order amidst competitive contention by accepting a framework of agreed-upon constitutional rules. Incomes policies must now be added to those rules.

The history of the years since 1945 is littered with failed efforts by democratic societies to sustain incomes policies. There have been periods of success for a good many countries; and four have sustained their success quite well over a longer span: Japan, Austria, the Federal Republic of Germany, and Switzerland. But the second most important point to be made about incomes policies is that they are difficult and pose deep-seated political and institutional problems.

The most important thing to be said about incomes policies, however, is that, whatever the difficulties, we shall have to overcome them if we are to sustain viable and civilized societies in the present and foreseeable environment of the world economy.

Politically, our societies must be brought together around a palpable, fully shared, overriding, long-run interest—an interest in sustained noninflationary growth—at the cost of abandoning chimerical short-run interests and zero-sum game attitudes. Institutionally, an incomes policy requires that we install arrangements for annual wage bargaining at the national level, where the common requirement of avoiding inflation is there on the table, to replace the fragmented sectoral wage negotiations that have emerged out of our histories, where the rate of inflation is taken essentially as an exogenous variable beyond the negotiatiors' control or responsibility. A national wage norm cannot, or course, be universally applied. There must be a range of flexibility in money wage increases to permit rapidly growing, high productivity industries to draw labor while others (as, indeed, at present) increase real wages at less than the average rate of productivity increase. Each country will have to work out these arrangements in terms of its own history, circumstances, and inherited institutions. What we know from the relatively successful cases is that incomes policies need not impose undue rigidities on the working of markets nor otherwise prevent vital private sectors from operating.

Obviously, judgments on the capacity of our societies to make such institutional changes and sustain them will differ; and there is room for legitimate debate. I would only say that, under strong presidential leadership, I believe the United States, as a society, is now capable of mounting and sustaining such arrangements once the stakes involved are fully and well explained.

There are policy implications of my call for a civilized synthesis that transcend the fundamental question of reconciling control over inflation with regular growth. I will cite three, all of which would require a significant change in attitude among some of the leaders of the counter-revolution that we have been experiencing on both sides of the Atlantic. One of the banners of the counter-revolution is that governments can do no economic good. I, for one, am prepared to argue that, in some directions, government actions have been excessive; a weighing of costs and benefits is appropriate along with a pruning out of dead weight. I would also argue that governments should not intrude if the private sector can do the job. But, against the background of firmly installed incomes policies, there are legitimate tasks to be performed that only governments can perform:

- Tax and other government initiatives could accelerate the diffusion of the Fourth Industrial Revolution, including a government role in retraining those components of the workforce displaced by the new technologies.[24]
- Government policies and negotiations are required to set an appropriate framework for a North-South partnership of the kind I have suggested, although a substantial part of the increased capital flows to the South could be private.
- The rehabilitation of infrastructure is, evidently, a task for public authorities.

VI

I conclude, then, this tentative and exploratory analysis with the judgment that there are no objective, economic reasons why the advanced industrial societies should experience high chronic technological unemployment in the generation ahead. The potential boom of the 1980s and 1990s would be driven initially by expanded investment rather than by real incomes lifted by favorable terms of trade, as was the case in the the 1950s and 1960s. To set the process in motion, we would be relying, in a sense, on the multiplier rather than the accelerator.

Like all of us, I wish profoundly that Postan was among us to respond. He might have said: "Look here. You've assumed away the problem. You have made effective incomes policies a condition for generating the flows of domestic and foreign investment necessary fully to employ our workforces. Look about you. Only rarely in modern history have our electorates been more divided. Most of those in power are committed to what you call the barbaric counter-revolution. Their opponents protest the consequences of the counter-revolution; but the remedies they propose look backward and are feeble. The leadership capable of reintegrating our societies and generating the consensus that incomes policies demand is nowhere in sight except in a few advanced industrial societies."

I would respond to such a legitimate charge with two final observations. First, if one has a patient faith in the democratic process, it is possible to believe that, with the passage of time, our citizens will, in one way or another, demand of their governments that they do something about high unemployment and eroding social services and infrastructure. That process may have begun in the United States with the recent congressional elections. Pressed between a rejection of the consequences of exclusive reliance on monetary policy as a means of controlling inflation and the consequences of resumed inflation if old formulas are applied, political leaders may begin to think afresh. Despite failures of the past, they may decide that much more serious and resolute approaches to incomes policies must be initiated. I am appalled by the domestic costs and the costs to the international community of our slow adjustment to the post-1973 environment; and I am haunted by the memory of the role that such a slow adjustment to new circumstances, after 1920, played in the process that yielded World War II. But I retain a faith that the dynamics of the democratic process will move us toward an approximation of better answers.

Second, in the meantime, we economists have a job to do, which we are not currently doing, if we are to be, in Keynes's good phrase, "the trustees of the possibility of civilization." We must break out of the narrow macro-economic terms in which we have tended to examine the employment-inflation trade-off (and the role of incomes policies in a possible reconciliation) and join with others to examine, each in his own society and in the light of prior failures and successes, the political and institutional as well as economic conditions for making an incomes policy work. Those conditions should include equity for the workforce and minimum interference with the workings of the private sector. When the political process forces those who bear political responsibility to look in new directions, we should be able to provide better guidance than we can at present. This is clearly one of the most difficult and important challenges we economists have confronted over the past two centuries—perhaps *the* most important. And it is clearly an exercise in political economy in the widest sense. But that, after all, is what economics at its best has always been.

NOTES

1. For elaborations, see these volumes by W. W. Rostow: *The World Economy: History and Prospect* (London: Macmillan, 1978), Parts Three and Six; *Getting from Here to There* (London, Macmillan, 1979), Chapters 1, 2, 8, and 9; *Why the Poor Get Richer and the Rich Slow Down* (London: Macmillan, 1980), Chapters 1 and 2. All three volumes were originally published by the University of Texas Press.
2. See *Why the Poor Get Richer and the Rich Slow Down*, p. 213.
3. For discussion, see *The World Economy: History and Prospect*, pp. 247–59.
4. Bankers Trust Company, "Energy Viewpoint," New York, May 1981, pp. 2–3.
5. W. W. Rostow, *The Process of Economic Growth* (Oxford: Clarendon Press, 1953, 1960), pp. 135–36.
6. British Petroleum Company, *BP Statistical Review of World Energy, 1981*, London, 1982, p. 32.
7. Taking precisely this view of raw material prospects, the World Bank has estimated that 1977–2000 capital requirements for additional capacity in seven key minerals would come to $278 billion (in U.S. 1977 dollars), of which $96 billion would constitute investments in the developing countries. (In 1980 dollars the figures would be about $353 billion and $122 billion, respectively.) World Bank, *World Development Report, 1981*, Washington, D.C., 1981, p. 27.

8. World Bank, *Energy in Developing Countries*, Report No. 3076, July 1980, pp. 6-8.
9. Inter-American Development Bank, *The Role of the Bank in Latin America in the 1980s*, Washington, D.C., April 1981, pp. 56-58.
10. W. W. Rostow, "Energy Target for the United States: A Net Export Position by 1990," ORBIS, Vol. 24, no. 3, Fall 1980, pp. 481-82.
11. Ingvar Svennilson, *Growth and Stagnation in the European Economy* (Geneva: United Nations Economic Commission for Europe, 1954), pp. 21-22.
12. Christopher Freeman, John Clark, and Luc Soete, *Unemployment and Technical Innovation, A Study of Long Waves and Economic Development* (Westport, Conn.: Greenwood Press, 1982), pp. 44-63.
13. Gerhard Mensch, *Stalemate in Technology: Innovations Overcome the Depression* (New York: Ballinger, 1979). This is the English translation of Mensch's German edition, which was published in 1975.
14. The heart of Freeman et al.'s theory is presented in *op. cit.*, Chapter 4; illustrated with respect to the macro-molecular chemistry and plastic industry in Chapter 5; and illustrated with respect to electronics in Chapter 6.
15. *Ibid.*, p. 102. To illustrate this proposition Freeman et al. include (p. 112) a chart exhibiting the course of electronics miniaturization over the period 1940-1975, with a kind of second stage booster after 1960.
16. Looking forward, Freeman et al. observe: "it is by no means unreasonable to link together the electronic computer, semiconductor technology, automation and information technology and to describe them collectively as a new industrial revolution or an 'information revolution'" *Ibid.*, p. 119.
17. Appendix C in *The World Economy: History and Prospect*, pp. 670-75, presents a variety of estimates that seek to establish the scale of the U.S. automobile industry in the U.S. economy measured by both value added and employment.
18. This estimate, from various sources, is derived from the following table published in *Newsweek*, October 18, 1982, p. 83.

Sectors with High Employment Growth Prospects

Occupation	Estimated Employment 1990
Industrial-robot production	800,000
Geriatric social work	700,000
Energy technicians	650,000
Industrial-laser processing	600,000
Housing rehabilitation	500,000
Handling new synthetic materials	400,000
On-line emergency medical	400,000
Hazardous-waste management	300,000
Genetic engineering	250,000
Bionic medical electronics	200,000
Laser, holographic and optical-fiber maintenance	200,000

19. U.S. Department of Labor, Bureau of Labor Statistics, *Occupational Outlook Quarterly*, Summer 1981, p. 1. Analyses of computer job prospects take up the whole issue.

20. See, for example, Max L. Carey, "Three Paths to the Future," U.S. Department of Labor, Bureau of Labor Statistics, *Occupational Outlook Quarterly*, Winter 1981, especially p. 7.

21. The present state of knowledge, speculation, and debate about the employment implications of the diffusion of robots is well summarized in Gail M. Martin, "Industrial Robots Join the Work Force," U.S. Department of Labor, Bureau of Labor Statistics, *Occupational Outlook Quarterly*, Fall 1982, pp. 2–11.

22. Angus Maddison, "Capitalist Economic Performance since 1820," in L. Jörberg and N. Rosenberg (eds.), *Technical Change, Employment and Investment*, papers prepared for the Eighth International Economic History Congress, Budapest, 1982 (Lund: Lund University, 1982), p. 155.

23. W. W. Rostow, "Comment from a Not Quite Empty Box," *The Economic Journal*, Vol. 92, no. 365, March 1982, p. 159.

24. Freeman et al., *op. cit.*, pp. 191–95, lay out a three-point policy to accelerate the diffusion of new technologies and maximize their positive employment effects.

TWENTY-TWO

Reflections on the Drive to Technological Maturity (1987)

In addition to requests for contributions to festschriften, academics are reminded of their advancing years by polite demands for reflective essays in intellectual autobiography. The following essay was my contribution to a series published by the Banca Nazionale del Lavoro Quarterly Review.

As the reader will perceive I devoted about 40 percent of the essay to the theme as defined by the editors and 60 percent to reflections that arose from my work on the present and foreseeable implications of the stage of growth I call the drive to technological maturity—that is, the sometimes protracted stage beyond take-off at the close of which a country finally achieves the capacity to apply efficiently and across the board virtually all relevant technology. By my calculations most of the population of the developing regions now live in countries in this stage, as Chart 1 seeks to dramatize; and that fact has, I believe, some significant implications that are briefly specified in this essay.

Once again, this essay is suffused by a theme that runs through a good many chapters in this book: the need to treat economic growth in terms of the generation and diffusion of the uneven but continuous flow of new technologies generated by the economic system itself, and the inability of highly aggregated concepts and measurements effectively to grip this process.

I. INTRODUCTION

Having accepted the invitation of the editors of the *BNL Quarterly Review* to reflect on the evolution of my "intellectual developments,

---

This chapter was published in the June 1987 issue of the *Banca Nazionale del Lavoro Quarterly Review* (no. 161). Reprinted with permission.

theoretical debates, and so on," I was, for a time, puzzled as to how to proceed. The unlikely catalyst proved to be a single sentence written by two respected old friends:[1] "Rostow's book, published in 1960, generalized to all human history and to all the future a model based on the experience of eighteenth- and nineteenth-century Britain, partially repeated by the United States." So far as the intellectual basis for *The Stages of Economic Growth*, its structure and pretensions to universality are concerned, they are quite wrong; and I shall shortly indicate why. But I have not responded to much more extreme and colorful misstatements of my views. As I said in the introduction to the volume of the International Economic Association reporting the 1960 Konstanz conference on the take-off:[2] "As for the take-off, it will have to look after itself . . . Like all intellectual constructs it will survive only if it meets the hard pragmatic test of usefulness to others—if it illuminates problems that deeply concern them. No market is—or should be—more ruthlessly competitive than the market place for ideas . . ."

I have replied temperately to critics on a few occasions for sake of the record or because editors or publishers insisted.[3] But I do not, in fact, believe such defenses much matter. The market for ideas is, indeed, oligopolistic; but over a reasonable period of time I don't think attack or defense (the equivalent of advertising) much affects the elasticity of the demand curve facing a given author.

Thus, the offending sentence generated by my friends on the Charles River triggered this piece not because it stirred me to gladiatorial combat but because it recalled that in my current research and writing one little discussed stage is proving highly relevant to a key phenomenon in the world economy.[4] The neglected stage is the drive to technological maturity.[5] The key phenomenon is the rapidly emerging capacity of the more advanced developing countries to absorb sophisticated industrial technologies and, with the special advantage of lower wage rates, to compete successfully in a widening array of manufactures with the older industrial states of Western Europe, North America, and, increasingly, Japan as well. They are collectively beginning to repeat the process whereby, say, Germany and the United States closed the gap separating them from Britain as of 1815; and Japan closed the gap separating it from Western Europe and the United States as of 1955.

In this perspective, the drive to technological maturity has thus moved on to center stage, to a degree replacing with the passage of time and progress the much-discussed take-off. This has happened for two underlying reasons: because most of the population of the developing regions now lives in countries experiencing the drive to technological maturity; and because it is in this stage that technological absorptive capacity accelerates and the efficient use of the most modern technology spreads from a few sectors across the whole terrain of industrial and agricultural output and the services. At its close, an economy must normally rely for growth on the flow of new technologies emerging from the global investment sector we call R&D.

I shall begin by responding to our editors' request by briefly recalling the origins and character of *The Stages* analysis, with special attention to the drive to technological maturity; and then suggest briefly the relevance of this stage to three major problems on the world scene: development assistance policy; managing the competition between older and newer industrial societies; and phasing out the Cold War.

II. HOW *THE STAGES* CAME ABOUT

I am skeptical that anyone—including the creator—can provide a full and accurate account of how he hit upon a given idea. It's generally a messy, only half rational business. But I am reasonably confident that the following sequence was the framework from which my notion of the stages of economic growth emerged.

The story begins with a kind of informal black market economic theory seminar in 1933–1934, when I was a sophomore, majoring in British history, at Yale. The seminar was conducted on Thursday nights by a talented graduate student, Richard M. Bissell Jr., fresh from a year at LSE. (As I recall, this meant we read Wicksteed as well as Marshall.) I was one of Bissell's four students. He was one of the most gifted expositors I have ever known, presenting to us the bone structure of both micro- and macro-theory, a good deal of it in mathematical terms.

Before the year was out, I decided, aged seventeen, to devote my professional life to combining history with economic theory in two senses: using economic theory systematically both to illuminate economic history and to explore the complex interactions of the economy with the non-economic sectors of society. And this is what I have tried to do ever since.

I set to work immediately on the British economy and British society of the nineteenth century. By the time I had completed my doctoral thesis (formally 1940, in fact 1939) I had concluded that neither British growth nor fluctuations could be explained without introducing the large forces at work in the world economy, including the interaction of British growth with growth in other countries. When I came, after the Second World War, to publish my first book, I stated the proposition as follows:[6]

> Much of Britain's investment was foreign investment, related to development on distant continents, in which Britain participated, but which British initiative did not wholly determine. And the course of events at home, in other respects as well, derived in part from forces generated abroad. The fluctuations and trends in Britain were shared, with variations, by most other areas in the world. It is likely that the optimum unit for the study of economic history is not the nation, but the whole inter-related trading area. . . .

While teaching at Cambridge, England, 1949–1950, and preparing to settle down as an economic historian in the United States, I began to work out a way to make good that vision; that is, to capture the interplay between the forces of national development and those generated in the world outside. Two conclusions emerged: the task required the study of certain pervasive international phenomena (*e.g.*, cycles, prices of major commodities which enter in international trade on a large scale, the impact of wars); and, equally, it required a method for analyzing the stories of national growth. It was in contemplating the latter requirement that I decided I had to formulate my own theory of economic growth—a process carried forward by a memorable discussion with D. H. Robertson.[7]

I had also concluded by that time that conventional economic theory suffered from four weaknesses which rendered it grossly inadequate as a framework for studying and teaching the history of the world economy as it had evolved since the mid-eighteenth century. First, it could not accommodate within its structure the process by which major new production functions were generated and diffused. It provided no credible linkage between science, invention, and the production process. And there is no way a serious economic historian can accept the evasions which seem to have satisfied a good many theorists; for example, to render innovation exogenous or embody it in gross investment; or to treat it as an incremental consequence of widening the market or learning by doing; or to bury it in the "residual," or the marginal capital-output ratio, or "intermediate production." Second, mainstream theory provided no credible explanation for trend periods, longer than conventional business cycles, in the prices of basic commodities relative to manufactures. Third, it provided no credible linkage of conventional business cycles to the process of growth. For a historian it is palpable that cycles are simply the form growth historically assumed. The separation of cycle and trend, of the Marshallian short from the long period, is an act of intellectual violence that cuts out the heart of the problem of both cycles and growth. But it will be recalled that 1950 was a time when mainstream business cycle theorists were ringing the changes on the interaction of the multiplier and the accelerator, thereby effectively separating growth from cycles, relegating innovation to exogenous investment.[8] Fourth, contemporary economic theory provided no mechanism for introducing non-economic factors into the analysis of economic growth when it was quite clear that economic growth—notably in its early phases but, in fact, throughout—could not be understood except in terms of the dynamics of whole societies.

Thus, as I began teaching the history of the modern world economy at M.I.T. in September 1950, I worked simultaneously on *The Process of Economic Growth*, which, among other things, tried to remedy these weaknesses. That study has remained the theoretical framework for my work in historical and contemporary economic analysis down to *The World Economy: History and Prospect* and beyond.

The first modest, unnoticed appearance of the take-off was in *The Process*, first published in 1952.[9] The take-off arose as an inescapable discontinuity from my own research and the papers of my seminar students, as together we turned around in our hands the stories not simply of Britain and the United States, but also of Belgium and France, Germany and Japan, Sweden, Russia, and Italy, Argentina, Brazil, Mexico, Turkey, Canada, Australia, and others. The discontinuity was inescapable because I began with the proposition that modern economic growth resulted from the generation and efficient absorption of increasingly sophisticated technologies. And if one studies the introduction into the economy of new technologies, one must disaggregate down to the level of the sectors (sometimes even to particular factories) where the new technologies are introduced. The discontinuity induced in those sectors—and related sectors—by the absorption of new technologies is then obvious; and it is quite possible to trace out in rough approximation at least the consequences for the aggregate performance of the economy induced by these multiple linkages.

Parenthetically, I would note that modern economic theory has focused on either the firm or the national economy; and it has not successfully linked micro- to macro-analysis. That is, in part, because it had no place in its formal structure for the analysis of sectors. Alfred Marshall wrestled with, but never solved, the problem with his representative firm and other devices. As an examination of any contemporary mainstream economic textbook reveals, modern economists generally ignore the problem. Behind this evasion is, explicitly or implicitly, the assumption of a Walrasian equilibrium in which, with technology and other Marshallian long period factors fixed, labor and capital yield equal marginal returns in all uses. Indeed, with such assumptions, why bother with sectors?

Dynamic growth analysis, embracing the generation and absorption of new technologies, requires the sectors because it is in the sectors that the dynamism initially occurs, altering the marginal rates of return in substantial segments of the economy and, therefore, patterns of investment, the allocation of labor, and other structural and institutional characteristics of the economy. That is why serious economic history is full of sectoral analysis for which there is no counterpart in mainstream economic theory where, via micro- and macro-theory, we blithely take our students from "one side of the moon—[to] the other without knowing what route or journey connects them. . . ."[10]

In any case, my seminar students and I went about our business in the early 1950s by trying to link technological, sectoral, and aggregate analysis as we examined growth patterns, case by case. If any one country in this initial array of case studies was of particular importance, it was neither Britain nor the United States. It was Japan. Here was a nation rooted in a wholly non-western culture whose movement through the pre-conditions and take-off could be analyzed within precisely the same framework—by answering the same matrix of questions—as the nations of the West. After Japan, the major Latin American countries and Turkey which entered take-off in the 1930s were most illuminating.

By 1955, having conducted projects and written books on Russia, China, and U.S. policy towards Asia while teaching economic history,[11] and having worked over the concept for five years in my seminar and applied it—and seen it applied by my students to many countries—I was ready to write an article on "The Take-off into Self-Sustained Growth."[12]

III. THE DRIVE TO TECHNOLOGICAL MATURITY EMERGES

Up to this point I did not attempt to distinguish any stages beyond take-off and the arrival of self-sustained growth. This, for example, is the formulation in the 1956 *Economic Journal* article:[13]

> ... The sequence of economic development is taken to consist of three periods: a long period (up to a century or, conceivably, more) when the preconditions for take-off are established; the take-off itself, defined within two or three decades; and a long period when growth becomes normal and relatively automatic. These three divisions would, of course, not exclude the possibility of growth giving way to secular stagnation or decline in the long term.

But as I worked forward with my seminar students, two further definable stages emerged within the general rubric of self-sustained growth; the drive to technological maturity and high mass consumption. The former was defined as follows in *The Stages* (1960):[14]

> After take-off there follows a long interval of sustained if fluctuating progress, as the now regularly growing economy drives to extend modern technology over the whole front of its economic activity. Some 10–20% of the national income is steadily invested, permitting output regularly to outstrip the increase in population. The make-up of the economy changes unceasingly as technique improves, new industries accelerate, older industries level off. The economy finds its place in the international economy: goods formerly imported are produced at home; new import requirements develop, and new export commodities to match them. The society makes such terms as it will with the requirements of modern efficient production, balancing off the new against the older values and institutions, or revising the latter in such ways as to support rather than to retard the growth process.
>
> Some sixty years after take-off begins (say, forty years after the end of take-off) what may be called maturity is generally attained.

The essentially non-economic process behind this stage, permitting it to happen, is the build-up within the society of scientists and engineers, workers and entrepreneurs, foremen and managers, capable of absorbing—and motivated to absorb—the backlog of relevant, hitherto unapplied technologies. This implies not only an extension of education at every level and the emergence of a wide range of modernized institutions, but also a succession of generations each born into and taking for granted a technologically more sophisticated world. The upshot is the progressive diffusion, beyond the relatively few leading sectors of take-off (quite often confined to one or a few regions), of modern attitudes and motivations as well as modern technologies. The emphasis on the process by which the expanding backlog of technologies comes to be absorbed should be contrasted with the virtually universal assumption of mainstream economics that all profitable inventions are incorporated into the capital stock as innovations and, therefore, no technological backlog exists. Moreover, since neo-classical economics assumes that net value product is equated at the margin in all uses, it is quite unnecessary to consider the allocation of investment resources as opposed to the aggregate proportion of GNP invested and the overall marginal capital-output ratio.

In the three academic years beginning in September 1955, as I elaborated and refined the processes beyond take-off, I directed a project and wrote a rather long book focused on the interplay of American domestic life and foreign policy.[15] It included a substantial introductory historical section covering that interplay from the beginning of the American republic to 1940. As I noted in the preface to *The United States in the World Arena*, it was my wife who suggested that I use the emerging, refined version of the stages of economic growth to help frame the analysis. (The other two concepts used for that purpose were the national style and the national interest.) *The Arena* went off to the publisher in August 1958; and we left for a sabbatical year in Cambridge, England.

It was initially my intention to use the year to begin writing a two-volume book on the stages of economic growth, embracing the full historical and contemporary evidence then available bearing on the concept; but I agreed to a request of the Cambridge economics faculty that I deliver eight lectures to undergraduates in the Michaelmas term of 1958 on "The Process of Industrialization" and packed what I had to say about the stages into those lectures. Since I wrote them during each week in a small office in the tower above the Marshall Library, for delivery on Friday mornings, they were rather fresh—a fact, I think, appreciated by students, who are shrewd in these matters.

After an interval in public service (1961–1969), I returned to academic life, resumed in Austin my seminar on the history of the world economy, refining along the way my theory of economic growth and its various components, including the stages.

So far as the drive to technological maturity is concerned, those refinements can be tersely summarized as follows:

- The identification of the political and social problems which typically characterize the drive to technological maturity (and other stages).[16]

- The demonstration, from post-1945 experience, that the drive to technological maturity, typically requiring about forty years beyond take-off in the pre-World War Two era, could be transitted more briskly under appropriate conditions.[17]
- Confirmation from improved historical and cross-sectional statistical data that a sharp rise in the proportion of GNP invested occurred during take-off and a further rise in the drive to technological maturity after which the investment rate tended to level off.[18]
- Evidence from improved historical and cross-sectional statistical data that the drive to technological maturity was typically the stage characterized by the maximum rate of growth.[19]

IV. DEFINING STAGES: GNP *PER CAPITA* VERSUS TECHNOLOGICAL VIRTUOSITY

Before turning to the contemporary relevance of the drive to technological maturity, it may be useful to compare briefly how stages of economic growth have come to be defined by the World Bank, by Kuznets and his followers, and by me.

The World Bank uses as its over-riding criterion GNP *per capita* in constant U.S. dollars.[20] It then arrays nations as "low income," "lower middle income," "upper middle income," "industrial market economies." Aware that this criterion involves some important anomalies, the Bank provides some corrective calculations and categories. For example:

- Calculations are presented indicating how GNP *per capita* would vary if purchasing power parity rather than exchange rates were used in making the conversion from local currencies into U.S. dollars.
- For unexplained reasons China and India are lumped together in a separate category as well as arrayed with other "low income economies." In my view, the separation is legitimate because these two most populous nations in the world combine vast low income rural sectors with some of the most technologically sophisticated industrial sectors in the developing world.
- Oil exporters and importers are averaged separately as well as among "middle-income economies." This is presumably because the World Bank is conscious that, depending on the oil price, an oil export or import position can distort the implied linkage between GNP *per capita* and stage of development. "High income oil exporters" are also separated out to distinguish them from poorer developing countries which export oil (*e.g.* Nigeria, Indonesia).
- "East European Non Market Economies" are separately presented because of dollar conversion and more general data difficulties.

Kuznets, in his apparently head-on, across-the-board clash with my concept of take-off at Konstanz, argued rather modestly in the end that the data were simply not sufficient as of 1960 to validate the assumed course of the investment rate and that the concept of entrance into the "early phase of modern growth" was a better designation than "take-off."[21]

But an important difference did exist between us. It lay in his insistence on measuring the critical transition primarily in terms of a sustained rise in income *per capita* and a shift of labor out of agriculture *versus* my insistence that such aggregate movements reflected a deeper process which required explicit analysis; *i.e.*, the absorption of new technologies in particular sectors which, along with their multiple linkages, accounted for the structural changes Kuznets used to identify modern economic growth.[22] Here is Kuznets' summary statement of his criteria.[23]

> Let us begin by agreeing that modern economic growth displays certain observable and measurable characteristics, which in combination are distinctive to it, i.e., were not evident in earlier economic epochs ... What these characteristics are is a matter for discussion; but I believe that agreement could easily be reached on some of them, e.g., those relating to rates of growth of national product, total and *per capita*, and to structural shifts that commonly accompany them. Let us assume for purposes of illustration that identification of such growth requires a minimum rise in *per capita* income sustained over a period of at least two or three decades, a minimum shift away from agriculture, and any other identifiable indispensable components of modern economic growth that we may specify.

Later Kuznets used the single criterion of accelerated urbanization to date "the beginning of modern growth" emerging with dates virtually identical with my dates for the beginning of take-off.[24]

Kuznets himself did not define stages beyond the beginning of modern growth; but Ohkawa and Rosovsky, in an evidently Kuznetsian spirit, arrayed three phases of modern growth in Japan in a fashion easily reconciled with my stages, the dating being, for all intents and purposes, identical.[25]

The primary criterion for defining my stages of growth, up to the stage of high mass consumption (which is a joint product of the level of consumption *per capita* and the income elasticity of demand), is the degree to which an economy has or has not absorbed efficiently the pool of then existing technology relevant to its natural resource base and the sectoral structure of its economy.

Thus, the difference between Kuznets' approach to growth measurement and mine is simple enough. Kuznets and I wholly agreed that the systematic application of science and technology to specific sectors was the basis for the sustained rise in real income *per capita* and structural change that distinguished modern growth from all previous history. By his own description, "frustrated" by the difficulties of measuring formally the generation and sectoral diffusion of technology, he settled for GNP

OHKAWA-ROSOVSKY	W. W. R. STAGES OF GROWTH
A. *The First Modern Phase of Modern Economic Growth, 1868-1905*	
I. Transition, 1868-1885	Pre-conditions for take-off (late period)
II. Initial Modern Economic Growth, 1886-1905	Take-off
B. *The Second Phase of Modern Economic Growth, 1906-52*	
III. Differential Structure: Creation, 1906-30	Drive to technological maturity (choice of military option;
IV. Differential Structure: Economic and Political Consequences, 1931-52	postwar recovery; completion technological maturity on civil basis)
C. *The Third Phase of Modern Economic Growth, 1953-present*	High mass-consumption

per capita and structural change, notably under the highly aggregated headings of primary, secondary, and service sectors.[26]

Although Chenery has refined these categories somewhat and, especially, characterized growth patterns according to the development strategy pursued, he has generally dealt with technological absorption on a highly aggregated structural basis.

Using statistical and other data, I have preferred to deal with the evolution of national economies by disaggregating down to the sectors in which the major technologies are actually introduced and then linking sectoral to aggregate national income analysis and structural change. In effect, Part Five of my *World Economy: History and Prospect*, covering the history of twenty countries, containing about two-thirds of the world's population, generating perhaps 80 percent of global product, is a sustained exercise in that method. This disaggregated approach, coming to rest on the rapidly changing pool of existing technologies, is, I believe, highly relevant to the three contemporary issues to which we now turn.

V. IMPLICATIONS FOR INTERNATIONAL DEVELOPMENT POLICY

The first of these issues is development policy. It arises because, as noted earlier, most of the population of the developing regions lives in countries experiencing the drive to technological maturity. By the method of identification I applied in *The World Economy*, this group includes China and India; the major countries of Latin America; a considerable group of countries in the Pacific Basin (*e.g.*, Taiwan and South Korea); Turkey and, potentially, some other countries of the Middle East now caught up in the tragic pathology of the region.

This is a quite different state of affairs than in the 1950s when a good deal of development thought and policy was generated and, to a degree, institutionalized. Then most of the developing world (including China and India) was struggling to get into take-off, moving through, or completing that phase. Under heavy pressure from relatively falling export prices for basic commodities after 1951, some of the Latin American countries were also experiencing rapid deceleration in their leading sectors of take-off. They were, it turned out, in a rather painful transition to the more diversified and sophisticated technologies and sectors of the drive to technology maturity, a fact which became apparent in the 1960s. Turkey was in a similar transition.

In his engaging Presidential Address delivered at the meeting of the American Economic Association in December 1983, W. Arthur Lewis cited the following "list of new models invented by development economists of the 1950s and 1960s":[27]

Two-gap model	dependency
unbalanced growth	indicative planning
vent for surplus	appropriate technology
Dutch disease	big push
dual economy	growth pole
disguised unemployment	rising savings ratio
structural inflation	low-level equilibrium trap

Almost all of these concepts arose from analyses of countries struggling to move from what I would call the pre-conditions for take-off into the take-off or to make the transition from take-off into the drive to technological maturity. After that transition, one hoped, they could rely increasingly on private international capital markets, rather than official aid, to supplement capital formation from domestic sources. And to a significant degree that has happened.

The developing world can now be roughly split between countries in or beyond take-off and those often hard cases which have not yet entered take-off; and this fact is, indeed, reflected in the increasing reliance of the former group on private rather than official capital imports.[28]

The shift of the more advanced developing nations to private capital markets has not, of course, ended the need for formulating international development policies towards them. Immediate problems posed for such nations by excessive debts, slow OECD growth, high OECD unemployment, and the consequent rise of protectionism are all on the agenda and by no means resolved. Before the debt burden is somehow lifted and rapid growth resumed in the more advanced developing nations (with important advantages to the OECD countries) large additional official as well as private aid transfers will be required; although higher OECD growth rates and lower interest rates combined with liberal trading arrangements would do just as well in most cases.

We shall return to OECD relations with developing countries in the drive to technological maturity in dealing with the second issue of policy identified in this paper. Before doing so, I would note one problem of domestic development policy which has risen autonomously in more advanced developing countries in every region; i.e., the need to shift the balance in the economy from the state to the private sector, from planning to market.

The existence of excessively large public sectors resulted from the convergence of technical economic and political forces and certain strongly held attitudes in the developing countries of the 1950s.

On the economic side, there was the pattern, set for some in the 1930s by the inability to earn or borrow, at tolerable rates, sufficient foreign exchange to avoid highly protectionist import substitution policies. These led directly to insufficient competition in domestic markets, idle industrial capacity, damping the entrepreneurial quality of both the private and public sectors. Foreign exchange rationing was also a policy that required large powerful bureaucracies to decide what should be imported. In many countries that process was the heart of what passed for "planning." On the political side there was the fear of explosions in the volatile cities and a decision, in effect, to exploit the farmer on behalf of the urban population. This had, of course, the effect of reducing incentives in the agricultural sector and slowing the rate of increase of agricultural production, forcing increased grain imports at the expense of manufactured good imports required for industrial development.

With respect to attitudes, the 1950s were times when, on balance, capitalism was an unpopular word, socialism a popular word among the educated élite in the developing regions. Capitalism was associated with colonial or quasi-colonial status, representing an intrusive external power. There was also considerable sentimental appeal in socialism during the 1950s: some of the European social democratic governments were doing quite well; Mao's Great Leap Forward and Chinese Communist policy in general generated a considerable appeal among those who did not investigate it too deeply; and even Khrushchev's boast that the U.S.S.R. would soon outstrip the U.S. in total output had a certain credibility in the late 1950s. To all this one can add that many of the emerging political leaders were intellectuals or soldiers, both types inherently suspicious of the market process and inclined, for different reasons, to have excessive faith in the powers of government administration.

Obviously, the answer now is not and should not be a compulsive Friedmanesque reliance on the market process. But the time has come to examine afresh and skeptically the accumulated economic functions of government, and to strike new balances between the public and private sectors—balances which would exploit the potentialities of private enterprise and competitive markets a good deal more than they are exploited at present.

The drive to technological maturity is peculiarly relevant to the public-private sector balance because public authorities have proved everywhere clumsy and inefficient in trying to manage the production of the increasingly diversified manufactures which characterize the drive to technological maturity; and, much more than was the case a generation ago, the private entrepreneurs now exist in the developing world capable of producing diversified industrial products competitively for world markets.

Although this complex and rather sophisticated set of problems confronts a good many countries in the drive to technological maturity, others have still not moved into take-off. Indeed, some of these, notably in Africa, have regressed in terms of real income *per capita* in recent years.

Their plight was made vivid by a question put to me by an African agricultural technician attending an international center in India where I spoke in 1983. He said in effect: "Many African countries became independent twenty years ago but have not entered take-off. What's wrong with your theory?" When laughter had subsided I discussed the wide range of mainly non-economic forces which have historically determined the length of the period I call the pre-conditions for take-off; short for Japan (32 years from Commodore Perry's arrival, only 17 from the Meiji Restoration); long for China (110 years from the Opium Wars), even longer for Mexico (120 years from independence). Evidently no uniform time period could be defined for developing the pre-conditions for take-off. I concluded that, basically, the people of each country, suffused with their respective cultural, social, and political heritages, would determine if, when, and how their entrance into sustained growth would begin; each case would be different; but the advanced countries—especially their development economists—owed the lagging aspirants more thought and attention than they had been thus far given plus a good deal of patience. The African heritage, including arbitrary boundaries derived from colonial history, was likely to make the interval between independence and take-off rather long but, I would guess, less than for China or Mexico.

By definition, the problems the Africans confront are extremely difficult. If not, they would have long since been solved given the aspirations of the people, the efforts of many dedicated men and women on the spot, and almost forty years of sustained international political and social science attention to development.

These laggard cases, of course, transcend Africa. At one end of old Hispaniola is the Dominican Republic whose political and economic progress since 1965 far exceeds the visions of the greatest optimists, of whom there were few; at the other end, Haiti. There are the two Yemens, Burma, and Bangladesh. And, intellectually as challenging as any, the Pacific Islands, some of which are even denied tourism by their geography.

A part of the challenge posed by these hard cases is that our profession cannot usefully come to grips with them unless we economists are willing to make cultural, social, and political factors—as well as history—a living part of our analyses. We paid a price in our studies of and prescriptions for more advanced developing countries when we set these factors aside, as we have often done. But still we could find areas of usefulness. This is much less likely to be the case in analyses of the pre-conditions for take-off.[29]

But my point here is that the emergence of a large part of the developing world into the drive to technological maturity has dramatized the wide range of countries we have traditionally included in the rubric "developing." *The World Development Report, 1986* records among countries called "developing" a GNP *per capita* range from $110 (1984) *per annum* (Ethiopia) to $7,260 (Singapore). (This range of $1/66$ compares to a range of less than ¼ among "industrial market economies.") The average for "low income" developing countries is $260; for "upper middle income," $1,950. Clearly, in dealing with a spectrum of this sweep a uniform "development economics" does not suffice. Shiva Naipaul wrote: "To blandly subsume, say, Ethiopia, India, and Brazil under the one banner of Third Worldhood is as absurd and as denigrating as the old assertion that all Chinese look alike. People only look alike when you can't be bothered to look at them too closely."[30]

So far as development aid policy is concerned, the major conclusion is that, while each country, like each student or doctor's patient is unique, we need, broadly, two types of policy: one addressed to pre-take-off countries, the other to countries in the drive to technological maturity, a subject to which we now turn.

VI. BROAD IMPLICATIONS OF THE CONTEMPORARY DRIVE TO TECHNOLOGICAL MATURITY FOR OECD RELATIONS WITH DEVELOPING REGIONS

My second proposition is that the developing countries now in the drive to technological maturity are destined to be at once a major source of trade and growth for the OECD world and a major challenge to its primacy. This is because they can be expected to experience their maximum growth rates; and these are almost certain to be higher than those in OECD. These countries are also moving quickly into a position where they will be able to absorb the technologies of the Fourth Industrial Revolution (micro-electronics, genetic engineering, etc.). This is, in one sense, repetition of an old story. Britain, for example, experienced a mixture of economic opportunities and strains as the United States, Belgium, Germany, France, and Italy acquired the technologies of the Second Industrial Revolution (railroads, steel, etc.). The Atlantic world as a whole confronted a similar adjustment when Japan and Russia acquired those of the Third (electricity, internal combustion, chemicals, etc.). Now the whole of the industrial North confronts in the decades ahead a parallel challenge as the more advanced countries of Latin

TABLE 1
INCOME LEVELS AND GROWTH RATES, 1960-1970

	Population 1967 (millions)	GNP per capita 1967 US $	Average Annual Growth Rate 1960-1970	Approximate Stage of Growth
		$	%	
United States	199	3,670	3-2 ⎤	High Mass Consumption
Group 1 ($ 1,750 - $ 3,670)	307	3,120	3-4	
Group 2 ($ 1,000 - $ 1,750)	238	1,490	3-5 ⎦	
Group 3 ($ 700 - $ 1,000)	444	930	6-5 ⎤	Drive to Technological Maturity
Group 4 ($ 400 - $ 700)	161	550	4-4	
Group 5 ($ 200 - $ 400)	299	270	2-9 ⎦	
Group 6 ($ 100 - $ 200)	376	130	2-6	Take-off
Group 7 ($ 50 - $ 100)	1,580	90	1-7	Pre-conditions
World	3,391	610	3-2	

Source: THORKIL KRISTENSEN, *Development in Rich and Poor Countries* (New York, 1974), pp. 156-9. Stages added by W. W. R.

America (led by Brazil), of the Pacific Basin (including China), plus India, having pretty well caught up with the first three industrial revolutions, acquire the fourth.

This proposition requires a bit of elaboration. First, then, growth rates. Table 1 and Chart 1 exhibit the behavior of growth rates *per capita* in relation to real income levels (and roughly equivalent stages of growth) for the period 1960–1970. Historical sequences of growth rates exhibit similar patterns of rise and subsidence with the growth rate surge of 1950–1972 something of an explicable exception in the OECD world.[31]

The reason for the peak growth rates during the drive to technological maturity is, as suggested earlier, that the progressive expansion in the size and quality of the cadres of entrepreneurs, engineers, foremen, skilled workers, etc. increases the society's capacity to absorb rapidly the backlog of unapplied technologies. That accelerated absorption elevates growth rates in the affected sectors and those linked to them. The investment rate rises not because the savings rate rises with the rise in average income *per capita*, as the generalized Keynesian consumption function suggests, but because profits rise in the new, more sophisticated, fast-moving leading sectors; and a high proportion of profits are ploughed back by ebullient entrepreneurs. Thus, as I have argued since the 1956 *Take-off* article, rising investment rates are substantially a result of accelerated growth *via* the absorption of new technologies in key sectors, rather than its initiating cause.[32]

The question then arises: Are the more advanced developing countries likely to be able to absorb and apply efficiently the technologies of the Fourth Industrial Revolution?

These technologies have four distinctive characteristics: they are closely linked to areas of basic science also undergoing revolutionary change; they are galvanizing the old basic industries as well as agriculture, forestry, animal husbandry, and the whole range of services; they are

CHART 1

INCOME LEVELS, ANNUAL GROWTH RATES, AND APPROXIMATE STAGE OF GROWTH, 1960-1970

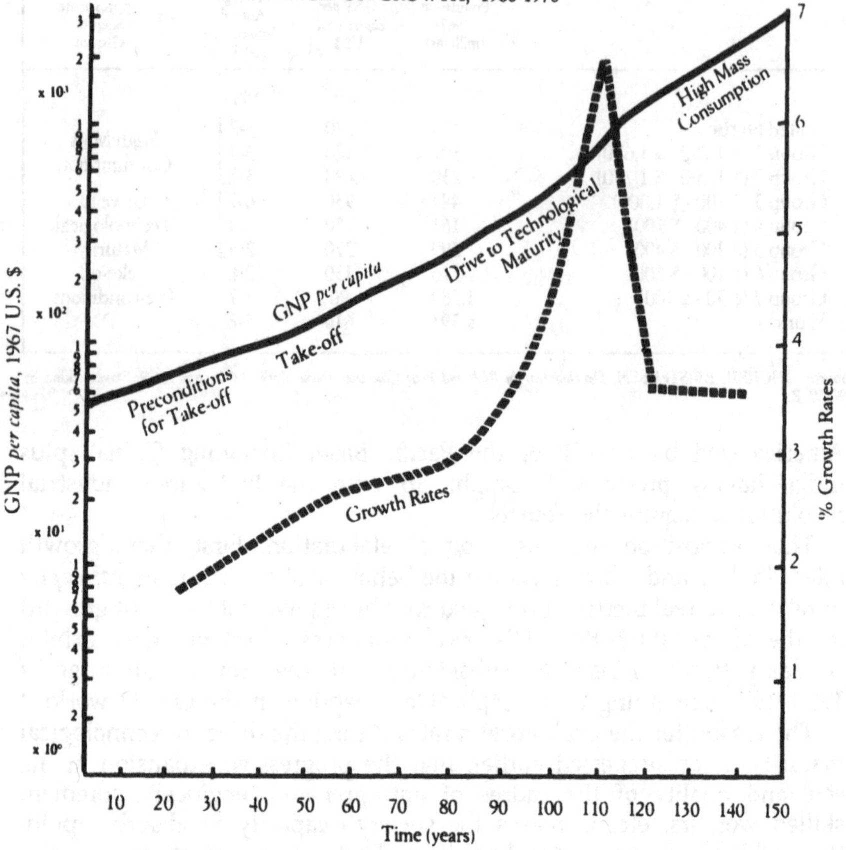

Source: Same as for Table 1.
Note: The US price level (GNP deflator) increased by approximately 3 times between 1967 and the third quarter of 1986.

immediately relevant to developing countries to a degree depending on their stage of growth; and they are each so diversified that no single country is likely to dominate them as, for example, Britain dominated the early stage of cotton textiles and the United States the early stage of the mass produced automobile.

Meanwhile, the developing regions have been mounting a human revolution of their own. Over-all, the proportion of the population aged 20–24 enrolled in higher education in what the World Bank calls "lower middle income" countries rose from 3 to 10% between 1960 and 1982; for "upper middle income" countries the increase was from 4 to 14%. The increase in India, with low income *per capita* but a vital educational system, was from 3 to 9%. For Brazil, fated to be a major actor in this drama, the increase from 1965 to 1982 was from 2 to 12%. To understand the meaning of these figures it should be recalled that in 1960 the proportion for the U.K. was 9%, for Japan 10%.

There has been, moreover, a radical shift towards science and engineering. In India, for example, the pool of scientists and engineers has increased from about 190,000 in 1960 to 2.4 million in 1984—a critical mass only exceeded in the United States and the Soviet Union. In Mexico, for example, the annual average increase in Mexican graduates in natural science was about 3%, in engineering 5%, in the period 1957 to 1973. From 1973 to 1981 the comparable figures were 14% to 24%, respectively—an astonishing almost five-fold acceleration.

Even discounting for problems of educational quality, the potential absorptive capacity for the new technologies in the more advanced developing countries is high. Their central problem—like that of most advanced industrial countries—is how to make effective the increasingly abundant scientific and engineering skills they already command. This requires, in turn, an ability to generate and maintain effective, flexible, interactive partnerships among scientists, engineers, entrepreneurs, and the working force.

I would guess that, despite current vicissitudes, the developing countries of the Pacific Basin (including China), India, and those containing most of the population of Latin America will absorb the new technologies and move rapidly forward over the next several generations. Much the same would happen, I believe, if the Middle East could find its way from its chronic, tragic bloodletting to a twentieth century version of the Treaty of Westphalia.

Thus, if my view of what lies ahead is broadly correct, and the latecomers continue to gain ground, the world economy and policy face an adjustment familiar in character but unprecedented in scale. The advanced industrial countries (including the U.S.S.R. and Eastern Europe) now constitute about 1.1 billion people, or, say, 24% of the world's population. At least 2.6 billion people, or about 56%, live in countries which will, I would guess, acquire technological virtuosity within the next half century. Moreover, population, in the decades ahead, will increase more rapidly in the latter than the former group. We are talking about a great historical transformation.

The phenomenon of poor countries catching up with the rich goes back, in fact, at least three centuries from, say, the rise of Britain relative to the initially more advanced Netherlands and France. But the dynamics of the process has attracted less attention than it deserves.

David Hume was, at once, the first analyst of what has been called the rich country-poor country problem and the most eloquent advocate of reconciliation rather than confrontation.[33]

> It ought . . . to be considered, that, by the encrease of the industry among the neighbouring nations, the consumption of every particular species of commodity is also encreased; and though foreign manufactures

interfere with them in the market, the demand for their product may still continue, or even encrease. And should it diminish, ought the consequence to be esteemed so fatal? If the spirit of industry be preserved, it may easily be diverted from one branch to another; and the manufacturers of wool, for instance, be employed in linen, silk, iron, or any other commodities, for which there appears to be a demand. We need not apprehend, that all the objects of industry will be exhausted, or that our manufacturers, while they remain on an equal footing with those of our neighbours, will be in danger of wanting employment. The emulation among rival nations serves rather to keep industry alive in all of them. . . . I shall therefore venture to acknowledge, that, not only as a man, but as a British subject, I pray for the flourishing commerce of Germany, Spain, Italy and even France itself. I am at least certain, that Great Britain, and all those nations, would flourish more, did their sovereigns and ministers adopt such enlarged and benevolent sentiments towards each other. . . .

Nor needs any state entertain apprehensions, that their neighbours will improve to such a degree in every art and manufacture, as to have no demand for them. Nature, by giving a diversity of geniuses, climates, and soils, to different nations, has secured their mutual intercourse and commerce, as long as they all remain industrious and civilized.

Hume's elaboration of his argument came to rest on two propositions for the short and medium run:

a) the composition of trade would change, but the rich country should benefit in an open trading system from the two-way expansion of trade with the up-and-coming poor country; but
b) to cope with the inevitably increased competition in certain sectors, the rich country would have to adjust its output and use of resources, exploiting its advantages in "the mechanic arts," transport facilities, banking institutions, etc.

In the long run, Hume granted that economic leadership might prove transient; but he regarded that proposition as part of a philosophy of history rather than a guide to current policy.

Adam Smith's position on the rich country-poor country problem was close to Hume's but not identical.

1. A rich country had a number of inherent advantages over a poor country which ought to permit it to retain its lead, barring failure to conduct correct policies.

2. Despite higher real wage rates, these advantages included lower unit labor costs, resulting from the greater division of labor, in turn made possible by the abundance and cheapness of capital. They included also a more elaborate and efficient transport system, reducing the relative prices of basic commodities.

3. Therefore, a rich country could afford to move towards free trade where it would enjoy the advantages of a large and productive commerce

with its partners in the world economy, even with its potential military adversaries.

The flavor of Smith's views is well captured in the following passages:[34]

> The more opulent therefore the society, labour will always be so much dearer and work so much cheaper, and if some opulent countries have lost several of their manufactures and some branches of their commerce by having been undersold in foreign markets by the traders and artisans of poorer countries, who were contented with less profit and smaller wages, this will rarely be found to have been merely the effect of the opulence of one country and the poverty of the other. Some other cause, we may be assured, must have concurred. The rich country must have been guilty of some error in its police [policy].
>
> * * *
>
> A nation that would enrich itself by foreign trade, is certainly most likely to do so when its neighbours are all rich, industrious, and commercial nations. A great nation surrounded on all sides by wandering savages and poor barbarians might, no doubt, acquire riches by the cultivation of its own lands, and by its own interior commerce, but not by foreign trade.

With Britain's primal take-off of the 1780s and its post-1815 widened lead in the new technologies, the rich country-poor country debate shifted to the legitimacy of tariff protection for infant industries in a country lagging technologically behind the front runner. The seriousness of the issue was heightened by the perception of Alexander Hamilton in 1791 that more than money was at stake:[35] "Not only the wealth but the independence and security of a country appear to be materially connected with the prosperity of manufactures." By and large, Hamilton's formula, with its security as well as welfare strand, was to be the fundamental rationale for industrialization in relatively underdeveloped countries over the subsequent two centuries. It was first accepted in countries of the Atlantic world conscious by 1815 of the widened technological gap with Britain. Thus the American and Continental tariffs of the post-Napoleonic period.

Britain was the only nation to move into take-off in the first graduating class in the last quarter of the eighteenth century. The next graduating class of, say, the second quarter of the nineteenth century included the United States, Belgium, France, and Germany. It was the movement of this second class to the drive to technological maturity—the stage beyond take-off—that revived the rich country-poor country anxiety in Britain. In the last quarter of the nineteenth century, post-Civil War America drove its railroads to the Pacific, rounded them out with feeder lines, and pushed population to the limits of the frontier; Bismarck, consolidated his empire, which exploited fully its potentialities in the age of coal and steel, surpassing British steel production in the 1890s. Britain became conscious that its time of lonely primacy was passing and that latecomers did indeed command the potentiality of catching up with early-comers. Alfred Marshall was one of the most thoughtful commentators on the process. He reflected not only on the long run industrial prospects of the United States, Germany, and France but also of the British dominions and Japan, Russia and China (with "great futures"), and India.[36]

In the more than two centuries since Hume generated a lively discussion among his contemporaries of the rich country-poor country problem, two important empirical studies bearing directly on the economic issues it poses were conducted: *Industrialization and Foreign Trade*, mainly the work of Folke Hilgerdt, and Eugene Staley's *World Economic Development*.[37] They were products of the League of Nations and the International Labour Office, respectively, as their secretariats looked to the future with considerable prescience during the Second World War. Hilgerdt's study constitutes, in effect, a systematic analytic test of Hume's propositions, based on statistical data covering the years 1870–1938.

Its three major findings were:[38]

first, that until about 1930 the growth of manufacturing, far from rendering countries independent of foreign manufactured goods, stimulated the import of such goods;

secondly, that again up to about 1930, those countries in which manufacturing developed most rapidly as a rule increased their imports of manufactured goods more than did other countries; and

thirdly, that after the breakdown of multilateral trade early in the 'thirties', this relationship between the growth of industry and of trade in manufactured goods was severed.

But Hilgerdt's story was distorted by the pathology of the inter-war years as well as by the autarchic economic policies of the Soviet Union. Nevertheless, the process of mutual adjustment envisaged by Hume went on and is well captured in Hilgerdt's conclusion on the changing composition of manufactures as "poor countries" industrialize, and on the related problem of "adaptation" in "rich countries."[39]

> While normally the import from older industrial countries is thus not likely to decline as a result of industrial growth elsewhere, these imports are likely to change in character, for the countries in which industry develops will diversify their demand for consumption goods and increase their demand for manufactured capital goods. Different supplying countries will thus be differently affected; and even those able to raise their sales may experience some difficulty in affecting the necessary adaptation. Under normal conditions, however, time for adaptation is likely to be afforded, for in the majority of countries, particularly those with a dense population, there are strong forces resisting the industrial development which is accordingly, as a rule, relatively slow.

The resistance to industrial development appears to have diminished sharply in the second half of the twentieth century.

Staley's substantial monograph is, in fact, a policy manual on the rich country-poor country problem. His objective was to define policies which would yield the greatest mutual benefit to advanced industrial and developing countries. With a barrage of statistical data he drove home the first of Hume's *dicta*; i.e., growth in less advanced countries enlarges exports from more advanced countries that, however, must adjust to the expanded competitive exports of the rising, less advanced countries.

The take-offs of the major Latin American countries and Turkey, beginning in the 1930s, inaugurate the fourth graduating class. They were joined in the 1950s and 1960s by India and China as well as by the extraordinarily dynamic smaller countries along the western rim of the Pacific. Although strongly affected by the rise and subsidence of the relative price of oil, their role in world trade for the period from the early 1960s to the early 1980s broadly validates the three basic Hilgerdt propositions:

- The period down to 1981 was marked by an extraordinary expansion in manufactured exports from developing countries;
- This surge was accompanied by continued high (but lesser) rates of increase in exports of manufactures to developing countries;
- There was an evident sensitivity of exports from developing countries to the rate of growth of advanced industrial countries; but the shift towards manufactured exports altered the relationship.

> This diversification away from primary products does not mean that foreign demand no longer matters. Developing countries depend on developed-country markets for their manufactured exports; short-run fluctuations in the demand for their exports due to fluctuations in growth in industrial countries can still be important. But the diversification of exports toward manufactures has changed the medium- and long-run competitive position of developing-country exports in developed-country markets. . . . Developing-country exports increased twice as fast in relation to developed-country income in the 1970s; for each 1 percent change in real income in developed countries, the volume of developing-country exports increased by only 0.9 percent in the 1960s, but by 1.7 percent in the 1970s.[40]

As we all know, things have not gone as well in the 1980s. Both the rich and the poor have slowed down to their mutual disadvantage, under the weight of chronic high unemployment in the Atlantic community and severe debt problems in important parts of the developing regions. Protectionist pressures have palpably strengthened. The world economy, taken as a whole, does not appear particularly industrious or civilized.

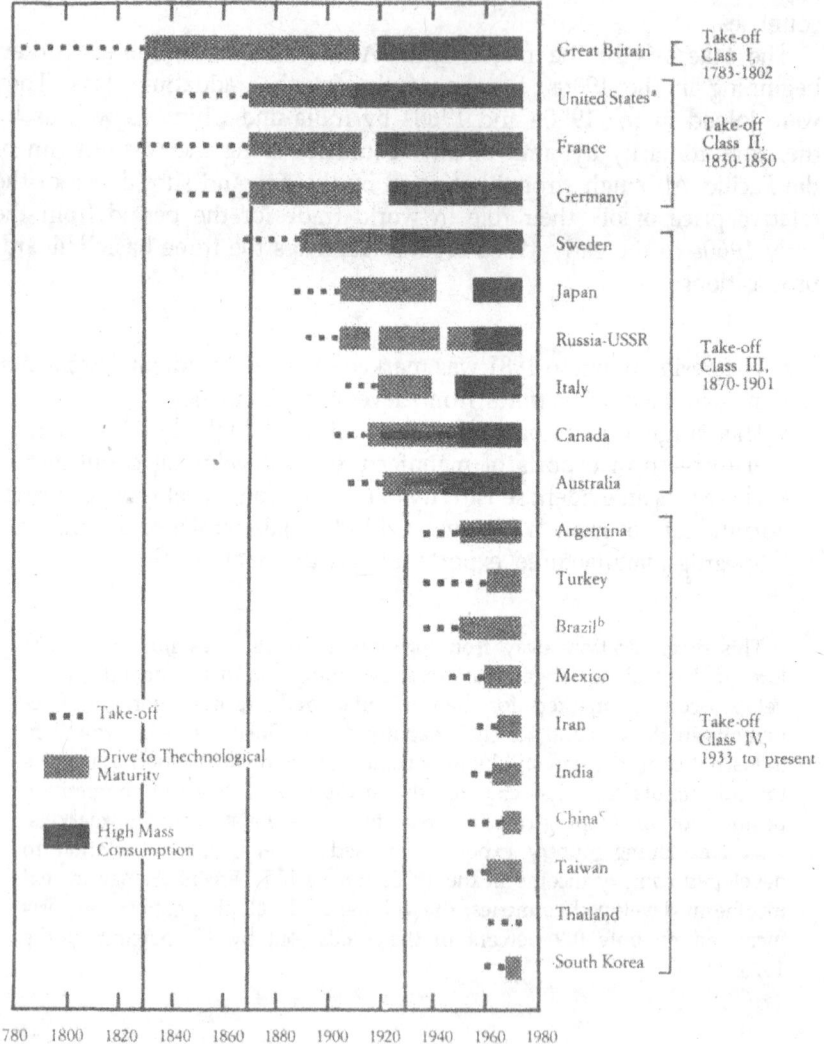

CHART 2

FOUR GRADUATING CLASSES INTO TAKE-OFF:
STAGES OF ECONOMIC GROWTH, TWENTY COUNTRIES

[a] New England regional take-off, 1815-1850.
[b] São Paulo regional take-off, 1900-1920.
[c] Manchuria regional take-off, 1930-1941.

Source: See *The World Economy, History and Prospect* (Austin: University of Texas Press, 1978), p. 51 and Part Five.

VII. HOW TO ORGANIZE AN INDUSTRIOUS AND CIVILIZED WORLD ECONOMY

Jean Monnet used to say that nations should not come together to negotiate but to stare at a common problem. When they have explored the problem together a solution will emerge. When the solution is translated into action, legitimate areas for negotiation will naturally appear at the margin.

Right now we are dealing, after a fashion, with some of the most acute short run problems in the world economy. We are, for example, buying time by rolling over the international debts of important developing countries; and we have co-operated to bring the dollar down closer to purchasing power parity. But we are still far from long run solutions to these problems, and others are being swept under the rug. International gatherings of Common Market and OECD leaders—let alone the United Nations—are still mainly dialogues of the deaf. In good part, that is because we are without a clear agreed vision of our great common problem. Lacking a common vision working politicians concentrate on the short run idiosyncratic problems of their own economies and their possible impact on the next election. Such parochial considerations never wholly disappear. But solutions to national problems would come easier if consensus were reached that the great long run common task is to work together to assure that the inevitable transition in the contours of the world economy takes place without either a neo-mercantilist fragmentation or war, both of which are clearly possible. When we stare at the hard, inescapable facts long enough, the solution likely to emerge—if we have the will to seize it—is to set about organizing together an industrious and civilized world economy which will exploit the large constructive opportunities open to us and fend off the dangers. One of the straightforward, immediate common interests that should render this vision potentially attractive even to the least visionary politicians is the significant degree to which prosperity in developing countries still depends on momentum in the advanced industrial countries and the fact that high momentum in the countries moving well through the drive to technological maturity should render exports to those countries a substantial leading sector in the next OECD boom.

Briefly, the larger task of Humeian reconciliation has three dimensions: First, within the advanced industrial countries there must be an acceptance of the fact that the great era of expansion of the welfare state (from, say, the 1870s to the 1970s) is over. Historians are likely to judge a limit was reached in the mid-1970s when the great surge, which had brought welfare outlays in the major OECD countries from 14% of GNP to 24%, peaked out. Politics addressed to the division of a pie assumed to be automatically expanding must give way in significant degree to concerted national efforts to assure the pie will continue to expand.[41]

Second, if we are to find solid ground between hegemony and chaos, something new and difficult but not impossible will be required. Western

Europe, Japan, and the United States will have to generate the collective leadership no one can now provide on his own. They will have to work with each other and the developing regions to exploit the possibilities and make the peaceful adjustments cooperation could render realistic and mutually profitable.[42]

Third, the intensified co-operation required between the more and less advanced nations requires some institutional innovation. Although I can not argue the case fully here, I am inclined to believe that the process of adjustment is likely to be pursued most effectively through greatly strengthened regional organizations containing societies at different stages of modernization. The United Nations, as a whole, is too big for serious business and lends itself to sterile and over-simplified political polarization. Regional organizations are smaller, closer to the day-to-day pragmatic problems which must be solved and, potentially, their operation can be softened and the risk of confrontation reduced by a sense of a neighborhood.

Specifically, strengthened enterprises should be encouraged in the Pacific Basin, the Western Hemisphere, and Euro-Africa. In happier times, a Middle East regional organization might be envisaged and one for South Asia, the basis for which already exists. In the Pacific Basin, the Asian Development Bank might be the organizing center; in Latin America, the Inter-American Development Bank and the OAS; in Africa, the African Development Bank and OAU. The World Bank and IMF would engage actively in each region. The advanced industrial countries might work with all these groupings although their relative roles would evidently vary with their historic and current interests.

There would be no lack of items for serious regional agendas: urgent debt, trade, and balance of payment problems; co-operative exploration of possible applications of new technologies; co-operation to deal with acute environmental problems; and co-operation in assisting the pre-take-off hard cases in which more advanced developing countries of the region should play a major role.

VIII. IMPLICATIONS FOR THE COLD WAR[43]

Historically, completion of the drive to technological maturity has proven to be a dangerous age. We have seen in this century two efforts by Germany, one by Japan, and one by Russia to seek hegemony in their regions when they, as late-comers, finally caught up technologically with early-comers, and were led to challenge the primacy they had earlier established. As its imperialist stirrings round about the turn of the twentieth century suggest, the United States was by no means exempt from this temptation to assert itself in the global arena of power and did not wholly resist that temptation.

Evidently in a nuclear age, both the pursuit of hegemony by a new major power and the defense of their interests by resistant older powers must be conducted with restraint if a cataclysm for the human race is to be avoided. Thus, the Cold War has proceeded now for four dreary decades in three rough cycles marked by successive phases of vigorous but still cautious Soviet efforts to exploit perceived laxness or weakness in the non-communist world and belated and rather restrained efforts to retrieve their positions by the United States and others who shared its interest in preventing Soviet hegemony in Europe, Asia, or elsewhere. We are now in the third relatively quiet interval in the Cold War, the other two being 1953–1955, 1969–1972. The question is: Can we convert this interval into a progressive liquidation of the Cold War or will we behave in such a way as to induce a fourth downswing? Is a soft landing possible? The answer relates in part to a fairly steady trend which operated quietly as these noisy, dangerous, and often bloody cyclical phases proceeded; i.e., the diffusion of effective power away from both the United States and the Soviet Union. This resulted not only from higher postwar growth rates in Western Europe and Japan than in the United States—and their catching up in technological virtuosity—but also from the dynamism of the developing countries that moved successfully into technological maturity. The combined total of U.S. and U.S.S.R. GNP may have declined from about 44% to 33% of the global product between 1950 and 1980.

First, Soviet difficulty in absorbing effectively the new technologies and, more broadly, reversing the protracted decline in the productivity of its economy poses searching political and institutional problems which may divert its energies to domestic concerns unless the non-communist world provides temptations to adventure too attractive to resist, too easy to exploit.

Second, the dynamism of the countries caught up in the drive to technological maturity is likely to strengthen a perception already widespread in Moscow; namely, that the power of nationalism, the diffusion to the developing regions of increasingly sophisticated technologies, and the diminished attraction of communist development dogma and methods make it increasingly clear that the emerging world community is not going to be dominated by the Soviet Union or by any other single power.

Third, if the non-communist world can mount a reasonable approximation of the three dimensional policy required to fulfill Hume's injunction to be "industrious and civilized," a rather good foundation exists for initiating evenhanded, serious negotiations with Moscow to bring the Cold War peacefully to an end.

The narrower conclusion to be drawn is for development economists. In retrospect, the pioneers of development economics of the 1950s focused sharply (and understandably) on how to make the transition into Simon Kuznets' Modern Economic Growth, Arthur Lewis' Industrial Revolution, Paul Rosenstein-Rodan's Big Push, my Take-off. Our common task two generations later is to understand better and prescribe more wisely for two cases: where the pre-conditions for take-off have proved particularly difficult and for the drive to technological maturity.

NOTES

1. Richard E. Neustadt and Ernest R. May, *Thinking in Time: The Uses of History for Decision-Makers* (New York: The Free Press, 1986), p. 207.
2. W. W. Rostow (ed.), *The Economics of Take-off into Sustained Growth* (London: Macmillan, 1963), p. xiii.
3. For those who may be interested, my responses to critics are to be found (beyond the Konstanz volume) in *The Stages of Economic Growth* (Cambridge: at the University Press, 1971) (second edition), Appendix B; *The World Economy: History and Prospect* (Austin: University of Texas Press, 1978), pp. 778–79 (note 2); "Development: The Political Economy of the Marshallian Long Period" in Gerald M. Meier and Dudley Seers (eds.), *Pioneers in Development* (New York: Oxford University Press, 1984), pp. 232–237 and 247–249; and my review of Angus Maddison, *Phases of Capitalist Development*, in *The Journal of Economic History*, December 1985, Vol. 45, No. 4, pp. 1027–1028.
4. I say "little discussed" because a recent study substantially focused on "semi-industrial" countries is much concerned with what I would call the drive to technological maturity. The study is: Hollis Chenery, Moise Syrquin and Scott Robinson, *Industrialization and Economic Growth* (New York: Oxford University Press, for the World Bank, 1986). Bela Balassa's, *The Newly Industrializing Countries in the World Economy* (New York: Pergamon Press, 1981) is also focused on specific countries beyond take-off. These valuable studies, however, are primarily concerned with the relative success of export-oriented (if not export-led) growth patterns. Chenery and his colleagues have more to say about the progressive absorption of sophisticated technologies than Balassa; but their method for dealing with the degree of technological absorption in the course of the whole growth transition is highly aggregated; i.e., via the relative scale of "intermediate" industrial production in the structure of GNP.
5. Characteristics of the drive to technological maturity are defined and illustrated in *The Stages of Economic Growth*, Chapter 5. See also *Politics and the Stages of Growth* (Cambridge: at the University Press, 1971), Chap. 4.
6. *Essays on the British Economy of the Nineteenth Century* (Oxford: at the Clarendon Press, 1948), pp. 12–13.
7. For reference to my discussion with D. H. Robertson, see *The Process of Economic Growth* (Oxford: at the Clarendon Press, 1953, 1960), pp. 5–7.
8. For my reaction at the time to mainstream cyclical analysis of the period, see "Some Notes on Mr. Hicks and History," *American Economic Review*, Vol. XLI, No. 3, June 1951, pp. 312–324.
9. *The Process of Economic Growth* (Oxford: at the Clarendon Press, 1953), pp. 17, 71, 103–108.
10. J. M. Keynes, *General Theory* (New York: Harcourt Brace, 1936), p. 292.
11. These enterprises yielded *The Dynamics of Soviet Society* (New York: W. W. Norton, 1953, 1967); *The Prospects for Communist China* (New York: Technology Press, M.I.T., John Wiley, 1954); and *An American Policy in Asia* (New York: Technology Press, M.I.T., John Wiley, 1955).
12. *Economic Journal*, Vol. 66, February 1956, pp. 25–48.
13. *Ibid.*, p. 27.

14. *Stages of Economic Growth*, p. 9.
15. *The United States in the World Arena* (New York: Harper and Row, 1960).
16. *Politics and the Stages of Growth*, pp. 98–183 and 196–218.
17. See, for example, the extraordinary rates of technology absorption and growth of Taiwan and South Korea in Chapters 45 and 47 of my *World Economy: History and Prospect*.
18. See, *ibid.*, pp. 55–59, and my *Why the Poor Get Richer and the Rich Slow Down* (Austin: University of Texas Press, 1980), pp. 275–288.
19. *Why the Poor*, etc., Chapter 6 as a whole.
20. See Table 1 and relevant notes in 1980's editions of World Bank's *World Development Reports*.
21. W. W. Rostow (ed.), *The Economics of Take-off Into Sustained Growth*, p. 43. In his 1971 *Economic Growth of Nations: Total Output and Production Structure* (Cambridge, Mass.: The Belknap Press of the Harvard University Press), pp. 61–69, Kuznets quietly capitulated to the Rosenstein Rodan-Arthur Lewis-Rostow view. He concluded that the net domestic capital formation proportion rose "from about 5 or 6 percent at the beginning of the modern growth process" to a "characteristic" 15 percent as a peak terminal value (pp. 64–65).
22. Here is how I compared Kuznets' full criteria for modern growth *versus* my criteria for take-off in *The World Economy: History and Prospect* (p. 778 n. 2):

"Kuznets' full criteria for modern growth are: the application of modern scientific thought and technology to industry; a sustained and rapid increase in real product per capita, usually associated with high rates of population growth; a shift of the working force out of agriculture to industry and services; significant contacts with the outside world. My view of what lies at the heart of take-off and the beginning of modern growth is the effective absorption of a limited range of modern technologies, yielding a high rate of expansion and significant scale in an identified leading sector complex, with evidence of spreading effects, bringing about in the usual case an acceleration of increase in GNP per capita, a rise in the investment rate, and an acceleration of the pace of urbanization. I regard accelerated urbanization as evidence of the 'lateral spreading effects' of leading sectors."

23. *Economics of Take-off*, p. 42.
24. *World Economy: History and Prospect*, pp. 778–779, where sources are indicated and minor discrepancies between Kuznets' dates and mine discussed.
25. Kazushi Ohkawa and Henry Rosovsky, "A Century of Japanese Economic Growth," in W. W. Lockwood, *The State and Economic Enterprise in Japan* (Princeton: Princeton University Press, 1965), pp. 52–53. The comparison of the two sets of stages is presented and discussed in my *Politics and the Stages of Growth*, pp. 378–379.
26. For discussions of Kuznets' dilemma and his acknowledgment of it, see, for example, my review of his *Economic Growth of Nations: Total Output and Production Structure* (Cambridge, Mass.: The Belknap Press of Harvard University Press, 1971), in *Political Science Quarterly*, Vol. LXXXVI, No. 4, December 1971, pp. 654–657. Kuznets' discussion of the problem is on pp. 314–343.
27. W. Arthur Lewis, "The State of Development Theory," *American Economic Review*, Vol. 74, Number 1, March 1984, p. 3.
28. For a full discussion of the changing structure of the international capital accounts of developing countries, see, especially, *World Development Report, 1985*

(New York: Oxford Press for the World Bank, 1985). Virtually the full text is devoted to the evolution of foreign borrowing, repayment, rollovers, etc.

29. The reader of Part Five of my *World Economy*, providing short economic histories of twenty countries plus stages of growth identifications, will note the disproportionate amount of space allocated to the pre-conditions period and the inevitably large part played by non-economic factors in the argument.

30. Shiva Naipaul, *An Unfinished Journey* (London: Hamish Hamilton, 1986), pp. 34–35.

31. For a full discussion, see my *Why the Poor Get Richer and the Rich Slow Down*, Chapter 6, "Growth Rates at Different Levels of Income and Stage of Growth." The accumulation during the depressed inter-war years and the Second World War of unapplied technologies makes the acceleration of growth rates for post-1945 Western Europe and Japan somewhat less of an exception than at first appears.

32. For further discussion, see *ibid.*, especially pp. 275–288. Also, *Pioneers in Development*, pp. 232–237 and 247–249.

33. *David Hume Writings in Economics*, edited and with an introduction by Eugene Rotwein (Madison: University of Wisconsin Press, 1955), pp. 79–82. For an account of Hume's and other views, see, especially, Istvan Hont, "The 'rich country-poor country' debate in Scottish classical political economy," Chapter 11 in Istvan Hont and Michael Ignatieff (eds.), *Wealth and Virtue: The Shaping of Political Economy in the Scottish Enlightenment* (Cambridge: at the University Press, 1983).

34. The quotations are to be found, respectively, in Istvan Hont, *op. cit.*, p. 300 (where original sources are provided), and Adam Smith, *The Wealth of Nations*, edited by Edwin Cannan (New York: Random House, 1937), p. 462.

35. Alexander Hamilton, "Report on Manufactures" (1791), in *Alexander Hamilton's Papers on Public Credit Commerce and Finance*, edited by Samuel McKee (New York: Columbia University Press, 1934), p. 227.

36. Alfred Marshall, *Industry and Trade* (London: Macmillan, 1919, reprint, New York: Augustus M. Kelley, 1970, *Reprints of Economic Classics*), Chapters III-V, especially pp. 95–106, 157–162.

37. League of Nations, *Industrialization and Foreign Trade* (New York: distributed in the U.S. by International Documents Service, Columbia University Press, 1945), with a Preface by A. Loveday, Director of Economic, Financial and Transit Department, dated July, 1945. The full reference for Staley's study, commissioned by the I.L.O, is: *World Economic Development* (Montreal: International Labour Office, 1944).

38. *Op. cit.*, p. 5. This summary passage is from Loveday's Preface.

39. *Ibid.*, p. 117.

40. *World Development Report, 1984* (New York: Oxford University Press for the World Bank, 1984), p. 43.

41. This argument is elaborated, for example, in my article published in *The Washington Post*, December 28, 1986.

42. This argument is elaborated in "Is There Need for Economic Leadership?: Japanese or American?" *American Economic Association Papers and Proceedings*, Vol. 75, No. 2, May 1985.

43. The following argument is elaborated in "On Ending The Cold War," *Foreign Affairs*, Vol. 65, No. 4, Spring 1987, pp. 831–851.

TWENTY-THREE

Beware of Historians Bearing False Analogies: A Review of Paul Kennedy, The Rise and Fall of Great Powers *(1988)*

Pointers from the Past: Kennedy's Comment (1988)

Reviewer's Reply (1988)

I was diverted from more conventional academic work in the spring of 1988 by a request that I review Paul Kennedy's well-known book for Foreign Affairs. The result and the subsequent exchange speak for themselves, and I do not intend, in the manner of a parliamentarian, to "extend my remarks" for the record in the analytic and policy terms Kennedy and I deployed in our debate.

I do wish to add three brief academic observations that were ruled out by limited space and the understandable policy orientation of Foreign Affairs.

1. The economics of power potential changed after the 1780s. Before the first industrial revolution, technology did play a role in military affairs; e.g., "Greek fire" in the defense of Constantinople, the stirrup, the crossbow, gunpowder, etc. But these and nonmilitary innovations were occasional, and, essentially, nations conducted their

---

This review was first published in the Spring 1988 issue of Foreign Affairs (vol. 66, no. 4); Kennedy's comment and my response appeared in the Summer 1988 issue (vol. 66, no. 5). Reprinted with permission.

affairs in a framework of relatively fixed technology. Their economies could (as in Chinese dynastic theory) be eroded not only by excessive military engagements but also by population pressure and loss of energy and virtue among the rulers and their civil servants. The extreme case in early modern Europe was seventeenth-century Spain, which suffered something like a 25 percent decline in population.

Once new technology became a flow—from, say, the 1780s forward—relative power became a matter not only of population size and natural resource availabilities (as well as geography, political organization, etc.) but also of the degree to which the pool of (then) modern technologies had or had not been efficiently absorbed. In the primal case of Britain's struggle against Napoleon, for example, Malthus was able to argue against Ricardo that exertions that would have earlier bankrupted the country were easily carried because of revolutionary technological changes and greatly expanded capacity in the cotton and iron industries. In fact, Malthus defined Britain's problem in terms not of war destruction or exhaustion of resources, but of inadequate purchasing power and excess capacity. Thus, in Chapter 8 of The Stages of Economic Growth I addressed the connection between the relative stages of growth and aggression, delineating three types of wars essentially in terms of relative degrees of technological virtuousity: colonial wars; regional aggression; and struggles to achieve—or to prevent others from achieving—a definitive grasp on the Eurasian balance of power. The latter objective could only be envisaged by a few nations whose size and geographical location converged with their arrival at technological maturity.

2. But the arrival of nuclear weapons and long-range delivery capabilities diluted the relative power of large, well located, technologically mature nations. *Nuclear weapons can be rationally used only in quite unlikely circumstances. Their primary functions are (a) to deter use of such weapons by others or (b) to help deter attack by conventional forces through the threat of using nuclear weapons in retaliation.* The history of the postwar world is full of examples of lesser powers successfully frustrating nuclear powers.

3. In a nuclear age, the increasingly crowded global stage of technologically mature (or foreseeably mature) nations [see Chart 2 in Chapter 22] makes the recurrence of efforts to achieve Eurasian or global hegemony less likely than it has been since the 1780s. *The diffusion of technological, industrial, and military power has been, in my view, the central phenomenon in the global community since the end of World War II; and this diffusion seems fated to continue well into the twenty-first century.* Although a world of diffuse power may not lend itself to monopoly, it is thoroughly capable of bloody conflict that is mortally dangerous to all. Therefore, the critical question to address, in my view, is not: Which country will be the next hegemon or hegemonic aspirant? It is: How do we organize, in a nuclear age, a reasonably orderly and peaceful world community within which power is widely diffused.

BEWARE OF HISTORIANS BEARING FALSE ANALOGIES: A REVIEW OF PAUL KENNEDY, THE RISE AND FALL OF GREAT POWERS

Professor Kennedy, a British scholar translated to New Haven, has written a massive book around a grand theme: the relation between the rise and fall of major powers over the past five centuries and the shifts in their relative economic strength and technological virtuosity. It is both a work of historical analysis, in which the author seeks to discern recurrent patterns upon which to base defensible generalizations, and a policy prescription, notably for the United States. Understandably, it is the latter strand that is receiving current attention; but before examining Kennedy's advice it is worth surveying briefly the other dimensions of his work.

First comes a survey of the world scene circa 1500, with quick portraits of Ming China, the Muslim world including Mogul India, pre-Tokugawa and Tokugawa Japan, pre-Petrine Russia, and Europe before the rise of the modern nation-states. Kennedy then brings to the stage his succession of quasi-Wagnerian melodramas of rise and fall: the Hapsburgs (1519–1659), the Anglo-French struggle in the wake of brief Dutch primacy (1660–1815), post-Napoleonic British primacy (1815–1885) and its erosion (1885–1918), the rise of the United States and the U.S.S.R. at the expense of the middle powers (1919–1942), the bipolar world and the beginning of its erosion (1943–1980). (My own opinion is that the erosion of the bipolar world began as early as 1948, when the U.S. Congress passed the Marshall Plan legislation and Tito successfully broke with Stalin.)

This survey involves the mobilization of a large volume of evidence, much of it not directly related to Kennedy's central theme. Sensing the diffuse character of his exposition, he provides a terse ten-page introduction. There he confronts two of the major unresolved analytic problems that run through his study, and there he fails to confront a third.

First, he asks, how much generalization is justified by this tale of battle and blood and wasted resources? The evidence, he finds, is too conflicting for any tidy laws of history. He limits himself to three unsurprising propositions:

- There is a causal link between economic strength and the power position of states in the international system.
- In the long run, the rise and fall of states reflect their relative economic position in the world economy.
- There is a time lag between the trajectory of a nation's relative economic strength and its relative military-territorial influence.

Second, Kennedy draws back a bit even from this degree of "crude economic determinism." He lists other factors that have affected relative national success and failure in the arena of power: geography, military organization, national morale and alliance systems, among others. These are, however, not pursued systematically in the analyses that follow.

Third is his missing insight: he fails to distinguish sharply those states which pursued policies of regional hegemony from those content with a balance-of-power policy (that is, a policy which aimed to prevent the hegemony of any other power in their region). In the post-1500 era—marked, above all, by the triumph of nationalism—it has made quite a difference whether a power set out to suppress the nationalism of others or rather to help mobilize the nationalism of allies to resist suppression by a third party. It is a distinction worth making.

The central problem of Kennedy's analysis and, later, prescription concerns his treatment of Great Britain in relation to the other cases of rise and decline. There is a subsection in Kennedy's book whose title poses a good question: "Britain as Hegemon?" It evokes Britain at the height of its power, with Europe in reasonable diplomatic equilibrium aided notably by Bismarck's restraint. It was an equilibrium about to break down, but it represented a technique for exercising power in a mulipolar arena quite different from that of Britain's predecessors or would-be hegemonic successors in Europe. A balance-of-power state may not be liked, but it is almost certain to find allies when it confronts another power intent on regional hegemony.

The British decline thus differs from the others. Britain's relative role in fending off attempts by a succession of powers to gain hegemony in Europe was, indeed, reduced by the progressive industrialization of other states. But its relative decline as a European and Atlantic power is not the result of pursuing a hegemonic dream in Europe. It did exercise hegemonic powers in the Empire, despite the recognition after the American Revolution that such powers would progressively wane as nationalism gathered strength. While the end of the British imperial dream was psychologically and politically traumatic, it saved money.

Nevertheless, the trauma of imperial decline postponed Britain's recognition that its destiny lay primarily with the European continent. The problem that had to be overcome was captured in Dean Acheson's somewhat cruel analysis and challenge late in 1962; namely, that Great Britain had lost an empire but not yet found a role.

The most obvious generalization from Kennedy's saga is political rather than economic: the pursuit of hegemony strengthens nationalist resistance, renders the expansionist effort increasingly costly, and out of its own dynamics may drive a state to extend its exertions to a point where failure is inevitable, as the hegemonic power reaches beyond its relative economic capacity. A state pursuing a balnce-of-power policy may find its relative status shifting due to the spread of industrial innovations, but it is not destined to repeat the fate of Hapsburg Spain, Napoleonic France, imperial and Hitlerite Germany, or militarized Japan.

In short, Kennedy's generalizations from the historical record down to 1942 suffer from a confusion of the British case with the others, and a confusion of two quite different links between economic resources and power in the world arena: the progressive economic strains imposed by the pursuit of hegemonic dreams in the face of affronted nationalism; and the progressive dilution of relative economic power as the British demonstration of industrial and commercial takeoff, starting in the 1780s, was followed during the succeeding two centuries by a sequence of takeoffs in continental Europe, North America, Latin America, Asia and the Middle East.[1]

This distinction becomes central when Kennedy moves beyond 1942. Kennedy's theory takes the form of a double analogy: he treats the post-1945 rise in U.S. power by analogy with hegemonic empires of the past; its decline by analogy with his interpretation of the decline of Britain. Neither analogy, in my view, is applicable.

Now, his stylized portrait. From 1943, he argues, the United States and the Soviet Union interpreted the world in bipolar power and ideological terms and acted accordingly. The two nations are presented as having equally fallen prey to "globalist" thinking. An unnamed "American official" is evoked from a secondary source to explain: "It is now our turn to bat in Asia," in succession to British and Dutch imperialists. American postwar economic policy is presented as an effort to exploit free trade and laissez-faire, at a time of European weakness, to consolidate American postwar economic primacy. This is the not-unfamiliar litany of some on both sides of the Atlantic since the end of the Second World War.

A full response to this caricature is not appropriate here. But it is worth recalling that the political instinct of the United States in 1945–46 was to come home from the world as much as it could and rely to the greatest possible extent on its membership in the United Nations to keep the peace. In the actions taken in Europe the United States was not engaged in an obsessive, bipolar duel for world power with the U.S.S.R. It was acting in continuity with its policy since 1917; namely, that it would move to redress the balance of power in Europe at times of acute crisis when that balance was palpably threatened. And it acted in a particular way.

In 1945–46 the issue debated in the U.S. government was whether to support the unity of Europe at the certain cost of creating a great economic competitor, gambling that the United States would have a strong partner in holding the balance of power. Well before the Marshall Plan offer, the U.S. government had decided on this course, and it has remained American policy in Europe for more than forty years. Washington was the steady friend of Jean Monnet, with his plans and dreams for a strong Europe—not exactly the posture one would expect from a power caught up in a hegemonic seizure.

In Asia, too, if one examines what the United States did, as opposed to the rhetorical sound track, it is clear that since the late nineteenth century the nation acted quite consistently in terms of the balance of power, and has continued to do so during the more than forty years since the end of the Second World War: the defense of South Korea; the U.S.-Japanese Mutual Security Treaty; the Southeast Asia Treaty; the defense for twenty critical years of South Vietnam, Laos and Cambodia; and the reaffirmation by Presidents Carter and Reagan of the Southeast Asia Treaty as it applies to Thailand, despite the tragic outcome of the engagement in Vietnam. There is great continuity in this story.

Just as Professor Kennedy does not capture the balance-of-power roots of American policy, he fails to deal clearly with the U.S. nuclear role. The preservation of a balance of power in Europe and Asia was, of course, complicated and rendered more expensive for the United States by its role as nuclear guarantor for its allies and others opposing Soviet hegemony in both regions. No other nation could or can foreseeably assume that function—and an abandonment of it would plunge the world into a dangerous, unstable phase of nuclear proliferation.

Now Kennedy's prescription: the United States should shift resources from "security" to "investment," sacrificing short-run military security to longer-run economic security. It is here that his analogy shifts from Russia and its predecessor hegemonic powers to his view of post-1945 Britain. There are four observations to be made about this advice.

First, of course, U.S. miltary outlays should be the minimum compatible with the protection of American vital interests. As a proportion of GNP, U.S. military expenditures have declined from 13.2 percent at the peak of the Korean War, to 8.9 percent at the peak of hostilities in Southeast Asia (1967), to 6.5 percent in the fourth quarter of 1987. This trend decline is no cause for complacency, but it is often forgotten amid rhetorical charges of a spiraling arms race.

Kennedy is quite aware of the trend but argues it does not take into account the relative rise in the economic power of other countries. His view would only be valid, however, if the United States were seeking hegemony over those countries. In fact, the relative rise in economic power has mainly occurred in countries allied to the United States, or where important common balance-of-power interests exist (e.g., India and China).

Second, the prospect is that the proportionate burden of the United States may decline further in the future, as the result of arms control agreements and other arrangements which reduce military burdens for both the United States and the U.S.S.R. The image that emerges from Kennedy's rhetoric and analysis—of an America in the grip of compulsions to pursue a linear expansion in its military outlays until it self-destructs—is justified neither by past trends nor by reasonable expectations for the future.

Third, desirable as it is, a relative reduction in military outlays does not automatically translate into a higher growth rate, nor is a relatively high rate of growth incompatible with a relatively high rate of military expenditures. For example, the burden of U.K. military expenditures declined in the years down to 1978, while the economy continued to deteriorate. Something of the same could be said of the American economy in the 1970s, when military expenditures declined to a trough of just under five percent of GNP in 1979. On the other hand, Taiwan, with 20 percent of U.S. GNP per capita and a proportionate military outlay higher than the United States, enjoys a per capita rate of growth almost four times higher. The situation of South Korea is similar. The capacity to reconcile a high rate of growth with a nation's security requirements is a much more complex affair than Kennedy allows.

Fourth, the challenge confronting the United States as it faces a protracted phase of increasing competition from the emerging powers requires much deeper and more radical change than Kennedy suggests: for example, improvement in the quality of the American educational system; increased cooperation between business and labor as well as bipartisan approaches to balancing the federal budget; intensified ties between the universities and the private sector. Incidentally, despite a high military claim on U.S. research and development resources, the United States seems to be maintaining its position in the generation of new technologies reasonably well. The critical dimension of competition lies in the pace at which entrepreneurs actually bring to bear the new technologies in production, a process not closely related to the military budget.

My conclusions about this book, then, are the following:

- The author's failure to distinguish a balance of power from a hegemonic policy is a fundamental flaw in his analysis and prescription.
- His familiar but still curious view of American diplomatic history conceals the fact that—rhetoric to the contrary notwithstanding—the United States has, ever since its alliance with France during the Revolution, pursued a balance-of-power policy.
- Such pursuit has permitted the United States to avoid the vicious circle which engulfed all true hegemonic powers over the past five centuries. I would add that nuclear weapons and a certain historically rooted caution have thus far also saved the Soviet Union from that fate, although its society has been greatly strained by its hegemonic efforts.
- For a balance-of-power country a satisfactory defense and a vital economy are not incompatible if, in David Hume's phrasing, they remain "industrious" at home and conduct a "civilized" alliance policy abroad.

A final word: Kennedy closes with a passage in which he tries to define the narrow margin open to statesmen (and their societies) in dealing with historical forces they can "neither create nor direct": a parable drawn from Bismarck, who once, in a Hegelian mood, set the limit of the possible as steering "with more or less skill and experience" on "the stream of time."

Kennedy seems to have somewhat more central European pessimism in him than the majority of Americans. As I went through the endless tables of relative economic power that characterize the text—some incorporating my own calculations—I thought from time to time he was taking these trends a bit too seriously. This came to me even more strongly while reading in his 1983 work, *Strategy and Diplomacy 1870-1945*. Its lead essay argues that Britain wisely followed a policy of "appeasement"—of adjustment to the inevitable rise of other powers—as it felt its primacy waning in the latter part of the nineteenth and early twentieth centuries; that Neville Chamberlain was on the right track with Germany—but for Hitler's actions, which "discredited" appeasement and gave leverage to the "unholy alliance" of left and right that came to oppose Chamberlain.

In fact, there was more to British policy over the whole period Kennedy analyzes than passive adjustment to economic and military power trends; for example, the alliance with France after 1900 and the beginning of a sense in British policymaking circles that an American alliance might in time be necessary to redress the balance of power in the old world.

But my most fundamental disagreement with Kennedy is his tendency to regard history as linear. He clearly believes, for example, that societies cannot regenerate. He regards calls for regeneration as the province of right-wing patriotic politicians trying fruitlessly to swim against the tides of history.

To Bismarck, I prefer Churchill ("the course of history ... is always being altered by something or other"). Without a conviction that man has a somewhat larger control over his destiny than Bismarck and Kennedy suggest, Britain's defeat of Napoleon and its remarkable World War II performance would have been impossible—as would the quite unpredicted postwar regeneration of Western Europe and Japan, and a great many other heartening historical events.

There is a special reason that Americans should lean toward the Churchillian view that our margin of control over our destiny is, to a degree, more generous than Kennedy allows. It was expressed in 1961, at a difficult moment in the wake of the Bay of Pigs debacle. President John Kennedy told me: "The British could have a nervous breakdown in the wake of Suez, the French over Algeria. They each represent six to seven percent of the free world's power—and we could cover for them. But we can't afford a nervous breakdown. We're forty percent, and there's no one to cover for us. We'd better get on with the job." And so we did.

What is the job now? The United States should stick with a new positive version of the balance-of-power policy that we have pursued with some success for more than two centuries. Such a new version lies in the broad direction Western Europe took, at long last, in the wake of the Second World War, after five centuries and more of internecine bloodletting. In order to balance the power of Germany on the one hand, and the United States and the Soviet Union on the other, Western Europe moved toward intensified, institutionalized cooperation, leading ultimately, perhaps, to unity. Great Britain could have and should have led that effort. For explicable although unfortunate reasons it did not, but the fact is that the European Community represents a more civilized version of the balance-of-power policy Britain pursued for centuries at times of power crisis in Europe.

The answer for the United States at this historical interval, when its relative power and influence, while diminished, still transcends by far that of any other power, is, in a sense, to pursue on a wider basis the policy Britain should have pursued toward Europe after 1945; that is, to move forward with others to give institutional substance to the profound common interests that suffuse the Pacific Basin and tame forehandedly the tensions which exist or might emerge; to move similarly in a new spirit of authentic partnership within the western hemisphere; to tighten the ties of partnership within the Atlantic community; and to hold out to the Soviet Union a vision of a soft landing from the cold war.

In more immediate terms there is a case for adjusting carefully and maturely the economic burdens within the alliances across the Atlantic and Pacific, in light of recent shifts in relative economic and technological capacity. There is no case for radical change in the structure or purposes of those alliances, committed as they are to both defense and conciliation, arms and arms control. On the contrary, their steadiness and continuity are fundamental to the possibility of a successful transition from where we are to a liquidation of the cold war. Another blind American retraction, as in 1945–46 and the 1970s, which Paul Kennedy's false analogies tend to encourage, could destroy that possibility.

NOTES

1. For a visual presentation of this sequence, see . . . [Chart 2 in Chapter 22 of this book].

POINTERS FROM THE PAST: KENNEDY'S COMMENT

To the Editor:
Interpreting the larger tendencies and broader patterns of world history is, by its very nature, an intellectually risky business. The mere fact of generalizing across centuries and continents disturbs the orthodox professionals, whose own focus upon a single decade or region probably represents over 99 percent of all historical studies. The necessity to synthesize and make sense of vast amounts of secondary literature

irritates the narrow specialist, who holds that it is improper to comment on, for instance, the policies of Gustavus Adolphus without years of research in the Swedish archives. Above all, perhaps, an author's attempt to point to the broader patterns of world history will provoke a response from critics who have their own, and very different, interpretations. Such disagreements will be the livelier if those critics sense that a new publication may also challenge their beliefs about the present and the future. As Marxists recognized long ago, just how the past is interpreted will always be a significant part of contemporary political disputes. "Pointers from the past" are, after all, trying to point us in a particular direction.

To that extent, W. W. Rostow's lengthy assault upon *The Rise and Fall of the Great Powers* in the Spring 1988 issue of *Foreign Affairs* is both perfectly natural and welcome. To be sure, anyone who reads a sustained critique of one's latest book in a journal as eminent as *Foreign Affairs* is bound to have mixed feelings: a dissatisfaction at the reviewer's failure to appreciate the volume in question, and a (admittedly only compensatory) satisfaction at the fact that one's arguments are getting such an airing. Ultimately the feelings of satisfaction must prevail; for does not the present heat generated by the debate over "lessons from the past" (or more accurately, over which "lessons" should be drawn from the past) suggest that we finally may be having our revenge on Henry Ford's well-known aphorism that history is bunk? If he had been right, then why should syndicated columnists across the country now be jostling to offer their opinions on the extent to which the past can offer pointers to the future?

Perhaps the real answer to the second question is that, while demonstrating by their very actions that they do not think history is bunk, journalists, politicians, reviewers and other sorts of pundits know that it is a very useful "grab bag" out of which materials for all sorts of interpretation can be plucked. In this connection, Ernest May's 1973 publication, *"Lessons" of the Past* still merits careful reading, perhaps especially by those who continue to use the term "appeasement" as if nothing in the historiography of the 1930s has altered since Churchill's *The Gathering Storm*.

Into this historical grab bag, of course, all reviewers have the right to grope, in the hope of bringing up evidence to counter the author's own interpretation of the past. But whatever counterargument they then produce deserves the same scrutiny they have given the book in question, especially when they make such a point about the problems of using analogies from the past.

This seems particularly necessary in the case of Professor Rostow's critique because of the peculiar but ultimately unsatisfactory emphasis he places upon the distinction between "hegemonic" and "balance-of-power" states in the 500-year story of *The Rise and Fall of the Great Powers*. Laymen who have not noticed this distinction raised in any other review of my book may be bemused at such an emphasis, as well they should; professional scholars, well used to the way in which history is raided for examples and counter-examples, will be far less moved.

The idea that great-power politics since the Renaissance can be seen as a struggle between certain states that strive for continental "hegemony" and others that counter with a "balance-of-power" policy is not a new one. It is, perhaps, best described in its "pure" form in Ludwig Dehio's 1962 classic *The Precarious Balance*. In Dehio's rendition of events, Philip II of Spain, Louis XIV, Napoleon, Kaiser Wilhelm II and Hitler led the five successive attempts to achieve European (and, to some degree, global) mastery, but they all were finally brought down by a coalition of "flank" powers, most notably Britain and Russia, and later the United States, which combined to oppose such hegemonic strivings. It was very much a tale of the good guys defeating the bad guys; and for a post-1945 German author fearful that the Soviet Union might become the new "hegemon," it was a useful one to lay before Anglo-American readers.

But the problem about employing such categorizations, as Mr. Rostow should well know, is that the issue is far more complex than those simple distinctions allow. After all, much of the recent interest in studying "hegemons" and "hegemonic regimes" in world politics has come from scholars in the field of international political economy, seeking to analyze the periods when the global trading and financial system appeared to center on one preeminent national economy. From this perspective, it is Great Britain itself, and later the United States, that are seen as the "hegemonic" powers, and the others that somehow have to relate to that hegemony. This is a point of more than semantic interest, since it is possible that many great-power clashes in the past were caused chiefly by one nation's fear of a rival's *economic* power. According to Mr. Rostow's fixed categorizations, one might conclude that the English should not have engaged in the three Anglo-Dutch wars of the seventeenth century (which were overwhelmingly "trade" wars), because their job was to preserve the European balance of power from the growing ambitions of France. Alas, nations often do not understand their function in world affairs in the way later interpreters do.

One might go on for a long time here, delving into the grab bag of history to show that the distinctions Mr. Rostow makes are all too often subjective rather than objective in nature; or, to put it crudely, that one nation's "balance-of-power" policy is viewed in another capital as a "hegemonic" striving. Denmark in the late-eighteenth and early-nineteenth century so often gravitated toward a French alliance because it resented Britain's overweening, "hegemonic" policies at sea. A century later, Germans under Wilhelm II spluttered with indignation at what they considered to be the British hypocrisy of wanting a balance of power on land but undisputed mastery for the Royal Navy at sea. The Russian equivalent of this twin-track policy in the eighteenth and nineteenth centuries was to preserve the power equilibrium within Europe while systematicaly expanding across Asia; to the peoples of Transcaucasia, the tsarist regime could hardly be viewed as a "system-stabilizing" flank power.

Yet even if we leave aside these cautionary remarks about Mr. Rostow's categorizations, the chief flaw in his critique still remains to be noted: it is the questionable relevance, in terms of a great power's capacity to remain successful and flourishing for generation after generation, of whether it sees itself (or is seen to be) as either a "hegemonic" or a "balance-of-power" nation. To be sure, an arrogant, hubristic state (like Napoleon's France or Wilhelm II's Germany) that tries to swallow more than it can chew is likely to exhaust its resources more swiftly than a power with fewer ambitions; and if that arrogance is sufficient to provoke a counter-coalition of great powers to mobilize their larger combined resources to prevail, it will meet its fate. If it fails to match its ends with its means—as hubristic powers have a greater tendency to do—it will pay the penalty.

But what Mr. Rostow apparently does not see is that this inability to match ends with means has brought down all sorts of countries, whether "hegemonic" or not, and whether they sought to revise or maintain the existing order. What ultimately counted was not their status, but their relative national strength. From the 1660s onward, for example, the Dutch found that they had increasingly to concentrate on beating back the "hegemonic" strivings of Louis XIV's France; a half-century later, that aim had been achieved (by a coalition), but the United Provinces was no longer in the ranks of the great powers. Again, from 1871 onward, and more particularly after 1919, the chief aim of French statesmen was to preserve a European balance of power in the face of Germany's massive economic and military expansion. It was a natural, and one might say worthy, sentiment—only partly aided by France's allies. But it could not gainsay the fact that the wellsprings of French power no longer sufficed to carry out its policy successfully. A "balance-of-power" strategy, like a "hegemonic" strategy, still required the power concerned to have the strength to achieve its aims.

We can now see why Mr. Rostow's singling out of Britain's historic "balance-of-power" role, and his argument that the United States since 1945 has occupied much the same position, is both less pertinent because Britain itself, all the Churchillian rhetoric and leadership notwithstanding, found it impossible to carry out an effective "balance-of-power" strategy when its own relative economic strength had ebbed. By 1945 Hitler's power had been destroyed much more comprehensively than Louis XIV's power in 1714; but Britain, like the Dutch Republic before it, was stepping out of the first ranks.

And Mr. Rostow's analogy is also much less comforting for the United States as it heads toward the 21st century—not because his proposed diplomacy of working with allies in Europe and East Asia to preserve the "balance of power" is wrong, but because he brushes aside the relative erosion of this country's manufacturing and financial strength since the 1950s. By a supreme irony, Mr. Rostow's little anecdote about President Kennedy's 1961 remark weakens rather than strengthens his case: "We've forty percent [of the free world's power]. . . ." Are we still far ahead now? And will we still be so in 2000 or 2020 if we fail to renew the wellsprings of our national strength, produce our own engineers, and manufacture our own microchips?

There is much to be debated about how far the United States needs to go in restructuring both its external diplomatic and military policies and its internal economic policies, in order to readjust to the changing global order and to preserve its more essential national interests. But that discussion cannot be initiated in the brief space permitted here, and will have to wait for another time. It is encouraging that in some of those areas, it seems to me, Mr. Rostow and I are not too far apart in our prescriptions. But moving toward such long-term policies will not be aided by evoking dubious historical analogies, especially of the Churchill v. Chamberlain category. Nor will it be aided by reading into history's grab bag to produce bemusing distinctions of a country's status in the international system, rather than focusing on those underpinnings of power that have affected *all* nations, whatever policy they choose to pursue.

PAUL KENNEDY
Yale University

REVIEWER'S REPLY

The reviewer replies:

In response to Mr. Kennedy, I shall deal with only four major points:

1. *Hegemony v. balance of power.* Kennedy first sets out to blur the distinction between a hegemonic and balance-of-power policy, but he evades an issue fundamental to his book and my review; i.e., the charge that U.S. foreign policy post-1945 sought hegemony in Europe and Asia. From his response I conclude that he has dropped that characterization and substituted a new charge: that Britain and the United States were each, in its time, hegemonic "global and financial" powers. As I have pointed out elsewhere, the pre-1914 world economic system did *not* depend on British economic hegemony (see, particularly, my *Rich Countries and Poor Countries*, 1987, Chapter 9). After all, British foreign trade fell from 25 percent to 16 percent of the world total between 1870 and 1914; its industrial production, from 32 percent to 14 percent. The system nevertheless worked because all the major players accepted rules of the game that kept the world's prices and business fluctuations roughly in step. The point is currently relevant. If the major economic states are in time to create a successor to the Bretton Woods system—as they should—they will have to focus on rules of the game acceptable to all

rather than on the instructions of an economic "hegemon" that never existed except for a few post-1945 years.

2. *Resources and a balance-of-power policy.* Accepting my distinction, Kennedy next argues that even a balance-of-power nation can be "brought down" for lack of adequate "relative national strength." He cites, in particular, France after 1919 and Britain after 1945. The tragedy of interwar France was not that it commanded in 1936–38 only five percent of the world's industrial production rather than Germany's 11 percent. It was that at Versailles the United States refused to give France the security guarantees it demanded as the price for a generous treaty with Germany. Interwar Britain, as well, took its distance from France at critical moments. At that time, Britain, France and the United States commanded 46 percent of the world's industrial production. If they had stood in firm coalition in the 1930s, the Second World War could have been prevented. Similarly, the failure of Britain to seize leadership in the movement toward European unity after 1945 was not the result of its having stepped "out of the first ranks." It failed to lead Europe because British political life was divided on postwar foreign policy; and an even more gravely weakened pre-1958 France took the European lead.

In short, relative economic power is not irrelevant; but countries are "brought down" by ill-advised pursuit of hegemony or by failure to form and sustain adequate anti-hegemonic coalitions—not by the numbers.

3. *Can the United States sustain an economic base for a successful long-term balance-of-power policy?* I was pleased that Kennedy, in his letter, aligns himself with "right-wing patriots" (and Democratic presidential candidates) in calling for a renewal of the wellsprings of the nation's economic strength. But one doesn't have to go back to the Hapsburgs to perceive that the U.S. fiscal and trade deficits of the 1980s and the Third World debt problem constitute major challenges. Whether or not they and the related Japanese and German surpluses are handled wisely by the world community will evidently have far-reaching strategic consequences. Linked to these concerns is the problem of adjusting to and exploiting productively the massive and pervasive technological revolution now under way. More than any other single factor, it is the challenge of the technological revolution that explains the curious fact that "restructuring" is going on quite self-consciously in every major economy. And, as Mr. Gorbachev insists, the outcome will affect the relative Soviet power position in the world. That is true for every other major nation-state.

As for the American *perestroika*, one can be as pessimistic or optimistic as one chooses concerning a process still under way. But on the specific points Kennedy cites, the American position is somewhat better than he suggests. Manufacturing, for example, is now leading American growth; and a good many American industries virtually written off a few years back are proving internationally competitive after re-equipment and the emergence of a more rational exchange rate. We did lose a good deal of the standard mass chip market; but demand is shifting to custom chips, where our position and prospects are better. More generally, the country is alive with more than 50 substantial high-technology concentrations, each the product of a partnership among universities, industry, state or local governments, and, often, the unions. We remain a vital continental society with many centers of initiative. As for the "supreme irony" of President Kennedy's quote, the latest World Bank data indicate that in 1985 the United States produced 45.9 percent of the output of the noncommunist industrial world; France, 6.4 percent; Britain, 5.5 percent.

These are among the assets that a strong and purposeful national administration could organize to accelerate revival at home and, in cooperation with others, to rebalance a distorted international economy. As I wrote in my review, there is a place in this process of domestic and international renewal for some redistribution of the burdens of the common defense and assistance to developing nations. But there is every reason to strengthen—not weaken—the structure of our alliances.

Does America command the resources and technological competence to sustain such a policy? Of course it does. Whether it will do so is a matter of nerve, will and leadership.

4. *Churchill v. Chamberlain and all that.* It is evident that Kennedy is preoccupied with what he regards as the failed wisdom of Chamberlain and the pre-1939 wrongheadedness of Churchill. Since none of us has a monopoly on truth, historical analysis jerkily moves forward on waves of revisionism and counter-revisionism. As one who spend 1936–38 in England, heard William Joyce ("Lord Haw-Haw") orate fascist doctrine at Carfax and Churchill urge a pact with the U.S.S.R. at the Oxford Union, was harangued by Ambassador Joseph Kennedy at Rhodes House and Nancy Astor at Cliveden on the inevitable destruction of capitalism if we were to fight Hitler, and then discussed these matters in great detail with my contemporaries, I can, perhaps, be excused if I am unimpressed by the new "historiography of the 1930s" as exemplified by A.J.P. Taylor and Paul Kennedy. There is no perspective generated by the recent revisionist literature that was not a familiar part of the intense discussion among students at the time.

I raise the issue not to reargue the past but because I believe the debate is relevant to the choice of policy before the United States. Brought up as our generation was on *Journey's End, What Price Glory* and other antiwar literature, none of us had any illusions about the probable costs of the war that would follow a confrontation with Hitler. Some were attracted by the time Britain might buy if, in effect, the Continent were turned over to Hitler; others by the dream of a stalemated war between Germany and the U.S.S.R. What tipped the balance for most of my contemporaries were two considerations: the long-run consequences for Britain of accepting the status of a dependent island off a Hitler-dominated mainland; and, equally, a sense that a Britain that made such a deal would not be worth living in.

Kennedy's counsel that the United States should risk unhinging the delicate balance of its alliances to increase marginally the resources available for the domestic economy also, it seems to me, fails to take into account accelerated nuclear proliferation and other dangerous and expensive longer-run consequences of a dilution or withdrawal of our commitments to others. It also risks demeaning the quality and purposes of our national life.

W. W. ROSTOW
University of Texas

PART FIVE

The Evolution of Economic Doctrine

TWENTY-FOUR

Technology and the Economic Theorist: Past, Present, and Future (1989)

I was delighted to participate in a symposium that led to a festschrift in honor of David Landes. We are not only old friends but—despite the domination of Keynesian income analysis, the neoclassical synthesis, and all that in the intellectual world around us—we also have held stubbornly in our work to the palpable, old-fashioned truth that the heart of modern economic life lies in the creation and diffusion of new technologies. And we gladly have accepted the consequence of that insight: namely, that, in D. H. Robertson's phrase, we had "to wallow" in the grubby details of how things were produced in particular times in particular sectors.

The theme of my essay was, therefore, quite appropriate for the symposium that was held early in September 1987 in the Villa Serbelloni, Bellagio, Lake Como. The text was subsequently revised (and improved) in light of admirably autocratic instructions from Henry Rosovsky and Patrice Higonnet, editors of the festschrift.

THE 1870 FORK IN THE ROAD

A celebration of the remarkably fruitful career of David Landes is a good moment to pause and contemplate a striking paradox in the history of economic thought. On the one hand, economic theorists are inclined to regard the formulation of marginal analysis round about 1870 as a decisive, creative benchmark in the life of the profession.[1] On the other hand, since that splendid intellectual revolution, mainstream economics has never been able to deal in a satisfactory way with what virtually all economists and economic historians agree is the central distinguishing characteristic of modern economies since the British industrial revolution of the late eighteenth century; that is, the regular generation of inventions and, for the first time in recorded history, their absorption into the economy as profitable innovations in an unbroken, if not continuous, flow. Blessedly, economic historians, unencumbered with elegant but illusory dreams of stable equilibrium, have gone on not merely chronicling but also analyzing and debating the origins and consequences of this flow for the performance of economies and the societies of which they are a part.

Part of the problem lies in the fact that modern economic theory moves from the firm to the economy, from micro- to macro-economics, blithely skipping the sectors on the Walrasian assumption that the net value product for all productive activity is equated at the margin. But invention and innovation happen primarily in particular sectors rather than in either discrete firms or the economy as a whole. That is why works in economic history are full of homely references to coal mining and cotton textiles, railroads and steel, automobiles and, even, clocks.

Down to the 1930s, macro-economics consisted almost exclusively of one version or another of the quantity theory of money. It was structured in such a way as to effectively conceal technological change by burying it in Q (or T); i.e., the quantity of total output of goods and services. In quantity theory analyses the production variable was treated as exogenous, and, as a matter of trend, its rate of change often taken to be constant. The Austrians—from Böhm-Bawerk to Hayek—dramatized technological change via the somewhat awkward concept of capital deepening.

As macro-economics evolved in the wake of the Keynesian revolution, it yielded, via Harrod-Domar and then neo-classical growth models, formulations that, in effect, were an aggregate production function. Technological change was subsumed in a marginal capital-output ratio or productivity variable. And when theorists and statisticians sought to account for the determinants of the rate of increase in output they did so by throwing technological change into a residual left after measuring the believed contributions of labor and capital inputs. But a modern economy is not driven forward by some sort of productivity factor operating incrementally and evenly across the board—be it called capital deepening, the marginal capital-output ratio, the residual, or what. It is driven forward by the complex direct and indirect structural impact of a limited number of rapidly expanding leading sectors within which new technologies are being efficiently absorbed and diffused. And it is this process of technological absorption that substantially generates, directly and indirectly, the economy's flow of investment via the ploughback of profits for plant and equipment, which helps generate enlarged public revenues for infrastructure and enlarged private incomes for residential housing. It is a process fundamental to any serious analysis of growth.

The incapacity of mainstream economic theory to cope with technological change in a useful way is a peculiarly unfortunate deficiency in the present era. Starting in about the mid-1970s, the fourth major clustering of innovations in the past two centuries moved into the economy from the R&D process: micro-electronics, genetic engineering, the laser, and a range of new materials. These are already restructuring the economies of the older industrial and more advanced developing countries. Their further elaboration and diffusion promise to remain central to the dynamics of the world economy over the next half century.

Against this background, the present essay sketches briefly how technology was dealt with by a selected sequence of major economists in these periods: pre-1870, from 1870 to 1939, and in the decades after the Second World War. It then isolates a series of problems that require solution if economic theory is to come to grips successfully with the problem of technology in the future.

PRE-1870

Hume and Adam Smith

Once upon a time economists were pretty sensible. First, David Hume. I believe the only explicit reference in Hume's economic essays to a particular technology is the following:[2] "Can we expect, that a government will be well modelled by a people, who know not how to make a spinning-wheel, or to employ a loom to advantage?" But he has a good deal more to say about the "mechanic arts" in broader but still discriminating terms. For example, he evokes as a central phenomenon the stimulus provided to invention not only by "necessity"[3] but also by the demonstration effect of imported "luxuries";[4] he suggests the likelihood of higher rates of increase in productivity in manufacturing than in agriculture, with important consequences for relative price trends;[5] and, perhaps of greater relevance to our own day, he analyzes in considerable detail the consequences for and the appropriate response to the narrowing of the technological gap between more and less affluent countries, including the need of the former, in the face of intensified international competition, to make prompt and efficient structural adjustment among the sectors.[6] Hume's great dictum, to which we shall return, is that, on balance, an earlycomer can gain from the technological and economic rise of a latecomer so long as the earlycomer remains "industrious and civilized."[7]

On this point, as with many others, Adam Smith carried forward along distinctive lines that, nevertheless, reflected the work of his older friend, David Hume:[8]

> The more opulent therefore the society, labour will always be so much dearer and work so much cheaper, and if some opulent countries have lost several of their manufactures and some branches of their commerce by having been undersold in foreign markets by the traders and artisans

of poorer countries, who were contented with less profit and smaller wages, this will rarely be found to have been merely the effect of the opulence of one country and the poverty of the other. Some other cause, we may be assured, must have concurred. The rich country must have been guilty of some error in its police [policy].

But Smith, in his treatment of technology, introduced a distinction not to reappear until Schumpeter's *The Theory of Economic Development* more than a century and a quarter later. As we are all correctly brought up to understand, the general thrust of Smith's doctrine suggested invention and innovation as an incremental improvement in ways of doing things, evoked by profit possibilities that almost automatically accompanied the widening of the market and the division of labor. He did recognize, however, that over long periods of time one could identify a few major technological innovations whose high productivity constituted an identifiable discontinuity helping to explain a long period decline in price. For example, surveying the woolen industry over three centuries, since the time of Edward IV, he identifies "three very capital improvements":[9] the exchange of rock and spindle for the spinning wheel, machines for winding and arranging the yarn before being put into the loom, and the fulling mill that supplanted treading in water to thicken the cloth. In both his *Lectures* and *The Wealth of Nations*, Smith drew a distinction between inventions contrived by those who actually operated the machines—a kind of incremental learning by doing—and those created by "philosophers" [scientists] that involved "new powers not formerly applied."[10] He cited the water wheel, fire machines [steam engines], and wind and water mills as examples of major discontinuous inventions. In *The Wealth of Nations* Smith also allows for creative inventions by specialized "makers of Machines."[11] In this passage Smith's terse evocation of the creative process is just and memorable: "combining together the powers of the most distant and dissimilar objects."

While recognizing the possibility of major, discontinuous inventive breakthroughs and even the likelihood, for a time, of increasing returns in manufactures, Smith envisaged nations reaching their "full complement of riches"; that is, a limit to growth. Diminishing returns won out in the end.

Malthus and Ricardo

Although Malthus and Ricardo are generally accounted the creators of the view that economics is the dismal science, their work after the great post-1812 decline in food prices, while focused on Britain's economic *malaise* from, say, 1815 to 1820, clearly reflected the enlarged role of machinery that had emerged during the generation of warfare with the French and was quite sanguine about the economy's long-run prospects. Their immediate concern was unemployment, which they interpreted in different ways.

The progress of technology bears in particular on the important final section of Malthus's *Principles*. Written in 1820, it is entitled "Application of Some of the Preceding Principles to the Distresses of the Labouring Classes Since 1815, with General Observations." He notes that, unlike the situation during the American and earlier wars, there was "a more rapid and successful progress in the use of machinery than was ever before known"; and the "vast increase of productive power" thus generated permitted the burdens of war to be carried while the nation's capital and real income per capita increased. He then argued that the postwar decline in public expenditures and incomes in agriculture reduced the capacity of the rural population to purchase both British manufactures and imports from abroad:[12] "The failure of home demand filled the warehouses of the manufacturers with unsold goods, which urged them to export more largely at all risks."

Malthus not only introduced the rise of the machine age into his underconsumptionist explanation for post-1815 distress but also addressed directly the question of whether the introduction of machinery led to chronic unemployment in the long run. Here he inverts Adam Smith by arguing that, with a "most usual" elasticity of demand, the widening of the market and increased employment can be a function of cost and price reduction brought about by the invention and efficient introduction of machinery.[13]

> When a machine is invented, which, by saving labour, will bring goods into the market at a much cheaper rate than before, the most usual effect is such an extension of the demand for the commodity, by its being brought within the power of a much greater number of purchasers, that the value of the whole mass of goods made by the new machinery greatly exceeds their former value; and notwithstanding the saving of labour, more hands, instead of fewer, are required in manufacture.
>
> This effect has been very strikingly exemplified in the cotton machinery of this country. . . . But it is known that facilities of production have the strongest tendency to open markets, both at home and abroad. In the actual state of things, therefore, there are great advantages to be looked forward to, and little reason to apprehend any permanent evil from the increase of machinery.

Ricardo also took for granted that he lived in a world where machinery and other methods of production were subject to improvement. He regarded total output as a function of "the application" of land, labour, machinery, and capital. The separation of the latter two thus dramatized the distinction between fixed and working capital. It was on this distinction that Ricardo constructed his analysis of the possibility of technological unemployment on which Marx was to build his concept of the reserve army of the unemployed.

Ricardo treated improvements in agricultural machinery and scientific knowledge as instruments, like cheap grain imports, for fending off diminishing returns in agriculture,[14] but his fundamental proposition was more stark:[15]

> The natural price of all commodities, excepting raw produce and labour, has a tendency to fall, in the progress of wealth and population; for though, on one hand, they are enhanced in real value, from the rise in the natural price of the raw material of which they are made, this is more than counterbalanced by the improvements in machinery, by the better division and distribution of labour, and by the increasing skill, both in science and art, of the producers. . . .
> From manufactured commodities always falling, and raw produce always rising, with the progress of society, such a disproportion in their relative value is at length created, that in rich countries a labourer, by the sacrifice of a very small quantity only of his food, is able to provide liberally for all his other wants.

Thus, in the wake of the Napoleonic Wars, Ricardo, as well as Malthus, became notably more hopeful about Britain's long-run prospects.[16]

> The richest country in Europe is yet far distant from that degree of improvement [The Stationary State], but if any had arrived at it, by the aid of foreign commerce, even such a country could go on for an indefinite time increasing in wealth and population, for the only obstacle to this increase would be the scarcity, and the consequent high value, of food and other raw produce. Let these be supplied from abroad in exchange for manufactured goods, and it is difficult to say where the limit is at which you would cease to accumulate wealth and to derive profit from its employment.

Ricardo's famous argument about machinery and technological unemployment has received attention for more than a century and a half when technological change converged with unemployment generated by cycles or other forces at work in the economy.[17] In terms of a microeconomic case, Ricardo argued, in effect, that if technological improvement permitted a radical shift in the ratio between fixed capital and labor in manufactures, an increase in unemployment might result. He then went on to adduce wider considerations that might make the introduction of the new machinery to the advantage of workers as well as capitalists, including reductions in the price of manufactures and enlarged employment opportunities.[18]

In general, Malthus, much influenced by the indirect as well as direct expansion of employment induced by the new cotton textile machinery, was a long-run optimist about fixed capital, but he allowed for the possibility of a net reduction in the demand for labor if the shift in factor proportions was sudden. Formally, Malthus's analysis of the machinery case is, essentially, macro, Ricardo's micro; although Ricardo's concluding, more hopeful observations on the longer-run impact of machinery embrace structural changes in employment and relate to the economy as a whole. Despite the formal character of their efforts, both were brought to confront the problem by the reality of severe unemployment and a Luddite machine-breaking mood in the working force, notably in the years 1816 and 1819.

J. S. Mill and Marx

Even though Mill and Marx differed radically on certain fundamental matters, they had, nevertheless, a good deal in common: The first edition of Mill's *Principles* and Marx's *Communist Manifesto* appeared in 1848; both were profoundly affected by the emergence of the railway age, in particular, and, in general, by the rapid diversification of new technologies as the mid-century approached; both reflected a heightened consciousness of the new industrial society crystallizing about them; both reacted against the harshness of the emerging industrial system, and Mill seriously contemplated but did not fully embrace socialism as an alternative to capitalism; both envisaged rather romantic, highly affluent, more or less stationary states as the appropriate end product of the process of technological progress and consequent economic growth. But unlike their classical predecessors (and Marshall as well), their stationary states were envisaged as the product of declining relative marginal utility for material goods rather than diminishing returns to natural resources. Taken together, both reflect the end of the first century of modern political economy—focused on growth itself—and the beginning of a second that, assuming growth based on automatically expanding technological virtuosity, centered on how best to reconcile its imperatives with enlarged social welfare.

So far as technology is concerned, both Mill and Marx were much influenced by Charles Babbage's best-seller *On The Economy of Machinery and Manufactures*, published in various printings and editions over the period 1832–1841.[19] It was read at a time when the Reform Bill of 1832 dramatized the political rise of a class whose power was rooted in the new technology—a fact to which Babbage refers. Consciousness of a distinctive phase was also heightened by the testimony laid before the 1833 parliamentary select committee on manufacture, commerce, and shipping and by Edward Baines's excellent *History of the Cotton Manufacture* and Andrew Ure's *The Philosophy of Manufactures*, both published in 1835.

Babbage's study of machinery and manufactures is remarkable because it combines scientific and engineering expertise with detailed knowledge of production processes, business practice, and basic economic principles. It includes a chapter "On Over-manufacturing" that finds in the manufacturing sector, rather than the commercial and financial sectors, the roots of the business cycle. There is, in fact, nothing quite like Babbage's book in the literature of economics. Mill's vigorous advocacy of public support for scientific (and other) research in British universities almost certainly owes a good deal to Babbage. But his most important influence on Mill was more general. Like Marx, Mill was a bookish man. Neither had a direct, hands-on knowledge of factories, machines, or technology. Babbage supplied them valuable, concrete, even if vicarious, knowledge of processes of great importance going forward.

The upshot of Mill's reflections, which, of course, were grounded more widely than on Babbage's study, was a firmer confidence than even post-1812 Malthus and Ricardo that a stationary state would not be imposed by diminishing returns, with which, in best classical style, he nevertheless begins.

Diminishing returns is introduced as "the most important proposition in political economy."[20] Then comes the "antagonist principle": "the progress of improvements in production."[21] He deals with the accelerated decline in the cost and prices of manufactures due to "the mechanical inventions of the last seventy or eighty years," which he judges to be "susceptible of being prolonged and extended beyond any limit which it would be safe to specify."[22] But he deals also at greater length than any of his major predecessors with the full range of inventions and innovations capable of exercising "an antagonist influence to the law of diminishing return to agricultural labour."[23] Among these innovations are improved education of the working force, improved systems of taxation and land tenure, and "more solid instruction" of the "rich and idle classes" that would increase their "mental energy," generate "stronger feelings of conscience, public spirit, or philanthropy: and qualify them for roles of constructive social as well as economic innovation."[24]

Mill was also aware that in the course of the 1830s the emergence of new technologies began to hold out the hope of rendering British farming profitable again after the long period of declining and stagnant agricultural prices that started in 1812: but it was only from about 1837 that the application of the new methods began to yield substantial results and create a new mood.[25] By the time Mill's *Principles* was published in 1848, it was clear that British agriculture would profitably survive despite the repeal of the Corn Laws.

As one might expect, Mill flatly rejected Ricardo's judgment that a shift toward fixed relative to circulating capital is likely to be "at the workers' expense."[26]

> (T)he conversion of circulating capital into fixed, whether by railways, or manufactories, or ships, or machinery, or canals, or mines, or works of drainage and irrigation, is not likely, in any rich country, to diminish the gross produce or the amount of employment for labour.... All capital sunk in the permanent improvement of land, lessens the cost of food and materials; almost all improvements in machinery cheapen the labourer's clothing or lodging, or the tools with which these are made; improvements in locomotion, such as railways, cheapen to the consumer all things which are brought from a distance.

The British railroad boom of the 1840s, with its massive expansion in fixed capital and its diffuse, strong positive effects on output and productivity, made it clear that Ricardo's proposition held only under extremely restricted assumptions.

So far as I am aware, Marx only once visited a factory. But he was, evidently, fascinated by machinery; and, like Mill, he drew heavily on Babbage as well as on others writing in this phase of increasing awareness of the ongoing revolution that had unfolded since the 1780s. Engels, actively engaged in manufacture, was evidently a vicarious but important source of information. But Marx went farther back into the history of machinery in earlier times. He viewed machinery as a great achievement of capitalism; as a satanic instrument for keeping labor in subjection; and, ultimately, as a major instrument for capitalism's undoing, via the forces set in motion by the rising organic composition of capital.

Marx's ambivalence toward machinery is well reflected in the following passage in which he begins with an evocation of invention as the business of generating practical applications from science and ends with an analogy from Goethe in which labor is sexually possessed by machinery.[27]

> ... it is, firstly, the analysis and application of mechanical and chemical laws, arising directly out of science, which enables the machine to perform the same labour as that previously performed by the worker. However, the development of machinery along this path occurs only when large industry has already reached a higher stage, and all the sciences have been pressed into the service of capital; and when, secondly, the available machinery itself already provides great capabilities. Invention then becomes a businesss, and the application of science to direct production itself becomes a prospect which determines and solicits it. But this is not the road along which machinery, by and large, arose, and even less the road on which it progresses in detail. This road is, rather, dissection ... through the division of labour, which gradually transforms the workers' operations into more and more mechanical ones, so that at a certain point a mechanism can step into their places. Thus, the specific mode of working here appears directly as becoming transferred from the worker to capital in the form of the machine, and his own labour capacity devalued thereby. Hence the workers' struggle against machinery. What was the living worker's activity becomes the activity of the machine. Thus the appropriation of labour by capital confronts the worker in a coarsely sensuous form; capital absorbs labour into itself—"as though its body were by love possessed."*

Despite Marx's profound interest in and almost obsession with invention and machinery and despite his awareness of the link between science and invention, his analysis of the historical transition to modern industrial capitalism is curiously incomplete and his linkage of technology to capital formation excessively simple. Historically, he moves from the widening of international markets, the "primitive accumulation" brought about by colonization, the slave trade, the expansion of the public debt,

---

*"Als hatt' es Lieb im Leibe," Goethe, *Faust*, Pt. I, Act 5, Auerbach's Cellar in Leipzig.

and other mercantilist policies to the diversion of this pool of resources—"dripping from head to foot, from every pore, with blood and dirt"—to machinery and the expansion of fixed capital.[28] There is no role in this story for the scientific revolution, Newton, and the new perception of man's capacity to understand and manipulate nature to his advantage—the Faustian Bargain in Landes's good image. This gap in Marxism was not filled until B. Hessen, a Soviet historian of science, delivered a paper in London in 1931.[29] Hessen argued that Newton "was the typical representative of the rising bourgeoisie" and that "the scheme of physics was mainly determined by the economic and technical tasks which the rising bourgeoisie raised to the forefront." Somewhat similarly, in dealing with the technological change in modern industrial capitalism, Marx subsumes the generation and diffusion of new technology in the whole process of accumulation, driven, as he saw it, by the capitalist's need to maintain the scale of his profits—in the face of intense competition and a falling profit rate—by labor-saving machinery that would sustain the reserve army of the unemployed and assure a flexible and compliant labor force. Put another way, Marx shared with his classical predecessors and his successors in mainstream economics a tendency to structure his analysis in ways that obscured the complex interplay of science, invention, and innovation despite the critical role it played in his system.

Conclusion

Thus, the work of the pre-1870 classical economists was marked by two characteristics. First, they all assumed that technology and the pace of technological change lay close to the center of economic analysis. This holds even for the pre–take-off economists, Hume and Adam Smith. They introduced technology in a direct unembarrassed way because the formal structures of their analyses were inherently dynamic. With the exception of Ricardo they all knew a good deal of history, and the great questions on which they focused all concerned movement through time. Under what circumstances would population rise or fall? What were the prospects for technological change and productivity in the economy's major sectors? Would the forces making for increasing returns triumph over those making for diminishing returns; and, if so (in the cases of Mill and Marx), should or would human beings ultimately create an affluent quasi-stationary state? How should more and less technologically advanced countries make the structural adjustments required for them to live together in a civilized way as the latter closed the technological gap separating them from the former (Hume and Smith)?

In short, they had not yet sold their birthright for a mess of equilibrium.

The second characteristic of the classical economists is that they focused on the great issues of their day and, in effect, wrote tracts for the times reflecting those issues: How the expansion of international trade could stimulate technological change to mutual advantage and cease to be a source of bloody conflict; how technological change could expand the market (e.g., cotton textiles) as well as vice versa, as Smith thought; how technological change could fend off diminishing returns in agriculture as well as manufactures; how revolutionary technological change could restructure whole societies not merely their economies (Mill, Marx, and the railroads); would the workers gain or lose from the progress of labor-saving technology?

These issues did not wholly disappear from view after 1870, but they ceased to be central.

1870-1937

Alfred Marshall

In terms of the 1870 fork in the road Alfred Marshall is a central figure. Trained as a mathematician, he was, on the one hand, an important participant in the marginalist revolution. Almost a century after the publication of his *Principles*, micro-economics, as conventionally expounded, still bears Marshall's imprint; and he had a firm grip on general equilibrium analysis as well. On the other hand, rooted as he was in J. S. Mill and the century-old classical tradition that lay behind him, he not only understood but refused to evade the conflict between mathematically formulated equilibrium economics— requiring short-period assumptions—and the economics of the wealth of nations in which the size and quality of the working force, the size of the capital stock, and technology are constantly changing. Although mainly remembered for his elaboration of partial equilibrium analysis, Marshall, from his own perspective, was primarily a growth economist.

At the micro-economic level he perceived and exposed the clash between the static equilibrium analysis—in which the seductive charms of differential calculus could be brought to bear—and the pervasive circumstance of increasing returns in industries; that is, in sectors "... which show a tendency to increasing return. Its limitations are so constantly overlooked, especially by those who approach it from an abstract point of view, that there is a danger in throwing it into definite form at all. But, with this caution, the risk may be taken; and a short study of the subject is given in Appendix H."[30]

Appendix H then demonstrates that under conditions of increasing returns (decreasing costs)—the normal condition of many firms and sectors in an economy regularly absorbing new technologies—no single stable equilibrium position exists for price and output; when "a casual disturbance" results in a substantial increase in capacity and output (and, thereby, lower costs), a cessation of that disturbance does not result in a return to the initial capacity-output-cost position; and, with respect to demand, a sharp reduction in costs and price may result not merely in increased purchases but an irreversible outward shift of the demand curve as consumers become accustomed to the commodity whose price has been greatly reduced.[31] A reversal in cost and price will, under these circumstances, not return the demand curve to its initial equilibrium position. Thus, not ony do both demand and supply curves slope downward but they cease to be independent of each other; and conventional equilibrium micro-economics becomes, in the Watergate phrase, inoperative.

Marshall created various devices for dealing with increasing returns—the trees in the forest, the representative firm, internal and external economics, a historic success of short period cost curves moving downward through time in response to improving technology but permitting a definition of equilibrium at a moment of time. With these he could more or less cope with the analysis of firms in existing industries. But he never found a way to deal formally with what he knew to be a major characteristic of technological history; namely, the emergence from time to time of inventions so radical as to create new industries (e.g., the railroad and electricity) or profoundly to transform old industries (e.g., cotton textiles and steel). Moreover, Marshall was extremely sensitive to the fact that, at any particular period of time in a given country, there were fast growing, slow growing, and declining sectors; and that their pace was often related to the historical stages of their underlying technologies.

In the end, he was acutely aware that he had not fully met his own challenge and woven the element of time into "a continuous and harmonious whole." At the close of Appendix H in the *Principles* he reflects on "the imperfection of our analytical methods" and, as often, throws out a clue as to how progress might be made in dealing scientifically with the long run; i.e., by dating the time a certain volume of production became "normal." In one sense, the large body of historical and empirical material in Marshall's three major volumes reflects the extraordinarily high goal he set for himself. It was to produce a set of principles that matched reality in its full complexity. Unlike Marx, he visited many factories and met many businessmen, labor leaders, and workers. He understood and often said that the study of "organic growth," which lay at the center of the problem of time in economic theory, was a biological field, not a derivative of or parallel to Newtonian physics.

Marshall, then, firmly brought technological change in the sectors into micro-economic analysis, but he left the gap of "epoch-making" innovations for Schumpeter to fill.

Joseph Schumpeter

In his youthful *The Theory of Economic Development* (1911), Schumpeter seized a nettle none of his predecessors and virtually none of his successors in mainstream economics were willing to grasp; namely, that the processes of invention and innovation were often neither exogenous nor incremental; or, in his own words, innovation was "spontaneous and discontinuous." Schumpeter does not tell us what led him to make major discontinuous innovations generated by economic incentives the center of his system.[32] Perhaps he didn't know. But, objectively, we can identify three suggestive antecedents:

- Adam Smith's distinction between incremental inventions contrived by those who actually operated the machines and those created by "philosophers" that involved "new powers not formerly applied."
- Karl Marx's exposition of a circular flow and, then, a dynamic economic model at the opening of Volume II of *Capital*.
- Alfred Marshall's explicit recognition—even dramatization—of the case of increasing returns, the severe theoretical problems it posed, and his effort to resolve them, a recognition Schumpeter respected while regarding Marshall's solution as unsatisfactory.

Schumpeter begins his exposition in *Economic Development* with a particular version of a static equilibrium Walrasian (or Marxian) system in a state of circular flow. He introduces (or accepts from Walras) a powerful simplifying assumption; namely, that "we shall think of a commercially organized state, one in which private property, division of labor, and free competition prevail."[33] The acceptance of this assumption blocked off Schumpeter throughout his career from the analysis of the process of growth from underdeveloped beginnings and thereby limited his range as a growth economist.

Schumpeter's circular flow system is, however, not quite as static as it might at first appear. It does not imply that "year after year 'the same things' happen."[34] It allows for incremental changes in technology that displace the equilibrium point of the system so marginally as to permit new equilibrium positions to be reached from the old "by infinitesimal steps" with which unimaginative managers (as opposed to heroic innovating entrepreneurs) can deal.[35] It also allows for changes in response to powerful exogenous events with economic implications; e.g., bad harvests, wars, revolutions.

Chapter II ("The Fundamental Phenomenon of Economic Development") focuses with great clarity on the one concept that distinguishes development from circular flow—the concept that remained the core of Schumpeter's subsequent work:[36]

> Development in our sense is a distinct phenomenon, entirely foreign to what may be observed in the circular flow or in the tendency towards equilibrium. It is spontaneous and discontinuous change in the channels of the flow, disturbance of equilibrium, which forever alters and displaces the equilibrium state previously existing....
>
> This concept covers the following five cases: (1) The introduction of a new good—that is one with which consumers are not yet familiar—or of a new quality of a good. (2) The introduction of a new method of production, that is one not yet tested by experience in the branch of manufacture concerned, which need by no means be founded upon a

discovery scientifically new, and can also exist in a new way of handling a commodity commercially. (3) The opening of a new market, that is a market into which the particular branch of manufacture of the country in question has not previously entered, whether or not this market has existed before. (4) The conquest of a new source of supply of raw materials or half-manufactured goods, again irrespective of whether this source already exists or whether it has first to be created. (5) The carrying out of the new organization of any industry, like the creation of a monopoly position (for example through trustification) or the breaking up of a monopoly position.

Schumpeter was quite conscious that his assumption that the major economic changes of the capitalist epoch occurred in an irreversible revolutionary way rather than by continuous adaptation was theoretically explosive. He referred, for example, to Marshall's failure to overcome "the difficulties which surround the problem of increasing return."[37] But he proceeded forward courageously to explore the implications of his proposition that "spontaneous and discontinuous changes in the channel of the circular flow," rooted in technological change, were the heart of capitalist development.

Schumpeter's *Business Cycles* was published in 1939, some thirty years after he had arrived at the basic concepts that form the substance of his *Theory of Economic Development*. The later study is a massive two-volume work of eleven hundred pages, almost four times the size of the earlier book. The later study focuses on business cycles, although Schumpeter notes "the subtitle really renders what I have tried to do":[38] *A Theoretical Historical and Statistical Analysis of the Capitalist Process*. On the whole, there can be few examples of an economist so faithfully trying to turn the "scaffolding" of his youth "into a house."[39]

Schumpeter's historical passages are designed to buttress his three-cycle theory, which does not concern us here. They reflect much scholarship and a good many debates about both theory and history; but, as he was fully aware, they are peculiarly indecisive.[40]

The one element in his scheme that comes through persuasively is the three periods of relative concentration of major innovations: cotton textiles, good iron made from coke, and Watt's steam engine starting in the 1780s; the railroads, starting (awkwardly for Schumpeter's interpretation of the Kondratieff cycle) in the 1830s and 1840s, leading on to steel, in the late 1860s; and then, round about the turn of the century, electricity, a batch of new chemicals, and the internal combustion engine.

In dealing with the interwar years, Schumpeter lays out an important argument bearing on technology and innovation. It starts by reviewing the technical case made, in the late 1930s, for the arrival of secular stagnation. The expansion of the U.S. economy between 1933 and 1937 still left 14 percent unemployed at the peak of what Schumpeter called "The Disappointing Juglar."[41] Then came the partially self-inflicted wound of the sharp American recession of 1937–1938. In the latter year Alvin

Hansen published his *Full Recovery and Stagnation*. For our present purposes, what is significant is that Schumpeter argued that in no objective, technological sense had investment opportunities diminished:[42] "Nor can it be urged that fundamentally new opportunities of first-rate magnitude are not in prospect. Barring the question whether that is so, it is sufficient to reply that in the eighteen-twenties hardly anybody can have foreseen the impending railroad revolution or, in the eighteen-seventies, electrical developments and the motor car." After making his case that capitalism was imperiled not by a waning of investment opportunities but by a hostile political, social, and intellectual environment plus self-generated degenerative forces, Schumpeter concludes:[43] ". . . if our schema is to be trusted, recovery and prosperity should be more, and recession and depression phases less strongly marked during the next three decades than they have been in the last two. But the sociological drift can not be expected to change." That was a quite remarkable economic prognosis to make in 1939 even if the period of extraordinary prosperity occurred in a Kondratieff downswing (1951–1973) and the sociological drift toward socialism began to reverse from, roughly, the mid-1970s.

The Young Simon Kuznets

Simon Kuznets's *Secular Movements in Prices and Production* (1930) shares with Schumpeter's *Theory of Economic Development* and *Business Cycles* a few striking similarities and is marked by several equally striking differences.

Like *Economic Development*, *Secular Movements* is a young man's book incorporating a large vision of the terrain the author intended to explore in his professional career and a definition of his proposed strategy. Both Schumpeter and Kuznets aimed to contribute to the generation of intimately linked dynamic theories of economic growth and business cycles that would combine historical and statistical analysis with theory. Above all, they identified innovation as the critical dimension of growth; they perceived the inherent unevenness of the process of innovation as key to an understanding of cycles of differing lengths; they accepted that the pursuit of these insights required not merely aggregate analysis but also detailed analysis of the sectors where innovation actually happened; and they based their analyses on the inescapable path of deceleration followed by a sector caught up in radical innovational change.

In building on these insights both men broke away from the mainstream preoccupations of their day; although Kuznets had available (and acknowledged the influence of) Schumpeter's *Economic Development*; and, in *Business Cycles*, Schumpeter had available Kuznets's *Secular Movements*.[44]

Kuznets begins with a set of observations on the empirical evidence.[45]

... if we single out the various nations or the separate branches of industry, the picture becomes less uniform, some nations seem to have led the world at one time, others at another. Some industries were developing most rapidly at the beginning of the century, others at the end. ... Great Britain has relinquished the lead in the economic world because its own growth, so vigorous through the period 1780–1850, has slackened. She has been overtaken by rapidly developing Germany and the United States.
... As we observe the various industries with a given national system, we see that the lead in development shifts from one branch to another. The main reason for this shift seems to be that a rapidly developing industry does not continue its vigorous growth indefinitely, but slackens its pace after a time, and is overtaken by industries whose period of rapid development comes later. Within any country we observe a succession of different branches of activity leading the process of development, and in each mature industry we notice a conspicuous slackening in the rate of increase. ... But contrasted with our belief in the fairly continuous march of economic progress, it raises a frequently overlooked question. Why is there an abatement in the growth of old industries? Why is not progress uniform in all branches of production, with the inventive and organizing capacity of the nation flowing in an even stream into the various channels of economic activity? What concentrates the forces of growth and development in one or two branches of production at a given time, and what shifts the concentration from one field to another as time passes?

These questions can best be answered by an inspection of the historical records of industrial growth, focused upon the processes that underlie economic development.

At this point Kuznets, having used a series of empirical observations to come to rest on the process of sectoral retardation, introduces some economic theory; but he slides it in with the reference to "factors discussed by economic historians" and traces a path that permits him, like Schumpeter, to assert that changes in technique are the decisive factor in growth.[46]

... technical progress comes to be realized in response to some felt needs, which may be brought about by the pressure of population or by changes in demand. ...

While all three forces are interdependent, the changes in technique most clearly condition the movements in both population and demand, while the dependence of technical progress upon population and demand is less clear and immediate. In the chain interconnection of the three, this link seems to be most prominent.

Thus, a similar focus on innovation leads Kuznets to much the same hypothesis that had governed Schumpeter's *Economic Development* a generation earlier; but their conceptual framework differed rather sharply.

The second major difference between Schumpeter and the early Kuznets is much narrower. Schumpeter made the creative entrepreneur and the progressively lesser breeds that swarmed after him the center of the innovational process; for Kuznets, at the center were his logistic curves (or three constants Gompertz curves) capturing statistically the process of retardation that suffused the life of sectors in a technologically dynamic economy. Retardation in a sequence of leading sectors was an observed statistical uniformity. He identified four reasons for retardation: the slowing down of technical progress, dependence of the innovational sectors on slower-growing sectors supplying raw material inputs, a relative decline in the funds available for expansion of the innovational sectors, and competition from the same industry in a younger country. Schumpeter's analysis of the waning contribution of an innovational sector to overall growth is not inconsistent with that of Kuznets, but it is distinctively different in its emphasis on certain nonstatistical and sociological factors at work.[47]

A third difference between the two approaches to innovation and cycles concerns what might be called the technical or intermediate objective of their work. For Schumpeter, in *Business Cycles*, the major objective was to give substance to his innovational interpretation of the long, half-century (Kondratieff) cycle, suggesting also its linkage to sequences of strong and weak decennial (Juglar) cycles. He found that primary trends in production and prices reflected systematically the life cycle of a given technical innovation (or opening up of a new territory or natural resource); that is, a phase of rapid, then decelerating, increase in output and of rapid, then decelerating, decrease in price.

Kuznets did not link his analysis of sectoral retardation to data on the course of national output during the time period with which he dealt. In dealing with secondary movements in production and prices, however, he did speculate at some length on the possible reasons for the concurrence of rapidly expanding output and constrained real wages in the period of rising prices, 1896–1914.

Walther Hoffmann

Hoffmann's *The Growth of Industrial Economies*, in effect, made the linkage between sectoral and aggregate growth analysis that Kuznets failed to make.[48] Growth emerges as a process carried forward by a succession of sectors of increasing technological sophistication, with a progressive relative expansion in capital goods. Specifically he finds the following:[49]

> Whatever the relative amounts of the factors of production, whatever the location factors, whatever the state of technology, the structure of the manufacturing sector of the economy has always followed a uniform pattern. The food, textile, leather and furniture industries—which we define as "consumer goods industries"—always develop first during the process of industrialization. But metal working, vehicle building, engineering and chemical industries—the "capital-goods industries" soon develop faster than the first group. This can be seen throughout the process of industrialization. . . .

For the purposes of our analysis we have divided this gradual process into the following four stages:
Stage I has a ratio of 5(5 ± 1):1
Stage II has a ration of 2.5 (5 ± 1):1
Stage III has a ratio of 1 (± 0.5):1
The fourth stage has a still lower ratio.

In Stage I the consumer-goods industries are of overwhelming importance, their net output being on the average five times as large as that of the capital-goods industries. In Stage II the initial lead of the consumer-goods industries has diminished to a point where their net output is only two and one-half times as large as that of the capital-goods industries. In Stage III the net output of the two groups of industries are approximately equal and in Stage IV the consumer-goods industries have been left far behind by the rapidly growing capital-goods industries. The main purpose of this book is to show that these stages of economic development can be identified for all free economies.

By seizing on and pursuing a measurable ratio—the proportion of value added in a selected group of consumer goods industries relative to a similar group of capital goods industries—Hoffmann produced an original morphology of growth in four stages and, along the way, arrayed a wide spectrum of countries with respect to the timing of their entrance into industrialization. His work in this area—generally ignored in the literature on development—clearly belongs among the authentic pioneering efforts.

A Conclusion

There is a certain shapeliness in the work of this array of four economists of the period 1870–1939 who, in different ways, took technology seriously. Marshall, who helped create modern mainstream micro- and macro-economics, almost alone confronted the challenge posed for formal theory by increasing returns. He says clearly how it arose inevitably from the process of technological innovation; but, despite considerable effort, he could never bring that process comfortably into the framework of conventional theory. In particular, he found the problem posed by large revolutionary innovations insoluble. His successors didn't try as hard as Marshall: they simply treated such innovations as exogenous.

Schumpeter seized on that problem and sought to solve it by dynamizing the Walrasian equilibrium system. His method was to relate the long cyclical waves in prices, interest rates, and money wages discerned by Kondratieff to the disequilibrium paths set in motion by clusters of major innovations. He also tried to relate the decelerating path of these innovations to fluctuations in the rate of increase in aggregate output via strong and weak Juglar (nine-year) cycles. As Schumpeter perceived, his effort did not succeed and, until the end of his life, his unfulfilled dream was to dynamize the Walrasian model by rendering technological innovation endogenous.

Kuznets was less haunted than Marshall and Schumpeter by theoretical challenges. He was primarily a skilled statistician and empiricist, but like his mentor Wesley Mitchell, he was also a thoroughly literate economic theorist. In his *Secular Movements* he explored in greater statistical depth than Kondratieff and Schumpeter the actual paths of output and prices in major sectors driven along their decelerating paths by major technological innovations.

He also harbored a dream of moving toward a dynamic theory of production and prices and, indeed, tried to apply his insights to national income accounting and highly aggregated statistical analyses of growth.

Walther Hoffman, also primarily a statistician, came at technological change from a quite different direction. Using historical data on consumers and capital goods sectors and sub-sectors, he developed an intriguing stage theory based on the rising relative scale of the latter.

While these four creative figures wrestled directly with the process of technological innovation, the greatly enlarged flow of economists in the seven decades after 1870 focused on other matters: long-term price trends; the refinement of partial equilibrium analysis in factor as well as commodity markets; welfare economics, which led quite directly to efforts to measure national income and its distribution; business cycles and the extraordinary pathology of the world economy during the interwar years. A good deal of this work touched on technological change, and some, at least, of those who did it thought seriously about innovation; e.g., D. H. Robertson. But the nature of the most searching policy problems of these decades and the inescapable awkwardness of equilibrium economics in dealing with technological change left the work to be carried forward by a handful of mavericks plus, of course, the economic historians, some of whom foreshadowed the post-1945 approaches to the analysis of technology and growth.

TECHNOLOGICAL CHANGE AND GROWTH ANALYSIS SINCE 1945

Three Types of Post-1945 Growth Analysis

Growth analysis returned to fashion in three forms in the post–World War II era: Harrod–Domar and neoclassical growth models; statistical analyses of average structural changes associated with different levels of real income per capita, pioneered by Colin Clark, carried forward in the postwar era by Simon Kuznets, Hollis Chenery, and their associates; and development economics, which drew a host of economists to prescription as well as analysis in support of heightened economic modernization efforts in Latin America, Africa, the Middle East, and Asia. There was also, as we shall see, a narrower field of growth accounting, associated notably with the work of Edward F. Denison, which sought to fill the empty boxes of neoclassical growth models.

For our narrow purposes it is sufficient to indicate how each of these three major fields dealt with or failed to deal with the problem of technology. It is almost, but not quite, a catalogue of convenient evasions.

Growth Models

Broadly speaking growth models have been of two types that aimed to dramatize two quite different problems. The Harrod-Domar model, reflecting the anxieties of the 1930s and an anticipated relapse into depression after the end of the war, aimed to illuminate the inherent instability of a growing capitalist economy. It did so by asserting the unlikelihood (in Harrod's terms) that the warranted rate of growth (G_w), which would satisfy private entrepreneurs, would match the natural rate of growth (G_n), the maximum long-run rate of advance—required for full employment and determined by the rate of population growth and the flow of innovations. Both the flow of innovations and their productivity (the marginal aggregate capital-output ratio) were given and fixed as were the proportions of capital and labor in production. The operational focus was on the requirements of public policy to force G_w to approximate G_n.

By the mid-1950s it was apparent that the world economy was not moving along on a knife's edge but enjoying a protracted, robust boom. Neoclassical growth models of two types emerged to explain this cheerful but unexpected circumstance. Type A introduced the assumption of variable proportions between capital and labor to keep growth on an approximation of a full employment path. Type B evoked the shape of the Kahn-Keynes consumption function to achieve a similar outcome: in a boom the rise in income and shift to profits yielded an increase in the savings proportion and a salutary reduction in effective demand; in a slump, the process was reversed and the system was pushed back toward its long-run full employment path by a fall in the savings proportion and rise in effective demand.

With an exception noted below, the various methods used to cope with the role of invention, innovation, and technology in growth modeling were designed, in a sense, to bypass what might be called the Schumpeter Problem; namely, his assertion that a significant number of innovations are large, endogenous, and discontinuous and have their initial impact on particular sectors but, in their larger consequences, affect not only the structure of the economy as a whole but virtually all of its major variables; e.g., the rate of growth of output, the demand for credit, the price level, real wages, the profit rate. The major growth modelers fastened their attention firmly on forces making for instability or stability in the overall growth path when the determinants of growth were defined in highly aggregated and arbitrary terms.

Here are the major devices for bypassing the problem of technological innovation:

- Assume no technical progress and treat growth as a product of an expanding working force and capital stock.
- Assume technical progress is incremental, exogenous, and a function of the passage of time (disembodied).
- Assume technical progress is embodied in investment and a function of the rate of investment—a kind of return to Smithian incremental technological change in response to the expansion of the market.
- Assume all technical change is endogenous but incremental, induced by factor prices, cumulative experience in production, education, and other improvement of human capital, and/or by R&D investment.

This world of incremental technological change, exogenous or endogenous, was rendered even more manageable by the generous use of the assumption of neutral technical progress, which is usually defined as an unchanged ratio of the marginal products of capital and labor so long as the overall capital-labor proportion is constant. But capital-saving and labor-saving forms of technical progress were, in some cases, introduced.

It should be noted that one major growth modeler (Type B), Nicholas Kaldor, did, to his credit, seek to reconcile Schumpeter's insight with growth modeling.[50] His line of argument can be summarized tersely as follows:

- All (then) current growth models consisted in the superimposition of an exogenous unexplained linear trend on an otherwise trendless model. In no sense do the resultant theories provide "the basis for a theory of economic growth."
- A theory of growth must explain variations in rates of growth "in different ages or in different parts of the world."
- Variations in rates of population growth, technical progress, and capital accumulation are not independent of human action but are a function of "basic social forces," especially "human attitudes to risk-taking and money-making."
- Thus, it is not the trend rate of growth that determines the strength and duration of booms but "the strength and duration of booms which shapes the trend rate of growth. . . . Schumpeter's hero, the 'innovating entrepreneur' . . . is found, after all, to have an honourable place, or even key role, in the drama. . . ."

Kaldor drew back from the profound implications of this bold foray into what he regarded as the forbidden fields of sociology and social history, but in the rather arid world of model-building his essay is something of an oasis.

Growth modeling fell away rapidly in the 1970s and 1980s. It provided in none of its variants either an explanation for the great postwar boom of the 1950s and 1960s or for its demise. The three great forces yielding the unexampled postwar boom were:[51] the large backlog of hitherto unapplied technologies available to Western Europe, an even larger backlog for Japan; an array of new technologies, mainly prewar in origin but available to all advanced industrial states for rapid innovation (television, synthetic fibers, plastics, new pharmaceuticals, etc.); and protracted improvement in the terms of trade for advanced industrial countries after 1951. The latter sharply reversed at the close of 1972; the stimulus of the old and new innovations waned from the mid-1960s forward in a perfectly natural way.

Without including an explanation for trend movements in relative prices and a much more disaggregated analysis of the generation and diffusion of technologies, growth models of the post–World War II quarter century were not particularly useful; although they provided considerable high-grade economic talent relatively innocent fun for some time. But there is an element of truth in A. K. Sen's rather bitter summation:[52] "It is as if a poor man collected money for his food and blew it all on alcohol."

The Statisticians of Growth

The statisticians of growth are certainly not vulnerable to Sen's charge of frivolous self-indulgence. Kuznets, picking up from Colin Clark's work and backed from 1949 forward by the Social Science Research Council, carried forward one of the great social science enterprises of the century, embracing eleven countries, aside from the United States. The purpose, as we all know, was to assemble in a uniform, comparable manner and analyze the data on the structural changes accompanying the process of modern economic growth. The latter is conventionally measured in terms of real national income per capita. The degree of disaggregation varies in Kuznets's studies of structural changes in demand, production, trade, and employment. But a good deal of his analysis is conducted in terms of the three Colin Clark categories: agriculture, industry, and services.

Kuznets did not confine himself, however, to reporting the average behavior of growing economies at different levels of real income per capita. He analyzed the fundamental nature of accelerated modern growth itself. He concluded, like most analysts, that, at its core, it was caused by the application of modern scientific thought and technology to industry. Thus, Kuznets regarded the measurable statistical phenomena he cited as evidence of entrance into modern growth as a result of a deeper process. These secondary, measurable phemonena were, notably, an accelerated rate of urbanization (which he used to date entrance into modern growth), a sustained and rapid increase in real product per capita usually associated with high rates of population growth, a shift of the working force out of agriculture to industry and services, and enlarged contacts with the outside world.

For the author of *Secular Movements*, some thirty years earlier, Kuznets's analytic emphasis on the application of modern scientific thought and technology to the economy is wholly comprehensible, focused as that book was on the sequence of leading sectors resulting from the diffusion of a succession of new technologies. But two aspects of Kuznets's massive exercise in statistical morphology denied him access to what he himself regarded as the Hamlet of the story of modern economic growth. First, his three basic categories were so broad that they could not be directly linked to the introduction and diffusion of major, particular technologies. Second, having made reasonably precise statistical measurability the overriding criterion for his work, Kuznets found it impossible to deal with technological changes within the framework of his enterprise. In his 1971 *Economic Growth of Nations*, near the end of his most productive period, Kuznets, after some three hundred pages of statistical and analytic summary of previous findings, suddenly expresses his frustration.[53]

> Since the high and accelerated rate of technological change is a major source of the high rates of growth in per capita product and productivity in modern times and is also responsible for striking shifts in production structure, it is frustrating that the available sectoral classifications fail to separate new industries from old, and distinguish those affected by technological innovations. . . .

In the following twenty-eight pages, Kuznets illustrates the need for greater disaggregation, if growth is to be linked to the coming in of new technologies. He discusses leading sectors, old and new, and presents a highly disaggregated table to capture their evolution in the United States over the period 1880–1948. Against that background he then sets up a model to illustrate the impact on aggregate growth rates of new rapid growth sectors and new products. It is a joy to be back with the author of *Secular Movements* and to observe his sensitive appreciation of the innovational process hitherto masked by his overriding preoccupation with large national income aggregates.

But, in fact, Kuznets was never able to resolve his fundamental dilemma: He defined modern growth in terms of the effective absorption of new technologies; but he measured it in terms of product per capita, a quite different, if related variable. And his successors in comparative statistical growth analysis, led by Hollis Chenery, productive in many ways, were also not able to break out of this prison of their own construction.

With respect to uniformities Chenery's 1975 *Patterns of Development, 1950–1970*, written with Moises Syrquin, perhaps best captures his method and achievement; although Chenery moved beyond in several major subsequent publications.

Its cross-sectional method differs from Kuznets's comparison of long historical time series in several respects. Chenery and Syrquin use correlation analysis to establish their average patterns (or "stylized facts");

disaggregate systematically a bit beyond Kuznets' strictly economic categories; and helpfully include several social categories, notably education and demographic transition.

Chenery went further in three major directions. First, in an article written with Lance Taylor, he disaggregated industries into "early," "middle," and "late."[54] These roughly approximate the sequence of leading sectors that characterize my take-off, drive to technological maturity, and high mass consumption, as well as Walther Hoffman's industrial stages. Second, Chenery gave a great deal more attention to trade and capital flows (including foreign aid) than Kuznets and defined categories for developing countries according to the relative scale and composition of their foreign trade. Third, Chenery had the advantage of having worked intensively on the problems of particular countries, e.g., Italy, Japan, Pakistan, Israel. He was a substantial figure in policy-oriented development analysis from the late 1950s forward. He understood better than some the gap between average behavior (and deviations) derived from correlation analysis and the kind of data required to render responsible policy recommendations. Analytically, he quite consciously sought to combine the virtues of historical and cross-sectional analysis with a sense of the uniqueness of particular cases.

Evidently, I find the Chenery extension of Clark-Kuznets structural analysis of growth more useful than the Harrod-Domar and neoclassical growth models. The two major weaknesses are, in my view, the inadequacy of the treatment of technological change and the failure to relate its findings to the relevant noneconomic factors that often are the major source of deviations from average behavior. But this is, after all, an almost universal weakness in formal growth modeling as well as in statistical analyses of the morphology of growth.

Growth Accounting: Edward F. Denison

A method for analyzing changes in the determinants of growth on the basis of painstaking disaggregation was developed by Edward F. Denison of the Brookings Institution. His method is incorporated in six books of his own (the first published in 1978) plus similar studies by others. Taken all together this literature embraces recent experience in the United States, Canada, Western Europe, Japan, India, and the Republic of Korea. Denison's most recent study is of the United States over the period 1929–1982.[55]

Table 1 indicates the extent of Denison's disaggregation as well as his estimate of the various sources of American growth over the fifty-three years for which he has developed comparable data.

For our purposes, the key variable is quantitatively the most important: "advances in knowledge." It covers both technological change and improvements in "managerial and organizational knowledge."[56] Despite heroic efforts, including linkage to the estimates of the productivity of R&D by Edwin Mansfield and others, Denison has thus far been forced

TABLE 1

Contributions to 1929–82 growth rates

	Potential national income				Actual national income			
	Total		Per person employed		Total		Per person employed	
	Whole economy	Nonresidential business	Whole economy	Nonresidential business	Whole economy	Nonresidential business	Whole economy	Nonresidential business
	(1)	(2)	(3)	(4)	(5)	(6)	(7)	(8)
Growth rate	3.2	3.1	1.6	1.7	2.9	2.8	1.5	1.6
Percent of growth rate								
All sources	100	100	100	100	100	100	100	100
Labor input except education	34	25	−13	−23	32	20	−12	−25
Education per worker	13	16	26	30	14	19	27	34
Capital	17	12	15	10	19	14	20	13
Advances in knowledge	26	34	54	64	28	39	55	68
Improved resource allocation	8	11	16	19	8	11	16	18
Economies of scale	8	11	17	20	9	12	18	22
Changes in legal and human environment	−1	−2	−3	−4	−1	−2	−3	−4
Land	0	0	−3	−4	0	0	−3	−3
Irregular factors	0	0	0	0	−3	−5	−7	−8
Other determinants	−5	−7	−10	−13	−5	−8	−10	−13

Source: Edward F. Denison, Trends in Economic Growth, 1929–1982 (Washington, D.C.: The Brookings Institution, 1985), p. 30.

to settle for treating advances in knowledge as a residual.[57] Denison provides reasonably convincing reasons for believing his residual is a fair approximation of improvements in knowledge for the period 1948–1973. With admirable candor, however, he finds the collapse in the rate of productivity increase after 1973 beyond the explanatory power of his analytic system.[58]

In short, growth accounting is a promising method for studying economic progress; but, like mainstream economic theory and the statistical morphology of growth, it has not yet developed a grip on the process by which new technologies are generated in particular sectors and diffused.

Development Economics

There is a certain paradox in the field of development economics as it enjoyed its period of glory in the 1950s and 1960s and experienced subsequently a period of retrospective criticism, debate, and even counter-revolution. In essence it was, in its heyday, the study of and prescription for societies that had failed to absorb substantially (or fully) the pool of relevant technologies that had been cumulatively created over the two previous centuries.

On the other hand, with an exception noted below, the great issues of analytic and policy debate in the field of development economics have not focused directly on technology, its generation and diffusion. The three major, partially related issues in contention were, stated crudely:[59]

- national planning versus reliance on the market;
- import substitution versus export-led growth;
- priority for agriculture versus priority for industry.

All relate to the central question: the pace at which a developing society absorbs efficiently the pool of hitherto unapplied, relevant technology available to it. But that question was mainly debated at one remove.

The question of technology did arise directly, however, around the issue of "appropriate technology" centered on Ernst Schumacher's "small is beautiful" doctrine. The now familiar Schumacher argument was that the capital/labor ratios prevailing in advanced countries generated capital-intensive, labor-saving technologies inappropriate to developing countries with quite different capital/labor ratios: "intermediate technologies" were, therefore, required: more sophisticated than those of the traditional society, more labor-intensive (and more human) than those of the advanced industrial world.

There is a strong *prima facie* case for Schumacher's view. An economic historian immediately thinks of Japan's great success with two-tier industrial development, starting with the silk industry, combining labor-intensive production in the villages with modern factory production.

This system, requiring a literate farm population, efficient organization, and good quality control, has never been duplicated on a large scale elsewhere. And, in general, the extent to which Schumacher's proposition could be efficiently applied has never been satisfactorily established. In one sense, Mao's disastrous Great Leap Forward of 1958 was a romantic, ill-conceived experiment in this direction. As the backyard iron furnaces of the Great Leap Forward demonstrated, the production possibility curves of micro-economic textbooks, with their array of incremental gradations of technology, do not exist in real life. Nature and human ingenuity may not be capable of providing efficient possibilities between a backyard iron furnace and a modern steel mill. On the other hand, it can be and has been argued, that we do not know. The technology now generally available has been generated in the labor-expensive North. Thus, some creative talent in the South might focus usefully on filling in the production possibility curves at the labor-intensive end.[60]

Economists often fail to take account, however, of an important mitigating circumstance. The working force involved in a production process is much larger than those actually engaged with machines on the floor of the factory or steel mill. Factory production has a large and usually long logistical tail engaging not only administrative personnel but material handling, transport, the production of essential raw material inputs, infrastructure, housing and other services to the working force, etc.—in short, the whole Leontief input chain. As anyone knows who has observed economic and social life in a low-wage developing country these activities are normally and quite sensibly much more labor intensive than in advanced industrial countries. Thus, the whole production process associated with a final product may conform much better to Schumacher's criteria than the final production or assembly stage.

The Direct Study of Technology: Its Generation and Absorption

For differing reasons, then, the growth modelers, statistical morphologists, and development economists for the most part dealt with technology as an exogenous aggregate. As Jacob Schmookler wrote:[61]

> While neoclassical economic theory has many important applications, it is poorly related to what really happens in the long run. It suffers from this deficiency mainly because it makes no provision for changes in technological knowledge. . . . Technological change has to be introduced into the analysis from the outside. It is assumed, not explained.

For example, the best known theoretical formulation and statistical measurement of the contribution of technology ("knowledge") to growth is "the residual," to which concept a whole series of economists contributed over three decades.[62]

On the other hand the paradox incorporated in Schmookler's observation quoted above was recognized by many postwar scholars who, in one way or other, set about studying directly the generation and diffusion of technology.

This is not the occasion for a bibliographical essay on a quite massive field,[63] but some examples should be noted.

Among economic historians, for example, Paul A. David and Nathan Rosenberg have carried forward in more sophisticated style the pioneering studies of Abbot Payson Usher, who had considerable impact on Schumpeter's formulation of Kondratieff cycles.[64]

In this field it is somewhat difficult to separate economic historians from other analysts of technological generation and diffusion because virtually all thoughtful students are driven back into history to track out the inherently prolonged dynamic processes involved. W. Rupert Maclaurin, architect of the remarkable post-1945 rise of the economics department at M.I.T., was also a pioneer in the analysis of change in communication technology.[65] Jacob Schmookler made a number of sophisticated contributions to the study of technology, perhaps most strikingly to the complex relations between science and inventions.[66] Edwin Mansfield and Svi Griliches pioneered the effort to measure the rate of return from research and development.[67]

From a quite different perspective, several major analysts have attempted to isolate the disproportionate impact on overall output, investment, and productivity change of sectors incorporating relatively new, rapidly diffusing technologies; that is, the young Kuznets's leading sectors of *Secular Movements*. Here the NBER study of Daniel Creamer and his colleagues and W.E.G. Salter's *Productivity and Technical Change* have been invaluable, as well as Solomon Fabricant's earlier NBER analysis of industrial production growth rates.[68]

There have also been those who, in the past two decades, have returned to the study of innovation and its diffusion under the inspiration of Schumpeter's *Business Cycles*. Here the stimulus was, clearly, the end of the great boom of 1951–1972 and the emergence of a protracted period of deceleration and irregular fluctuations that fit no pattern familiar in mainstream economics. Gerhard Mensch and Christopher Freeman and his colleagues at Sussex have been major figures in this branch of the invention-innovation renaissance.[69]

Finally, there has been a great deal of work addressed directly to the generation, diffusion, and impact on output and employment of the clustering of innovations that asserted itself in the mid-1970s. The immensely fertile IC^2 Institute at the University of Texas at Austin is one major source of work of this kind.[70]

Nathan Rosenberg has written fruitfully about almost all these dimensions of the study of technology, but neither he nor his colleagues in this specialist exploration of the field have produced a unified view of the various phenomena they have isolated or linked technology generation and diffusion to the main body of economics.

PROBLEMS FOR THE FUTURE

The Fourth Technological Revolution: Character and Significance

The unification of technology analysis and its linkage to micro- and macro-analysis is, as suggested at the beginning of this essay, urgent as one looks at the present and speculates about the future. We are living in the midst of the fourth great technological revolution of the past two centuries and the relative fate of both advanced industrial and developing countries will depend over the next half century and beyond on the pace at which its scientific potentialities are unfolded and, especially, the pace at which the subsequent inventions are efficiently woven into the societies of the world economy, rich and poor alike.

Following the sequence Schumpeter derived from economic historians—which should be taken seriously but not too seriously—there were three distinct concentrations of major innovations between the 1780s and, say, the 1960s. Factory-manufactured textiles, Cort's method for making iron from coke, and Watt's steam engine all came on stage in a substantial way in Britain of the 1780s; then the railroads, making considerable commercial headway in the 1830s but generating substantial booms in Britain, the American Northeast, and Germany in the 1840s and leading on to the revolution in steelmaking in the 1860s; finally, electricity, a new batch of chemicals, and the internal-combustion engine. These became significant round about the opening of the twentieth century and, in its various elaborations, carried economic growth forward through the 1960s in the advanced industrial countries.

The measurement of degree of development in terms of the capacity to absorb and apply efficiently the global pool of relevant technologies is heightened, as suggested earlier, by the character of the fourth technological revolution. The new technologies have four distinctive characteristics: a close linkage to areas of basic science also undergoing revolutionary change; a capacity to galvanize the old basic industries as well as agriculture, forestry, animal husbandry, and the whole range of services; an immediate relevance to developing countries to a degree depending on their stage of growth; and a degree of diversification such that no single country is likely to dominate them as, for example, Britain dominated the early stage of cotton textiles and the United States the early stage of the mass-produced automobile. The diversified character of this cluster of technologies is already yielding large-scale trade and cooperation across international boundaries as comparative advantage asserts itself, as well as evident intense international competition.

While the old industrial countries of the North have been spawning this glamourous, much discussed revolution in technology, the developing regions of the South have been mounting a little-noted human revolution of their own.

Overall, the proportion of the population aged 20–24 enrolled in higher education in what the World Bank calls "lower middle income" countries rose from 3 percent to 10 percent between 1960 and 1982; for "upper middle income" countries the figure increased from 4 percent to 14 percent. For Brazil, fated to be a major actor in this drama, the proportion rose from 1 percent in 1965 to 12 percent in 1982. In India, with low per capita income but a vital education system, the figure rose from 3 percent to 9 percent. To understand the meaning of these figures, it should be recalled that in 1960 the proportion for the United Kingdom was 9 percent, for Japan 10 percent.

There has been, moreover, a radical shift toward science and engineering. In India, for example, the pool of scientists and engineers has increased from about 190,000 in 1960 to 2.4 million in 1984—a critical mass exceeded only in the United States and the Soviet Union. In Mexico the annual average increase of graduates in natural science was about 3 percent, and in engineering 5 percent, in the period 1957 to 1973. From 1973 to 1981 the comparable figures were an astonishing 14 percent and 24 percent, respectively—an almost fivefold acceleration.

Even discounting for problems of educational quality, the potential absorptive capacity for the new technologies in the more advanced developing countries is high. Their central problem—like that of most advanced industrial countries—is how to make effective use of the increasingly abundant scientific and engineering skills they already command. This requires, in turn, an ability to generate and maintain flexible, interactive partnerships among scientists, engineers, entrepreneurs and the working force.

These figures, signaling a surge in technological absorptive capacity, mark the arrival of a stage when national growth rates are, under normal circumstances, at a maximum. Despite current vicissitudes, India, the developing countries of the Pacific Basin (including China), and those containing most of the population of Latin America are likely to absorb the new technologies and move rapidly forward over the next several generations. Much the same would happen, I believe if the Middle East could find its way from its chronic bloodletting to a twentieth-century version of the Treaty of Westphalia, which ended the Thirty Years' War in 1648.

Thus, the world economy and polity face a familiar adjustment in which late comers narrow and finally close the gap with front-runners. But this time it is likely to occur on an unprecedented scale. The advanced industrial countries (including the U.S.S.R. and the East European nations) now constitute about 1.1 billion people, or approximately one-quarter of the world's population. At least 2.6 billion people, about 56 percent, live in countries that will, I estimate, acquire technological virtuosity within the next half century. Moreover, population growth rates in the decades ahead will be higher in the latter group than in the former. We are talking about a great historical transformation, and technological generation and diffusion is at the heart of the process.

Eight Tasks Ahead

If economic historians and economists are to make a maximum contribution to an understanding of the technological dimension of the process underway, they must unify the eight following dimensions of the task and link them to the main body of economic theory; although it should be immediately noted that linkage will transform and dynamize micro- and macro-economics. For purposes of clarity, conservation of space, and, perhaps, to stimulate controversy I shall state them tersely and bluntly, without reference to their roots in the literature already summarized earlier in this essay.

First, and most fundamental, invention—that is, the whole R&D process—should be regarded as a sub-sector of total investment; that is it represents current allocation of human talent and other resources to achieve an expected future rate of return over cost that, taking risk and appropriability into account, at least matches allocations in other directions. It is possible to argue, as Schumpeter did, that not all inventions are born of Mother Necessity. Some represent creations that generate a hitherto unsuspected market. But we are dealing, in the end, with an investment governed by not unfamiliar laws of expected future profitability.

Second, R&D is a complex spectrum in which investment is involved at each stage from basic science to pilot projects. The criteria governing investment in each type of activity in the spectrum will vary; and the relations among them are complex, notably the often oblique relation between basic science and invention. For present purposes it is sufficient to note that a range of conceptually distinguishable but interacting creative investment activities are in play within the R&D spectrum, and that the linkages and interactions have never been as close as they are in the Fourth Technological Revolution.

Third, it is useful if oversimple to regard inventions and innovations as made up of two broad types: incremental and discontinuous, in the tradition of Adam Smith and Schumpeter. In fact, however, we are dealing with a spectrum of degrees of discontinuity and, therefore, degrees of creativity and heroism in innovation. Nevertheless, the distinction between profit maximization under conditions of fixed production functions and entrepreneurship under degrees of risk imposed by the need to change production functions should not be wholly lost.

Fourth, scientific and inventive as well as entrepreneurial talent tends to cluster, but none of us can yet explain precisely and confidently why this important phenomenon exists. The literature contains various notions of clustering as well as various explanations for the degree to which the phenomenon exists. A good deal of further work on this problem is required. Three clues appear worth pursuing: the working out and refinement of a given innovational breakthrough is clearly a long-term process, transcending a number of conventional (say, nine-year) business cycles; the logistical path of a sector affected by a major innovational breakthrough results in a withdrawal from that sector of R&D creative talent as the sector's rate of growth decelerates; the clusters of apparently independent technological systems may not be as independent as they look. Thus, for example, the impact of Watt's steam engine on both the cotton textile and iron fabrication industries; the impact of the railroad on the modernization of both the iron and steel and engineering industries as well as on agriculture and raw material production; the internal combustion engine on chemical, electricity, steel, and machinery industries; and the ubiquitous role of the computer in the current technological revolution.

Fifth, we must find a way to deal systematically with the phenomenon of a technological backlog: its size and the circumstances that determine whether and at what pace that backlog can be efficiently absorbed. This proposition obviously relates to the analysis of underdevelopment but also to the problems that underlie the current Soviet aspiration for *perestroika* and those underlying the challenge faced by certain U.S. sectors that have failed to absorb promptly and efficiently the full potentialities of the technologies of the Fourth Technological Revolution.

Sixth, clarification of the relation between the pace of technological absorption and the investment rate. A high proportion of investment in plant and equipment is financed in advanced industrial societies by the ploughback of profits. There is considerable evidence that industrial investment is disproportionately concentrated in sectors rapidly absorbing new technologies or technologies, hitherto out of reach, drawn from the technological backlog. The pace of technological absorption in leading sectors also substantially determines the rate of growth of real GNP, thus public revenues and thus also real private income available for consumption. One can argue, therefore, that the rate of investment is substantially (not wholly) determined by the pace of technological absorption: plant and equipment outlays directly, infrastructure investment via the course of public revenues, residential housing via the course of real private income net of taxes.

Seventh, official statistical data on employment should be reorganized to permit measurement of total employment associated with a given sector or innovation. The Standard Industrial Classification (SIC) numbers cannot be easily grouped to measure, for example, total employment associated with steel, or computer output. One needs estimates for each stage in the Leontieff input-output chain, including services. The motor vehicle industry in the United States is virtually the only sector for which such estimates have been made.[71] The inability to make such calculations is felt with particular strength at a time of technological revolution like the present.

Eighth, more research is required on the impact of innovations generated by problems and profit possibilities in one sector on productivity and output in other sectors. As noted earlier both history and the contemporary scene are full of examples of such unforeseen, secondary benefits—from the steam engine to the computer. In particular, such linkages help explain why the phenomenon of diminishing returns to basic commodity production—built into classical economics—has been fended off for the better part of two centuries in the advanced industrial world.

These eight problems embrace virtually all of the issues to which historians and other analysts of technology have addressed themselves. I believe that, if pushed further, these areas for research would yield not only a more coherent specialist field but also a way of linking technological generation and diffusion to mainstream economics.

The keys to the linkage are, of course, the treatment of the whole R&D process as a complex endogenous investment sub-sector or sectors, the distinction between incremental and discontinuous innovations, the tendency of major innovations to cluster, the phenomenon of the technology backlog, and the multi-dimensional role of the pace of technology absorption in determining the rate of investment.

When made, these linkages would of course, rather radically transform existing growth models—indeed, contemporary mainstream economics as a whole. But so much the better.

NOTES

1. W. S. Jevons and Carl Menger published their formulations in 1871 and Leon Walras in 1874; although Jevons' "coefficient of utility" made its appearance as early as 1862.

2. Eugene Rotwein (ed.), *David Hume: Writings on Economics* (Madison: University of Wisconsin Press, 1955), p. 24.

3. *Ibid.*, pp. 17–18.

4. *Ibid.*, p. 13.

5. David Hume, *History of England* (London: Strahan [printer], 1802), Vol. III, pp. 402–403; Vol. IV, p. 327.

6. E. Rotwein (ed.), *op. cit.*, pp. 80–82. The lively and theoretically fruitful eighteenth-century debate on this subject is well summarized in Istvan Hont, "The 'rich country–poor country' debate in Scottish classical political economy," in Istvan Hont and Michael Ignatieff (eds.), *Wealth and Virtue, The Shaping of the Scottish Enlightenment* (Cambridge: at the University Press, 1983).

7. Rotwein (ed.), *op. cit.*, pp. 78–79.

8. This quotation is to be found in Hont, *op. cit.*, p. 300, where original sources are provided. See also *Wealth of Nations*, edited by Edwin Cannan, with an introduction by Max Lerner (New York: Random House, 1937), p. 462.

9. *Wealth of Nations*, pp. 245–246.

10. Edwin Cannan (ed.), *Lectures by Adam Smith* (Oxford: at the Clarendon Press, 1896), pp. 167–168; and *Wealth of Nations*, pp. 9–10. The meaning of "philosophers" in Smith's usage, "whose trade it is not to do anything, but to observe every thing," is suggested by his listing of their several areas of specialization (*Lectures*, p. 168): "mechanical, moral, political, chemical."

11. *Wealth of Nations*, p. 10.

12. T. R. Malthus, *Principles of Political Economy*, Second edition (New York: Augustus Kelley, 1951), p. 416.

13. *Ibid.*, pp. 352 and 360.

14. Piero Sraffa and M. H. Dobb (eds.), *The Works and Correspondence of David Ricardo* (Cambridge: at the University Press, 1955), Vol. I, pp. 94, 120, and 132.

15. *Ibid.*, pp. 93–94 and 97.

16. *Ibid.*, Vol. IV, p. 179.

17. See, for example, Chapter V in W. W. Rostow, *British Economy of the Nineteenth Century* (Oxford: at the Clarendon Press, 1948, reprinted by Greenwood Press, Westport, Connecticut, 1981).

18. Sraffa and Dobb (eds.), *op. cit.*, pp. 389–392 and 395.

19. Charles Babbage, *On The Economy of Machinery and Manufactures* (London: Charles Knight, first edition 1832). The first edition sold some 3,000 copies in two months—the equivalent of about 40,000 copies in the United States of the mid-1980s. Two further printings shortly followed. An enlarged fourth edition was published in 1841. Babbage is quoted on eight occasions by Mill in his *Principles*, sometimes at length.

20. *Principles*, p. 134.

21. *Ibid.*, p. 136.

22. *Ibid.*, p. 182.

23. *Ibid.*, p. 183.

24. *Ibid.*, p. 184.

25. See, for example, A. D. Gayer et al., *The Growth and Fluctuations of the British Economy 1790–1850* (Oxford: at the Clarendon Press, 1953), Vol. 1, pp. 295–296. Also R.C.O. Matthews, *A Study in Trade Cycle History, Economic Fluctuations in Great Britain 1833–1842* (Cambridge: at the University Press, 1954), p. 32.

26. *Principles*, pp. 750–751.

27. K. Marx, *Grundrisse: Foundations of the Critique of Political Economy* (Rough Draft), translated with a foreword by Martin Nicolaus (London: Allen Lane, 1973), p. 704.

28. See, especially, "Genesis of the Industrial Capitalist," Chapter XXXI of *Capital*, Vol. I, pp. 750–760 (Moscow: Foreign Languages Publishing House, 1954. Published in Great Britain by Lawrence and Wishart, London, 1954).

29. For precise references and discussion, see W. W. Rostow, *How It All Began* (New York: McGraw-Hill, 1975), pp. 148–151 and 251. These passages and references include G. N. Clark's reply to Hessen's interpretation of Newton.

30. Alfred Marshall, *Principles of Economics*, eighth edition (London: Macmillan, 1930), p. 461.

31. *Ibid.*, pp. 805–812.

32. Loring Allen points out that there are foreshadowings of *The Theory of Economic Development* in Schumpeter's first book *Das Wesen und der Hauptinhalt der Theoretischen Nationaloekonomie* (Munchen and Leipzig: Duncker und Humbolt, 1908). In his most vivid comment (pp. 182–183), Schumpeter argues that statics and dynamics are completely different fields, with different problems, methods, and subject matter. He notes that his current work is within the terrain of statics; but he concludes: "Dynamics, still in its infancy [Anfangen], is a 'Land of the Future.'"

33. *Economic Development*, p. 5.

34. *Ibid.*, p. 62.

35. *Ibid.*, pp. 61 and 64 n. 1.

36. *Ibid.*, pp. 63–64, 66, and 132ff.

37. *Ibid.*, p. 63 n. 1. The reference to Marshall is in the later English edition. It is unclear whether Marshall's bold confrontation of the problem on increasing returns—and failure fully to solve it—influenced Schumpeter's thought when formulating *The Theory of Economic Development*.

38. *Business Cycles* (New York: McGraw-Hill, 1939), Vol. I, p. v.

39. *Ibid*. Two examples come to mind: Adam Smith's *The Wealth of Nations* (1776); and Karl Marx's *Communist Manifesto* (1848) and the first volume of *Capital* (1867).

40. *Ibid.*, p. v.

41. *Ibid.*, pp. 1011–1050.

42. *Ibid.*, pp. 1037.

43. *Ibid.*, p. 1050.

44. S. Kuznets, *Secular Movements* (Boston: Houghton Mifflin, 1930), pp. 299–300, includes a brief paraphrase of Schumpeter's development theory in a section entitled "Innovations, Progress, and the Cyclical Fluctuations." He notes that it is among the theories he is using "as a point of departure for our reasoning" (*ibid.*, p. 300 n. 1).

45. *Ibid.*, pp. 1–5.

46. *Ibid.*, pp. 5, 6, and 9.

47. Schumpeter, *Business Cycles*, pp. 497–500. There is a certain grudging character to Schumpeter's references to Kuznets on retardation. He refers to it as an "old idea" (*ibid.*, p. 497, n. 2) and characterizes Kuznets' analysis as a "partial success."

48. The 1931 edition, entitled *Stadien und Type der Industrialisierung*, was published in Kiel by the Institut für Weltwirtschaft of the University of Kiel. The 1958 edition, *The Growth of Industrial Societies*, translated from the German by W. O. Henderson and W. H. Chaloner, was published in Manchester by the Manchester University Press.

49. *Ibid.*, pp. 2–3 and Chapter II ("The Process of Industrialization"), pp. 24–41.

50. Nicholas Kaldor, "The Relation of Economic Growth and Cyclical Fluctuations," *Economic Journal*, Vol. LXIV, March 1945, pp 53–76.

51. For an elaboration of this argument, see my "The World Economy Since 1945: A Stylized Historical Analysis," *Economic History Review*, Second Series, Vol. XXXVII, No. 2, May 1985, pp. 252–275.

52. A. K. Sen (ed.), *Growth Economics* (Harmondsworth: Penguin, 1970), p. 9.

53. *Economic Growth of Nations*, p. 315. One of Kuznets's final scientific papers ("Driving Forces of Economic Growth: What Can We Learn From History?") focused substantially on the same theme; i.e., the centrality of technological innovation and its structural consequences, in Herbert Giersch (ed.), *Towards an Explanation of Economic Growth* (Tubingen: J.C.G. Mohr, 1981).

54. "Development Patterns: Among Counties and over Time," *Review of Economics and Statistics*, Vol. L, November 1968, pp. 391–416; Chenery's 1960 "Patterns of Industrial Growth," *American Economic Review*, Vol. L, September 1960, pp. 624–654, foreshadowed to a degree the conclusions of the later (1968) article (1971 edition), pp. 230–234.

55. Edward F. Denison, *Trends in American Economic Growth, 1929–1982* (Washington D.C.: The Brookings Institution, 1985).

56. *Ibid.*, p. 28.

57. See, especially, *ibid.*, pp. 27–32, including notes on Edwin Mansfield and others.

58. *Ibid.*, pp. 29–30.

59. For a more extensive list of "Development Dichotomies" and an interesting effort to reconcile them, see Paul Streeten in Gerald M. Meier and Dudley Seers (eds.), *Pioneers in Development* (New York: Oxford University Press, for the World Bank, 1984), pp. 337–361.

60. See, for example, Victor L. Urquidi, "Scientific and Technological Cooperation for Development: Towards a New Outlook," The Lincoln-Juarez Lecture 1982, Washington, D.C., November 13, 1986. This issue was also taken up in the report by an international commission chaired by Felipe Herrera, Organization of American States (OAS), "Hemispheric Cooperation and Integral Development," OEA/Ser. T/11, OIC 15-80 (Washington, D.C., August 6, 1980).

61. Jacob Schmookler, *Patents, Invention, and Economic Change Data and Selected Essays*, edited by Zvi Griliches and Leonid Horowicz (Cambridge: Harvard University Press, 1972), p. 70.

62. The work of Edward F. Denison (e.g., *Trends in American Economic Growth*) and others in growth accounting has a considerable intellectual background including the following: J. Schmookler, "The Changing Efficiency of the American Economy, 1869 to 1938," *Review of Economic Statistics*, August 1952, pp. 214–231; S. Fabricant, "Economic Progress and Economic Change" in 36th Annual Report (New York: NBER, 1954); A. K. Cairncross, "The Place of Capital in Economic Progress" in L. H. Dupriez (ed.), *Economic Progress* (Louvain: Institut de Recherches Economiques et Sociales, 1955), pp. 235–248; M. Abramovitz, "Resources and Output in the United States Since 1870," *American Economic Review, Proceedings*, Vol. 46 (1956); R. M. Solow, "Technical Change and the Aggregate Production Function," *Review of Economics and Statistics*, Vol. 39 (1957). See also, a critical response to emphasis on technology rather than total physical inputs as the source of productivity increase, D. W. Jorgensen and Z. Griliches, "The Explanation of Productivity Change," *Review of Economic Studies*, Vol. 34 (1967).

63. The bibliographical references at the close of each chapter of Paul Stoneman's *The Economic Analysis of Technological Change* provide a useful sense of the scale and directions of recent analytic work on the economics of technological change (Oxford: Oxford University Press, 1983). But Burton H. Klein's *Prices, Wages, and Business Cycles: A Dynamic Theory* (Elmsford, N.Y.: Pergamon Press, 1984) should be added, despite its title.

64. See, notably, Paul A. David, *Technical Choice Innovation and Economic Growth* (Cambridge: at the University Press, 1976). These works provide a good view of the perspectives of both scholars incorporated in other books and essays. For an effort to bridge the gap between mainstream economics and economic historians, including considerable discussion of problems posed by technology, see William N. Parker (ed.), *Economic History and the Modern Economist* (Oxford: Blackwell, 1986).

65. Maclaurin focused primarily on various aspects of radio and television technology. See, for example, *Invention and Innovation in the Radio Industry*, (New York: Macmillan, 1949).

66. In addition to his *Patents, Invention and Economic Change*, cited in Note 61, see Jacob Schmookler, *Invention and Economic Growth* (Cambridge: Harvard University Press, 1966).

67. See, for example, Edwin Mansfield, *The Economics of Technological Change*, (New York: W.W. Norton, 1968), and his *Industrial Research and Technological*

Innovation, (New York: W.W. Norton, 1968). Zvi Griliches' seminal study was an effort to measure the social rate of retun for 1910–1955 on R&D resources invested in the development of hybrid corn: "Hybrid Corn: An Exploration in the Economics of Technological Change," *Econometrica*, October 1957. Also, "Research Costs and Social Returns: Hybrid Corn and Related Innovations," *Journal of Political Economy*, October 1958.

68. Solomon Fabricant, *The Output of Manufacturing Industries, 1899–1937* (New York: NBER, 1940); Daniel Creamer, Sergei P. Dobrovolsky, and Israel Berenstein, *Capital in Manufacturing and Mining: Its Formation and Financing* (Princeton: Princeton University Press, 1960); and W.E.G. Salter, *Productivity and Technical Change* (second edition with an addendum by W. B. Reddaway; Cambridge: at the University Press, 1966). In his belated return to a disaggregated approach to the linkage of technology to growth, Kuznets uses extensively the study of Creamer et al. (*Economic Growth of Nations*, pp. 314–343).

69. Mensch's hypothesis is incorporated in his *Stalemate in Technology: Innovations Overcome the Depression* (New York: Ballinger, 1979), English translation of the 1975 German Edition. Freeman's views are fully elaborated in C. Freeman, John Clark, and Luc Soete, *Unemployment and Technical Innovation* (Westport, Conn.: Greenwood Press, 1982). The references in the latter (pp. 203–210) list the principal recent work on long cycles as well as the older literature, although work on long cycles has continued to swarm in the 1980s. My evaluation of the Mensch-Freeman debate is in my review of the latter's study in *The Journal of Economic Literature*, Vol. XX, March 1983, pp. 129–131. See also Alfred Kleinknecht, foreword by Jan Tinbergen, *Innovation Patterns in Crisis and Prosperity. Schumpeter's Long Cycle Reconsidered.* (New York: St. Martin's 1987).

70. A few of IC²'s many monographs in this terrain are: Pier A. Abetti, Christopher W. LeMaistre, Raymond W. Smilor, and William A. Wallace (eds.), *Technological Innovation and Economic Growth* (Austin, Tex.: IC² Institute, The University of Texas at Austin, 1987); Pier A. Abetti, Christopher W. LeMaistre, and Raymond W. Smilor (eds.), *Industrial Innovation, Productivity, and Employment* (Austin, Tex.: IC² Institute, The University of Texas at Austin, 1987); Eugene B. Konecci, George Kozmetsky, Raymond W. Smilor, and Michael D. Gill, Jr. (eds.), *Commercializing Technology Resources for Competitive Advantages* (Austin, Tex.: IC² Institute, The University of Texas at Austin, 1986); Eugene B. Konecci, George Kozmetsky, Raymond W. Smilor, and Michael D. Gill, Jr. (eds.), *Technology Venturing: Making and Securing the Future* (Austin, Tex.: IC² Institute, The University of Texas at Austin, 1985); Eugene B. Konecci and Lawrence Kuhn (eds.), *Technology Venturing: American Innovation and Risk-Taking* (New York: Praeger Publishers, 1985); George Kozmetsky, *Transformational Management* (Cambridge, Mass.: Ballinger Publishing Company, 1985); and Vijay Mahajan and Yoram Wind (eds.), *Innovation Diffusion Models of New Product Acceptance* (Cambridge, Mass.: Ballinger Publishing Company, 1986).

71. See *The World Economy: History and Prospect*, Appendix C, pp. 670–675, where various estimates for the U.S. motor vehicle industry have been assembled.

TWENTY-FIVE

Development, Efficiency, and Equity in Historical Perspective (1989)

This essay was written for a festschrift organized in honor of Benjamin Higgins ("Equity and Efficiency in Development: Essays in Honor of Benjamin Higgins," Donald J. Savoie, ed.). In the 1950s we shared a good deal of the exciting first decade of the Center for International Studies at MIT under the graceful and effective leadership of Max Millikan. The center launched a program addressed to both development analysis and policy, including sustained field research in India and Indonesia. Higgins directed the work on Indonesia from 1954 to 1959.

As for most of us trained in the 1930s, economic development was a kind of second marriage for Higgins. Among Higgins's early and abiding interests was welfare economics, which is evidently relevant to policy in developing as well as advanced industrial countries. The links between welfare and development economics, therefore, was a felicitous choice for a volume in honor of Higgins. I was pleased to be asked to contribute a general historical essay on development, efficiency, and equity.

In writing this essay I thought often of Higgins's task in dealing with Indonesia of the 1950s. It had underlined for us all a memorable lesson: the primacy as well as complexity of politics in developing countries. Where politicians saw advantages to themselves and their political objectives in granting priority to economic development—as did, among others, Nehru in India, Park in South Korea, and most of the post-1940 Mexican presidents—progress, even quite rapid progress, was possible. Where the political objectives of leaders clashed with the imperatives of development, politics almost always won and development lost—thus, the economic fate of their respective countries under Ben Bella, Nasser, and Nkrumah as well as Sukarno.

The problem in Indonesia was neatly summed up by Sukarno during his visit to Washington in April 1961. President Kennedy urged him to concentrate his energies on developing his country, which was rich in resources but whose people were impoverished and ill prepared for modernity by the colonial power. Sukarno replied that development was too slow. He needed an external victory to unify his people. They were united in wishing to take over West Irian, so Sukarno begged "Give it to me, Mr. President." Sukarno's extreme but not untypical concentration on devices of quick political gratification led directly to the tragic events in Indonesia of 1965.

At work on development in this setting Higgins managed to accomplish a good deal that later contributed to post-1965 progress in Indonesian development; but it had not been an easy assignment. In fact, as I note in this essay, development economics lacked and still lacks a satisfactory linkage to political analysis; and the building of a political economy of development—which is where economics took its start in the eighteenth century—should be a major objective in the generation ahead.

INTRODUCTION

In responding to my assigned task, I shall proceed in five steps as follows:

- defining the eighteenth-century roots of development and welfare policy.
- tracing schematically the evolution of thought and policy from 1776, when Hume died and the *Wealth of Nations* was published, to the marginalist revolution round about 1870.
- tracing similarly the rise of welfare economics and the welfare state over the subsequent century.
- commenting on the debate about development, efficiency, and equity in post-1945 development theory and practice.
- making a few final observations on future tasks.

FOUNDING FATHERS: DAVID HUME AND ADAM SMITH

Modern political economy was created as part of a much larger venture: the shifting of the Heavenly City of mediaeval Christianity "to earthly foundations."[1] This secular redefinition of the good life and the good society forced the leaders of the Enlightenment back to first principles and led them into philosophy, psychology, politics, sociology, and culture as well as economics. David Hume, in fact, began with psychology, as this quotation from his youthful *Treatise of Human Nature* suggests:[2] "These principles of human nature you'll say, are contradictory. But what is man but a heap of contradictions."

His view of the human condition is directly in the line from Plato to Freud. In a powerful simplification Plato analyzed the problem of balancing the "spirited" side of human beings, "appetite," and "reason." The roughly analogous elements for Freud were, of course, the id, ego, and super-ego. In a graceful move from micro- to macro-analysis economists have never been able to emulate, Plato linked politics and psychology by regarding his tripartite view of the individual as "the state within us" on which public life is built. Freud made a similar linkage of the two domains in *Civilization and Its Discontents*.

Hume's tripartite simplification consisted of "action," "pleasure," and "sympathy." (He also included "indolence" as a requirement of respite from the sustained pursuit of action and pleasure to which diminishing relative marginal utility evidently applied.) He used his system as the basis for some propositions of considerable substance.

- He identified action as well as pleasure as "causes of labour," action constituting the exercise of physical, mental, or artistic talent in a setting of challenge, for some practical purpose. In this Hume evokes Keynes's later dictum:[3] "If human nature felt no temptation to take a chance, no satisfaction (profit apart) in constructing a factory, a railway, a mine or a farm, there might not be much investment merely as a result of cold calculation."
- Hume saw, quite particularly, that the rise of urban life, as increasing commerce expanded the cities, would bring human beings together in more closely knit, interdependent societies and heighten the power of "sympathy" on which civilized life ultimately depended. More generally, he argued that the expansion and diversification of manufactures and the increase in productivity brought about by the expansion of commerce and exploitation of comparative advantage not only enriched private life, by expanding the range of choices open for the pursuit of action and pleasure, but also had wide-ranging, benign social consequences for the noneconomic dimensions of society, including provision of the foundation for human liberty and "mild" if not wholly democratic government. Thus Hume saw economic change as fundamental to social and political change, but he also saw economic change as dependent rather more on noneconomic than economic motives.
- Hume also enunciated clearly one of the most powerful of all propositions in welfare economics that, again, flowed directly from his perception of people:[4] "Every person, if possible, ought to enjoy the fruits of his labour, in a full possession of all the necessaries, and many of the conveniences of life. No one can doubt, but such an equality is most suitable to human nature, and diminishes much less from the happiness of the rich than it adds to that of the poor." This perception later converged with a realization of the inherently psychological and social forces that determined the subsistence wage

leading Ricardo, for example, to argue: ". . . the friends of humanity cannot but wish that in all countries the labouring classes should have a taste for comforts and enjoyments, and they should be stimulated by all legal means to procure them. There cannot be a better security against a superabundant population."[5]

Adam Smith derived much from Hume, and in many ways both were pre-Bentham utilitarians.[6] They both were deeply troubled by gross inequality of income distribution. Indeed, *The Wealth of Nations* refers on its second page to the fact that ". . . a great number of people do not labour at all, many of whom consume the product of ten times, frequently of a hundred times more labour than the greater part of those who do work. . . ." But they were puzzled as to how a more just system could be reconciled with the need for competition. After all, they were at war against excessive bureaucracy and battling for a greater degree of privatization. They saw competition as the most efficient way to tame the evil monopolizing instinct of entrepreneurs; and with some reluctance, they accepted the inequality that competition yielded but groped for ways to mitigate it. There was also a strong, untamed nonutilitarian strand in Smith. The opening sentence of his *Theory of Moral Sentiments* was: "How selfish soever man may be supposed, there are evidently some principles in his nature, which interest him in the fortune of others, and render their happiness necessary to him, though he derives nothing from it, except the pleasure of seeing it." Istvan Hont and Michael Ignatieff have been correct to remind us that Hume and Smith were committed to justice—albeit in a world of human beings moved by conflicting impulses and consequently confronting forces that often did not converge.[7]

On utilitarian grounds both Hume and Smith found a substantial legitimate role for government. As early as 1739, in his *Treatise of Human Nature*, Hume set out the case for the public role in a substantial array of enterprises as well as it has ever been done:[8]

"Two neighbours may agree to drain a meadow, which they possess in common; because 'tis easy for them to know each others mind. . . . But 'tis very difficult, and indeed impossible, that a thousand persons shou'd agree in any such action; it being difficult for them to concert so complicated a design, and still more difficult for them to execute it. . . . Political society easily remedies both these inconveniences. Magistrates find an immediate interest in the interest of any considerable part of their subjects. They need consult no body but themselves to form any scheme for the promoting of that interest." Thus, concludes Hume, "bridges are built; harbours open'd; ramparts rais'd; canals form'd; fleets equip'd; and armies disciplin'd. . . ." All this was crystallized in Smith's famous tripartite description of the three legitimate functions of government under a system of natural liberty: national defense; the provision of justice; and erecting and maintaining public works and institutions needed and profitable for "a great society" but unprofitable for private enterprise.[9] The third category included strong support for popular education in which, once again, Smith embraces but goes beyond the utilitarian argument:[10] "Though the state were to derive no advantage from the instruction of the inferior ranks of people, it would still deserve its attention that they should not be altogether uninstructed. The state, however derives no inconsiderable advantage from their instruction"—an advantage he proceeds to specify. In fact, welfare economics for two and a half centuries has had a dual character. Economists have argued that providing for equality of opportunity and otherwise struggling against poverty was good for society—a profitable investment; but they also argued, as did Adam Smith on education, that it was morally right and necessary for a decent, civilized society.

The classical tradition in political economy emerged from the Enlightenment and all that had preceded it. It included strands from Greece and Rome; from Christianity slipped in through the back door; it reflected inspiration from the Scientific Revolution, and lessons learned from the brutal seventeenth-century struggles from Britain to Bohemia. It thus created canons of private and public ethics that remain to the present day in the Atlantic community, but with influence far beyond.

That tradition was rooted in Hume's sense of the almost impenetrable complexity and diversity of individuals and the respect society ought to accord that uniqueness within the limits permitted by the minimum imperatives of social organization. From those propositions flowed a claim for mild and permissive government; but they also led to a bias against monopolistic power and to reliance on the discipline of competition—where competition was possible. In this bias, efficiency and virtue seemed to converge but with acknowledged and troubling costs in equity. As for development, the classical tradition unashamedly reversed the view that the good, uncorrupt society must be spartan. It argued that commerce in luxuries was essential to expanding the wealth of nations; and expanded wealth was necessary for human freedom, mild government, and an increasingly civilized life based on enlarged "sympathy" for one another among the citizenry.

Embedded in this panoramic view of the individual in relation to society was a theory of economic growth.

In Hume's case his quite recognizable production function emerges from the series of short often polemical policy essays that incorporate most of his contribution to economics.

Output in Hume's system is a function of labor, land, and manufactures; the productivity of labor and of land are determined by the scale of manufactures; and the scale of manufactures is determined by the scale of trade, foreign and domestic, and the productivity increases provided by the exploitation of comparative advantage. The productivity increases reflect the increased human effort induced, in the first instance, by the availability of a widened range of "luxuries" and, then, by the cumulative experience of merchant, worker, farmer, and manufacturer operating within a progressively more diversified economy, offering both heightened challenges and rewards that, in Hume's view, were the optimum setting within which men stretched their capacities to the limit and came to prefer frugality and gain to the immediacy of pleasure.

As for capital and technology Hume argued that it is the general prosperity of a country, not the money supply, that yields low rates of interest; that rates of interest are a product of demand and supply; and in generating the necessary supply of savings, once again the merchant emerges as hero, this time as miser rather than the exploiter of comparative advantage:[11]

> There is no craving or demand of the human mind more constant and insatiable than that for exercise and employment; and this desire seems the foundation of most of our passions and pursuits. . . . But if the employment you give him be lucrative, especially if the profit be attached to every particular exertion of industry, he has gain so often in his eye, that he acquires, by degrees, a passion for it, and knows no such pleasure as that of seeing the daily encrease of his fortune.[12] And this is the reason why trade encreases frugality, and why, among merchants, there is the same overplus of misers above prodigals, as, among the possessors of land, there is the contrary.

Hume assumed that, in stimulating diversified manufactures by the exploitation of comparative advantage, the "mechanic arts" would flourish and even his normally prodigal proprietors of land would divert some of their surplus from consumption to investment and "study agriculture as a science, and redouble their industry and attention." One fundamental and abiding proposition relating to technology was enunciated by Hume with clarity: "necessity . . . is the great spur to industry and invention."[13]

Smith's growth theory, incorporated in a large treatise, is more explicit and extensive. It has lent itself to a good deal of formal modeling.[14] Labor, land, and capital are unambiguously his three factors of production. The system is driven forward, as in Hume, by the savings of the frugal, who are assumed to invest all savings, without leakage. Leakage occurs when the rich and government indulge in expenditures that employ "unproductive" labor. Capital permits the widening of the market and, thereby, the division of labor. Capital is mainly envisaged as working capital supplying labor with necessaries, raw materials, and simple tools. "Machines" appear somewhat more explicitly in Smith than in Hume, but they come to much the same thing as Hume's "mechanic arts." In explaining how the division of labor increases productivity, Smith identified three forces:[15] the worker's increase in dexterity; the saving of the worker's time as he concentrates on a single task rather than moves from one task to another; and "the invention of a great number of machines which facilitate and abridge labour, and enable one man to do the work of many." These significant refinements of familiar technologies he distinguishes from occasional, rare major technological breakthroughs accomplished by "philosophers" (scientists)—an important quasi-Schumpeterian distinction to the best of my knowledge not to be found earlier in the literature of economics.

Both Hume and Smith had a good deal to say in dynamic terms about the rich country–poor country problem; that is, the effect on a more advanced country of an effort by a less advanced country to close the gap in per capita income and technological competence.[16] They urged the more advanced country, in Hume's phrase, to be "civilized and industrious"; that is, to enjoy the expansion in exports and income per capita to be derived from the rise of the less-developed country and to compensate for the inevitable increased low-priced imports from that country by shifting rapidly to production and export of technologically more sophisticated products and otherwise exploiting the assets developed during its period of unchallenged primacy.

The Smithian model asserted in effect that a society could, for a time, expand its output and (for a shorter time) its real income per capita; but that, in the end, a limit was reached at its "full complement of riches." A limit to growth was reached for three reasons: technological progress was constrained by geographical or other limitations on the expansion of the market (and thus on incremental technological change) and by the fact that major technological change was judged to be an occasional once-over event; the rise in real income per capita was constrained by the rise in population that resulted, after a lag, from an initial rise in the real wage; diminishing returns (in different degree) constrained the expansion of production of basic commodities.

1776–1870

As welfare economists, Hume and Smith inveighed, above all, against the domestic and international aspects of mercantilism. Their enemies were monopoly, war, and (in Smith's case) empire. In welfare terms their hope for all humanity, in Hume's good phrase, was "liberty, industry, and good government." They wished to see all nations achieve their "full complement of riches" in peace.

But that ceiling—based on technological, population, and resource constraints—began to lift less than a decade after the publication of *The Wealth of Nations*. In the 1780s, after a generation's inventive ferment, major innovations began to unfold as a flow, starting with the convergence of the new textile machinery, Watt's more efficient steam engine, and Cort's method for fabricating iron. British patents sealed averaged 29 per annum in the 1770s. They moved up as follows in the next four decades: 48, 65, 92, 101. By the 1840s the annual average was 458. Invention and innovation had become a substantial if erratic flow, which had never happened before in human history.

Then, in 1812, a second constraint was broken: the price of wheat fell from its peak of 152s (per quarter) in August 1812—the Napoleonic

War peak—to 75s in December 1813. It proceeded erratically to a further trough in 1822 when it leveled off as a matter of trend down to the price explosion of 1852–1854. The post-1812 decline combined with the gradual emergence of the United States and other major overseas suppliers of food and raw materials and an awareness that British population growth was decelerating. These developments ended, for a time, the concern with population and the food supply that had understandably obsessed Malthus and Ricardo down to 1812. Their post-1815 writing and debate were, in one sense, neither Malthusian nor Ricardian: They argued over the character of the postwar malaise and the impact of machinery on employment. But the stationary state (or worse) that had haunted them in the most acute period of wartime pressure of population on the food supply was pushed far down the road. If not quite ebullient over the human prospect, they ceased to be dismal scientists.

This late phase in the work of Malthus and Ricardo constitutes a significant transition; for a generation later, John Stuart Mill and Karl Marx, from quite different perspectives, accepted invention and innovation as an on-going almost automatic process; Marx assumed that it was possible indefinitely to defeat the power of diminishing returns in agriculture, Mill that there was time to bring population and growth under control before diminishing returns forced on the world economy a stationary state. They both focused on a quite different welfare problem; that is, how best to ameliorate the evident harshnesses of the industrial society emerging in their time on the continent and the United States as well as in more advanced Britain. Like Smith and Hume, pre-1813 Malthus and Ricardo, Mill and Marx believed there were (or should be) limits to growth. But their limits arose not from diminishing returns but from diminishing relative marginal utility for real income itself, conventionally defined. Mill looked to a time when birth control would render labor rather than land the scarce factor of production, real wages (rather than rent) would rise to a point where men and women chose an affluent but essentially static real income in a physical environment unstrained by excessive population or excessive industrialization. Marx's equally romantic notion of communism was a time when all material wants were satisfied and work itself had become a psychological necessity.

Mill was not merely the first no-growth environmentalist but also an early articulator of major aspects of what was to become the welfare state. While retaining a fierce loyalty to individual human liberty and the disciplining virtues of competition, he set out the legitimate welfare functions of government in much greater detail than his major predecessors.

- Cases in which the consumer is an incompetent judge of the commodity, of which education is the major example cited.
- Cases of persons exercising power over others, notably the protection of young persons and the insane.

- Cases of contracts in perpetuity in which an individual is not in a position to judge his interest at some future and distant time.
- Cases of delegated management where public surveillance and limited powers over joint stock companies are judged legitimate to assure that inherently monopoly powers are not abused. Mill judged public ownership and operation of economic units to be "jobbing, careless, and ineffective"; but he thought private joint stock companies little better, if better at all.
- Cases where public intervention is required to achieve a broadly agreed objective; for example, the reduction of hours of work that, if not accomplished by law, could be disrupted by a minority of workers or factory owners. Mill also cites the control over the disposition of land in land-rich population-poor colonial areas.
- Poor laws, where it is necessary to reconcile the need to aid the destitute with the need to avoid generating habitual reliance on such aid.
- Colonization, where it is necessary to reconcile the legitimate private interests of those planting or developing colonies with "a deliberate regard to permanent welfare of the nations afterwards to arise from these small beginnings."[17]
- Finally the Hume-Smith category: support for enterprises, installations, or institutions clearly in the public interest but not capable of generating adequate private support; e.g., voyages of discovery, light houses, scientific research in universities, etc. And similar public activities in areas in which private agencies "would be more suitable" but where the society has not developed the experience and habits of private cooperative action; e.g., roads, docks, harbors, canals, etc.

In the meanwhile a whole array of ameliorative actions were, in fact, generated as modern industrialism diffused. Welfare policy, in the widest sense, became increasingly important if not yet as central to politics in the Atlantic world as it was to become in the century after 1870. Nevertheless, the political, legal, and intellectual foundations of the welfare state were laid in the more advanced industrial countries before 1870.

This is the case because those foundations lay in universal male suffrage, a recognition of the legitimacy of labor unions, and mass public education. None of these conditions were fully achieved before 1870. And movement in these directions after 1870 among Britain, France, Germany, and the United States was certainly not uniform. The pace was much affected by the degree of industrialization and urbanization. France, for example, with its continued rural majority tended systematically to lag, and in the United States, where the states assumed primary responsibility for welfare policy, they moved fairly consistently in the order of their industrial experience; i.e., Massachusetts, New York, Pennsylvania, etc.

By 1870, or thereabouts, universal male suffrage was more or less accepted as a principle, although hedged about in various ways; e.g., inhibitions on Black voting in the South, the continued control of the budget by the German executive rather than parliament. And, of course, the vote for women was several generations away.

Similarly, after initial legal inhibitions on the formation of labor unions they had established what might be called inhibited legitimacy by 1870 with chronic challenge or harrassment by the courts, the executive authorities, or both.

In terms of the British urban worker's round of life, the limitation of hours of work was the most substantial achievement, a parliamentary effort begun in 1802 reaching its climax with the quite well policed Ten-Hours Bill of 1847. In the United States the Federal government symbolically led the way with a ten-hour limitation in the navy yards; but the arrangements in the states not only varied but the laws, where put on the books, were not well enforced. Excepting Britain, the issue was placed on the agenda of politics, but awaited further industrialization, urbanization, and agitation before it was resolved.

The most fundamental issue in welfare economics of this era, however, was the debate over socialism; that is, the comparative merits and demerits of socialism and capitalism for the long pull. Marx was formed, Mill was strongly influenced by the ferment generated by socialist literature that emerged on both sides of the Channel, notably in the 1840s. This is not an occasion to rehearse the fine-grained balance sheet drawn up by Mill, an assessment heightened by Harriet Taylor's sympathetic assessment of socialism.

Essentially Mill took the view that despite the likelihood of "jobbing, careless, and ineffective" enterprises under socialism, the balance, when set against capitalism, in Mill's time tipped to socialism because of capitalism's gross inequity and harshness. Over the long pull, however, he judged capitalist societies would reduce these blemishes and, besides, the disciplining virtues of competition were required. His verdict:[18] "If a conjecture be hazarded, the decision will probably depend mainly on one consideration, viz, which of the two systems is consistent with the greatest amount of human liberty and spontaneity." And so, it was in arguing for a reduction in the blemishes of capitalism—including a battle for women's voting rights—that J. S. Mill became one of the founding fathers of the democratic welfare state.

1870–1975

In historical retrospect, the century that began with Bismarck's pioneering social legislation of 1871 (accident insurance) and ended with the leveling off of transfer payments as a proportion of GNP in most advanced industrial countries in the mid-1970s, might well be called,

Table 1. **APPROXIMATE SOCIAL SERVICE EXPENDITURES: ADVANCED INDUSTRIAL COUNTRIES, 1890–1981**
(All levels of government: Percentage of GNP [or GDP])

	United States	United Kingdom	Germany	Seven major OECD countries
1890	1.8	1.9	--	--
1913	2.1	4.1	5.1	--
1929	3.2 (1927)	9.5	19.3	--
1940	6.9	11.3	--	--
1950	6.2 (1948)	18.0	24.2	--
1960	[10.9]	[13.9]	[20.5]	[14.3]
1970	--	--	--	[19.5]
1975	--	--	--	[22.0]
1981	[21.0]	[24.9]	[31.5]	[24.0]

Sources: Unless otherwise indicated, data are from Richard A. Musgrave, *Fiscal Systems* (New Haven: Yale University Press, 1969), pp. 94–95 (Table 4–1). Social Services include education, welfare programs, and housing as well as social insurance. There are no estimates for total German social expenditures for 1890 and 1913. The more narrow category of social insurance expenditures appears to have increased as follows as a proportion of GNP. 1891, 0.7%; 1901, 1.3%; 1913, 1.8%. These figures were calculated from Supan Andic and Jindrich Veverka, "The Growth of Government Expenditure in Germany Since the Unification," *Finanzarchiv*, Vol. 23, No. 2, January 1964, pp. 199–200 (per capita total budget expenditures in constant [1900] prices and per capita social insurance as % of total expenditure; p. 238 [population]; and p. 241 [GNP at 1900 prices]). Bracketed figures for 1960–1981 are from an OECD study summarized in the *OECD Observer*, no. 126, January 1984, "Social Expenditure: Erosion or Evolution?" pp. 3–6. These figures include expenditures for: education, health, pensions, unemployment insurance, family allowances and other programs. They are related to GDP rather than GNP.

in one of its dimensions, The Age of Social Welfare. Table 1 provides some indication of the timing and scale of this massive phenomenon.

These figures rise down to the mid-1970s under a sequence of quite dissimilar impulses:

- In response to political pressure from urban constituencies as the relative rise in food and basic commodity prices decreased or limited the rise in real wages from the mid-1890s to 1914.
- In a typical postwar surge in social outlays during the 1920s as if in compensation for hardships endured.
- In response to the depth and severity of the depression of the 1930s.
- Another postwar surge in social outlays after 1945.

Table 2. **SOCIAL EXPENDITURE BY COUNTRY, 1960–1981**

	Social expenditure as a percentage of GDP		Annual growth rate of real GDP		Annual growth rate of real social expenditure	
	1960	1981[a]	1960–75	1975–81[a]	1960–75	1975–81[a]
United States	10.9	21.0	3.4	3.2	7.7	2.9
Japan	8.0	17.5	8.6	5.1	9.7	8.9
Germany	20.5	31.5	3.8	3.0	6.7	1.9
Canada	12.1	21.7	5.1	3.3	9.5	2.9
France[b]	13.4	23.8	5.0	2.8	7.4	7.6
Italy	16.5	29.1	4.6	3.2	7.4	3.1
United Kingdom	13.9	24.9	2.6	1.0	5.6	3.3
Australia	10.2	18.6	5.2	2.4	8.6	2.4
Austria	17.9	27.9	4.5	2.9	6.0	4.6
Belgium	17.0	38.0	4.5	3.0	9.1	4.6
Denmark	10.2	29.0	3.7	2.2	9.3	4.4
Finland	13.2	n.a.	4.5	2.9	7.3	n.a.
Greece	8.7	12.8	6.8	3.5	7.8	2.3
Iceland	11.7	27.1	4.3	3.5	8.2	5.2
Norway	11.7	27.1	4.3	4.1	9.5	5.6
Netherlands	16.3	36.1	4.5	2.0	9.2	1.4
New Zealand	13.0	19.6	4.0	0.4	4.4	3.7
Sweden	14.5	33.5	4.0	1.0	8.4	4.0
Switzerland	7.7	14.9	3.4	1.8	6.9	2.5

Notes: [a] or latest available year. [b] Excluding education expenditure. n.a.: not available.
Source: OECD, as in Table 1.

- Then the majestic expansion in the unexampled boom of the 1950s and 1960s in which the citizens of advanced industrial societies chose more or less consciously to take a substantial proportion of their rise in real incomes in the form of enlarged social services.

The sequence ends with the pressure on real wages of the oil price and other shocks of the 1970s in which the citizenry tried to protect their real incomes, accepted a halt in the expansion of social services but resisted a drastic reduction in their proportionate share in total output. The post-1975 deceleration is captured in Table 2.

Evidently nations have differed in the proportion of their resources they have chosen to allocate to social services. For example, in 1977 transfer payments were 15.4 percent of GDP for the United States, at the bottom of the league, 39.3 percent for the Netherlands, at the top.[19] And differences extended to the various components that make up social services. But the sustained high priority for outlays of this kind in the advanced industrial countries is, evidently, one of the most remarkable

Table 3. **INCOME ELASTICITY OF GOVERNMENT SPENDING IN CONSTANT PRICES: 1950–1977**

	Total[1]	Consumption[2]	Transfers[3]
Austria	1.80	0.54	3.23
Canada	1.96	1.17	2.90
Denmark	2.25	1.54	3.09
Finland	1.70	1.20	2.30
France	1.61	.60	2.54
Germany	1.46	.92	2.06
Greece	1.27	.68	2.11
Ireland	2.47	1.21	4.33
Netherlands	2.46	.63	4.38
Sweden	2.70	1.42	4.43
Switzerland	1.89	.79	3.41
United Kingdom	1.37	.77	2.07
United States	1.74	1.18	2.59
Median	1.80	.92	2.90

[1] Total current disbursements of general Government.
[2] Government final consumption expenditure.
[3] Transfer outlays of general Government.
Source: United Nations, *Yearbook of National Accounts Statistics*, 1977 and 1964; also, replies to questionnaire for 1978 yearbook (unpublished).

aspects of political and economic history over the past century, as is the tendency of this proportion to level off in the course of the 1970s. The power of the thrust for expanded social welfare services during the great OECD boom of the 1950s and 1960s is captured in Table 3, which exhibits the income elasticity of government spending for thirteen countries.[20]

The average elasticity of almost three for transfer payments whose movements are dominated by changes in social welfare outlays is an extraordinary figure, which evidently could not persist for long.

This climactic surge was rooted in an intellectual and policy revolution that occurred a century earlier. Historians of economic thought almost universally recognize a clearly marked turning point round about 1870.

The turning point had two not necessarily convergent dimensions, although Alfred Marshall captured both: a new and more formal emphasis on the optimum allocation of resources and the conditions for equilibrium, set out in terms of marginal analysis; and a heightened concern with issues of social welfare. 1870 comes close to the time when Jevons (1871), Menger (1871), and Walras (1874) published their respective formulations of marginal analysis, although Jevons's "coefficient of utility" dates back to 1862. In addition, the date approximates 1867 when the first volume of *Capital* appeared and Marshall began his serious study of economics; it is close enough to 1871 when the seventh edition of Mill's *Principles*, the last edited by the author, was published. As turning points go, then, 1870 is a reasonable if somewhat arbitrary symbol.

It is also the time when the advanced industrial societies of that era began to come seriously to grips with problems of welfare, income distribution, monopoly power, and other contentious matters that forced themselves to the center of the political stage. Operationally, these issues were posed by the rise of new political forces often linked to an extension of the ballot: the Populists, Grangers, and Progressives in the United States; the Labour Party and the invigorated Liberals in Britain; the Socialists on the Continent; the labor unions everywhere; and, down to the mid-1890s, the embattled American farmers.

The relation of mainstream economics to this essentially political process was complex. The demonstration that differential calculus was a viable tool in economics had a powerful impact. It proved capable of expressing with precision certain fundamental economic propositions and, especially, defining, under strict limiting assumptions, conditions of stable equilibrium in both specific markets and for an economy as a whole. The major economic figures—in Britain, on the Continent, and in the United States—became caught up in the authentic adventure of refining market analysis for both final output and factors of production under what came to be known as Marshallian short-period assumptions—excluding the dynamic supply forces, as well as changing incomes and tastes, at work in the process of economic growth. Without these complications, pure theories of production and distribution could be brought together in splendid symmetry; but political economy gave way to economics. The discipline became the evolving methods of analysis, not the great problems demanding solution in the active world; and the increasingly refined methods of analysis led, in most—not all—cases, away from, rather than toward, the issues of political economy in active contention. What John Williams had to say after an exhaustive test of the classical theory of foreign trade could be said of mainstream economics as a whole in the wake of the revolution of 1870 and after:[21] "The classical theory assumes as fixed, for purposes of reasoning, the very things which, in my view, should be chief objects of study. . . ."

Moral and ethical issues did not, of course, disappear from economics, and economists certainly did not abandon the right to hold strong personal views on issues of policy and social justice. Even Léon Walras was an advocate of wide-ranging economic and social reform, but this stance was clearly divorced from his work as an economist. Economists did not become less concerned with the fate of their societies, but the linkage of theoretical formulation to problems of policy was attenuated by the seductive elegance of the new concepts and methods of analysis. There is an important sense, in fact, in which the intellectual underpinnings of the movement for what we might broadly call welfare reform were quite precisely related to the gaps between the formal assumptions underlying post-1870 mainstream economics and reality.

The central propositions of mainstream economic theory assumed perfect competition and steady full employment; the dissidents dramatized the reality of monopolies and severe cyclical unemployment. Formal theory linked income distribution to the net marginal value product of the economic functions performed by individuals; the dissidents dramatized (as had Mill) the institutions, patterns of land ownership, inheritance law, relative access to education, and other noneconomic determinants of income distribution emerging from the history of particular societies.

Among the inequities they identified was the asymmetry in the labor market of the individual worker vis-à-vis the more concentrated power of the employer, operating individually or collectively. The market-oriented theory of distribution in its pure form was silent on such vicissitudes as accidents at the work place, health facilities and educational opportunity for the poor, old-age insurance. By one form of argument or another, the dissidents dragged these issues toward the center of the political arena. The examples could go on to embrace Henry George's powerful polemic built on an interpretation of the Malthus-Ricardo theory of rent; Thorstein Veblen on conspicuous consumption, the monopolistic corporation, and technology; Upton Sinclair on the Chicago slaughterhouses; the American institutionalists, the Fabians, including Shaw; the German and British historical schools, including R. H. Tawney. And then—sometimes over-lapping these examples and categories—there were various kinds of socialists, including some writing and arguing in the tradition of Marx as they chose to interpret him.

I would emphasize again that the mainstream economists did not universally and systematically oppose the measures that arose from these heterodox sources. Some, in fact, supported them. But the formal constructs of mainstream economics were a poor basis for crusading zeal; and the social welfare movement, which progressively gathered momentum down to the First World War, was, in fact, nourished mainly by an array of iconoclasts who were crusading not only on behalf of the less advantaged but also against the inadequacies they thought they perceived in mainstream economics.

It does not follow that the quiet acknowledgment of the inhumanities of capitalism, the exploration of possible remedies, and authentic concern for the less advantaged that motivated Mill, Marshall, Pigou, and others in that nonpolemical tradition were unimportant in democratic societies. They did not provide the banners and rhetoric for the ardent reformers. But they helped persuade the critically important "moderate, decent, conservative margin" in the middle of the political spectrum that major reforms were legitimate and necessary.[22] And, indeed, when Pigou came to formalize welfare economics, a good deal of the machinery of marginal analysis—including the distinction between marginal net social and private products—could be mobilized for a strongly felt but well-mannered crusade.

Alfred Marshall (1842–1924) holds a special place in this story. He is, clearly, the founder of modern welfare economics, although quite consciously in the classical tradition. Moving on proximately from J. S. Mill he took problems of welfare very seriously, indeed. His contribution to theory is generally reckoned primarily in the field of partial equilibrium analysis. But he came to economics by a route that led him from mathematics to metaphysics to ethics, and finally, without enthusiasm, to political economy. The heart of his commitment lay in a deeply rooted desire to lift from the working classes the burden of poverty—the psychological, social, political, and cultural, not merely the economic burden. Thus, in the first edition of *The Principles* (1890):[23] "The study of the causes of poverty is the study of the causes of the degradation of a large part of mankind." Writing late in life about his transition to economics Marshall recalled:[24] "I had doubts about the propriety of inequalities of *opportunity*, rather than material comfort. Then, in my vacations I visited the poorest quarters of several cities and walked through one street after another looking at the faces of the poorest people."

In his studies rooted in this concern, Marshall asserted a good many propositions of substance; for example:[25]

> There is no extravagance more prejudicial to the growth of national wealth than that wasteful negligence which allows genius that happens to be born of lowly parentage to expend itself in lowly work. No change would conduce so much to a rapid increase of material wealth as an improvement in our schools, and especially those of the middle grades, provided it be combined with an extensive system of scholarships, which will enable the clever son of a working man to rise gradually from school to school till he has the best theoretical and practical education which the age can give.

He systematically explored the implications of perhaps the most fundamental proposition in welfare economics—already present in Hume:[26] "... The same sum of money measures a greater pleasure for the poor than the rich." All this built up to one of the boldest calculations in the history of welfare economics.[27]

> It is a common saying that we have more reason to be proud of our ways of making wealth than of our ways of using it. . . .
> Opinions are not likely to agree as to the amount of private expenditures which is to be regarded as socially wasteful from this point of view. Some may put it as high as four or even five hundred millions a year. But it is sufficient for the present that there is a margin of at least one or two hundred million which might be diverted to social uses without causing any great distress to those from whom it was taken; provided their neighbours were in a like position, and not able to make disagreeable

remarks on the absence of luxuries and of conventional "necessaries for social propriety" which are of little solid advantage. . . .

By Marshall's calculation U.K. annual income was £1.7 billion. His proposed additional social allocation would, therefore, be 5.9–11.8 percent of national income—by no means a trivial proposition.

But it was certainly through his pupils (and their pupils) that Marshall's influence was carried forward: A. C. Pigou, D. H. Robertson, and Keynes, above all, but also, less directly, Bickerdike, Colin Clark, and many others. It was, in fact, an issue in welfare economics—income distribution—that forced the pace of national income accounting on both sides of the Atlantic.[28] But, of course, chronic high unemployment in Britain and most of Western Europe in the 1920s and then the Great Depression of the 1930s came to dominate the welfare concerns of both orthodox and unorthodox economists. Here Marshall's three great pupils at Cambridge played a central role, moving on from Marshall's incomplete monetary theory to grapple with the business cycle and chronic high unemployment in real as well as monetary terms; but Swedish, Continental, and American economists, of different or more diversified lineage, made significant contributions to an increasingly international effort climaxed in 1936 by the publication of Keynes's *General Theory*.

Meanwhile the debate on the relative merits of socialism versus capitalism, now just about a century old, was heightened during the interwar years by the existence of a socialist state and economy in the Soviet Union and by the extraordinary disarray of the capitalist world that, evidently, played a substantial role in bringing on World War II.

In the wake of that war, as we have already noted, there was an immediate expansion of social services in Britain and the United States followed, as the boom of the 1950s and 1960s took hold, by a generation-long surge in welfare outlays throughout the advanced industrial world.

Table 4 captures the average composition of welfare outlays in 1960 and 1975, for seven major OECD countries, with some indication of the factors determining changes between those two years. The unexpected, sustained vitality of the economies of Western Europe, Japan, and the United States permitted this rounding out of the welfare state, one of whose most striking characteristics was a revolutionary extension of higher education that moved the advanced industrial societies a good deal closer to the criterion that no young man or woman capable of and interested in acquiring a higher education should be denied that experience. Table 5 suggests the scale of the expansion and, in most cases—with Japan a notable exception—the deceleration or leveling off after 1975.

The post-1945 years also saw a great deal of theoretical refinement in the field of welfare economics on which Ben Higgins and others have commented. I would only note here that the massive expansion in welfare outlays in, say, the quarter-century 1950–1975 was, as nearly as one can perceive, quite independent of this intellectual development. The

Table 4. GROWTH RATE OF SOCIAL EXPENDITURE 1960-1990
Averages for the 7 Major OECD Countries

	For reference: Social expenditure as a per cent of GDP	Growth of social expenditure at current prices	Of which:			... due to:		
			Change in overall price level	Change in relative cost of welfare benefits	Increase in real social expenditure...	Change in demographic pattern	Change in coverage	Change in real benefit levels
1960					*Annual Change 1960-75 (%)*			
Education	4.2	14.7	5.4	2.57	6.1	0.29	1.90	3.83
Health	2.7	17.1	5.4	1.35	9.6	1.03	0.60	7.83
Pensions	4.5	14.3	5.4	0	8.4	2.23	1.62	4.35
Unemployment insurance	0.4	18.0	5.4	0	12.0	5.08	0	6.60
Family allowances and other programmes	2.5	14.0	5.4	0	8.2	n.a.	n.a.	n.a.
Total Social Expenditure	14.3	15.0	5.4	1.0	8.0	1.36	1.43	5.03
1975					*Annual Change 1975-81 (%)*			
Education	5.1	12.9	9.65	1.14	1.8	-1.74	0.20	3.40
Health	5.1	14.2	9.65	1.02	3.1	0.26	0	3.10
Pensions	7.3	16.9	9.65	0	6.6	1.77	0.78	3.94
Unemployment insurance	1.1	16.7	9.65	0	6.4	7.84	-2.30	1.00
Family allowances and other programmes	3.4	13.4	9.65	0	3.4	n.a.	n.a.	n.a.
Total Social Expenditure	22.0	14.8	9.65	0.50	4.2	0.75	0.22	3.20

Source: *The OECD Observer*, January 1984, No. 126, p. 4.

Table 5.   **INDUSTRIAL MARKET ECONOMIES**
Number enrolled in higher education as percentage of relevant age group

	1960	1965	1975	1984
Industrialized countries (average)	16	21	34	38
Spain	4	6	21	26
Ireland	9	12	16	22
Italy	7	11	25	26
New Zealand	13	15	27	29
Belgium	9	15	22	31
United Kingdom	9	12	17	20
Austria	10	9	25	26
Netherlands	13	17	26	31
France	8	18	24	27
Australia	13	16	23	27
Finland	8	11	19	31
Germany, Fed. Rep.	6	9	20	29
Denmark	10	14	30	29
Japan	9	13	17	30
Sweden	9	13	28	38
Canada	16	26	39	44
Norway	7	11	22	29
Switzerland	7	8	14	21
United States	32	40	58	57

Source: *World Development Report, 1979*, p. 111; *World Development Report, 1987*, p. 263.

expansion appears to have been a quite pure product of the income elasticity of demand expressing itself through the democratic political process. But woven into that process was a strand of Hume and Adam Smith's "sympathy"; that is, a willingness of citizens to see a margin of the increment to their real incomes, at a time of rapid increase, diverted to the less advantaged without expectation of direct or indirect private advantage.

From the turbulent mid-1970s, however, a Proposition 13 mentality began to prevail. As the OECD study cited earlier observed: "Some slowing down of this rapid growth [in social expenditure] was to be expected, but what could have been an acceptable evolution instead assumed aspects of a financial crisis. Economic circumstances have forced an earlier, more severe, and more urgent re-examination of social policies than would have been the case if high rates of economic growth had persisted and inflation been avoided."

As for that part of the welfare economics debate concerned with the relative virtues of capitalism versus socialism, socialism continued to lose ground not because capitalism's performance in the 1970s and 1980s was particularly glamorous, but because the performance of the socialist economies was markedly worse. The candid acknowledgment of socialism's failure in China and the struggle there to acquire the benefits of competitive markets was particularly influential in shifting the climate of opinion in the developing regions of the world economy. For reasons we shall shortly consider, the common enemy in an astonishing array of countries became the "state bourgeoisie" rather than the capitalist bourgeoisie.[29]

Economic growth theory came back into intellectual fashion for the first time since 1870 in the period, roughly, 1949 (when the United Nations and the United States launched technical assistance programs) to 1973 when the great postwar boom was distorted by the explosion of grain and oil prices. Work on growth took the form of a kind of three-ring circus, with some, but relatively limited, communication among the rings: Harrod-Domar and then neoclassical growth models; statistical analyses of the morphology of growth pioneered by Colin Clark carried forward after the war by Simon Kuznets; and analyses addressed directly to the aspirations and problems confronted in Latin America, Africa, the Middle East, and Asia as governments and peoples sought to move forward in the complex, many-sided process of development.

Here I shall only consider the development ring of the postwar growth circus. In particular, I shall examine three quite different links between welfare economies and development analysis and policy and draw a broad conclusion.

First, there is the link between welfare economics in advanced industrial countries and development economics. The link was strong because, for most major figures in the field, development economics was a kind of second marriage; and a good many were permanently marked by their experiences in wrestling with the severe economic and social problems of the 1930s and of the immediate postwar years in Europe.

Among the ten "pioneers in development" who contributed essays to the first volume on that theme organized by the World Bank, seven cited the formative role of such linkages.[30] Typically, Gunnar Myrdal was most explicit in articulating the somewhat Marshallian value premise that underlay both his rationale for the Swedish welfare state and his approach to development:[31]

> In the 1920s and 1930s, when my research and policy work had focused on conditions in Sweden, I held the view that an equalization in favor of the lower-income strata was also a productive investment in the quality of people and their productivity. And I found support for this opinion in comparisons of different rich nations' growth statistics. It seemed clear that income equalization would have an even greater effect in this direction for underdeveloped countries, where the masses of people are suffering

from very severe consumption deficiencies in regard to nutrition, housing, and everything else. *The productivity of higher consumption levels stands for me as a major motivation for the direction of development policy in underdeveloped countries. Higher consumption levels are a condition for a more rapid and stable growth.*

In underdeveloped countries such a redistribution of income cannot, however, be carried out by taxing the rich and transferring money to the poor via social security schemes and other such measures to raise their levels of living. The poor are so overwhelmingly many, and the wealthy so relatively few—and tax evasion among them so common. What is needed in order to raise the miserable living levels of the poor masses is instead radical institutional reforms. These would serve the double purpose of greater equality and economic growth. The two goals are inextricably joined. This implies a fundamental difference from developed countries, where the two goals can be, and often are, pursued separately.

This is not an appropriate occasion to explore all the explicit and implicit linkages between welfare economics in advanced industrial countries and development economics as it emerged in the 1950s and 1960s. But it is worth noting one respect in which development economists were directly in the line of welfare economists reaching back to Adam Smith: they sought (like Myrdal in the quotation above) to demonstrate that what was morally right was also good for the economy. But, again like their predecessors, there was a quite independent strand of moral or religious commitment to assist the less advantaged, heightened by what might be called historical excitement at the drama of intensified efforts at modernization that began to unfold in Asia, the Middle East, Latin America, and Africa.

By the end of the 1960s a second, quite different linkage between development and welfare economics emerged. It began with an intellectual revolt against what might be called the orthodox development position of the 1960s, which took the form of the "basic human needs" strategy. It arose, in turn, from two sources. First, and most important, because in a good many countries high, overall real growth rates were accompanied by considerable mass poverty, unemployment and partial unemployment, and by other social ills. Second, there was a strand within the "basic needs" movement of limits-to-growth doctrine; that, to preserve the human habitat, growth must stop, income be redistributed, real income be stabilized at a level that would provide for basic human needs. And there was also sometimes a touch of romanticism about Mao's China and Castro's Cuba in the exposition of this doctrine.

One of the best and most lucid articulations of the basic needs doctrine came in response to the report of the Pearson Commission: *Partners in Development: Report of the Commission on International Development* (1969). That report, financed by the World Bank, was an effort to dramatize the need for continuing and even enlarged development assistance at a time when political support in the advanced industrial countries was weakening.

The Pearson Commission recommended that an average growth target for the developing countries of 6 percent be set for the 1970s; official development assistance be targeted at 0.7 percent of GNP for the advanced industrial countries with 20 percent allocated through multilateral agencies; and that the terms of ODA be limited to 2 percent interest (with 25–40 year maturity). The quantitative target percentage of GNP was twice the current level. In that sense, the Pearson Commission report was ambitious.

The report was reviewed at an international conference organized by Columbia University and held at Williamsburg and New York, February 15–21, 1970. These gatherings yielded a document called the Columbia Declaration, which captures well the themes and mood of the basic needs doctrine:[32]

> In incomes, living standards, economic and political power, one-third of the world has in recent decades been pulling steadily ahead, leaving the remainder of mankind in relative poverty, in many cases to live without clean water, education, basic medical facilities or adequate housing. Yet with modern technology and existing productive capacity, none of this need continue if mankind would develop the will and organization to use the resources at hand. . . . New objective criteria for effective development assistance are required. An over-all minimum growth rate for all countries is, no doubt, a desirable objective. But it is essential also to develop targets designed to achieve a minimum average per capita income of $400 to be reached by all countries not later than the end of the century. Criteria are also needed which focus on the living standards in the bottom quarter of each country's population. We also suggest setting up of a special fund devoted specifically to the fulfillment of social objectives in the areas of education, health, family planning, rural and urban works housing and other related programs.
>
> . . . There is an urgent need to strengthen the multilateral international framework in the fields of trade, aid, and relations between rich and poor nations. . . . Such strengthening necessarily involves the channeling of increased and independent finance and moves toward compulsory contributions by member countries. International power must increasingly be shared democratically; and this objective can only be attained by strengthening the role of institutions in which the developing economies have a representative vote.

This doctrine was not wholly ignored in the 1970s. The World Bank, for example, under Robert McNamara's direction allocated increased resources for social purposes and conducted sophisticated analyses of the relationship of poverty and excessively skewed income distribution to aggregate and sectoral growth rates. A great deal of both poverty and abnormally skewed income distribution was, in fact, linked to excessive rates of population increase and inadequate attention of governments to agriculture and to the modernization of rural life. Inadequate tax collection and the diversion of governments funds to a variety of dubious subsidies (thus constraining allocations for health, education, and other important social purposes) also played a role.

Where birthrates were rapidly declining and agricultural productivity and the modernization of rural life taken seriously, the lowest 20 percent of the population received proportions of total income comparable to distribution patterns in advanced industrial countries; e.g., South Korea and Taiwan.

Despite these deeper forces which largely determined the social outcome in developing nations, the rise of the "basic human needs" doctrine undoubtedly led to some reallocation of national and international development resources and, perhaps equally important, to intensified analyses of the anatomy of poverty in developing countries.

What was not accepted was the doctrine that the resources of the rich countries should come to some significant degree under political control of bodies substantially controlled by poor countries. This was a fundamental principle of the New Economic Order expounded year after year in United Nations bodies. It constituted an extension to an international community of the principle of declining relative marginal utility, more or less recognized within national societies. But the international community of the 1970s and 1980s was still rooted in jealously guarded sovereignties; and, on the whole, the asymmetrical assertion of rights and duties asserted under the banner of the New Economic Order proved unproductive or worse.

The "basic needs" doctrine and the thrust for a New Economic Order—related in fact but not necessarily in logic—can be regarded as an attack from the Left. The neoclassical assault on the "structuralists" can be regarded as a sortie from the Right. Ian Little reduced the neoclassical case to elemental terms as follows:[33] ". . . until fairly recently I see the story as one of the battle between structuralists who see the world as bounded and flat, and consisting of stick-in-the muds, who have to be drilled—and neo-classicists who see it as round and full of enterprising people who will reorganize themselves in a fairly effective manner."

The neoclassicists—Peter Bauer, for example—can find a splendid gallery of figures to caricature if from no other source than United Nations debates. But in an essay on development, efficiency, and equity, there is a bit more to be said.

First, those who argued that there was an important role for public policy in the early phases of development operated from premises rooted in Hume and Smith, Marshall and Pigou; and their case was made with some precision. Paul Rosenstein-Rodan, for example, isolated four issues arising from possible flaws in the working of private markets: disguised unemployment (or excess population) in the countryside; Marshall's "pecuniary" external economies, yielding economies of scale; the indispensable role of large blocks of infrastructure investment as a necessary foundation for profitable industrialization; and the importance of "technological external economies," notably public investment in education and training.

Taken all together, the reality of these forms of market failure constituted Rodan's case for planning the kind of "Big Push" he envisaged as necessary to lift a relatively stagnant underdeveloped country into sustained growth:[34]

> The market mechanism does not realize the "optimum" either in one nation or between nations because it relies on such unrealistic assumptions as linear homogeneous production function, no increasing returns or economies of scale or of agglomeration, and no phenomenon of minimum quantum or threshold. This obscures the nature of the development process and the risks involved. Nothing in theology or technology ordains that God created the world convex downwards.

Rodan's fourth public function should, in my view, be widened beyond education in the narrow sense to include all the dimensions of the expansion in technological absorptive capacity: institutions, tax and other incentives, and the encouragement of entrepreneurs capable of and willing to risk the introduction of new production functions.

This suggests a second point neoclassicists do not regularly address; i.e., the appropriate framework for policymaking in a developing country depends intimately on time and its stage of growth. For example, on a visit to Thailand in 1961 I found, as in much of Southeast Asia, modern entrepreneurship overwhelmingly in the hands of overseas Chinese sometimes "married" for protection to Thai military officers. Twenty-two years later modern entrepreneurship was much more widely spread and Thai planners could focus substantially on creating a benign macroeconomic framework for a vital private enterprise system.

If we accept, for a moment, Ian Little's definition of the dividing line among development economists as between structuralists and neoclassicists, the distinction becomes highly sensitive to time and the historical stage of the economy or economies one has in mind. A country in what I call the preconditions for take-off (say, Indonesia as of the 1960s) may not only lack, as did Thailand, an indigenous cadre of entrepreneurs, but also have a low level of literacy; a grossly inadequate secondary and higher educational system; a traditional agriculture essentially untouched by the productive methods available to modern labor-intensive farming; an infrastructure incapable of underpinning an efficient national market or a vital place in the international economy; a feeble if not obstructive and corrupt bureaucracy; and a flow of public revenues incapable of supporting the minimum irreducible functions of government, as defined, say, by Adam Smith.

The net investment rate may be 5 percent or less and concentrated in enclaves developed by foreign investors to expand raw material exports.

I cite this familiar array of the characteristics of underdevelopment to specify what I mean by "structural" problems, a term often used ambiguously. The first and obvious point to be made—somehow lost in Little's structuralist versus neoclassical paradigm—is that a sensible policy prescription for a country will vary greatly with its stage of growth: where it stands in the preconditions for take-off, in take-off (which is always a phenomenon limited by sectors and, often, by regions), or how far beyond in the drive to technological maturity, also a dynamic process that takes time. The role of the state is bound to be greater relative to the private sector, in the preconditions for take-off, than in, say, the drive to technological maturity. After all the proportion of investment allocated to infrastructure (excluding housing) is normally above 30 percent in all societies. The development theorists of the 1950s and the 1960s were visiting, staring at, prescribing for societies primarily at the lower end of the growth spectrum. Put another way, economies moving along well in the drive to technological maturity can, increasingly, be analyzed and prescribed for by the same techniques as those applied to more advanced industrial countries—although I would certainly not qualify neoclassical economics as adequate to either task.

Take for example, the following description of the situation in one developing country:[35]

> The Egyptian economy bears the legacy of economic policies dating from the 1950s which were motivated by concern for equity and assistance to the poor. These policies were characterized by price regulation, subsidization of consumer goods, a dominant public sector and state control. Subsequently the government has tried to insulate the average citizen from many of the shocks in the international economy and has not adjusted prices over the years . . . consumers have not faced world prices for energy or many basic commodities. Both prices and wages of government workers in particular have been held down significantly. As the gap between the market and the administered prices has grown, it has become more and more difficult and costly to maintain the current system.

This passage applies, of course, to a good many developing economies in Asia and Latin America as well as the Middle East.

The bloated public sectors that have been a legitimate target of critics—neoclassical and otherwise—must be viewed as the outcome of a historic process rather than misguided development theories. They resulted from the convergence of what might be called technical economic and political forces and certain strongly held attitudes in the developing countries of the 1950s.

On the economic side, there was the inability to earn or borrow, at tolerable rates, sufficient foreign exchange to avoid highly protectionist import substitution policies. These led directly to insufficient competition in domestic markets, damping the entrepreneurial quality of both the private and public sectors. Foreign exchange rationing was also a policy that required large powerful bureaucracies to decide what should be imported. In many countries that process was the heart of what passed for planning. On the political side there was the fear of explosions in the volatile cities and a decision, in effect, to exploit the farmer on behalf of the urban population. This had, of course, the effect of reducing incentives in the agricultural sector and slowing the rate of increase of agricultural production, forcing increased grain imports at the expense of capital goods for industry and transport.

With respect to attitudes, the 1950s were times when capitalism was an unpopular word, socialism a popular word in the developing regions. Capitalism was associated with colonial or quasi-colonial status, representing an intrusive external power; and it was systematically represented as such and denigrated by political leaders over a wide range. There was also considerable sentimental appeal in socialism during the 1950s: Some of the European social democratic governments were doing quite well; Mao's Great Leap Forward and Chinese Communist policy in general generated a considerable appeal among those who did not investigate it too deeply; and even Khrushchev's boast that the U.S.S.R. would soon outstrip the United States in total output had a certain credibility in the late 1950s. To all this one can add that many of the emerging political leaders were often intellectuals or soldiers, both types inherently suspicious of the market process and inclined, for different reasons, to have excessive faith in the powers of government administration.

In the present narrow context it is fair to ask to what extent, if any, structuralist development economists bear some responsibility for this outcome. Stripped of rhetoric the charges can be reduced to three:

- postwar "export pessimism" and excessive reliance on import substitution;
- inadequate incentives and support for agriculture combined with excessive subsidies to maintain low prices for "basic needs" in the cities;
- excessive reliance on government ownership and control of industry; inadequate encouragement of domestic competition and foreign private investment.

With respect to the first charge, it should be recalled that import substitution policies—if not traced back to Alexander Hamilton—were the product of a condition not a theory; that is, the Great Depression of the 1930s. Prebisch, trained as a classical economist, supported such policies on pragmatic grounds in the face of the overwhelming balance of payments crisis that confronted Argentina and a great many other developing countries of the period. The later homilies of, say, Jacob Viner or Peter Bauer would have sounded hollow, indeed, in Latin America of the 1930s. ECLA doctrine, which in a familiar pattern turned out to be fighting the last war, came later.

Export pessimism in the early postwar years was, in part, the result of a general expectation that depression in the world economy was likely to recur after a brief restocking boom. There was, moreover, a universal failure among economists to anticipate the pace of the global boom of the 1950s and 1960s: GDP per capita in the advanced industrial countries in the period 1950–1973 increased at an annual rate (3.8%) almost three times the highest previous sustained rate (1.4%, 1870–1913). Export pessimism suffused the view of prospects for certain advanced industrial countries (e.g., Italy, France, Japan) as well as the developing regions in the early postwar years.

As for the tilt of policy toward the cities at the expense of agriculture and rural life, development economists bear little or no blame. They did, of course, vary in the strength of their protests against these distortions; and Peter Bauer can argue legitimately that he should have been more strongly supported by his colleagues in protesting the damage to agriculture wrought by the African marketing boards. Moreover, most development economists did not appreciate fully the corrosive (as well as positive) consequences of U.S. agricultural products supplied under P.L. 480. But the relative neglect of agriculture and increasingly onerous subsidies to urban populations surely arose not from the propositions and prescriptions of development economists, but primarily from the political life of the developing regions and irrational reactions against real or believed distortions of the colonial (or quasi-colonial) past.

In short, politics was generally more important than economics in the developing world, and the critical political issues were substantially different than those of the advanced industrial countries. Here, I believe, is the reason for the inadequacy of, say, Bauer's plea that aid only be granted to those governments that relied on the market and thus moved toward democracy or, say, Myrdal's and Singer's easy transfer of the canons of the post-1945 social-democratic welfare state in North Western Europe to the developing world. In fact, seven of the nine World Bank pioneers I have evoked for present purposes ended up in puzzlement or disappointment at the extent to which politics frustrated the economic development outcomes they envisaged or hoped for.

SOME CONCLUSIONS AND COMMENTS ON THE FUTURE

By the time Adam Smith's *Wealth of Nations* was published certain propositions, after several generations of thought and intense debate about the political economy of growth, were established that bear directly on the subject matter of this book.

- Economic development was conceived as an essential part of a process of building morally good and civilized domestic societies and a peaceful and decent international society. Living in a mercantilist world in which, for example, Britain was at war for some forty years of the eighteenth century, a world in which the intrusions of government were often inefficient and driven by narrow special interests, those who created modern political economy saw in enlarged domestic and international competitive commerce not only a way to discipline and harness the self-seeking propensities of human beings and governments but also a way to strengthen within and across international boundaries the healing quality of "sympathy." They looked to governments with reduced but still substantial functions in the society that, to the maximum consistent with the security of others, respected the freedom of unique individuals.

- As for efficiency and equity, they found a good deal of potential convergence; but they also found some painful choices whose consequences might require mitigation on moral grounds. Efficiency, for example, required an acceptance of an unequal distribution of income and wealth; but it was also the part of efficiency to educate the children of the poor; and it was morally right to temper inequity further by recognizing Hume's dictum: "No one can doubt, but such an equality is most suitable to human nature, and diminishes much less from the happiness of the rich than it adds to that of the poor."

  Efficiency required specialization of function; but that process, in Smith's view, could narrow the range of human experience and sensibility. It was right to try to mitigate this cost with public education.

  Behind it all was an acute awareness of the brutal human consequences of poverty and of the more civil and freer life of widened choices economic development could bring.

- The world of Hume and Smith was one in which thoughtful observers were also conscious of societies at different levels of real income per capita: They recalled that England itself was, a few centuries back, a rather primitive upstart compared, say, to the Habsburg-dominated continent; they compared the North American to the Latin American colonies; the Dutch to all others in Europe; the still vital Chinese economy to decaying Bengal; and, indeed, England to Scotland, the latter progressing but in line astern. Thus, speculation on the dynamics of narrowing the gap between relatively rich and poor countries, and an appropriate efficient and equitable policy of the rich toward the upwardly mobile poor, were actively on the agenda of the third quarter of the eighteenth century. And the issue of growth in relation to the good society remained central to political economy through J. S. Mill and Marx down to Marshall, who uniquely belonged to both the pre-1870 and post-1870 worlds.

But putting Marshall aside there were few indeed who took development in its full classic sense seriously between 1870 and the post-1945 era. Indeed, there were not many who studied economic growth, in its narrower sense. Economic growth was assumed as virtually automatic in the advanced industrial world. It entered into analyses of the business cycle in one way or another and, occasionally, the terms of trade. But except for Schumpeter, the young Kuznets, Walther Hoffmann, and a handful of others, it moved for about eighty years to the periphery. And when Harrod produced a growth model in the 1930s it was to demonstrate the likelihood if not certainty of short-run instability in a capitalist economy.

When the concern for development moved on to the global agenda after World War II, few picked up where the classics left off—Arthur Lewis being a notable exception. For practitioners of development—including politicians in the developing regions—all the great classical issues were, in fact, alive: What kind of society should we try to build? How should we exploit convergences between efficiency and equity and what do we do when they don't converge? What priority should development enjoy versus the other imperatives of politics? How should poor and rich countries relate to each other? What is the correct role for competitive markets relative to that of government? Development economics inevitably got caught up in these problems because it became a field for practitioners as much as for theorists. But there was no common base, no agreed political economy of development. The debates over basic needs, the right of poor countries to allocate the income of rich countries, the market versus government planning provided, it's fair to say, only little illumination. Behind it all was an almost automatic carry-over of debates in the advanced industrial countries of the 1930s—Right, Center, and Left—to often irrelevant settings.

The line of argument set out in this essay suggests that the next generation ought to try to build a fresh political economy of development reaching back for inspiration, if not for definitive answers, to the spacious architecture of the eighteenth-century founding fathers. I suggest this course because the problems evidently on the agenda require a kind of treatment not provided by conventional growth theory or by neoclassical economics or by Marxism in its various versions. I believe there are five great problems ahead.

- The foreseeable arrival at technological maturity of what I call the Fourth Graduating Class (see Chart 2 in Chapter 22), embracing *inter alia* China and India, Brazil and Mexico. Their peaceful absorption into the world economy and world polity without the violence and tragedy that accompanied the rise of Germany, Japan, and Russia is a central challenge for the next generation and more—indeed, an imperative for survival in a nuclear age.
- The peaceful liquidation of the Cold War with the Soviet Union, a conflict clearly anchronistic in a world that does not lend itself either now or foreseeably to domination by any single nation or ideology.
- The maintenance of economic vitality and a high degree of cooperation in and among the countries of Western Europe, Japan, and the United States—a condition for successful management of

the first two tasks. The outcome will depend greatly on the pace at which the present round of new technologies is elaborated and efficiently applied in the advanced industrial world.
- Intense international cooperation to cope with the mounting pressures on the physical environment exerted by the movement to full industrialization of, say, 80 percent of a global population that could reach 11 billion by the middle of the next century.
- Patient assistance, where possible, to the nations that have found development particularly difficult; e.g., Africa south of the Sahara, Haiti, Yemen, Afghanistan, Burma, some of the Pacific Islands. These nations contain perhaps 20 percent of the human race and are an inescapable welfare charge on the more fortunate early-comers to modernization.

The old debate about the state versus the market is being settled by the movement beyond take-off into the drive to technological maturity of most developing countries combined with a belated recognition that an efficient agriculture is not only essential for an industrial society but requires strong private incentives including fair prices for the farmer. The increasingly sophisticated and diversified technologies of the drive to technological maturity simply do not lend themselves to state management, notably at a time when a powerful technological revolution imposes a vertiginous pace of obsolescence year after year.

Moreover, it may well be that the human impulse to exercise increased control over his or her destiny as modernization proceeds is pushing political communities increasingly toward one serious version of democracy or another. The passage of time in an environment of development—erratic, uneven, and ungainly as development has been—may be settling some of the old debates. But a fairly clear-cut triumph of private markets and democracy will not clear the development agenda, nor, indeed, in itself guarantee peace and a viable world economy. Above all, I suspect, the next phase will require, on a global scale, the maximum expression of the quality David Hume and Adam Smith called sympathy and regarded as the essential bond among human beings in a civilized society.

NOTES

1. Carl Becker, *The Heavenly City of the Eighteenth Century Philosophers* (New Haven: Yale University Press, 1932).
2. David Hume, *Philosophical Works*, T. H. Green and T. H. Grose (eds.) (London: Longman Green, 1912), Vol. 3, p. 238.
3. J. M. Keynes, *The General Theory of Interest, Employment, and Money* (London: Macmillan, 1936), p. 150.
4. David Hume, *Writings on Economics*, edited and introduction by Eugene Rotwein (Madison: University of Wisconsin Press, 1955), pp. 15 and 21–32.

5. Piero Sraffa (ed.) with the assistance of Maurice Dobb, *The Works and Correspondence of David Ricardo*, Vol. I (Cambridge: at the University Press, 1951), pp. 96–97.

6. For Hume's priority in utilitarianism, his great influence on the subsequent tradition among economists, and Adam Smith's distinctive characteristics in this field, see Lionel Robbins, *The Theory of Economic Policy* (New York: St. Martin's Press, 1952), especially pp. 176–178.

7. Istvan Hont and Michael Ignatieff (eds.), *Wealth and Virtue: The Shaping of Political Economy in the Scottish Enlightenment* (Cambridge: at the University Press, 1983), p. 7.

8. Hume, *Philosophical Works*, Vol. 2, p. 304.

9. *Wealth of Nations*, Edwin Cannan, ed., with introduction by Max Lerner (New York: Random House, the Modern Library, 1937), p. 651.

10. *Ibid.*, p. 740.

11. Rotwein, *David Hume*, pp. 52–53.

12. See, in Sraffa and Dobb, *The Works*, Vol. X, p. 90, the contrast between Nathan Rothschild's Humeian passion for business and Ricardo's temperance.

13. Rotwein, *David Hume*, pp. 17–18.

14. My *Growth Theorists from David Hume to the Present* (New York: Oxford University Press, 1989) discusses at some length the formal characteristics of Adam Smith's growth theory and presents in a mathematical appendix (done with Michael Kennedy) one-sector and three-sector Smithian growth models.

15. *Wealth of Nations*, p. 7.

16. See, especially, the extensive treatment of this issue in Hont and Ignatieff, *Wealth and Virtue*. The mathematical appendix referred to in Note 14 also contains a model of the rich country–poor country problem.

17. John Stuart Mill, *Principles of Political Economy*, Introduction by V. W. Bladen, Textual Editor J. M. Robson (Toronto: University of Toronto Press, 1965), p. 963.

18. *Ibid.*, pp. 208–209.

19. Morris Beck, "The Public Sector and Economic Stability," in *The Business Cycle and Public Policy*, A compendium of papers submitted to the Joint Economic Committee, November 23, 1980 (Washington, D.C.: G.P.O., 1980), p. 129.

20. *Ibid.*, p. 113.

21. John Williams, "The Theory of International Trade Reconsidered," *Economic Journal*, Vol. XXXIX, 1929, pp. 195–209.

22. The adjectives set off by quotation marks are from John F. Kennedy's often repeated definition of the group that had to be won over by a victorious candidate in an American presidential election. For context, see my *Diffusion of Power* (New York: Macmillan, 1972), p. 129.

23. Quoted, J. M. Keynes, "Alfred Marshall, 1842–1924," in A. C. Pigou (ed.), *Memorials of Alfred Marshall* (London: Macmillan, 1925), pp. 9–11.

24. *Ibid.*, p. 9.

25. Mill, *Principles*, p. 212.

26. *Memorials of Alfred Marshall*, p. 11.

27. *Ibid.*, p. 323.

28. On British pioneering, see J. C. Stamp, *British Incomes and Property* (London: P. S. King, 1916); A. L. Bowley, *Wages and Income Since 1860* (Cambridge: at the University Press, 1937); and Colin Clark's reminiscence in "Development Economics: The Early Years," in Gerald Meier and Dudley Seers (eds.), *Pioneers in Development* (New York: Oxford University Press for the World Bank, 1984).

On the American side, the story centers on a debate about income distribution that led to the creation of the National Bureau of Economic Research, well told by Solomon Fabricant, *Toward a Firmer Basis of Economic Policy: The Founding of the National Bureau of Economic Research* (Cambridge, Mass.: NBER, 1983). See also Carol S. Carson, "The History of the United States National Income and Product Accounts: The Development of an Analytic Tool," *Review of Income and Wealth*, series 21, No. 2, June 1975.

29. The phrase "state bourgeoisie" emerged from the debate on the appropriate relative role of public and private sectors in Latin America. It is referred to in William Glade, "Economic Policy-making and the Structures of Corporations in Latin America," offprint ser. no. 208 (Austin: Institute of Latin American Studies, University of Texas at Austin, 1981).

30. Gerald M. Meier and Dudley Seers (eds.), *Pioneers in Development* (New York: Oxford University Press, for the World Bank, 1984). The following "pioneers" explicitly linked their views on development to one aspect or another of their earlier professional and policy concerns: Colin Clark, Albert O. Hirschman, Gunnar Myrdal, Raul Prebisch, Paul N. Rosenstein-Rodan, Hans Singer, and Jan Tinbergen. P.T. Bauer's first professional work was on Southeast Asia and West Africa; Arthur Lewis, on Jamaica and the Caribbean; mine, in economic history.

31. Meier and Seers, *Pioneers in Development*, p. 154. Myrdal also notes that he applied the method of his *An American Dilemma* to his *Asian Drama*, which, in method, he described as a kind of "replica of *An American Dilemma*" (*Ibid.*, p. 153).

32. Barbara Ward, J. D. Runnalls, and Lenore d'Anjou (eds.), *The Widening Gap: Development in the 1970s* (New York: Columbia University Press, 1971), pp. 11–13.

33. Little's statement comes from a letter to Paul Streeten quoted in his "Postscript: Development Dichotomies," Meier and Seers, *Pioneers*, p. 345. Little's full critique of the structuralists is incorporated in his *Economic Development: Theory, Policy, and International Relations* (New York: Basic Books, 1982).

34. Meier and Seers, *Pioneers*, p. 209.

35. This passage comes from an unclassified U.S. government document written by an anonymous U.S. public servant. I quoted it in a lecture at the National Bank of Egypt in November 1983 (*Prospects for the World Economy*).